for Olivia

'so much worth blended with so much
sweetness'

Mark

14·iii·80

A fantasy of reason

Don Locke

A fantasy of reason

 The life and thought
of William Godwin

Routledge & Kegan Paul
London, Boston and Henley

First published in 1980
by Routledge & Kegan Paul Ltd
39 Store Street, London WC1E 7DD,
Broadway House, Newtown Road,
Henley-on-Thames, Oxon RG9 1EN and
9 Park Street, Boston, Mass. 02108, USA

Photoset in 10 on 11pt Linocomp Baskerville by
Rowland Phototypesetting Ltd, Bury St. Edmunds, Suffolk
and printed in Great Britain by
Page Brothers Ltd, Norwich, Norfolk

British Library Cataloguing in Publication Data

Locke, Don
A fantasy of reason
1 Godwin, William
I Title
192   JC176.G82   79-40937

ISBN 0 7100 0387 0

This, more than any
To Ann, more than ever

Contents

Illustrations

(between pages 212 and 213)

Acknowledgments

It was a brief passage in Alisdair MacIntyre's excellent *Short History of Ethics* which first aroused my interest in William Godwin. Since then I have benefited most from the work of Burton R. Pollin, and especially from his monumental bibliography of *Godwin Criticism*. Without that it would have been impossible for a novice in matters historical and biographical to have written a book such as this. Professor Pollin dug the ground for me, and planted the seeds; I have picked the fruit. I hope that he will regard the result as some tribute and reward for his labours.

Inevitably I also owe a great deal to the many scholars who have researched the life and works of Percy Shelley, and especially to the editors of the Pforzheimer Library manuscripts, whose *Shelley and His Circle* serves both as a guide and a model to anyone working in this area. For personal encouragement, advice and information I would like to thank Professor Pollin, Professor Christoph Clairmont, Professor Lewis Patton, Mr J. C. Sainty, Mr Peter Opie, Professor Marion K. Stocking, Lady Mander and Mme Mary Claire Bally-Clairmont, and the librarians and archivists of the Bodleian Library, Keele University, Norfolk County Records Office, Tullie House, Bristol City Art Gallery, Camden Library, the Guildhall, and the National Portrait Gallery. I also owe thanks to the University of Warwick, for a period of sabbatical leave, and to the Pforzheimer Library, the Dr Williams Library, Tullie House, the British Museum, and in particular Lord Abinger, for permission to use or quote from unpublished manuscript material.

But I would especially like to thank Alan Bainbridge, for extremely useful suggestions at an early stage of the manuscript, and my wife Ann, who had to endure William Godwin for some seven years, on and off, and still emerged game enough to comment in detail on a final draft.

1 ♣ Reason, truth and justice

I am bound to disseminate without reserve all the principles
with which I am acquainted, and which it may be of importance to mankind to know; and this duty it behoves me to
practise upon every occasion and with the most persevering
constancy. I must discharge the whole system of moral and
political truth, without suppressing any part under the idea of
its being too bold or paradoxical, and thus depriving the whole
of that complete and irresistible evidence, without which its
effects must always be feeble, partial and uncertain.[1]

Political Justice, 1793

♣ Hidden away in some old library or bookshop you might one day
come across the weighty volumes of *Political Justice*, a work as
obscure now as its author. Yet there was a time when it was a
popular sensation, a veritable prodigy of imagination and intellect,
and William Godwin the most famous, certainly the most notorious,
writer in the land. 'No work in our time', declared William Hazlitt,
'gave such a blow to the philosophical mind of the country as the
celebrated *Enquiry Concerning Political Justice*'.[2] For Godwin captured
the spirit of the age, that sense of radical reform and immediate
improvement that accompanied the revolutions first of America and
then of France, and carried it further, further perhaps than anyone
else has ever dared go, in a truly remarkable exploration of how
things are and what they yet might be. Even today the book is
astonishing, amazing or absurd according to taste, a striking survey
of issues both ancient and contemporary: government and law,
punishment and property, reason and revolution, benevolence and
justice, sincerity and marriage. But in its time it was a revelation,
not merely as a piece of moral and political speculation but as an
exercise in reason and argument. 'In the first fervour of my
enthusiasm', wrote Godwin himself, 'I entertained a vain imagination of "hewing a stone from the rock", which by its inherent
energy and weight, should overbear and annihilate all opposition,
and place the principles of politics on an immovable basis'.[3] And
that basis consisted in three fundamental values, three eternal
ideals: Reason, Truth, and Justice. *Political Justice* is a commentary,
a rhapsody – development and variation, digression and interlude –
on those three themes.

Truth, first of all, which we ignore at our peril. For error leads inevitably to evil and unhappiness, since 'all vice is nothing more than error and mistake reduced into practice, and adopted as the principle of our conduct'.[4] Godwin, like Socrates, believes that the man who acts wrongly has simply mistaken his true interests, that once we know the real nature and tendency of our conduct we will always act rightly. In fact virtue is the means to happiness, and once men appreciate that truth they will be virtuous because they want to be happy, and happy because they are virtuous. But truth also provides the means of social and political progress. The history of mankind has been, and will continue to be, a history of continual improvement, as men have come to learn more about their environment, their society and themselves. As knowledge increases and information is disseminated, more widely and more rapidly than ever before thanks to the invention of printing, man will arrive by degrees at a full and clear understanding of what he is, and what he can make of himself. Our social and political institutions, our very selves, will develop and change accordingly:

> There is no science that is not capable of additions; there is no
> art that may not be carried to a still higher perfection. If this
> be true of all other sciences, why not of morals? If this be
> true of all other arts, why not of social institutions?[5]

That is the faith on which *Political Justice* is founded.

Hardly surprising, therefore, that Godwin's prime concern in the practical politics of his day should be with freedom of opinion. He does not exactly believe in a right of free speech – indeed he does not believe in rights, as such, at all – but he does believe in a duty, the duty to speak the truth as plainly and as clearly as we can, without fear of the consequences. Accordingly, *Political Justice* devotes a chapter or two to the supreme virtue of sincerity, an absolute frankness and honesty in everything we say and do. But it is equally the duty of *Political Justice* itself to speak the truth about society and government, 'to disseminate without reserve all the principles with which I am acquainted',[6] and equally without fear of the consequences.

Truth, therefore, will make us wise, virtuous, happy and free. But how are we to arrive at truth? Not through authority, much less through force, but only through reason, through each individual's exercise of his capacity to think and judge for himself. The mere fact that someone tells me something is so cannot, by itself, establish that it is so; men cannot be made wise against their wills. Only reason can reveal the truth and bring us to act accordingly:

There is no effectual way of improving the institutions of any
people but by enlightening their understandings. He that
endeavours to maintain the authority of any sentiment, not by
argument, but by force, may intend a benefit, but really inflicts
an extreme injury. To suppose that truth can be instilled
through any medium but that of its own intrinsic evidence, is
the most flagrant of all errors. He that believes the most
fundamental proposition through the evidence of authority,
does not believe a truth, but a falshood [sic] . . . . All that he
believes is that it is very proper that he should submit to
usurpation and injustice.[7]

So if men are to recognize truth, they must be allowed to recognize it
for themselves. Yet the function of most social and political institutions is precisely to set some men in power over the rest, requiring
individuals to disregard their own reason and bow to the opinion of
others, 'the authorities', who know better than they. Even worse,
governments rely on falsehood, on secrecy and deception, and if
necessary on force, to control their subjects. 'This boasted institution', says Godwin, 'is nothing more than a scheme for enforcing by
brute violence the sense of one man or set of men upon another.'[8] It
can have no place in a world of reason and truth.
    And if governments must go, it is clear that laws cannot be far
behind. For the system of law and punishment — 'coercion', as
Godwin likes to call it – is contrary to justice and truth as well as to
reason. Contrary to justice because all conduct is determined by
laws of cause and effect, the inevitable result of the particular
education and environment that has made each man what he is, so
that ultimately we are no more responsible for what we do than an
apple is responsible for falling to the ground: 'The assassin cannot
help the murder he commits any more than the dagger.'[9] Contrary
to truth because courts depend for their existence on obscurity,
deception and dishonesty, as each advocate seeks to impose the
interpretation that best suits himself: 'Law was made that a plain
man might know what to depend on; and yet the most skilful
practitioners differ about the event of my suit.'[10] And contrary to
reason because punishment appeals to force and to fear, not to
argument:

It includes in it a tacit confession of imbecility. If he who
employs coercion against me could mould me to his purposes
by argument, no doubt he would. He pretends to punish me,
because his argument is strong; but he really punishes me,
because his argument is weak.[11]

Instead, in a world of truth and reason, men will do voluntarily, in the light of their own understanding, what at present we misguidedly, impossibly, try to force them to do:

> Reason is the only legislator, and her degrees are irrevocable and uniform. The functions of society extend, not to the making, but the interpreting of law; it cannot decree, it can only declare that, which the nature of things has already decreed.[12]

Reason is shared by all men, and truth too is one and uniform, the same for everyone in every country, so groups of people, meeting together freely and discussing their problems openly, relying on proof and not on power, appealing to argument and not to authority, will ultimately arrive at an agreement where each man can see the truth for himself and act appropriately. It will be a world with no governments and no need of them, no laws and no need of them, a world governed by truth and reason alone.

But there are other conclusions, no less surprising, to be drawn from the primacy of private reason. If it is essential that people learn to think for themselves, influenced solely by the evidence and uncorrupted by authority and the pressure of public opinion, then, as Godwin subsequently put it, 'we should avoid all those practices that are calculated to melt our opinions into a common mould.'[13] It follows, therefore, that 'everything that is usually understood by the term cooperation, is in some degree an evil', 'that all supererogatory cooperation is carefully to be avoided, common labour and common meals.'[14] And the argument extends to cohabitation, and even to marriage, an institution which – like punishment – is found to be contrary to reason, truth and justice, all three. A world of rational men will be a world of wholly independent, wholly self-sufficient individuals, prepared to regulate their conduct in accordance with their own opinions, and never deferring their judgment to that of another:

> For example: shall we have concerts of music? The miserable state of mechanism of the majority of the performers is so conspicuous as to be even at this day a topic of mortification and ridicule. Will it not be practicable hereafter for one man to perform the whole? Shall we have theatrical exhibitions? This seems to include an absurd and vicious cooperation. It may be doubted whether men will hereafter come forward in any mode gravely to repeat words and ideas not their own . . . . All formal repetition of other men's ideas seems to be a scheme for imprisoning for so long a time the operations of our own mind.[15]

Nothing was safe, nothing sacred, once Godwin set off in pursuit of reason and the truth!

But what will this world be like when, as it seems, none of our present institutions and conventions survive? The answer is that a world of pure reason will be a world of political justice, that is, a state of society organized along moral lines. As the very title of the book makes clear, morality is as important to Godwin as is politics, and the moral doctrines certainly pack as many surprises. For what, more specifically, *is* morality, or justice? 'If justice have any meaning', Godwin tells us, 'it is just that I should contribute every thing in my power to the benefit of the whole.'[16] Duty, likewise, is 'the mode in which any being may best be employed for the general good'.[17] Any other action will be unjust; in failing to produce all the good that I can, I perform an injustice against my fellow men.

To us, perhaps, this seems a curious use of a notion which seems to have more to do with equality and fairness than the benefit and welfare of everyone. But the fact that Godwin uses 'justice' as a synonym for morality in general already tells us much about the way he applies this test of the greatest possible good. Morality, for him, is not simply a matter of doing good unto others, but a matter of doing good unto all men equally, as befits their capacities and abilities. This means, in particular, that it must be immoral, unjust, to make exceptions of particular people just because they happen to be our family or our friends, let alone ourselves. 'If the extraordinary case should occur in which I can promote the general good by my death, more than by my life, justice requires that I should be content to die.'[18] Equally it would be wrong for me to do something for someone close to me just because he is close to me, when I might perhaps be of greater benefit to someone else; that too would be an injustice against my fellow men. So what Godwin came to call 'the private and domestic affections' are actually a source of vice and error, in so far as they lead me to favour my family and friends not because I can do them most good, but simply because they are mine. Nor has he qualms about remarking, in the midst of a discussion of the foundations of political obligation: 'It is of no consequence that I am the parent of a child, when it has once been ascertained that the child will receive greater benefit by living under the superintendance of a stranger.'[19]

Gratitude, likewise, 'can be no part either of justice or virtue.'[20] For gratitude leads us to prefer one man not for the good he can do mankind generally but for the good he has done us personally, when he might perhaps have been of more benefit to someone else. This is not to deny that it may sometimes be our duty to repay our benefactors, just as it is often our duty to help friends and family, when that will increase the general welfare. But it is to deny that we have a duty to our benefactor just because he has helped us. Indeed to act from a motive of gratitude, instead of for the good of all, would be positively immoral; so far from being a virtue, gratitude, as such, is a vice, so much more of absolute injustice. 'I would spare him commission of that vice', snapped Edmund Burke when he heard of this doctrine, 'by not conferring on him any benefit.'[21] Similarly, there can be no obligation to do something just because we have promised. If what I do promotes the general welfare then what I do is right, and I ought to do it whether I have promised or not; if what I do detracts from the general welfare then what I do is wrong, and I ought not do it whether I have promised or not. Either way promising makes no difference: the mere fact that I have said I will do it cannot make a right out of a wrong.

For much the same reason, there can be no rights of man, as they have been called, only duties, more exactly the one fundamental duty of doing all that good that is within your power. If by a right we mean the discretionary power to do something as and when we please, without incurring any blame – as I might claim the right to do what I like in the privacy of my own home – then there can be no such thing. Either what I do is right in itself, in which case there is no need of a right to do it; or it is wrong, and to claim the right to do it is a manifest absurdity: it is to claim the right of doing wrong. And this argument, too, goes further than first meets the eye. 'Few things have contributed more to undermine the energy and virtue of the human species', adds Godwin in his second edition, 'than the supposition that we have a right, as it has been phrased, to do what we will with our own.'[22] Property ought, in justice, to belong not to him who happens to own it, nor even to him who has earned it, but to him who can benefit most from it. So long as I possess something which would be of more good to another I have no right to retain it; that too can only be a wrong:

> To whom does any article of property, suppose a loaf of bread, justly belong? To him who most wants it, or to whom the possession of it will be most beneficial . . . . I have an hundred loaves in my possession, and in the next street there is a poor man expiring with hunger, to whom one of these loaves would be the means of preserving his life. If I withhold this loaf from him, am I not unjust? If I impart it, am I not complying with what justice demands? To whom does the loaf justly belong?[23]

In a just society, therefore, private property will no longer exist, gone the way of governments and their laws, whose main function is, after all, simply to preserve and protect it. But property is also a positive evil. So long as some depend for their own survival on the wealth of others there will always be 'a sense of dependence', 'a servile and truckling spirit'. Great wealth provides a 'perpetual spectacle of injustice', and perverts our values, emphasizing material possessions instead of intellectual and moral attainments. It fosters vice, envy, malice and revenge, as well as robbery and war. And ironically, as we shall see, Godwin sees a further objection to the established administration of property, in the fact that the poverty of the majority limits human happiness by holding down the natural growth of population.

Nor is there any 'Objection to this System from the Allurements of Sloth' to quote a chapter title, any danger that people will never exert themselves unless they stand to make some personal gain. In fact it is the institution of private property, the appeal to wealth rather than merit, which is responsible for man's selfishness. What ultimately motivates us is the love of distinction, a desire to stand out amongst our fellows and be admired by them. In our present corrupt and corrupting society this is easily achieved through wealth and extravagance. But in a state of equality personal riches will no longer provide the means whereby one man can set himself above others, and luxury and ostentation will lose their present spurious appeal. The love of wealth will be replaced by the love of reputation, so that men stand out for their intelligence or their benevolence, not their possessions. Yet the love of fame, too, is a delusion which, 'like every other delusion, will take its turn to be detected and abjured'.[24] In the end rational men will be motivated solely by the recognition that what they do is for the good of all, by a concern for justice itself. Then they will be content to live in 'a state of rigid simplicity'. There will be little call for physical labour, and such as is needed will be shared equally, so that no great exertion will be required of any one individual. Godwin is even prepared to do the arithmetic: 'Half an hour a day, seriously employed in manual labour by every member of the community, would sufficiently supply the whole with necessaries.'[25] In the *Enquirer*, four years later, the estimate is increased to two hours.

Thus reason will lead us to truth, and truth will lead us to justice, and we will arrive at a state of pure anarchism, in which there is not only no government, but no law and no punishment, no personal rights and no private property, no individual attachments and no promises, no collaboration and no matrimony, no constraints of any kind on the freedom of thought and action. And the result will not be anarchy, a word that has for Godwin the same negative connotations it has for us. Instead *Political Justice* presents a vision of wholly rational, wholly benevolent beings, each acting by the light of his

own reason, but each acting solely for the good of others, and all
living harmoniously together in a state of austere happiness:

> There will be no war, no crimes, no administration of justice,
> as it is called, and no government . . . . But beside this, there
> will be no disease, no anguish, no melancholy and no resent-
> ment. Each man will seek with ineffable ardour, the good of
> all.[26]

It was this Godwinian millennium that Shelley would depict at
one of the climactic points in his verse drama *Prometheus Unbound*:

> And behold, thrones were kingless, and men walked
> One with another, even as spirits do,
> None fawned, none trampled: hate, disdain or fear,
> Self-love or self-contempt on human brows
> No more inscribed, as o'er the gate of hell,
> 'All hope abandon ye who enter here' . . . .
> The loathsome mask has fallen, the man remains
> Sceptreless, free, uncircumscribed, but man
> Equal, unclassed, tribeless, and nationless,
> Exempt from awe, worship, degree, the king
> Over himself; just, gentle, wise . . . .

Others have given us more prosaic versions of the same noble scene:
Bulwer Lytton in *The Coming Race*, H. G. Wells in *Men Like Gods* – a
phrase borrowed from Godwin himself. But Wells, Lytton, Shelley,
even Godwin, were all anticipated by one Lemuel Gulliver who, on
his final journey of discovery, had found himself in the land of the
Houyhnhnms, a race of intelligent horses living the life of reason
much as Godwin describes it. They, too, believed 'that our institutions of government and law were plainly owing to our grave defects
in reason, and by consequence in virtue; because reason alone is
sufficient to govern a rational creature.' They, too, had 'no conception of how a rational creature can be compelled, but only
advised or exhorted; because no person can disobey reason, without
giving up his claim to be a rational creature.' They, too, could see no
grounds for favouring family or friends, but 'have it that nature
teaches them to love the whole species, and it is reason only that
maketh a distinction of persons, where there is a superior degree of
virtue'. (For further discussion of the similarities between Swift and
Godwin, see J. A. Preu, *The Dean and the Anarchist* (1963).)

Yet what Godwin presents as an indication of what we might one
day become, Swift intended as a demonstration of what men, mere
Yahoos by comparison, can never be. The vision is undeniably
attractive, even inspiring, but deeply implausible. Its poetic and

literary appeal is obvious, its philosophical and psychological justification more doubtful, and one feels more inclined to side with Swift: surely men just are not, and cannot be, like that? Godwin, however, is convinced that they are, or at any rate can be. For the improvement that truth will bring is not merely material, though he does find himself wondering whether one day 'a plough may not be turned into a field, and perform its office without need of super-intendance',[27] and so relieve us of even that half an hour seriously employed in manual labour which is all that our needs require or justice demands. It will also be an improvement in society, in morality, in man himself. Man, in a word, is perfectible, and perfectibility – what Godwin later preferred to call 'the progressive nature of man' – 'is one of the most unequivocal characteristics of the human species, so that the political, as well as the intellectual state of man, may be presumed to be in a course of progressive improvement.'[28] Reason must discover truth, and truth in its turn must produce justice: nothing can be more incontrovertible.

Godwin's faith in human reason was unbounded. He even thought it possible, by sheer strength of argument, to halt in his tracks the assassin bent on murdering us, though he does reluctantly admit that 'we are not yet wise enough to make the sword drop out of the hands of our oppressors by the mere force of reason'[29] – not yet! By the end of the book he begins to wonder whether mind might not prove powerful over matter in a more than metaphorical sense, and appealing to the way in which our state of mind can affect physical strength and stamina, conjectures that we may yet over-come sleep, sickness, and finally death, by power of thought alone – an idea later revived in Shaw's *Back to Methuselah*. Godwin is quick to add that this is mere speculation, in no way essential to his argument, and he deleted much of the discussion in a later edition. But to his critics it was but further evidence of an absurd extremism: a society without government, a morality without individual attach-ments, a plough that needs no ploughman, a man who will not permit himself to die. And that judgment has persisted, so that Godwin is regarded still as the supreme fantasist of reason. 'Reason seems to have had the same effect on him as mere enthusiasm has on other men', wrote the essayist John Churton Collins. 'What sobers most men intoxicated him. What quenches them gave him fire.'[30] And perhaps no other work carries reason to such patently un-reasonable lengths. 'It is a curious instance of extreme principles', complains the *Dictionary of National Biography*, 'advocated with the calmness of one-sided logic.'

Yet that is precisely *Political Justice*'s great value and virtue, at once its weakness and its strength. For this is no mere collection of fanciful utopian claims; it too appeals to reason and truth, and its theses are – or come to be – founded in proof and argument. More than any other British thinker of his time, more even than Burke or Bentham, Godwin was a political *philosopher*, concerned not with practical problems but with the universal principles that lie behind them, with the whole system of moral and political truth, and prepared to draw the necessary conclusions with a logical coolness that often takes the breath away. There is little in his thought that is entirely original – 'I am a true Englishman', he noted once, 'formed to discover nothing but to improve anything.'[31] But what is his own, and entirely characteristic, is the way that he systematizes ideas derived from a variety of sources, and the thoroughness and persistence with which he follows any line of thought, however forbidding, to its logical conclusion, however unexpected, until he becomes in turn a Utilitarian, an Anarchist, and a Communist, so far in advance of those movements that he does not even know the names.

To his contemporaries, indeed, the extraordinary thing was that these conclusions, however unacceptable in themselves, seemed to follow remorselessly from unquestionable premises:

> The principles contained in Political Justice had all the appear-
> ances, and many of the effects, of self-evident axioms. To
> understand the terms, and adopt the propositions of the work,
> were so nearly inseparable, that it was a fact that some very
> great and learned men, in expressing an abhorrence of its
> doctrines, could not conceal the secret that their detestation of
> Political Justice was chiefly occasioned by its subtlety in eluding
> their zeal to detect the radical error which, from certain
> propositions they held to be infallible, they were sincerely
> persuaded lay somewhere in the work. Political Justice at once
> tortured their feelings and baffled their reason.[32]

So much so that the left-wing *Cambridge Intelligencer* carried a long letter alleging that the fact that Godwin, his book and his publisher all escaped prosecution demonstrated that it was the work of an *agent provocateur*, hired by the government to provide a *reductio ad absurdum* of radical principles!

For a few brief years Godwin was the most celebrated – the most admired, the most controversial – writer in the country. But the puzzle is that this burst of fame should be at once so intense and so short-lived, to be followed by a deep and lasting obscurity. 'Five and twenty years ago he was in the very zenith of a sultry and unwhole-some popularity,' wrote Hazlitt in 1824;

he blazed as a sun in the firmament of reputation; no-one was more talked of, more looked up to, more sought after, and wherever liberty, truth, justice was the theme, his name was not far off. Now he has sunk below the horizon, and enjoys the serene twilight of a doubtful immortality . . . . He is to all ordinary intents and purposes dead and buried. But the author of *Political Justice* and *Caleb Williams* can never die; his name is an abstraction in letters; his works are a standard in the history of intellect. He is thought of now like any eminent writer of a hundred-and-fifty years ago, or just as he will be a hundred-and-fifty years hence. He knows this, and smiles in silent mockery of himself, reposing on the monument of his fame.[33]

Yet Hazlitt was writing some hundred-and-fifty years ago, and Godwin's obscurity has, if anything, only thickened and deepened.

The contrast with his close contemporary, Jeremy Bentham, could hardly be more marked. *Political Justice* was a sensation; Bentham's *Introduction to the Principles of Morals and Legislation*, published four years earlier, was barely noticed; the phrases 'the New Philosophy' or the 'Modern Philosophy', usually meaning what today we call Utilitarianism, referred always to Godwin, never to Bentham. But now it is Bentham and his *Introduction* that are celebrated for their contribution to political philosophy, while Godwin is recalled only as a somewhat shady character on the fringes of literary history, thanks to his friendship with Wordsworth and Coleridge, Lamb and Hazlitt, Sheridan, and especially Shelley. It is Bentham's undistinguished portrait that hangs in the National Portrait Gallery, while the noble head painted by Sir James Northcote is kept in store for the few who care to seek it out. Yet Godwin's philosophy is at least as stimulating as Bentham's, and may even be of greater contemporary interest and relevance.

So history has passed its own judgment on William Godwin. But that judgment is not founded in the evidence, the evidence of *Political Justice* itself. It is not enough to dismiss him as some idle dreamer, lost in his fantasy of reason. It is his arguments we must consider, for on them rests the fate of his book as a work of political philosophy, and as a contribution to the thought of man. Yet the collapse of Godwin's reputation and opinions lies not only there, but also in the history of the times, and in the man himself. The answer to the puzzle lies in all three. What, then, of William Godwin?

2 ♣ The most powerful instrument

It has appeared that the characters of men are determined in all their most essential circumstances by education. By education in this place I would be understood to convey the most comprehensive sense that can possibly be annexed to that word, including every incident that produces an idea in the mind, and can give birth to a chain of reflection.[1]

Political Justice, 1796

♣ William Godwin, preacher, teacher, journalist, novelist, philosopher, publisher, beggerman, hack, was born on 3 March 1756 in a neat redbrick house in Knowe's Acre near the heart of Wisbech, a small, prosperous farming town in the flat grey fenland between Peterborough and King's Lynn. It was a severe and daunting childhood, as drab and unrelieved as the landscape, and it left an indelible mark on the man. His father, John Godwin, like his father before him, was a Calvinist minister, 'extremely nice in his apparel and delicate in his food,'[2] convivial with his friends, but stern and unrelenting towards his children, and so far as Godwin himself was concerned, unlikable and unapproachable.

> One Sunday, as I walked in the garden, I happened to take the cat in my arms. My father saw me, and seriously reproved my levity, remarking that on the Lord's-day he was ashamed to observe me demeaning myself with such profaneness.

Godwin's mother Ann was more lively and more openly affectionate, relatively uneducated but probably more intelligent than her husband, but as a boy Godwin felt no closer to her. The seventh of thirteen children, but only the third to survive infancy, he was put out immediately to a wet-nurse in the village, and did not return home until the age of two. Even then he became the special charge of his father's cousin, an ex-schoolmistress who lived with the family, and when the other children resented this preference, his parents sided with them, or so it seemed to Godwin himself.

This Miss Godwin, too, was strict and rigorously pious, cold and undemonstrative, yet possessive to the extent that she 'made me her companion by night and by day', devoting herself to weeding and reading, and discouraging any sign of childishness or playfulness. Young Godwin even 'had the honour to be her bed-fellow', where 'she instructed me to compose myself to sleep with a temper as if I were never to wake again in this sublunary world. This lesson made a deep impression on my mind.' The lesson was reinforced by his first books, the *Pilgrim's Progress* and James Janeway's morbid *A Token for Children*, 'An Account of the Deaths of Many Pious Children', which relates the lives and exemplary deaths of children so God-fearing that they are constantly crying when they are not dying, all for sheer love of their maker. Godwin found it easy enough to identify with them, and 'felt as if I were willing to die with them, if I could with equal success engage the admiration of my friends and mankind.' And when Miss Godwin told him the life of a child was happier than that of an adult, 'I remember listening to her with much the same sort of sensation, as if she had told me that it was a more eligible lot to partake the fate of the damned, than to go to heaven.'

He grew up, inevitably, a shy, serious, pompous child, nervous with strangers and terrified by the size of the congregation in Norwich cathedral, finding his only pleasure in the books with which he hid himself from his cheerless world: 'I remember when I was a boy, looking forward with terror to the ample field of human life, and saying, When I have read through all the books that have been written, what shall I do afterwards?'[3] His precocious gift with language took the bizarre but predictable form of an obsession with preaching, and he would deliver whole sermons from his high-chair to whomever would listen. Later there was at school 'a poor lad of the village, whose name was Steele', to whom Godwin preached 'of sin and damnation, and drew tears to his eyes', even to the extent of sneaking the key to the meeting house so that he could admonish the unforunate boy from Godwin senior's pulpit.

With this for a childhood it is hardly surprising that the man should earn a reputation for coldness and remoteness. No wonder he placed so small a value on emotion, regarding the private and domestic affections as obstacles in the way of rational deliberation. The child, reared with firmness rather than love, distanced from both father and mother, reared in a severe and unrelenting Calvinism, his attention directed always towards what was good and true rather than what might be enjoyable, seems the true father of the man, the dispassionate intellectual who judged all things in the light of eternal and impartial truth. But this is only the official Godwin, author of a lofty treatise on political principles; the real Godwin scarcely lived up to that ideal. Behind the façade of pure reason lay a tangle of repressed doubts and fears, a desperate need of affection, an obsession with the good opinion of others, an all-pervasive desire to be noticed and admired. The philosopher who preached self-sufficiency in all things nevertheless depended for his own peace of mind on the companionship of others, and his novels would seethe with suppressed emotions: anxiety, despair, and above all, loneliness. Friendship, he once wrote, is a necessity of our nature, without which we are less than wholly human. Yet as a child he could secure affection only by securing approval, through achievements that demanded the admiration of his elders, and from that sprang his intense ambition, from even his earliest years, to be someone of note. He was thinking of himself, no doubt, when he maintained that the love of distinction is one certain mark of a child of talent and promise:

> He burns to be somebody. He cannot endure to be confounded in the crowd. It is the nature of the human mind never to be satisfied with itself, except so far as it can by some means procure to have its own favourable opinion confirmed by the suffrage of others.[4]

The admiration and approval that Godwin failed to find in his parents – 'They either did not see in me anything extraordinary, or made a conscience of not confiding it to me' – he found instead in his teachers, from Miss Godwin on. All were impressed by his ability and intelligence, and he became arrogant and conceited, 'having no doubt of being equal to everything I undertook'. Once, aged thirteen or fourteen, he had visited the local court, and when prevented from lounging on the cushion in front of the judge had 'silently remarked, if his lordship knew what the lad beside him will perhaps one day become, I am not sure that he would have removed my elbow'! And though that early self-conceit vanished once he was exposed to a wider and less easily impressed acquaintance, his pride remained, in the form of a certainty in the correctness of his opinions, a tendency to preach and moralize, an inability to accept criticism. He could not bear his father's sarcasm, of which he had a good deal, so sensitive to any rebuff that he would rather not ask for something than run the risk he might be refused, and all life long disagreement would throw him alternately into fits of petulance and bouts of depression. For all his stress on cool clear reason, the adult Godwin displayed a streak of obstinate conviction that could all too easily boil over into self-righteous anger at the folly, stupidity and consequent wickedness of those who disagreed with him.

Pride, ambition, the need of friendship, the desire for approval, self-righteousness, sensitivity to criticism, awkwardness and shyness, all combined to make Godwin morbidly anxious about what others thought of him.

The profoundest passion of my life seems to have been an acute sensibility to the good or ill opinion of others: this it was which generated in me the love of fame: this has been the source of my most lively joys and sorrow. It is this that has made me perpetually anxious to present to others the most favourable aspect of the opinion I have entertained of them.[5]

He needed to be somebody; without that he could face neither the world nor himself.

Doctrinal disagreement between preacher and congregation was a major occupational hazard among the Dissenting clergy, and twice John Godwin was obliged to leave his post. When Godwin was two-and-a-half the family moved from Wisbech to Debenham in Suffolk, and then again, two years later, to Guestwick in Norfolk, then as now 'a village of the lowest order, having nowhere the appearance of a street, no three of its houses being contiguous to each other, but all them thinly scattered over a space of about two miles in diameter'. Yet this out-of-the-way spot had, and still has, an imposing meeting house – all the more impressive for being so totally unexpected – whose long-standing congregation was currently without a preacher. It was an important post, and John Godwin held it until his death twelve years later.

William was now four and already reading. For formal schooling he went first to Mrs Gedge, a local widow who could recall the previous century, and then, after her death, to a school of about a hundred boys in nearby Hindolveston. In summer he would walk the two-and-a-half miles across the fields with his brother and the tormented Steele; in winter he would stay in town, though not as one of the school's thirty-odd boarders. The master, Robert Akers, was a tall, pale, wrinkled man, a self-educated tailor who prided himself on his penmanship. Strict and impersonal, he taught nothing but the three Rs, and Godwin was, he says, 'perhaps the only one of his scholars that ever loved him.'

Inevitably the childhood preacher first saw his career lying, like that of his father and grandfather, in the Nonconformist church. He claims to have made up his mind when he was six, but his father was against it, being 'seriously impressed with the notion that there was a sort of pride and unsubmittingness of spirit in me, incompatible with the humility of the gospel', while his mother was convinced that a boy who so loved reading must surely become a bookseller. Even so, once he had absorbed all that Akers could teach him, Godwin, aged eleven, was sent to Norwich as the private pupil of a prominent Dissenting minister, Samuel Newton – and there found himself no longer the favourite. For Newton was harsh and contemptuous, 'the most wretched of pedants', 'his chief passion . . . polemics, . . . his almost sole gratification to be admired for his controversial talents', and also, to Godwin's horror and indignation, an enthusiastic disciplinarian. It was the first time he had had to suffer this 'ignominious violation', and he resented the injustice and irrationality of it as much as the pain. 'The infliction of stripes upon my body can throw no new light upon the question between us', he would complain in *Political Justice*:

> I can perceive in them nothing but your passion, your ignorance and your mistake. If you have any new light to offer, any cogent arguments to introduce; they will not fail, if adequately presented to produce their effect. If you be partially informed, stripes will not supply the deficiency of your arguments.[6]

And to complete the chilling picture, Newton's wife was yet another of those unfeeling, unbending, not quite human characters that populated Godwin's youth:

> She may be compared to an animated statue of ice. She would never, like Newton, put herself out of the way for the delight of giving anyone pain, but she was indifferent to their pleasures, as she might be said, in a popular sense, to be indifferent to her own.

Godwin hated and feared them both, yet Newton's love of argument could not fail to take effect. There must have been many an angry dispute – if Godwin found Newton brutal and intolerant, Newton found him arrogant and unyielding – but in the end Godwin was persuaded. He had been reared a Calvinist, but Newton was something more than that: he was a follower of Sandeman, 'a celebrated north country apostle, who, after Calvin had damned ninety-nine in a hundred of mankind, had contrived a scheme for damning ninety-nine in a hundred of the followers of Calvin'. Characteristically, 'this scheme for damning those good simple souls, who never suspected a word of the matter, but thought themselves cocksure of everlasting life, was the favorite topic of Newton's discourse', and the God-fearing Godwin, obsessed with the thought of eternal damnation, could hardly ignore arguments that demonstrated that his beliefs would inevitably consign himself, his family, and most of those he knew, to the very Devil. So he became a Sandemanian, the advantage being, as he later put it, that of the Catholics over the Protestants: that the Protestants allow that Catholics might be saved, but not vice versa. Such considerations kept him a Sandemanian until he was twenty-five, but at the end of his life he looked back on those early teachings, Calvinist and Sandemanian alike, with almost total disgust.

That 'celebrated north country apostle' was actually a Scotsman, son-in-law and chief disciple of John Glas who had been expelled from the established Church of Scotland in 1728; thanks to ~~Spence~~ Sandeman's many writings, those known in Scotland as Glassites were called Sandemanians in England. His teachings seem to have meant different things to different worshippers, for the only other Sandemanian of note, the mild Michael Faraday, seems to have endorsed a faith very different from that of Godwin and Newton. But the sect's most distinctive tenet was that belief in God must be a matter of wholly intellectual assent, unpolluted by any element of emotion or unreasoned faith. Moreover the Sandemanians disapproved of private wealth, holding that property should always be subject to the needs and purposes, and always at the call, of the Church as a whole; and they believed that all decisions must be a matter of total unanimity, with no room even for abstentions – those with objections must state them and argue them, so that the necessary agreement can be reached through rational discussion. And all these doctrines – the superiority of intellect over emotion, the elimination of private property, a complete equality of status, universal agreement arrived at by open debate – would emerge as leading themes in the atheistical *Political Justice*. Such was Godwin's intellectual debt to Newton that, for all the harshness and brutality, he could still look back on him as 'certainly my friend'.

Nevertheless by June of 1770 he could stand it no longer, and telling his father that he had decided not to enter the ministry after all, he returned to Akers as senior pupil assisting with the education of his juniors. Nine months later he returned to Newton – 'I had nearly completed my fifteenth year, and now hoped for a somewhat more manly treatment, nor was I wholly disappointed' – only to be sent home again at the end of 1771, because Newton said he had nothing left to teach him. And so Godwin was working still as an assistant master in Akers's school when his father died, on 12 November 1772. 'It was', said Godwin grudgingly, 'with considerable reluctance that he quitted this sublunary scene.' But at last he was free to follow his original intention, and train for the ministry. (Godwin dated his father's death as both November and December, but the Guestwick Church Book, in the Norfolk Record Office, confirms that it was the former.)

As a Dissenter Godwin was barred from the established universities, but that was actually an advantage, since he could go instead to one of the celebrated Dissenting Academies, which provided the most balanced and up-to-date education of their time. He applied first to the most prestigious Academy of all, at Homerton, but to his surprise was rejected on account of his Sandemanianism – it was only then that he bothered to read Sandeman's writings, 'that I might compare them with my previous habits of thinking, and know whereof I was accused' – and in September 1773 he enrolled instead at the Academy at Hoxton, then a small village on the outskirts of London.

These Dissenting Academies tended naturally towards political radicalism, for what was a Dissenter but someone who rejected the Church with which the state identified itself, who believed instead in freedom of conscience and opinion, freedom from political inter-ference and control? But the Hoxton Academy was even more radical than most, 'growing much too unorthodox for the con-gregational fund'[7] by the time it was closed down in 1785, and Godwin's own tutor, Dr Andrew Kippis, was one of the more prominent left-wing intellectuals of the time. But though he was there five years Godwin remained, he insists, the institution's only Tory, just as he was its only Sandemanian, despite never attending the London chapel. Evidently Newton had been 'an intemperate Wilksite', but when Godwin read the reports of parliamentary debates in the *Gentleman's Magazine* he had been more impressed by the opposition's intemperance and extravagance, their 'repeated assertions that, if such and such a measure were adopted, our liberties were gone', and so had preferred to side with the govern-ment, an opinion reinforced by the friends of his mother with whom he had stayed in London before starting at Hoxton. But most of all, perhaps, he was temperamentally disinclined to toe any party line: 'Newton, my schoolmaster, and the young men at Hoxton College, almost with one voice proclaimed me as the most self-conceited, self-sufficient animal that ever lived.' So despite being 'famous in my college for calm and dispassionate discussion' and 'indefatigible in my search for truth', 'all my enquiries terminated in Calvinism', and he came out of Hoxton as he went in, still a Tory and still convinced that 'the majority of mankind were objects of divine condemnation, and that their punishment would be everlasting'. His Testimonial, or graduation certificate, is dated 25 May 1778; he was then twenty-two.

Godwin had done a spell of preaching at Yarmouth and at Lowestoft during his final summer vacation, and after a false start at Christchurch in Hampshire and a 'putrid fever' that almost killed him, he took up his first post at Ware. His sermons were eloquent but uninspired, fervently evangelical, but not notably Calvinist,

> nearer to the animated style of the French orators, than the generality of compositions for the pulpit in this colder climate.

They present many just and useful sentiments in no unpleasing dress. They are picturesque, and therefore entertaining; they are declamatory, but the declamation is not destitute of thought or good sense.[8]

Indeed the story goes that his congregations were more appreciative when he used his father's sermons in place of his own. But it was at Ware that he met another young preacher called Joseph Fawcett, 'almost the first man I had ever been acquainted with, who carried with him the semblance of original genius', and Fawcett, an admirer of the American philosopher-theologian Jonathan Edwards and of Edmund Burke, converted Godwin to them both. 'I became', he says, 'an oppositionist, chiefly influenced by my fervent admiration for the talents and virtues of Edmund Burke and James Fox' – suggesting, too, that those calm and dispassionate discussions at Hoxton included some measure of wilful obstinacy.

After little more than a year at Ware Godwin moved on to Stowmarket in Suffolk, where he read Swift and became in consequence a republican, and was introduced to the writings of the French philosophers – d'Holbach, Rousseau and Helvetius – by a local tradesman, Frederick Norman. Under their influence his religious beliefs began to alter too: 'my orthodoxy was sensibly declining; I rejected the doctrine of eternal damnation; and my notions respecting the trinity acquired a taint of heresy.' But Godwin was still enough of a Sandemanian to believe that you did not have to be an ordained minister, as he as yet was not, to administer the sacraments. When, finally, he was ordained, the outraged ministers of the neighbourhood refused to attend the ceremony, and in April of 1872 he was effectively expelled from his post. It was while waiting in London for another that he first turned his hand to writing for publication, with the encouragement of Fawcett and Kippis. The result was his *Life of Chatham*, William Pitt the Elder, who had died four years before, and still for Godwin 'the great commoner'. It was a grandiosely rhetorical tribute, successful enough to run immediately into a second edition, and when Godwin did find a post that December, at Beaconsfield where Burke had his country home, he sent a copy in the hope that Burke might endorse this first publication. But there is no evidence that Burke replied to the letter, or that the two men ever met.

Meanwhile the religious doubts that had begun with reading D'Holbach's materialist *Système de la Nature* increased with reading Joseph Priestley. D'Holbach led him to question orthodox Christianity, and especially the Church, but not, as yet, God himself. Priestley, with whom he corresponded, made him instead a Socinian, who denied the divinity of Christ, and once and for all he renounced Calvinism, 'a gloomy doctrine' as he later described it, 'equally condemned by the understanding, and revolting to the heart'.[9] He could remain in the Church no longer and in June of 1783 he resigned his ministry. He had lost his calling, but it would be another five years before he lost his faith. In later years Godwin was to trace over and again the minute details of his changing religious convictions, but at the time the break with his childhood vocation seems to have been surprisingly painless. He still had the support and approval of his Hoxton tutor Kippis, and as he explained to his mother, he now intended to devote his life to an equally noble calling, the benefit of mankind:

> I know of nothing worth the living for but the usefulness and service of my fellow-creatures. The only object I pursue is to increase, as far as lies in my power, the quantity of their knowledge and goodness and happiness.[10]

At Beaconsfield Godwin had written a first political pamphlet, his *Defence of the Rockingham Party*. It was a strange choice, with an even odder title, for Rockingham, who had used the defeat in America to end twelve years of Tory rule, was dead, and his 'party' had died with him, when Fox refused to serve under his successor. Instead Fox, the severest critic of the American war, had joined forces with his bitterest enemy, Lord North, the war's chief architect, to bring down his own side. It was this 'most unscrupulous coalition known in our history',[11] and especially its 'Rockingham connexion' – not just Fox, whom Godwin refers to by name, but also Edmund Burke, much commended despite a lamentable adherence to 'aristocratical principles' – that Godwin defends, as the party best fitted to govern at that moment. But his defence was as ill-conceived as Fox's grab at power. The ministry, hopelessly divided, fell at the end of the year, to be replaced by Pitt the Younger, then aged twenty-four, first minister for the next seventeen years. Fox, on the other hand, would never hold office again, until the final months of his life.

However, Godwin's ambition now was to found a school. He secured financial backing, hired a furnished house, and produced a brochure that proved to be the most significant of these early publications, his *Account of the Seminary* 'that will be opened on Monday the Fourth Day of August, at Epsom in Surrey, for the instruction of Twelve Pupils in the Greek, Latin, French and English Languages'. The title deserves to be given in full, for it is only there that Godwin provides any information about the school itself: you could read the entire pamphlet, otherwise, without realizing that it was meant as an advertisement. Nowhere is there mention of practical matters like classrooms, facilities, the teacher and his qualifications, fees, meals, or the length of terms. The *Gentleman's Magazine* might greet the project with approval – 'His plan is ingenious, without being romantic, and deeply speculative, yet strictly practical' – and recommend it to parents on the grounds that 'men of genius seldom will submit to the drudgery of education'.[12] But it was hardly a prospectus calculated to persuade fond parents, nor unkind ones for that matter, and the school never opened.

Instead the *Account of the Seminary* is an exercise in educational theory, an essay on the value of the humanities and the ancient languages in particular, together with some strikingly advanced suggestions on how they might best be taught. Nothing could differ more from the harsh and repressive schooling Godwin himself had received: the pupil should be governed by kindness not by fear; he should proceed at his own preferred pace; the emphasis should be on discovery, not on committing things to memory; free writing is to be preferred to formal composition, free reading to vocabulary and grammar; the teaching should be fitted to the particular capacities of the particular child; the teacher should concentrate on practical matters, on things that mean something to his pupil: history, for example, should deal not with dates and military campaigns, but with the changing manners of men.

Fourteen years later, in a volume of essays called the *Enquirer*, Godwin was able to develop these ideas at greater length. 'According to the received modes of education, the master goes first and the pupil follows. According to the mode here recommended, it is probable that the pupil should go first, and the master follow.'[13] The teacher, he says, has but two functions: to provide the student with the motivation to learn for himself; and to smooth out such difficulties as lie in his way:

> It is of less importance, generally speaking, that a child should acquire this or that species of knowledge, than that through the medium of instruction, he should acquire habits of intellectual activity . . . . The preceptor is in this respect like the incloser of uncultivated land; his first crops are not valued for their intrinsic excellence; they are sown that the land may be brought into order.[14]

This is why Godwin is against the memorizing of facts and figures. The sheer accumulation of information will never arouse interest. Instead the teacher's first task must be 'The Obtaining of Confidence', to quote one essay title, and once the pupil feels a sympathy with his master he will come to admire what he admires. It is only in this way, by example, that the child can be imbued with a love of learning; but when he has acquired that, he has acquired everything.

The debt in all this is obviously and explicitly to Rousseau, but there are differences between them, most notably in Godwin's emphasis on language and literature. Rousseau himself had little time for book-learning, holding that education must be concerned with things, not words. But for Godwin and *Political Justice*, literature is one of the three sources of moral improvement, to be ranked with politics and education itself. The desire to read, fiction as well as fact, provides the child with a key to all human knowledge and understanding, and therefore to virtue, inasmuch as the one depends on the other: 'He that loves reading has everything within his reach. He has but to desire; and he may possess himself of every species of wisdom to judge, and power to perform.'[15]

But there is another, more important, difference. According to Rousseau, the teacher must seem to be allowing the child to do as he pleases, when in fact he is directing his studies. 'Let him believe that he is always in control', he wrote in *Emile*, 'though it is always you who really controls. There is no subjection so perfect as that which keeps the appearance of freedom.' Yet for Godwin the original sin of social institutions is precisely that they try to control us by deceiving us; and equally we seek to manage our children, from even the youngest age, by lying to them:

> If the nurse find a difficulty in persuading the child to go to sleep, she will pretend to go to sleep along with it. If the parent wish his youngest son to go to bed before his brothers, he will order the elder ones up stairs, with a permission to return as soon as they can do it unobserved. If the mother is going out for a walk or a visit, she will order the child upon some pretended occasion to a distant part of the house, till she has made her escape.[16]

If education is to equip us for a life of truth and reason, it must be based in frankness and honesty, in the supreme virtue of sincerity. If we are to instil the proper, indeed necessary, respect for truth, we must conceal nothing, inhibit nothing, censor nothing. And if we are to encourage the use of reason, and devalue the appeal to blind authority, we must talk to children as to equals, and accord their opinions the same weight as our own. As things are

> the terms of the debate . . . . are, first, If you do not convince me, you must act as if I had convinced you. Secondly, I enter the lists with all the weight of long practice and all the pride of

added years, and there is scarcely the shadow of a hope that you will convince me.[17]

If he is to set the right example, the teacher must be prepared to reason with his pupils, to hear their arguments, and if necessary, concede defeat. He must be their friend and adviser, but never their master.

The main advantage of this approach to education is freedom, for both master and pupil: 'Three fourths of the slavery and restraint that are now imposed upon young persons will be annihilated at a stroke.'[18] Indeed Godwin feels as strongly about the tyranny that adults exercise over children as he does about that which governments exercise over their subjects: 'Dearly indeed, by twenty years of bondage, do I purchase the scanty portion of liberty, which the government of my country happens to concede to its adult subjects.'[19] But is freedom enough? Perhaps some children are not capable of benefiting from Godwinian encouragements; perhaps the only way to teach some is by dinning the crucial facts into them, by repetition, by authority, by force if needs be; perhaps the only way for a civilized community to survive at all is for its members to be inculcated with the same opinions and attitudes, rather than allowing each individual to go his own disruptive way. The controversy rages on, even now.

But Godwin is well aware of this objection, that school is 'the time to correct the native vices of the mind', when a modicum of pain and discomfort might mend errors which 'must otherwise fall with tenfold mischief upon the age of maturity'.

> But who is it that has told you, that the certain, even the probable consequences of this severity are beneficial? Nothing is so easily proved, as that the human mind is pure and spotless, as it came from the hands of God, and that the vices of which you complain, have their real source in those shallow and contemptible precautions, that you pretend to employ against them.[20]

This, in a nutshell, is the basis of his educational theories as it is of his political doctrines: the human mind, in itself, is good and pure; left to itself it cannot lead us astray; it is only when private judgment is distorted, by government or by education, that we fall into error:

> Speak the language of truth and reason to your child, and be under no apprehension for the result. Show him that what you recommend is truly valuable and desirable, and fear not but he will desire it. Convince his understanding, and you enlist all his powers animal and intellectual in your service.[21]

It looks, perhaps, the wildest optimism. It is certainly not obvious that we are all equally capable of rationality, equally capable of arriving at an accurate estimation of truth. Of course the fact that adults are not wholly rational proves nothing against Godwin, since he will explain that by the distorting pressures of existing educational practices and political institutions. But it has still to be proved that all men are equally rational, or at least that education can make them so. And Godwin believes that it can be demonstrated, that 'nothing is so easily proved': that, at any rate, was to be the argument of *Political Justice*. For the moment, however, he saw education as the main force for good or ill: a sound system the means by which everyone might be converted to reason and truth, a perverted system the main obstacle to human progress. Even when he began to doubt the supreme effect of environment, he remained convinced that education was of all others 'a most powerful instrument'. Yet as the *Enquirer* allows, education in the strict sense provides only a very small part of the variety of experiences that shape the infant mind and condition the adult. Accordingly his attention began to turn from schools to governments, to public institutions of every kind. It is politics, even more than education, which holds the key to man's future, the explanation of his present and his past.

3 ♣ Sincere friendships

How extensive an effect would be produced, if every man were sure of meeting in his neighbour the ingenuous censor, who would tell to himself, and publish to the world, his virtues, his good deeds, his meannesses and his follies . . . . Nor is it possible to say how much good one man sufficiently rigid in his adherence to truth would effect. One such man, with genius, information and energy, might redeem a nation from vice.[1]

Political Justice, 1793

♣ The school had failed, more exactly had never begun, but the *Life of Chatham*, the *Defence of the Rockingham Party* and now the *Account of the Seminary* had helped Godwin gain a toehold as a freelance writer, and one after another the little volumes poured eagerly forth: a booklet of clever literary parody called *The Herald of Literature*; a collection of his own sermons, under the misleading title of *Sketches of History*; a set of bitterly sarcastic *Instructions to a Statesman*, being the unprincipled Lord Temple whose intrigues on behalf of the King had brought down the Fox-North coalition; a translation from the French of the *Memoirs of Simon, Lord Lovatt*, which though 'refined and improved in every sentence, almost in every line, by Mr and Mrs Murray', the publishers, and put into print, was not actually released for another thirteen years; and three novels – *Damon and Delia* (ten days' work for 5 guineas), *Italian Letters* (three weeks' work for 20 guineas), and *Imogen, A Pastoral Romance* (four months' work for 20 pounds)—not to mention his 'principal employment', writing for the *English Review* (at 2 guineas a sheet, maximum income 24 guineas a year). And all in a single year!

Two of these early novels have survived, their florid melodrama far removed from the detailed restraint of Godwin's mature prose. *Italian Letters* is a story of love, seduction and corruption, told after the fashion of Richardson, through the correspondence of the main characters. But unlike his friend Holcroft, whose *Anna St Ives* has the villain dutifully writing his letters even as he waits outside the heroine's bedchamber, 'undressed and ready for combat', Godwin does not cheat with the form, apart from delaying one crucial note in the post. The narrative, however, is every bit as sensational, with the seducer writing of the sixteen-year-old virgin on whom he has set his sights, that 'the mellow fruit is ready to drop from the tree, and seems to solicit some friendly hand to gather it', while a friend warns of the danger – and injustice – of getting the girl pregnant. It might be expected to throw his family into consternation at what he was up to, alone in the big city, yet Miss Godwin – now become Mrs Sothren – seems to have thought it the best of his writings. But then she had herself introduced him to Richardson's *Clarissa*, and so inspired him to compose whole epistolary novels in his head as he walked the fields of Norfolk. Perhaps this was one of them.

In *Imogen* intrigue gives way to magic, in a flimsy tale of a wicked lord who uses sorcery to carry off the virtuous shepherdess, only to be thwarted by her honest shepherd lover. Such interest as there is lies only in the Preface, where Godwin pokes fun at a celebrated forgery of the day, by discussing with great seriousness the claim of his own text to be the work of an ancient Welsh bard, Cadwallo. Godwin was never noted for a sense of humour; he took himself altogether too seriously for that. But there was more than a streak of irony in him, and the wit of the *Herald of Literature*, the sarcasm of the *Instructions to a Statesman*, and the gentle mockery of the *Imogen* Preface, show that he was not always the dour pedant of later years.

The *Sketches of History* was the only one of these early works to bear Godwin's name, and none made him much money. The *Life of Chatham*, published on his own account, actually left him £40 in debt, and his only reward for the *Herald of Literature* and the *Sketches* was the job with Murray's *English Review*. So for the most part, as he says, 'I did not eat my dinner, without previously carrying my watch or my books to the pawnbrokers.' Nevertheless he had now proved himself sufficiently to give up, for a time, the unrewarding business of writing pot-boilers to order, and in 1784 George Robinson and Andrew Kippis, publisher and editor respectively of the *New Annual Register*, a Whig answer to the Tory *Annual Register*, invited him to take over their yearly historical survey. It was not the most rewarding work, but enough to enable him to move from the second to the first floor of his Soho lodgings.

Next year he began to write also for the *Political Herald*, a new monthly that was sponsored by Fox and Sheridan, who was as prominent an MP as he was a dramatist. Godwin, writing under the name of 'Mucius', toed the orthodox Whig party line, supporting the impeachment of Warren Hastings, attacking the ambition and hypocrisy of the younger Pitt, and positively gushing with praise of Edmund Burke, superior in both style and content even to Rousseau. In 1786 Godwin was for a time the *Herald*'s acting-editor, and was eager to continue permanently in the post, provided he could preserve his independence by sharing any profits rather than drawing a salary. But despite several discussions with Sheridan, the *Herald* was allowed to collapse at the end of the year.

So Godwin turned instead to the British Museum, where a post as under-librarian in the Department of Natural and Artificial Productions had just come vacant. He presented as impressive a front as he could muster, signing his letters 'the Rev. William Godwin', trusting that Lord Robert Spencer would remember him for his work on the *Herald*, and asking the Bishop of Llandaff, to whom he had dedicated his volume of sermons, to write in his support. (Watson's somewhat dubious reply, uncertain about recommending a Dissenter, is dated by Kegan Paul as 18 May 1790. But this must be an error, since Godwin had applied on 24 January 1787, and the post was filled a month later – unless Watson's letter relates to a second application in 1790, when a similar post did come vacant, or, perhaps, to some quite different transaction.) But the job went to another, and Godwin was left with the *New Annual Register* and its 60 guineas a year.

Soon, however, he was writing another political booklet, an anonymous *History of the Internal Affairs of the United Provinces* from 1780 up till the present, in which he detailed the steps by which the citizens of the Netherlands had been drawn into confrontation, and then open hostilities, with their ruler or Stadtholder, William V. To many it was a question of monarch versus aristocracy, but for Godwin – 'perhaps an impartial and just reasoner will not feel himself inclined warmly to espouse the cause of either of these parties' – its importance lay elsewhere, in the attempts of some Dutch cities to govern themselves by public meeting, by community council in effect, precisely as *Political Justice* would soon prescribe. But though he cares nothing for the Stadtholder, of whom he speaks always with the greatest contempt,

> that the aristocracy should remain is essential to the welfare of Holland. Wherever riches have been in any degree accumulated, and the inequality of mankind has made any considerable progress, a pure democracy cannot long exist. It is absurd for us to suppose to ourselves the poor giving laws to the rich, and the affairs of a country directed by those who possess the smallest share of property. The influence of property must in some manner be exerted; and it is better to open to it an easy and moderate channel, than to suffer it, either by its sinister proceedings to undermine the manner of the people or by the violence of its resentments, to shake the fabric of the state.

It is, as we shall see, the doctrine of his idol Burke, that political stability requires institutions that represent the sources of power

within the community. But at the same time Godwin is groping
towards the realization that private wealth lies at the root of political
authority, with the inevitable consequence that if the one is unjust, so
must the other be. However, Godwin's main concern was to argue
against external intervention by either England or Prussia: that
would be both unjust and useless, he insists, for 'there never was a
people that was enslaved, who were determined to be free'. But
events overtook him yet again. His book scarcely had time to be
published, much less read, before the Prussians had moved in with
British approval, to set William V back in undisputed control. It
would be his last personal publication for six years.

Godwin had now reached his thirties, still wearing his black
parson's garb, his frizzed hair sticking out from under a large cocked
hat, and with a passion for argument that impressed and annoyed in
equal measure those with whom he had to deal. For convinced as he
was that he possessed truths so obvious and proofs so certain that
only the wickedly stupid could fail to be persuaded, he was prepared
to challenge the whole world on the field of reason, if needs be, and
conquer it by sheer force of argument. But although he could argue a
principle vehemently enough, he was a poor conversationalist,
lacking any capacity for small talk, shy and consequently tactless in
unfamiliar company, sometimes afraid to advance an opinion for
fear he might be unable to back it up – 'too sceptical, too rational, to
be uniformly zealous' – yet liable to veer dramatically to the
opposite extreme and turn aggressive or rude, seeming at times a
frightened fool, at others a passionate ass. His childhood had made
him awkward, his religious training made him self-righteous, his
pride made him touchy: 'He reminded those who knew him of the
Metaphysician engrafted on the Dissenting Minister. There was a
dictatorial, captious, quibbling, pettiness of manner.'[2] Censorious of
others but uncertain of himself, and acutely sensitive to any
criticism, he could all too easily turn a theoretical disagreement into
personal offence, then lack the quick flash of repartee with which to
defend or extricate himself. He would turn peevish or petulant, or
stalk out in a rage and concoct a defence in the privacy of his study,
painstakingly recreating the challenges and counter-challenges of
the day before:

Your original charge against me was, that I never retracted my
opinion, but having once uttered it, always found some subter-
fuge by which to defend it. Whether you be at present disposed
to retract a part or maintain the whole of this charge, I do not
know. I know that I immediately stated back to you the precise

truth of the case, that the contrary of this is rather my characteristic . . .[3]

And so on, and on, and on.

Godwin's constant companion in these early years, and for most of their lives, was James Marshall, a fellow student from Hoxton days who had helped finance his first publication, the *Life of Chatham*. After an unsuccessful sortie to the West Indies, Marshall had returned to set up house with Godwin, to share their expenses, their earnings and their ambitions. But he proved the less successful, and remained all his life what Godwin had been at first, a literary odd-jobber, a translator and indexer. He was also, in effect Godwin's secretary, his manager almost, since it often fell to him to mollify the publishers and editors that Godwin had antagonized by his stormy petulance. Nor did Marshall himself escape those outbursts. According to Godwin's daughter, who remembered Marshall well, 'Godwin, whose temper was quick, and from an earnest desire of being in the right, somewhat despotic on occasion, assumed a great deal of superiority and some authority.'[4] But for his part Godwin put their difficulties down to the evils of cohabitation, whether it be between friend and friend, husband and wife, or master and pupil. 'It seems to be one of the most important arts of life', he would later argue with the vigour of personal experience, 'that men should not come too near each other, or touch in too many points. Excessive familiarity is the bane of social happiness.'[5]

The ill humour which is so prevalent through all the different walks of life, is the result of familiarity, and consequently of cohabitation. If we did not see each other too frequently, we should accustom ourselves to act reasonably and with urbanity.[6]

Yet for all his prickliness and awkwardness, his argumentativeness and lack of social graces, Godwin had begun to make himself a name in left-wing circles, and at Sheridan's he met the young political hopefuls of the day: the dandified George Grey, recently elected to parliament at the age of twenty-two, but more concerned with the look of his legs and the enormous square buckles of gold with which he adorned them; the eager George Canning, who would also become prime minister, albeit on the other side; and William Wilberforce, just then beginning his harassment of the slave trade through the House of Commons. For a time, perhaps, Godwin hoped he might make another of their number, for Sheridan had told him he should be in parliament. But rather to his disappointment, this close contact came quickly to an end, until there were other, different, reasons to revive it.

Instead it was at the regular dinner parties of his publisher Robinson that Godwin formed the friendships which would last into the 1790s: with the learned antiquarian and leading light of the Society for Constitutional Reform, Thomas Brand Hollis; with the bohemian beauty Helen Maria Williams, whose intellectual tea parties represented the height of radical fashion; with William Nicholson, a commercial agent who dabbled in chemistry and phrenology as well as politics and philosophy; and above all with the dramatist Thomas Holcroft. The self-educated son of a shoemaker, a jockey and actor turned playwright, Holcroft was already the successful man of letters that Godwin and Marshall hoped to become, with a formidable output of operas, comedies, novels and dramatic poems which would eventually total more than thirty works. They met first in 1786, and Godwin struck up an immediate intimacy with this swarthy, intense, passionate man, older by eleven years and already thrice married. 'His temper was acid, petulant and harsh . . .', wrote Godwin, describing his friend through the character of Mr Forester in his novel *Caleb Williams*.

At first sight all men were deterred by his manner, and excited to give him an ill character. But the longer any one knew him, the more they approved him. His harshness was then only considered as habit; and strong sense and active benevolence were uppermost in the recollection of his familiar acquaintance. His conversation, when he consented to lay aside his snappish, rude and abrupt half-sentences, became flowing in diction, and uncommonly amusing with regard to its substance.

Others testify equally to Holcroft's abruptness and outspokenness. Later in life, when he had had to endure more than his share of misfortune and vilification, he would march up to a new acquaintance and demand to know, straight out, whether he intended to be friendly or no; and Coleridge, asked whether he was not much struck with Mr Holcroft, replied that he felt more in danger of being struck *by* him. There is ample evidence, too, in his letters to Godwin, of Holcroft's sense of humour, and those snappish half-sentences. Disjointed phrases crowd surrealistically upon one another – he calls one such letter an 'olio', a stew of mixed vegetables – until the writer is forced to pull up in a string of etceteras, 'for I am quite out of breath. Observe, however, I will not vouch for the truth of a single syllable of all this: but I will cite you most grave and respectable authorities, viz. Herald and Post.'[7] Though they seem an unlikely pair, the aggressive and uncompromising Holcroft and the sensitive, diffident Godwin, at bottom they were two of a kind, equally fascinated by matters of man and morality, equally excited at the prospect of imminent political and social reform. It was Holcroft who made Godwin finally an atheist, and when Godwin went off to Guildford for the summer of 1788, armed with a copy of Campbell's *Answer to Hume on Miracles*, in order to make up his mind once and for all, Holcroft kept him up to date on the lively Westminster by-election that had among its high-spots the tossing of a lawyer from a committee room window into a passing sewage cart. At supper together, now at Godwin's, now at Holcroft's, in unending argument and discussion, they hammered out the views of government and society which would permeate their most important books, Godwin's *Political Justice* and Holcroft's *Anna St Ives*, published just a year apart. It was Holcroft, not Godwin, of whom Hazlitt said,

> He believed that truth had a natural superiority over error, if it could only be heard; that if once discovered, it must, being left to itself, soon spread and triumph; and that the art of printing would not only accelerate this effect, but would prevent those accidents which had rendered the moral and intellectual progress of mankind hitherto so slow, irregular and uncertain.[8]

And it was Holcroft, not Godwin, who once told a bemused Thomas Ogle that

> it is nonsense to say that we must all die; in the present erroneous system I suppose that I shall die, but why? because I am a fool! – Hurra! said I: but if a man chops your head off? – It will be impossible to chop your head off: chopping off heads is error, and error cannot exist. – But if a tree falls on you and crushes you? – Men will know how to avoid falling trees: – but trees will not fall: falling of trees arises from error.[9]

But their similarities ran still deeper, both equally convinced of the truth of their convictions, both equally tactless, both equally easily offended. 'I will certainly not fail you, God willing, on Tuesday', runs one note from Holcroft, followed immediately by another: 'Sir – I write to inform you that instead of seeing you at dinner tomorrow I desire never to see you more, being determined never to have *any* further intercourse with you of *any* kind.' To which he adds the postscript,

> I shall behave, as becomes an honest and honourable man, who remembers not only what is due to others but to himself. There are indelible, irrevocable, injuries that will not endure to be mentioned. Such is the one you have committed on the man who would have died to serve you.[10]

Godwin called Holcroft 'a man of iron' and Holcroft dubbed him

'Sir Fretful', but even in their anger true friendship shows through, and it was to Godwin that Holcroft turned in November 1789 when his son William ran away from home, taking with him £40 stolen from his father's bureau and a pair of pistols. They must have known that the boy intended to leave the country, for they went at once, fruitlessly, to Gravesend, and then a week later to Deal, where they boarded the *Fame*, lying at anchor, between one and two on a Sunday afternoon, 15 November. The sixteen-year-old boy, hidden below deck, heard Holcroft call that he was coming to look for him, and rather than face his father, put one of the guns to his mouth and pulled the trigger. Godwin's laconic diary records the tragedy, but records it in French: '*élopement de son fils*'; '*funérailles*'. (It is possible that the 'Jour de mauvaise nouvelle' listed for 4 September 1788, which evidently involved sending Marshall twice to Southampton, refers to the previous occasion on which William Holcroft ran away.)

Godwin had begun this diary the year before. At first it contained only occasional notes, but the entries soon became regular and more detailed, though always abbreviated and sometimes entirely cryptic. For this was no journal, but only the briefest record of each day's doings and readings, amounting by the end of his life to thirty-two notebooks, each carefully ruled and dated by hand, a week to the page, the dates and references to external affairs in red ink, the main entries in black. Yet these scrimpy jottings tell us much about Godwin, providing a key not merely to the events of his life but also to that rigid and methodical personality that needed to keep each detail in its proper, rationally ordained place. Emotion there is, sometimes, but emotion distanced by being recorded in French, with the word '*démêlé*', signifying a quarrel or disagreement, especially common.

Still, Godwin was argumentative rather than quarrelsome, prickly not aggressive, and these clashes tended to be short-lived, as upsetting to himself as they were to others:

31.W [i.e. diary entry for Wednesday 31 August 1791.] Holcroft dines. Fawcett expected. *démêlé*. Faintness.

Friendship, as ever, was a necessity of his nature, and the same insecurity that made him so sensitive, so anxious to impress and succeed, meant that he stood equally in need of constant re-assurance, sympathy and support, of someone who would admire his virtues, ignore his faults, and withstand the continual rows and recriminations with which he tested those closest to him: 'I am subject to long fits of dissatisfaction and discouragement; this also seems to be constitutional. At all times agreeable company has an omnipotent effect upon me, and raises me from the worst tone of mind to the best.'[11]

The strains of life with Godwin were further increased in the summer of 1788, when the household was joined by his twelve-year-old ward and pupil, Tom Cooper. Two years earlier Andrew Kippis had been the means of another 80 guineas for his protégé, when he found Godwin a private pupil called Willis Webb, who studied under him for a year, in between Eton and St John's College, Cambridge. Their first experience of private tutoring had been encouraging enough, and Webb continued to call on his teacher for many years thereafter, to continue their discussions of morality, self-love and the rest. But Cooper was a very different pupil, with a very different background. He was a second cousin whose father, a surgeon with the East India Company, had died recently in Bengal, leaving his wife and family penniless. Despite his own precarious finances Godwin willingly took charge of the boy, and devoted himself remorselessly to his education, making this his opportunity to put into practice what he had previously preached: education was a most powerful instrument, by which men could be made rational, just and free; and Tom Cooper would be the living proof of that proposition.

Unhappily Cooper himself felt otherwise, and went almost out of his way to resist his tutor. Moody, rude and spiteful, he was no doubt working out resentments of his own on the far from placid Godwin. But Godwin would not concede that any failure was due to faults in the student; it would take more than an obstreperous teenager to shake his faith in man's essential goodness, his natural perfectibility. 'Not to impute affected ignorance, lequel n'existe pas. not to impute dulness, stupidity', he reminded himself again and again; 'Do not impute intentional error, lequel n'existe pas.'[12] But naturally Godwin did not always heed his own warnings, and Cooper – whose apology to Marshall for disobedience once took the form 'I am glad that I have escaped doing that which your words naturally excited me to do' – would sometimes reply in kind. In one such fit of temper he carefully noted down the 'pointed and humiliating words' that Godwin had used of him, then left the note for Godwin to find:

He called me	*a foolish wretch*	in my presence
He said	*I had a wicked heart*	ditto
He would	*thrash me*	ditto. Does he think I would submit quietly?
I am called	*a Brute*	in my absence
I am compared to	*a Viper*	ditto

He went out	*merely to avoid me*	ditto
I am	*a Tiger*	ditto
I have	*a black heart*	ditto
	No justice in it	ditto
	No proper feelings	ditto

He has no enmity to my *person*, yet he hates me. I suppose he means by that that he does not find me ugly.[13]

Godwin's reaction to this piece of petulance was astonishing. 'My dear boy', he wrote,

I am more pleased than displeased with the paper I have just seen. It discovers a degree of sensibility that may be of the greatest use to you, though I will endeavour to convince you that it is wrongly applied. I was in hopes that it was written on purpose for me to see; for I love confidence, and there are some things that perhaps you could scarcely say to me by word of mouth. I have always endeavoured to persuade you to confidence, because you have not a friend on earth that is more ardently desirous of your welfare than I, and you have not a friend so capable of advising and guiding you to what is most to your interest . . .[14]

Godwin welcomed the outburst because it revealed the paramount virtue of sincerity. The fact that Cooper was not content merely to think ill of him, but actually told him so, and why, was for him a mark of the greatest merit.

For if happiness and a just society are to be possible only when people have regard to truth and nothing but truth, then speaking the truth as we see it must be the most important of all virtues. Too often we conceal what we think, from cowardice or a mistaken belief that there are some things better left unsaid; but the inevitable result is ignorance and mistake, and therefore evil. It is for Godwin a measure of the corruption of our society that a judge, Lord Kames, and a moralist, Archdeacon Paley, were prepared to allow that there are false oaths that are not objectionable, deliberate falsehoods that are not lies. But the practice that he personally takes most exception to is the 'established mode of excluding visitors' by sending a minion to declare that you are not at home, a practice cowardly of the master, corrupting of the servant, and irritating for the caller – and also, one imagines, one from which the earnest Godwin himself tended to suffer, albeit one he never adopted.

Accordingly Godwin, no less than Tom Cooper, was prepared to speak the truth as he saw it to friends and acquaintances, however unpleasant it might seem, however much their hackles might rise in the process. Of course if we are going to proclaim uncomfortable truths, it is best to do so in a pleasant and acceptable way. But Godwin believed also that an open frankness will carry its own excuse and justification, that no one will take offence once they recognize that you speak from sheer respect for truth. And here, inevitably, lay the origins of many a *démêlé*, with Holcroft in particular, especially because the morbidly sensitive Godwin was not a man to accept the truth with equal equanimity when levelled against himself. He could speak it well enough, but he could not so readily take it, a characteristic easily misunderstood. 'Godwin, whose very heart is cankered by the love of singularity, and who feels no disinclination to wound by abrupt harshness, pleads for absolute sincerity', complained Coleridge later, 'because such a system gives him frequent opportunity of indulging his misanthropy.'[15]

Later in life Godwin was more doubtful of the power, or the right, of unvarnished truth to carry all before it. 'He was by no means rugged and blunt', he says of a character in the novel *Mandeville*. 'His air was humane and his manner conciliating. But he held it for a sacred duty, to tell the plain and simple truth. This is the misfortune of the moral virtues. Whoever acts them scrupulously, overacts them.' But at the time of *Political Justice* he felt no such qualms: 'If every man today would tell all the truth he knows, three years hence there would be scarcely a falsehood of any magnitude remaining in the civilized world.'[16] Sincerity, therefore, is an absolute duty; lying must always be wrong, regardless of circumstances. Common sense may tell us that this cannot be so, that there will always be cases where a lie is the lesser of two evils, where the end will justify the means. But Godwin, typically, will have none of that: 'We must not be guilty of insincerity. We must not seek to obtain a desirable object by vile means.'[17]

But suppose that the husband of a seriously ill woman has been killed. Should not this information be kept from her, by deception if needs be? Not at all.

> The most that could possibly be conceded in a case like this is, that this perhaps is not the moment to begin to treat like a rational being a person who has through the course of a long life been treated like an infant. But in reality there is a mode in which under such circumstances truth may safely be communicated; and, if it be not thus done, there is a perpetual danger that it may be done in a blunter way by the heedless loquatiousness of a chambermaid, or the yet undebauched sincerity of an infant.[18]

Suppose, then, that a man can save himself from those who seek to kill him, only by telling a lie. Would he not be justified in telling that

lie? By no means: if, instead, he declares himself boldly and honestly
to his pursuers, 'would he not have done an honour to himself, and
afforded an example to the world, that would have fully compensated the calamity of his untimely death?'[19] Suppose, finally, a
resident of Portugal of the 'opinion that the established government,
civil and religious, of that country is in a high degree injurious to the
welfare of its inhabitants.' Ought he to say so, and suffer imprisonment or death for his pains? Here Godwin is at first more evasive,
since 'a person so far enlightened upon these subjects, ought by no
consideration to be prevailed upon to settle in Portugal; and if he
were there already, ought to quit the country with all convenient
speed.'[20] But if that should prove impossible, then again the sacrifice
must be made: 'It is by no means certain that the individual yet
existed, whose life was of so much value to the community, as to be
worth preserving at so great an expence [sic], as that of his
sincerity.'[21]

Yet as Godwin came eventually to see, this uncompromising
insistence on the importance of sincerity fits awkwardly with his
equally uncompromising adherence to the standard of justice as the
one true test of morality. We need only conceive a case where the
failure to tell the truth will actually promote human welfare – which
seems not so difficult to do – and one or the other must then give
way: either the deception will be right, in which case sincerity is not
an absolute duty; or it will be wrong, in which case justice is not
the only test of morality. For that matter there may even be cases
where frankness and honesty actually contribute to the survival of
injustice:

> Let us however suppose, a circumstance which is perhaps
> altogether impossible, that a man shall be a perfectly honest
> lawyer. He is determined to plead no cause, that he does not
> believe to be just, and to employ no argument, that he does not
> apprehend to be solid. He designs, so far as his sphere extends, to
> strip law of its ambiguities, and to speak the manly language
> of reason. This man is, no doubt, highly respectable, so
> far as relates to himself; but it may be questioned whether
> he be not a more pernicious member of society than the dis-
> honest lawyer. The hopes of mankind in relation to their future
> progress, depend upon their observing the genuine effects of
> erroneous institutions. But this man is employed in softening
> and masking these effects. His conduct has a direct tendency to
> postpone the reign of sound policy, and to render mankind
> tranquil in the midst of imperfection and ignorance.[22]

As Godwin points out, it is like the problem of the Imbecile

Monarch (George III had had one bout of insanity in 1765 and another in 1788–9, which had already prompted the question of whether he should be replaced by his son. Recurring attacks in the 1800s would culminate in the appointment of the Prince Regent, later George IV, in February 1811): if we are going to have a monarchy it might seem best to ensure that the office does not fall into the hands of a person of notorious imbecility, perhaps by making the post in some way elective; yet 'such is the strange and pernicious nature of monarchy, that it may be doubted whether this be a benefit', for to disguise the evils inherent in monarchy is 'perhaps one of the greatest injuries that can be done to mankind'.[23] At bottom it is the old problem of means and ends: sometimes, surely, it will be better to allow a temporary evil – an imbecile monarch, a dishonest lawyer, a judicious lie – in order to ensure a greater permanent good?

Moreover, this clash between justice and sincerity is echoed in later editions by a similar clash between justice and that absolute independence of thought and action on which Godwin also placed so much emphasis, a conflict between the welfare of all and the freedom of the individual which would recur the following century, in the tension between John Stuart Mill's two most celebrated works, *Utilitarianism* and *On Liberty*. For there are those who insist that it is only by ignoring the rights of the individual and striking directly towards the benefit of everyone, by means of a benevolent dictatorship if necessary, that social and political progress can be ensured. Which, then, should take precedence: utility or liberty, justice or individual independence?

Godwin, perhaps, should be in no doubt, since *Political Justice* explicitly rejects human rights, and rejects them precisely because no man has the right to do what conflicts with the general good, yet although he appears often as the most single-minded of Utilitarians, there seem also to be other values in his moral scheme of things. Indeed some have seen his insistence on independence and sincerity as fundamentally at odds with the surface Utilitarianism, as if he were merely disguising a morality of old-fashioned absolutes in fashionable Continental garb. But undeniably there are other values in his philosophy: there are reason and truth as well as justice, and the conflict between utility, sincerity and independence is simply the conflict between these three. The problem Godwin has to face is which is of most importance, most value: an adherence to truth; the exercise of private reason; or justice, the benefit of all? And once the problem is stated, the answer is obvious, as it gradually became obvious to Godwin himself: independence and sincerity have supreme value, but as means not as ends; their value lies precisely in their utility. So when, in the second edition, he returns to the problem of whether deception might sometimes be permissible to protect your own life – or even more crucially, that of another – there is much beating about the bush, but eventually the point is conceded. There are times, and there are situations, where sincerity must take second place: 'sincerity itself is a duty, only for reasons of utility.'[24] Godwin's insistence on those values of reason and truth is not an exception to his belief in justice, but a consequence of it. Sincerity and independence are necessary because they are necessary for justice.

But to return to Tom Cooper. Perhaps it was as a substitute for the son who committed suicide that Holcroft took a special interest in the boy, and though, Godwin intended him for an author, under Holcroft's influence he inclined more towards the stage. So when, in 1792, Cooper announced his intention of walking to Paris to join the new Revolutionary Army, Holcroft arranged instead for him to go to Edinburgh to join the travelling company of Stephen Kemble, younger brother to the more famous John. But this first venture proved something less than a success. After a few walk-on appearances, Cooper, still only sixteen, was given his big chance at Newcastle-on-Tyne, where he was to play Malcolm in *MacBeth*:

> I went through the part very well, and tolerably perfectly, till I came to within two lines of the end of the play (I speak the last speech), and there I wanted the word. The noise behind the scenes, the play being nearly over, prevented my hearing the prompter, and in an instance some people at the back of the gallery, as I guessed, began to hiss, and immediately everybody else began to clap, which lasted for a minute, and we were so near the end it was not advisable to wait the conclusion of the bustle to say the few words that remained. The trumpets sounded and the curtain fell.[25]

Cooper does not mention that it was left to the dead MacBeth, Kemble himself, to call the curtain down. He was given £5, and sent back to London.

He persevered, none the less, and with Holcroft's continued encouragement was for several years a touring player, writing regularly and affectionately to Godwin, their former animosity apparently forgotten. For a time, early in 1795, Godwin did persuade him to take a job as a clerk in Bristol, but to his distress Cooper ran away after only a few months and was soon back studying the stage under Holcroft. He even appeared with some small success as Hamlet at Covent Garden, and as a result was invited to perform in Philadelphia. Godwin and Holcroft were against the offer but Cooper accepted, and an anxious Godwin saw the youth off from the George and Blue Boar on 12 September 1796.

But Godwin need not have worried. Cooper introduced to America the histrionic style of John Kemble, and was within two years

> recognized as the unrivalled tragic actor of America, despite a faulty memory and careless study. During a period of at least thirty years Cooper was the most conspicuous figure on the American stage . . . . He possessed extraordinary beauty of face and form, and a magnificent voice.[26]

By all accounts a stern and forbidding man, the creation of his childhood as Godwin was of his, Cooper was also a figure of some social standing. But his return visits to England never matched his American success, and his career declined towards the end, though well-attended benefits show that he remained a major draw. Thomas Abthorpe Cooper, trained by Holcroft but educated in the full Godwinian sense by Godwin himself, died in America in April 1849.

4 ♣ The great debate

This was the year of the French Revolution. My heart beat
high with great swelling sentiments of liberty. I had read with
great satisfaction the writings of Rousseau, Helvetius, and
others, the most popular authors of France. I observed in them
a system more general and simply philosophical than in the
majority of English writers on political subjects, and I could
not refrain from conceiving sanguine hopes of a revolution of
which such writings had been the precursors. Yet I was far
from approving all that I saw even in the commencement of
the revolution. I never for a moment ceased to disapprove of
mob government and violence, and the impulses which men
collected together in multitudes produce on each other. I
desired such political changes only as should flow from the
clear light of the understanding, and the erect and generous
feelings of the heart.[1]

Memorandum on 1789, written around 1800

♣ Godwin's career as a political journalist had begun too late for
him to salute the American War of Independence, but he was
convinced that that revolution must quickly be followed by others,
each one more peaceful and more radical than the last, as reason,
truth and, finally, justice extended their domain across the world. 'A
new republic of the purest kind is about to spring up in Europe', the
Internal Affairs of the United Provinces had enthused;

> and the flame of liberty, which was first excited in America,
> and has since communicated itself in a manner more or less
> perfect to so many other countries, bids fair for the production
> of consequences, no less extensive than salutary.

Of course that particular confidence had been immediately crushed
by the armies of Prussia, but the memory of the democratic
revolution in Holland would soon be obliterated, relegated to a mere
footnote to history, by another revolution, as unexpected and
exhilarating as it would prove to be violent.

King Louis XVI, on the verge of bankruptcy and unable to raise
new taxes, had been obliged to convene the Estates-General, the
traditional assemblies of gentry, clergy and bourgeoisie, for their
first meeting since 1614. He had had to stand helplessly by while

those three Estates turned themselves into a single body, the commons forming a majority, and began to debate issues of economic and constitutional reform. And when he had seemed to threaten a *coup d'état* against this new Assembly, the people of Paris had seized arms with which to defend it, and so thrown open the dungeons of the infamous Bastille, and liberated all its hapless victims: four forgers, two madmen, one murderer. Then, in a single night, the extraordinary St Bartholomew of the Privileges, feudalism had been abolished, and a stream of nobles, clerics and civic dignitaries had vied with one another in renouncing all traditional rights and prerogatives. At first the king, 'a kindly man, with just enough brain capacity to know that he was unfit to be king in that crisis',[2] had refused to promulgate these resolutions, or the subsequent Declaration of the Rights of Man. But the women (perhaps) of Paris had marched on his palace at Versailles, home of the legendary Sun King, Louis XIV, and an international symbol of absolute monarchy, and forcibly taken him back to the capital, where they could keep an eye on him.

Even the most die-hard of Tories could hardly be expected to sympathize, when it had been Louis's costly support of the American rebels, as much as anything else, that had precipitated his present predicament. But those on the left were naturally ecstatic. The citizens of America had thrown off an unjust rule; now the citizens of France had humbled one of the world's mightiest despots. Where would it all end, what could halt the cause of liberty and equality now? 'How much the greatest event that ever happened in the history of the work, and how much the best,' enthused Charles Fox, leader of the parliamentary Whigs, while his great rival, Prime Minister Pitt, also found much that he could admire. 'The present convulsions in France must sooner or later culminate in a general harmony and regular order . . . ,' he declared. 'She will enjoy just that kind of liberty which I venerate,' the kind of liberty which 'it is my duty, as an Englishman, particularly to cherish.' To a predominantly Dissenting body like the London Revolution Society events in France were a positive inspiration, a model that they themselves might follow.

Not that these 'Revolutionists' intended any revolution. Instead they owed both name and origin to the Glorious Revolution of 1688, when the peaceful transfer of power from James II to William and Mary had also marked a transition both from Catholic to Protestant rule, and from absolute to constitutional monarchy. It was a similar peaceful double reform that the Revolution Society looked forward to now: the repeal of the antique Test and Corporation Acts which limited public office, in theory if not in practice, to members of the

Church of England; and the reform of parliament itself. After the collapse of the war against the American colonists, the political tide had seemed to be running their way: the repeal of the Acts was narrowly defeated in 1787, and came within twenty votes of success two years later; and the prime minister himself had formerly introduced a bill for parliamentary reform. So it was with a sense of imminent success that Andrew Kippis, once Godwin's tutor and now his editor, had addressed the Revolution Society in its centennial year of 1788, and proposed to his eager audience their three-fold right: 'to choose our own governors; to cashier them for misconduct; to frame a government for ourselves'.

That theme was taken up again the following year, by the venerable Richard Price, statistician and philosopher. But this time the Revolutionists were meeting in an atmosphere more heady, more hopeful, than ever before. 'I have lived to see a diffusion of knowledge, which has undermined superstition and error, Price enthused.

> I have lived to see the rights of men better understood than ever; and nations panting for liberty, which seemed to have lost the idea of it – I have lived to see THIRTY MILLIONS of people, indignant and resolute, spurning at slavery, and demanding liberty with an irresistible voice; their king led in triumph, and an arbitrary monarch surrendering himself to his subjects – After sharing in the benefits of one Revolution, I have been spared to be a witness to two other Revolutions, both glorious – And now, methinks, I see the ardour for liberty catching and spreading; a general ammendment beginning in human affairs; the dominion of kings changed for the dominion of laws, and the dominion of priests giving way to the dominion of reason and conscience.

At the dinner which followed there was a unanimous vote of congratulation to the National Assembly of France: the freedoms for which the English had striven in their own revolutions but had not entirely realized, the freedoms for which the French were striving now, they might yet achieve together.

It was the very day of Price's *Discourse on the Love of Our Country*, 4 November 1789, that a young Parisian councillor, Charles Jean-François de Pont, wrote to England to ask the opinion and advice of the man from whom, as he said, he had first acquired a great love of liberty, Edmund Burke. An aggressive and grandiloquent orator whose impassioned tirades could last for hours, if not for days, Burke had gained for himself the reputation of an intemperate radical, both for his vigorous support of the American colonists, and for his vitriolic campaign against oppression and misgovernment in India in the person of Warren Hastings. But his reply to de Pont, when finally it came, was scarcely as he had expected:

> I had certainly no idea that my letter would lead to the publication of the work which you have so kindly sent me. I will even confess that I should never have made the request, had I been able to forsee its effects; and that if I had at that time known your opinions, so far from begging you to express them, I should have besought you not to make them public.

For Burke made this his opportunity to reply to Price and all those like him, who sought inspiration in the French atrocity. 'I wish my countrymen rather to recommend to our neighbours the example of our British constitution', he declared, 'than to take models from them for the improvement of our own.' And his scathing critique of everything the events in France stood for and portended, his *Reflections on the Revolution in France*, would set off in its turn one of the most comprehensive wars of the written word in all British history. It was truly the Great Debate.

Burke's own political creed found its concrete expression in that same Glorious Revolution of 1688. Indeed it was Price's reference to other, more violent, revolutions as equally glorious, as much as the appeal to the imported doctrine of natural rights, that sparked off Burke's last outburst of political rage. He had supported the American colonists because they had evolved institutions of their own to which they therefore owed their allegiance, but he will have none of Kippis's 'new and hitherto unheard of Bill of Rights'. Established institutions had for him an almost divine legitimacy – it was Burke who proposed that the requirement of the Test and Corporation Acts be changed from that of taking the Lord's Supper in accordance with the rites of the Church of England, to the solemn declaration that the existing establishment was in harmony with the law of God, and not in any way to be tampered with! Not that Burke was opposed to change as such: 'a state without the means of some change is without the means of its conservation.' But as that phrase implies, conservation was for him more important than change. He is, therefore, the archetypal conservative, accepting no reforms but the most gradual and most considered. Burke believed that human society requires so complex a body of belief and practice that no simple solution, such as political theorists dream of, can be possible; no intellectual construction, no matter how ideal, no matter how rationally based, can compete with the solid realities of historical experience and conventional wisdom. To begin anew, without reference to what we have learnt from the past, is to 'set up your trade without a capital'.

It is here that the revolution in France cut at the very roots of civilized society. It was not the fact of change that Burke abhorred, but its speed and its manner. Writing in 1790, when the scattered violence of the preceding summer was passing into history and the course seemed set fair for some form of liberal democracy, Burke insisted on the implications of this sudden break in political continuity, this challenge to the very basis of the state. In the quietest months of revolutionary France, he predicted the most dire consequences: moderate constitutional reform will give way to republicanism, there will be proscription of enemies, civic anarchy and civil war, and, in the end, military dictatorship. To many these rash predictions seemed little short of insanity, and if Burke had been proved wrong, if France had halted at the point she had then reached, it is doubtful whether his extravagant claims would have taken their place as a major contribution to political philosophy. But events would prove him right, so dramatically and convincingly right, that his opinions have often seemed in need of no further support.

It was Burke, more than anyone else, through his writings and his parliamentary speeches, who polarized British opinion, raising the spectre of violence and revolution at home as well as abroad. Published in November 1790 at five shillings the copy, the *Reflections* had soon sold over 30,000 copies, provoking a stream of replies and counter-replies which would amount to some seventy pamphlets in all, not to mention heated discussion in the newsprints and in the streets. The majority proved hostile: a passing reference to the 'swinish multitude' was particularly resented, and the more spirited replies carry titles like *Hog's Wash* or *Pig's Meat* or *Pearls Cast Before Swine*. But Burke's manifest lack of sympathy for the plight of the poor under the *ancien régime*, contrasting markedly with his effulgent praise of Marie Antoinette, was exposed most successfully in one of the very first answers, published later the same month, Mary Wollstonecraft's *Vindication of the Rights of Man*. 'Among all your plausible arguments and witty illustrations', she complained, 'your contempt for the poor always appears conspicuous and arouses my indignation.' Burke tells them they

> must respect that property of which they cannot partake. They
> must labour to obtain what can by labour be obtained; and
> when they find, as they commonly do, the success dispro-
> portioned by the endeavour, they must be taught to find their
> consolation in the final properties of eternal justice.

Miss Wollstonecraft replies in her schoolmarm fashion, 'It is, Sir, possible to render the poor happier in this world without depriving them of the consolation which you gratuitously grant them in the next.' But we shall be hearing more of Miss Wollstonecraft.

The *Vindication of the Rights of Man* ranks as one of the three major replies to Burke, along with James Mackintosh's *Vindiciae Gallicae*, a work as dry and scholarly as its title, and the book which would rival Burke's as a classic of political theory, Thomas Paine's *Rights of Man*. Paine had been the prime propagandist of American independence, author of *Common Sense*, the biggest-selling pamphlet in the history of print. Now he was in Europe trying to interest someone in his revolutionary design for a bridge which would be held up by horizontal iron girders, instead of the conventional vertical supports. When he learnt that Burke was preparing an essay against the French Revolution he set himself up in rooms in Islington to produce a reply as soon as it should appear. Once, out walking, he came across Mackintosh's footman and told him to advise his master to discontinue work on the topic: once his own pamphlet was published no one would read any other. And so, in March 1791, after some trepidation and some delay, there appeared the first part of the *Rights of Man*.

It proved the opposite of Burke in more than content. Where Burke piled grandiloquent phrase upon grandiloquent phrase in passages designed to be recited rather than read, Paine's writing was simple and direct, often pungent and amusing. That familiar title of 'honest Tom Paine' carries just the right suggestion of blunt no-nonsense worthiness, a lack of affectation and even of sophistication, so that one contemporary complained, 'he writes in defiance of grammar, as if syntax were an aristocratic invention.'[3] But although his prose was more lively, because less ornate, than Burke's, Paine's argument was less systematic, and therefore less authoritative. The *Reflections* give the impression of a man struggling to come to grips with eternal verities; the *Rights of Man*, Part One especially, is little more than a piecemeal refutation of Burke's particular complaints against Price and the French. Paine intends to set the record straight, and to expound and defend the new French constitution and its Declaration of the Rights of Man and of Citizens, which he quotes in full. It is only in a final, aptly-titled 'Miscellaneous Chapter' that he tries to put the dispute in perspective. But he soon gave up the vain attempt to draw so many loose ends together, and decided instead to write a second, more systematic, treatise, to be published as the *Rights of Man*, Part Two.

The paradox of this confrontation is that while it is Paine who speaks with the voice of the plain practical man who will not be taken in by the high-falutin' nonsense of the intellectuals, and Burke sounds like a man who puts his faith in grandiose declarations and sophisticated theories, in fact their political stances were exactly the reverse. It is Paine who relies on an abstract doctrine of natural rights and an optimistic faith in human nature, while Burke appeals to the hard reality of social institutions; where Burke puts his trust in precedent and experience, Paine is content to rely on a scrap of paper drawn up by the French National Assembly. And Burke's authorities would prove the more reliable: his prediction of growing anarchy would be borne out more and more, while Paine's devout belief in imminent universal peace, the brotherhood of man, and the immediate collapse of monarchies and despotisms of every kind, proved just about as wrong as it could be.

Even so Paine's down-to-earth style was ideally tailored for his audience, plain folk interested not in the ultimate justification of political authority, but in their rights, as men and as citizens. Soon the *Reflections* had to be abbreviated, to enable it to reach the wider and poorer public that was reading Paine. But the *Rights of Man*, published first at three shillings and then, thanks to subsidies from political societies, in even cheaper editions, at sixpence or less, quickly outstripped sales of the *Reflections* by the order of two to one. Paine became the radical hero, the man who had spoken up for the common man, sharing with Burke the honour of being hung or burnt in effigy.

For Burke it was all 'pure defecated atheism,' 'the brood of that putrid carcass, the French Revolution', deserving 'no other refutation but that of the common hangman'. (Ford K. Brown's biography of Godwin mistakenly refers these remarks to *Political Justice*. In fact Burke took almost no notice of that book, see p. 62 below.) Yet, reading that first part of the *Rights of Man* today, it is difficult to see how it could ever have been considered a subversive document. Even if we are prepared to be shocked by its relatively mild attacks on monarchy and aristocracy as useless and unjust, Paine's republicanism amounts in context to government on behalf of the people as a whole: 'republican' and 'representative' government were often taken as synonymous, and the Britain of today would count as a republic in Paine's sense. But what was disturbing was not Paine's arguments, such as they were, but his precedents, his appeal to France as a model for Britain. The original publisher had second thoughts when he saw the book set up in print, and withdrew it when only a few dozen copies were done. Publication had to be delayed for a month, until another printer could be found.

Meanwhile, as Paine set to work on the second part of his *Rights of Man*, the debate was growing more heated. The second anniversary of the fall of the Bastille might seem to some a suitable occasion to express solidarity with the French, but several meetings had to be cancelled through government pressure, and an entirely respectable dinner in Birmingham sparked off several days of anti-radical – and more to the point, anti-Dissenter – rioting in which Joseph Priestley had his home and his laboratory, the best-equipped in Europe, burnt to the ground. When the more systematic, more visionary, and even more successful *Rights of Man* Part Two appeared in February 1792, it, too, had been delayed for a month by a change of publisher. The first had tried to buy the copyright and had then declined to proceed, clearly as a result of external pressure. Paine himself was sure that the prime minister had intended – and indeed managed – to delay publication until after the announcement in Parliament of a series of tax reforms, so as to steal some thunder from Paine's own proposals, which included family allowances, old age pensions, and a graduated property tax. But Pitt is more likely to have been worried by Paine's more developed and more outspoken attack on the existing form of government. For this time he pulls no punches: 'All hereditary government is in its nature tyranny'; 'Monarchy always appears to me a silly contemptible thing', and unpardonably expensive to boot. Only a fully representative government, grounded in human nature, reason and experience, can be relied upon to provide just and wise laws. But Paine remained unlucky in his predictions. 'I do not believe that Monarchy and Aristocracy will continue seven years longer in any of the enlightened countries in Europe', he proclaimed; France and Britain will become allies instead of enemies; and

> as revolutions have begun . . . it is natural to expect that other revolutions will follow. Revolutions are to be looked for. They are become subjects of universal conversation, and may be considered as the Order of the Day . . . . All attempts to oppose their progress will in the end be fruitless.

Passages like these, of course, were simply asking for trouble, and within three months the man who had eventually published both parts of the *Rights of Man* was summoned for printing and circulating seditious literature. He pleaded guilty, and on 21 May the pamphlets were outlawed and Paine himself charged with sedition. The trial was postponed until December and Paine at first intended to defend himself, but, as he prepared to leave a gathering on 13 September, the poet William Blake warned him that if he went home he would be going to his death. A speech of the previous evening had been noted by government spies, and a warrant was out for his arrest. Paine left immediately for France, where he had been made an

honorary citizen, and elected to the new National Convention by
four separate constituencies. Customs officials at Dover began a
search of his baggage, but were so impressed at finding a personal
letter from the president of the United States that they waved him on,
allowing just enough time for him to put to sea before the arrest
warrant arrived behind him. Two months later Paine was tried in
his absence. He had written an insulting letter to the Attorney-
General:

> that the Government of England is as great, if not the greatest,
> perfection of fraud and corruption that ever took place since
> government began, is what you cannot be a stranger to; unless
> the constant habit of seeing it has blinded your sense.

When this was read aloud in court Paine's counsel, Erskine, who
knew nothing of it, declared it must be a forgery, but despite an
impassioned speech for the defence, the foreman of the jury declared
that no further evidence was necessary, and Paine was duly found
guilty of High Treason and sentenced to death, should he ever be
apprehended in Britain or its colonies.

This conviction came as a watershed in Anglo-French affairs. As
late as January 1792, only three months before the outbreak of a war
that would last until 1815, Pitt had been publicly predicting fifteen
years of peace. Whatever his response to radicalism at home, he had
so far been following a conciliatory line with the French, and took a
firm stand only when the revolutionary armies seemed to threaten
Holland. But in January 1793, a month after Paine's trial, Louis
XVI was executed, and the following month the French declared
war against Britain too. It was in this highly charged atmosphere
that there appeared, on 14 February, the book that would mark the
culmination of the war of the pamphlets, and raise the whole debate
to a more reflective, more philosophic level. Its title, *An Enquiry
Concerning Political Justice and its Influence on General Virtue and Happiness*,
its size and its cost, all marked an essential difference in both style
and substance from Burke, Paine and their myriad commentators.

For this was something more than another reply to Burke. In fact
Political Justice was scarcely a reply to Burke at all, and the debt to
Burke's earlier writings is obvious and often explicit, even if Godwin
sometimes takes seriously what was meant only ironically. His
conclusions might stand at the opposite extreme from Burke's
appeal to convention and tradition, but in method he was still a
Burkean gradualist, relying on reasoned debate, not violent revolution. In the days of the *Political Herald* he had written again and
again in effusive praise of Burke's virtues and talents, the brightest
orator in the House of Commons, the most prominent and promising

of the true friends of mankind. And even now, when Burke was reviled as a traitor to the radical cause, the worst that Godwin can call him is 'this illustrious and virtuous hero of former times'.[4]

Indeed *Political Justice* might almost be a reply to Paine, for Godwin rejects out of hand both natural rights and written constitutions, the twin planks of Paine's political platform. Moreover, it is probably no coincidence that Godwin proposed his own 'Political Principles' a matter of months after reading the first *Rights of Man*. However much he shared Paine's faith in human nature and his optimism for man's future, he would have been little impressed by the scrappiness of the argument. When Paine invokes those Rights of Man he seems to be referring merely to a document drawn up by the French National Assembly; we look in vain for some account of how those rights arise or are substantiated. But that is not how Godwin's thought works. He believed, and with justice, that the debate had concentrated too much on purely local issues, on what had happened in France or might yet happen in Britain, when what was needed was a whole system of moral and political truth, within which each particular problem could find its due solution. The question was not whether we should introduce this or that reform, or provide this or that safeguard. The problem was not how to protect men from their governments, or the state from its citizens. The fundamental issue, quite simply, was how men ought ideally to live, what society ought ideally to be.

5 ♣ A true euthanasia
of government

When a man writes a book of methodical investigation, he does not write because he understands the subject, but he understands the subject because he has written. He was an uninstructed tyro, exposed to a thousand foolish and miserable mistakes when he began his work, compared with the degree of proficiency to which he has attained when he has finished it.[1]

Enquirer, 1797

♣ To Godwin and his like the events in France had been a revelation, an intoxication, an inspiration. 'Few persons but those who have lived in it', wrote Southey some thirty-five years later,

can conceive or comprehend what the memory of the French Revolution was, nor what a visionary world seemed to open upon those who were just entering it. Old things seemed to be passing away, and nothing was dreamt of but the regeneration of the human race.[2]

Godwin dined with the Revolution Society at the London Tavern in November 1789, when Price proposed his vote of congratulation to the French National Assembly. (Price delivered his *Discourse on the Love of our Country* at the Dissenting House in Old Jewry on 4 November, but the dinner at the London Tavern must have been the following evening. Godwin's diary lists 'Dine with the Revolutionists – Price, Kippis . . .' for 5 November, Guy Fawkes Night!) He dined with them again the following year, when the abrasive John Horne Tooke put a motion against the nobility, which Price personally opposed. And he was there once more in 1791, when Paine and his principles more than filled the gap left by Price's death. But most exciting of all, he and Holcroft had eagerly awaited J. S. Jordan's republication of the first *Rights of Man*, after the original publisher had changed his mind.

'I have got it', wrote Holcroft finally in breathless triumph,

– If this do not cure my cough it is a damned perverse mule of a cough – The pamphlet – From the row – But mum – We don't sell it – Oh, no – Ears and eggs – Verbatim, except for the addition of a short preface, which as you have not seen, I send you my copy – Not a single castration (Laud be unto God

50

and J. S. Jordan) can I discover – Hey for the New Jerusalem! The millennium! And peace and eternal beatitude be unto the soul of Thomas Paine.[3]

(The story is often told that Paine entrusted this republication to Godwin, Holcroft, and their friend Thomas Brand Hollis, while he went off to France. Yet Holcroft's well-known letter is hardly that of a man, or to a man, who had seen the book through the press, and when the story was put about at the time Brand Hollis said he had never seen the work in manuscript. Godwin did meet Paine, for the first time, five days after the original publication, and he 'borrowed Paine' a day or two after that, but there were no further meetings until November, and Paine would surely not have entrusted his book to a virtual stranger. In any case Paine did not leave for France until after its second publication.)

The following month Godwin wrote Sheridan an open letter, signed 'a well-known literary character', and Holcroft wrote similarly to Fox, 'to encourage those two illustrious men to persevere gravely and inflexibly in the career on which they had entered',[4] and not join the mounting witch hunt against Tom Paine. Yet all this excitement still left Godwin at something of a loose end. 'Even almost from boyhood', he later explained,

> I was perpetually prone to exclaim with Cowley, –
>> What shall I do to be for ever known
>> And make the age to come my own?

> But I had endeavoured for ten years, and was as far from approaching my object as ever. Everything I wrote fell dead-born from the press. Very often I was disposed to quit the enterprise in despair. But I still felt ever and anon impelled to repeat my effort.[5]

In 1790, 'being desirous . . . of inculcating those principles on which I apprehend the welfare of the human race to depend',[6] he had begun and abandoned a tragedy about St Dunstan; the following year he had suggested a Natural History to his employer Robinson, but that project ended in a *démêlé* a few days later. But it was politics that formed 'the almost constant topic of conversation between me and Holcroft',[7] and at dinner on 30 June 1791 Godwin 'proposed a Political Principles'. Robinson agreed to support him as he wrote, and so he 'abdicated, I hope for ever, the task of performing a literary labour the nature of which should be dictated by any thing but the promptings of my own mind.'[8]

By September he had completed his duties for the *New Annual Register* and was hard at work, writing his two or three manuscript pages a day, sometimes as many as six or seven, but revising carefully as he went along and discussing his ideas constantly, most often with Holcroft but also with a younger friend, George Dyson, not much older than Tom Cooper, and with the practically minded William Nicholson. It was not always easy work, for Godwin was a meticulous writer, and once, after twelve months' labour,

> there was one paragraph he wrote eight times over before he could satisfy himself with the strength and perspicuity of his expressions. On this occasion a sense of confusion of the brain came over him, and he applied to his friend Mr Carlisle, afterwards Sir Anthony Carlisle, the celebrated surgeon, who warned him that he had exerted his intellectual faculties to their limit. In compliance with his direction, Mr Godwin reduced his hours of composition within what many will consider narrow bounds.[9]

Other writers may consider Mr Godwin lucky that eight revisions was so uncommon an occurrence, but at least *Political Justice* does not require the reader to exert his intellectual faculties to their limit, until a sense of confusion of the brain overcomes him. The argument may sometimes be repetitive and poorly structured, but the writing is as clear and incisive as Godwin wanted it to be.

Nevertheless this slow and painstaking composition had important consequences for the development of Godwin's thought. When he began writing, the first stage of the French Revolution was just coming to its end, and as a democrat he had every reason to feel optimistic. Two years of intense discussion at all levels of society had culminated in a range of social, political and legal reforms that would permanently transform the structure of French society. A new constitution had been drawn up, prefaced by a solemn Declaration of the Rights of Man and of Citizens. The French monarch was now ruling in Paris with the consent of his National Assembly, not from Versailles by his own divine right. But while Godwin wrote, the situation had deteriorated. Before long France had declared war on her neighbours, and was well on the way to losing it. In August 1792 the people of Paris occupied the Tuileries Palace, to the loss of some 1200 lives, and the National Assembly nervously suspended Louis's rule, voting to replace itself with a National Convention to be elected by universal male suffrage: the celebrated French constitution, two years in the making, had lasted less than one. And when the conquering Prussians threatened those who might resist them with 'all the rigours of war', a rampaging mob had slaughtered more than a thousand 'enemies of the Revolution' in their Paris cells. Yet on the very day that the new Convention assembled the enemy advance was halted, the Prussians, miraculously, began to withdraw, defeated by rain, dysentery and their own poor supply lines, and the next day, 22 September, France proudly declared herself a republic. Within weeks she had voted her support for popular revolution wherever it might occur, and an enthusiastic people's army surged forward in a thrilling string of victories in the name of liberty, equality, fraternity. By the time that Godwin laid down his pen, on 29 January 1793, Louis XVI had been tried and executed. Three days later Britain, too, was at war with France.

These developments cannot help but leave their mark on the book. Arguments are included against the violent overthrow of governments, arguments which grow even more pointed in subsequent editions; and a footnote makes it clear that five chapters on the causes, object and conduct of war, unexpectedly inserted in the midst of a discussion of democratic government, owe their presence to France's original declaration of war against Austria. But more important than the impact of external events is the internal development of the argument. In its original version especially, *Political Justice* is a fascinating record of a thinker pushed further and further, to more and more extreme conclusions, by premises not at first explicit, and to some extent hidden from the author himself. Godwin explains in his Preface that, although the writing took him all of sixteen months, the urgency of the project meant not merely that he spent less time on it than he would have liked, but that the printing had begun before the manuscript was completed.

> Some disadvantages have arisen from this circumstance. The ideas of the author became more perspicuous and digested, as his enquiries advanced. The longer he considered the subject, the more accurately he seemed to understand it. This circumstance has led him into a few contradictions. The principal of these consists in an occasional inaccuracy of language, particularly in the first book, respecting the word government. He did not enter upon the work without being aware that government of its very nature counteracts the improvement of individual mind; but he understood the full meaning of this proposition more completely as he proceeded, and saw more distinctly into the nature of the remedy.[10]

At the beginning Godwin quotes approvingly from Paine's *Common Sense*, that 'society is in every state a blessing; government even in its best state but a necessary evil.'[11] By the end he has changed his mind about both.

Later stages of the book, moreover, show symptoms of a different disorder. The author becomes so immersed in his chain of reasoning, and so excited by the conclusions it generates, that he follows his arguments wherever they may lead, and eagerly adopts positions which on a little reflection might have seemed less plausible. With the heat of discovery upon him he decorates his text with the continual remark that 'nothing could be more evident', 'more simple', 'more incontrovertible', 'more unquestionable', and the more extravagant the claim, the more he insists on its obviousness. As he subsequently regretted:

> I am singularly fitted for a votary of paradoxes, without being eminently impelled to it by the pure love of paradox – I am viciously persuadable by the arguments of others, and want that quick and peremptory feeling which defends many men from absurdity and error.[12]

But Godwin was viciously persuadable not merely by the arguments of others, but also by his own, until *Political Justice*'s extraordinary closing chapters leave no institution of any sort safe from his devastating reason. In later editions he made some attempt to remedy these excesses, but even in its final form *Political Justice* remains something of an intellectual helter-skelter, in which both author and reader leave behind, with ever-increasing speed, the relatively secure position from which they began.

When Godwin set out to write his treatise on the first principles of politics, his concern was not with the rights of individuals, of which he felt rather too much had been made already, but with the moral basis and moral effects of different forms of government. He takes it as proven beyond question, by Locke and others, that there are no innate principles, that we are at birth neither virtuous nor vicious, that it is our circumstances – environment, experience, education – that make us what we are. Chief amongst these, 'of all the modes of operating upon mind . . . the most considerable,[13] are the political institutions through which governments seek to regulate our conduct. So originally Godwin saw his task as to discover which form of government will do most to encourage human progress and the eventual attainment of a state of political justice. 'A sound political institution was of all others the most powerful engine for promoting individual good',[14] to be ranked with education and literature – meaning by that, writing of all kinds – as one of the three major sources of moral improvement, for 'no man was ever yet found hardy enough to affirm that it could do nothing'.[15] But passages such as these have to be deleted in the second edition; Godwin discovers, somewhat to his surprise, that he is just that man.

He had known from the start that government counteracts individual improvement, partly because the sheer inertia of institutions acts as a brake on progress, giving 'substance and permanence to our errors', partly because any attempt by the government to interfere positively is bound to be self-defeating. If governments seek to encourage us to virtue by rewarding good conduct they simply change the nature of our action, and we are in danger of doing what is right not because it is right but because we stand to gain from it, of acting not from benevolence but from self-interest. Nor can the government promote progress by laying down for us what is true and what false, what right and what wrong. The appeal to authority, that the government has told us so, can never demonstrate that something is so; truth can be ascertained only through the exercise of reason.

So what is the justification of political institutions? What gives them their authority over individuals? How and why are we under any obligation to obey the government and its laws? There are, Godwin says, three theories as to the source of political authority – sheer force, divine right, social contract – and none is acceptable. He has little difficulty disposing of the first two. The appeal to force might explain how a particular government exacts obedience from its subjects; but it does nothing to show that it ought to be obeyed, that it has any legitimate authority. The appeal to divine right, likewise, is either a concealed appeal to force, or 'must remain totally useless, till a criterion can be found, to distinguish those governments that are approved by God, from those which cannot lay claim to that sanction.'[16] But the third theory raises questions that are far more fundamental.

The basic idea of a social contract is that, finding that individual interests can best be promoted by joint action, men came together in groups and agreed to operate as a community in accordance with various rules. It is from this original agreement, this primordial social contract, that legal and political obligations arise; this is why citizens have an obligation to obey the government under which they happen to find themselves. As history, of course, it is sheer fantasy, but it is doubtful whether even the most fervent of social contract theorists took himself to be describing an actual historical event, the first founding of civic government. And even if the theory were historically true, it is doubtful whether it would prove what it is meant to, since it is not clear why today's citizens should be bound by the decisions of their remote and primitive ancestors. Rather, the theory presents us with a fable, an image of how government and its obligations are to be understood. In so far as we each of us participate in a particular social organization and share its benefits, to that extent we each of us consent, at least tacitly, to be bound by the rules of the system; and it is this implicit acceptance that gives governments their authority over us.

Godwin sees the obvious difficulties: the problem of who, precisely, has consented to what; of how far and for how long such consent can be presumed to extend; and especially of what can be made to rest on such a tenuous notion as tacit consent. Does the mere fact that I live quietly under the protection of the laws indicate a tacit consent to be governed as I am, and hence generate an obligation to obey any government, no matter what laws it lays down? 'Upon this hypothesis every government that is quietly submitted to, is a lawful government, whether it be the usurpation of a Cromwel, or the tyranny of a Caligula.'[17] But Godwin has another, more novel, point to make. The theory is that we are under an obligation to obey our government because we have in some way promised or agreed to do so; but as he now proceeds to argue, there can be no such obligation. Only justice can generate obligations; agreements, promises, contracts, these can have nothing to do with the case.

It seems, then, that the authority of governments must lie in the consent of their citizens, in common deliberation and common agreement:

> to give each man a voice in the public concern comes nearest to
> that admirable idea of which we should never lose sight, the
> uncontrolled exercise of private judgment. Each man would
> thus be inspired with a consciousness of his own importance, and
> the slavish feelings that shrink up the soul in the presence of an
> imagined superior would be unknown.[18]

But if the demands of government are acceptable only when we agree to them, political authority will be legitimate only when it is unnecessary; beyond that it will be an unjustifiable interference with individual reason. So it emerges that governments have no legitimate authority after all: they can be justified only as a necessary evil, necessary to restrain the wilder members of the community from injustice against others:

> It is earnestly to be desired that each man was wise enough to
> govern himself without the interference of any compulsory
> restraint; and since government even in its best state is an evil,
> the object principally to be aimed at is, that we should have as
> little of it as the general peace of human society will permit.[19]

We have now reached the end of *Political Justice*'s third book, and it may well seem that the argument can stop here. Indeed Book Four, the last in the first volume, is rightly titled 'Miscellaneous Principles', dealing as it does with such leftovers as the value of sincerity, the mechanism of the human mind, the problem of free will, and the basis of morality. But literally and figuratively we are still only half way, and when Godwin turns in Book Five to a detailed critique of the three main forms of government – monarchy, aristocracy, democracy – surprises are in store, for him and for us. Both monarchy and aristocracy, under which Godwin includes any form of government by one or a few, even constitutional monarchies and presidential systems, are founded in falsehood, in secrecy, deception, and what Godwin calls 'imposture', the setting up of one man with a prominence and power over his fellows which he manifestly does not deserve. But even in democracy there are dangers. The example of ancient Athens shows how power can fall to an ignorant multitude, or even worse to the crafty and turbulent demagogue, so that decisions are rashly taken and constantly altered, while men of real ability are despised and distrusted, and distrusted all the more because they refuse to bow to the opinion of the majority. But the dangers of demagogy can be avoided through a system of representation: 'by this happy expedient we secure many of the presented benefits of aristocracy, as well as the real benefits of democracy'. Decisions will be made carefully and only after full deliberation by a body of

> persons of superior education and wisdom . . . not only as the appointed medium of the sentiments of their constituents, but as authorised upon certain occasions to act on their part, in the same manner as an unlearned parent delegates his authority over his child to a preceptor of greater accomplishments than himself.[20]

Godwin finds his ideal form of government, if government there must be – and as yet he thinks there must, for government is a necessary evil – in a reformed British Parliament, albeit without a divisive separation into Commons and Lords.

The obvious objection, even so, is that in thus securing the pretended benefits of aristocracy we also secure its main disadvantage, the setting of some individuals in authority over others. It seems that the only legitimate form of government on Godwinian principles must be a completely participatory, non-representative democracy after all. Yet even in a participatory democracy, people are not free to follow their own judgment. Instead they are forced into a fictitious unity by a blind appeal to majority opinion, and 'the whole is wound up, with that intolerable insult upon all reason and justice, the deciding of truth by the casting up of numbers.'[21] That is why Godwin prefers an elected parliament, which can proceed by debate rather than demagogy, its members persuading one another, not simply voting against one another.

Nevertheless, it now appears that all government, including even Godwin's preferred representative democracy, must be 'an usurpation upon the private judgment and individual conscience of mankind',[22] that 'all government corresponds in a certain degree to what the Greeks denominated a tyranny.'[23] The solution is to limit the powers of the elected assembly, so that its function becomes executive not legislative, its members managers not governors, dealing with the day-to-day details of organization and finance which the bulk of the people delegate to them. Beyond that government need have only two functions, 'the suppression of injustice against individuals within the community, and the common defence against external invasion'.[24] But the second of these is required only in emergencies, and the first is best left to small locally based groups – juries, in effect, or parish councils – which can arrive at a genuine unanimity through discussion and argument, not mere weight of numbers. And when governments are reduced to these small local councils, of the sort that Godwin had welcomed in the United Provinces, people will no longer be taking decisions which govern the conduct of others; they will be deciding for themselves, and only for themselves. At that point government, as such, will have disappeared: so far from being a necessary evil, governments are evil but unnecessary, ultimately dispensable in a world where men are allowed to think and decide for themselves. Somewhat to Godwin's surprise, the rational form of government is no government at all; or as the second edition would put it, with benefit of hindsight:

> The true supporters of government are the weak and uninformed, and not the wise. In proportion as weakness and ignorance shall diminish, the basis of government will also decay . . . . A catastrophe of this description, would be the true euthanasia of government.[25]

So far, perhaps, it looks more like a death from natural causes. But Godwin, in his first edition, is a man adrift in the middle of his argument, uncertain both where he is going and what carries him there, and there is still one more twist to the argument. Originally it had been a point against monarchy and aristocracy, and in favour of democracy, that 'implicit faith, blind submission to authority, timid fear, a distrust of our powers, an inattention to our own importance and the good purposes we are able to effect . . . are the chief obstacles to human improvement.'[26] But we see now that the point applies against all government, any government, against government as such. Political institutions are not simply dispensable or unnecessary in a world of truth and reason; they must actually be dispensed with, if men are ever to trust in their own judgment, if political justice is to be possible at all:

> With what delight must every well informed friend of mankind look forward to the auspicious period, the dissolution of political government, of that brute engine, which has been the only perennial cause of the vices of mankind, and which, as has abundantly appeared in the progress of the present work, has mischiefs of various sorts incorporated with its substance, and no otherwise to be removed than by its utter annihilation![27]

Godwin's analysis of the evil effects of government, of legal coercion and the political superintendence of opinion, is acute enough, and applicable still today. His stress on the value of private judgment and the supremacy of individual conscience accords man a worth and dignity denied him by any authoritarian system of government, including even the representative democracies of our own 'free' world. His belief that rational men ought to make for themselves the decisions which affect their lives, that only they can judge what is truly in their interests, is an idea currently being revived, after generations of allowing others to think and decide for us. Yet his conclusion, that political and legal institutions must one day be abolished if a just society is to be possible at all, still seems rather too much to swallow. The obvious objection is that some measure of authority and control will always be necessary, if the turbulence of human passion is to be restrained, if civilized society is to survive at all. Yet that, for Godwin, is precisely the essential error of political institutions, the mistake of thinking that man must always be controlled by force and deception, instead of by reason and truth. It is just this failure to trust individual reason which prevents human progress:

> Men are weak at present, because they have always been told they are weak, and must not be trusted with themselves. Take them out of their shackles, bid them enquire, reason and judge, and you will soon find them very different beings.[28]

Everything turns, therefore, on the perfectibility of man, yet that is something which Godwin, in this first edition, does not establish, nor even argue for. Instead he puts so much trust in the rapid march of events to prove him right that the chapter called 'Human Inventions Capable of Constant Improvement', so far from being a proof of future progress, is merely a history of the past triumphs of reason and truth. It is only in his second edition that Godwin recognized the need for a proof of this central, crucial, highly contentious assumption, and so added a key chapter on the omnipotence of truth. Without that proof the argument of the original edition floats in an intellectual vacuum, a remarkable piece of political and moral speculation, a fascinating but implausible account of what society would be like if men were truly rational, if they were indeed Houyhnhnms and not mere Yahoos. Without that proof *Political Jusice* remains, what at first it seems, more political fantasy than political philosophy.

The style of *Political Justice* provides a fitting expression of Godwin's faith in the power of truth and the primacy of reason; in accordance with its own precepts, the book generates light, not heat. He writes smoothly and clearly, with an air of lofty detachment, avoiding both the thundering righteousness of Burke and the shifts and sallies of Paine, his calm lucidity contrasting equally with the baroque elaborations of the *Reflections* and the sturdy roughness of the *Rights of Man*. Hazlitt's famous remark accurately captures the differing impacts of their literary styles, at least: 'Tom Paine was considered for the time as a Tom Fool to him . . . Edmund Burke a flashy sophist. Truth, moral truth, it was supposed, had here taken up its abode, and these were the oracles of thought.'[29]

No doubt, too, Godwin's faith in the irresistibility of truth, if only it is presented clearly, helped calm the doubts he must have felt in publishing his book so soon after Paine's conviction. The message of *Political Justice* was undoubtedly more radical than that of the *Rights of Man*, but its tone was less pointed, and its air of detachment from current controversies, together with its cost, appears to have saved him. It is said that when the Cabinet considered prosecution, Pitt declared that 'a three guinea book could never do much harm amongst those who had not three shillings to spare',[30] a principle to be revived in the Obscene Publications Act of 1959. (This story, told first by Mary Shelley, is repeated by all of Godwin's biographers. Unhappily *Political Justice*'s first edition sold for £1 16s. od. But the Cabinet did discuss prosecution, on 25 May 1793.) But although Godwin's sober argumentation was unlikely to encourage anyone to violent revolution – a course he in any case explicitly repudiated – Pitt was mistaken in thinking that *Political Justice* would not command a following, even among the relatively uneducated public that was reading Paine:

The work, though discussing its topics at great length and in very minute detail, was scarcely published when it was everywhere the theme of popular conversation and praise. Perhaps no work of equal bulk ever had such a number of readers; and certainly no book of such profound inquiry ever made so many proselytes in an equal space of time. Pirate editions were published in Ireland and Scotland; and people of the lower

classes were the purchasers. In many places, perhaps some
hundreds in England and Scotland, copies were brought by
subscription, and read aloud in meetings of subscribers.[31]

Its sales could hardly rival the *Reflections*, let alone the *Rights of Man*,
but *Political Justice* none the less ran to 4,000 copies and three
editions, and Godwin's fame soon eclipsed that of the absent Paine.

In fact Godwin's passion for argument, his eagerness to discuss
his ideas with anyone who could be persuaded to listen, had already
put him 'in the singular situation of an author, possessing some
degree of fame for a work still unfinished and unseen',[32] and the
intelligent interest of men like James Mackintosh, author of the
learned *Vindiciae Gallicae*, or the caustic and quick-witted Horne
Tooke, who divided his time between reformist politics and the
study of language, convinced him his book would be the success he
so desperately wanted it to be. Yet first reviews were mixed, often
favourable but seldom enthusiastic, endorsing the premises perhaps,
admiring the arguments certainly, but baulking at the conclusions.

> If his ardent enthusiasm in favour of truth and liberty, with a
> sanguine anticipation of the perfection of human nature, have
> betrayed Mr Godwin into a few extraordinary and chimerical
> propositions, though we may be disposed to smile at their
> singularity and extravagance, we can scarce censure the
> principle in which they originate,[33]

declared the liberal *Analytical Review*, drawing the line only at
Godwin's remarks on religion, too serious a topic to be dismissed so
lightly. His former employer, the *New Annual Register*, predictably
praised his 'well-informed, bold and vigorous mind', his 'fearless'
writing 'unfettered by system', but found that it too could not
'subscribe without exception to Mr Godwin's opinions', 'fanciful
and extravagant'[34] as some of them were. Even the most favourable
report, in the *Monthly Review*, admired 'the freedom of its inquiry, the
grandeur of its views, and the fortitude of its principles', but still
refused to 'subscribe to all the principles which the volumes contain':
'Many of the opinions which this work contains are bold; some are
novel; and some, doubtless, are erroneous.'[35] But this reviewer is the
only one to discuss the change in Godwin's views about government;
hardly surprising, for he is Thomas Holcroft.

Others greeted the book with the same bemused tolerance that lay
behind the Cabinet's decision not to prosecute. The *Critical Review*,
for one, could see no harm in 'a work which of its very nature and
bulk can never circulate among the inferior classes of society',[36]
especially since it rejects violence and is so lacking in topical

references and practical policies: it is a fascinating and provoking intellectual exercise, but increasingly eccentric and visionary. The *British Critic*, more hostile, insists that these bulky volumes will only gather dust and flies in the bookshop windows: 'a much heavier fate than persecution [sic] awaits him, and one for which perhaps his mind is not equally prepared; the worst fate that can attend ambitious authorship, and system making, neglect.' Yet even the *Critic*, more contemptuous than any of this 'perfectly chimerical' book, concedes that if you once grant Godwin his premisses, the conclusions inexorably follow. But, 'denying any one of them – and what reasonable man will not strenuously deny them all? – the whole fabric crumbles into dust, or vanishes into less than air!'[37]

The leading left-wing figures of the day reacted with the same mixture of praise and puzzlement, respect for Godwin's reason, amazement at his truths. Charles Fox found he could not read it, no more than could Burke, but where Burke imputed Godwin's 'absurd and extravagant theories . . . to vanity, and a desire of appearing deep when really shallow',[38] Fox simply returned his copy to the bookshop. Joseph Priestley, foremost of the radical Dissenters, told Godwin personally that the book 'contains a vast extent of ability – he admits all my principles but cannot follow them into all my conclusions',[39] yet Priestley's *Memoirs* would describe *Political Justice* as a laborious and injudicious defence of school-boy paradoxes. Horne Tooke, never one to pull his punches, added that

> my book is a bad book, and will do a great deal of harm . . .
> written with good intentions, but to be sure nothing could be so
> foolish . . . Holcroft and I had our heads full of plays and
> novels, and then thought ourselves philosophers.[40]

But perhaps the novelist Anna Barbauld came closest to the truth, when she summed it all up as 'borrowed sense and original nonsense'.

Yet the most significant reaction would come from Samuel Newton. When Godwin heard that his former tutor had found in *Political Justice* 'matter so peculiarly censurable that you could not bear to read it any further', he wrote at once to complain that 'when I knew you you were an ardent champion for political liberty . . . . It is impossible that you should not have perceived that the book in question is intended to promote that glorious cause.'[41] Newton's reply, more tolerant and more sympathetic than we might expect from Godwin's account of his teacher's love of polemics, was all too prophetic. He has, he writes, the greatest admiration for Godwin's elegance of style, his 'general idea of political justice and liberty'; it is simply not true that he had been unable to finish the book; and yet

there were several things you advanced concerning moral
obligations, gratitude, any public test of marriage, christianity
and one or two more subjects, that very much disgusted me.
My indignation was raised, not so much that you differed from
me, but because I conceived it would damn the book, which
contained in it so many useful and most interesting sentiments.[42]

His advice was that Godwin should tread more warily, should he
have the benefit of a second edition. Anxious as always to defend
himself against all criticism, however well-intentioned, Godwin
wrote testily back his old antagonism beginning to break through.
But Newton managed to mollify him, and Godwin came to visit
whenever he returned to Norfolk. And eventually he would admit
the justice of the charge:

I . . . am filled with grief when I reflect on the possibility that
any oversights of mine should bring into disrepute the great
truths I have endeavoured to propagate. But this is my mind
constituted. I have, perhaps, never been without the possession
of important views and forcible reasonings; but they have ever
been mixed with absurd and precipitate judgments, of which
subsequent consideration has made me profoundly ashamed.[43]

6 ♣ Things as they are

The moral of any work may be defined to be, that ethical sentence to the illustration of which the work may most aptly be applied. The tendency is the actual effect it is calculated to produce upon the reader, and cannot be completely ascertained but by the experiment.[1]

Enquirer, 1799

♣ The fame that Godwin still anxiously awaited would come not from the literary and political establishment, but from a younger, more idealistic, generation. His theories might seem fanciful to some, but who could have believed that France would move so rapidly from absolute monarchy to people's republic, who could say what man's future progress might be? Godwin's principles were their principles, and his conclusions, as inspiring as they were unorthodox, seemed inexorable. He had had the strength and the courage to gaze determinedly in that dazzling new day of which the revolution in France was only the dawn, and the independence of mind to set it down in print: 'Truth, moral truth . . . had here taken up its abode, and these were the oracles of thought.' When the Greenock Library purged its shelves of the works of Godwin and Holcroft, its younger members seized control of the management board and reinstated them, even raising the subscription so that they could buy more copies.

So singly and by twos the eager young radicals and their hangers-on came to seek him out: the hugely impressive Joseph Gerrald, dressed in the French style with his hair hanging loose and unpowdered and his shirt casually open at the neck; the enthusiastic Robert Merry, founder of the Della Cruscan school of poetry which survives only in anthologies of bad verse; the classicist Richard Porson, Oxford's Professor of Greek aged only thirty-three; the eccentric antiquarian Joseph Ritson, who adopted the French revolutionary calendar and took to addressing acquaintances as 'Citizen'. But two, in particular, would be of special importance. Thomas Wedgwood, son of the famous potter, was an amateur philosopher and psychologist, and a pioneer of photography who, in experiments with Humphry Davy, would discover how to produce images on paper prepared with nitrate of silver, though not how to make those images permanent. But more crucially, Wedgwood would inherit a personal fortune of £29,000 which, as a true Godwinian, he would be eager to devote to the greater good of his species. For the moment he might be Godwin's pupil, sending him regular essays on education and psychology for his comment; but one day he would also be a patron. There was even a suggestion that the two might set up house together at Wedgwood's expense, but it came to nothing, perhaps because Wedgwood's poor health required him to live at the coast, perhaps because the severe critic of cohabitation was never an easy man to live with. But Godwin was touchy on the subject of money too, and when Wedgwood offered to buy him a copying machine as newly invented by James Watt, he proudly declared himself against the receipt of gifts (there is, however, some evidence of such a machine among Godwin's papers), while Wedgwood went to pained lengths to defend the moral propriety of his offer. Godwin even objected to his wealthy friend prepaying the postage on his letters; but he would not always be so sensitive.

The other important new acquaintance was John Thelwall, founder and editor of the original *Tribune*, a man with a remarkable talent for passionate oratory and political agitation. Their opinions, by and large, were the same opinions – it was from Godwin that Thelwall acquired his belief in necessity, truth and the importance of sincerity, the injustice of punishment, gratitude and marriage – but in methods they stood at opposite extremes. Where Godwin argued, Thelwall declaimed; where Godwin reasoned, Thelwall organized; where Godwin urged deliberation, Thelwall urged action. Before long it would bring them into angry conflict, but for the moment they stood together, their ideals as yet untarnished by the deteriorating situation in France, the hard political realities of repression in Britain.

As an author of relatively independent means Godwin could now afford a place of his own, instead of having to change his lodgings once or twice a year, as he had done for a decade past, and at the end of 1792 he had moved into a small town house at 25 Chalton Street, in Somers Town behind St Pancras. (Godwin later reported that he moved to Chalton Street early in 1793, but his diary has 'Go to Somers Town' on Boxing Day 1792, followed by a 'Remove' on the 27th.) There, free at last from the evils of cohabitation, he could live as frugally as possible, with expenses not much above £100 a year – at a time when he himself had calculated the average price of labour at a shilling a day – and no servant except a cleaning woman who would warm him the occasional mutton chop. There he could devote himself to study and to writing, to the 'usefulness and service of my fellow creatures', increasing 'the quantity of their knowledge and goodness and happiness', precisely as he had promised his mother ten years before, precisely as *Political Justice* had demonstrated that one ought.

His existence now, and for most of his life, was as methodical and unvaried as the diaries in which he meticulously recorded it. Before breakfast he would read, sometimes in French, Latin or Greek as well as in English; every morning he would write for a few hours; every afternoon he would pay calls about the town, and read some more, often from a different book, sometimes in a different language; every evening he would take supper with friends, or visit the theatre, or both. Each day might be extraordinarily like the last, but the variety within kept his mind fresh and eager. 'I am then in the best health and tone of spirits', he said, 'when I employ two or three hours, and no more, in the act of writing and composition.'[2]

And so he began 'to look around and consider to what species of industry I should next devote myself'.[3] He began a *History of Rome*, but soon opted for another novel, no mere pot-boiler like those early efforts, forgotten already, but something which might spread his reputation and his opinions into places that *Political Justice* would never penetrate. 'I will write a tale', he told himself again and again, 'that shall constitute an epoch in the mind of the reader, that no one, after he has read it, shall ever be exactly the same man that he was before.' He wrote only in this mood, and when once it deserted him, instead of his usual two or three pages a day he managed only six in three months. 'I held it for a maxim', he says, 'that any portion that was written when I was not fully in the vein, told for considerably worse than nothing'; 'a passage written feebly, flatly, and in a wrong spirit, constituted an obstacle that it was next to impossible to correct and set right again,' and was therefore worse than nothing written at all.

This policy of writing only when the spirit drove him paid off amply, for much of Godwin's excitement gets into his story, making *Caleb Williams* a gripping tale of adventure even now, for all its verbose, old-fashioned and somewhat artificial style. 'No-one', declared Hazlitt, echoing the remarks of many another,

> ever began Caleb Williams that did not read it through: no one that ever read it could possibly forget it, or speak of it after any length of time but with an impression as if the events and feelings had been personal to himself.[4]

Godwin himself attributed this to the unorthodox way in which he had invented the story, working backwards from the climax to the beginning. He had commenced with the conception of a series of adventures of flight and pursuit; the fugitive in perpetual apprehension of being overwhelmed with the worst calamities, and the pursuer, by his ingenuity and resources, keeping his victim in a state of the most fearful alarm. This was the project of my third volume.

Young Caleb Williams had escaped from jail, and is pursued by his former employer Falkland, and more particularly by Falkland's agent Jones – later renamed Gines – who shows an almost supernatural ability to find Williams out, whatever his hiding place, whatever his disguise. Williams falls among thieves, conceals himself in London, secludes himself in Wales; he takes on the appearance of a beggar, an Irishman, a Jew; but always Jones tracks him down and Falkland's persecution continues, until Williams has finally to turn and face his oppressor directly.

I was next called upon to conceive a dramatic and impressive situation, adequate to account for the impulse that the pursuer should feel, incessantly to alarm and harass his victim . . . This I apprehended could best be effected by a secret murder, to the investigation of which the innocent victim should be impelled by an unconquerable spirit of curiosity.

Caleb's suspicions centre on a mysterious iron chest that Falkland agonizes over, but always keeps safely locked. The confusion of a chimney fire gives him his opportunity to break the chest open, only to be caught red-handed by Falkland himself. Falkland confesses his guilt, but warns Williams that, knowing what he does now, he will never again have peace or contentment. In fact Caleb has no desire to inform on his revered patron, but Falkland's supervision and severity force him to run away. He is overtaken, accused of theft, and placed in prison. Convinced that he will be found guilty and duly executed, Williams escapes – at the third attempt – and so begins his life of wandering.

The first and weakest volume sets the scene for all this. Falkland is introduced as a gentleman of the most conspicuous virtue and nobility, admired by everyone, not least by Williams himself. But Falkland's sense of honour and integrity bring him into conflict with his boorish neighbour, Tyrrel, who publicly knocks him down and kicks him. Later that same night Tyrrel is found murdered, and though Falkland is the obvious suspect the charge carries no conviction against a man of such manifest virtue, and another victim of Tyrrel's tyranny is hung for the crime.

This technique of backwards plotting has since become the stock in trade of the suspense writers, but later authors owe more than that to Godwin's inventiveness. *Caleb Williams* is the first of the thrillers, the ancestor of the detective novels. Its confrontations and courtroom settings initiated a mania for trial scenes in popular plays and novels that has endured until the present. It breaks new ground both in its theme of flight and pursuit, escape and capture, and in its almost total lack of romantic interest. 'He has no tale of rational love', complained the *Analytical Review*, hard put to account for the book's undeniable impact,

> no marked instance of personal attachment, no fondly anxious parent, or child devoted to filial duty . . . but by the exertion of genius, which is indeed astonishing, he rivets our attention to a minute dissection of the characters, feelings, and emotions of three insulated men . . .[5]

Wilkie Collins derived much of his suspense and claustrophobia from *Caleb Williams*; Balzac enthused over it equally, and Victor Hugo's Jarvet, in *Les Misérables*, is a direct descendant of the inexorable Jones; Poe copied Godwin's use of atmosphere, and even thought his plotting superior to Dickens's, to whom he pointed out the backwards plotting technique; and Dickens, in his turn, admired the elements of social realism he found in Godwin, though probably more influenced by that of Holcroft.

But it is not just the pace of events, with Caleb constantly discovering and being discovered, escaping and being taken again, disguising himself and still being detected, with all the agility and frequent implausibility of an eighteenth century James Bond, that makes *Caleb Williams* so enthralling. Godwin's intention is to take us inside his characters, to have us feel what they feel, and fear what they fear:

> The thing in which my imagination revelled the most freely, was the analysis of the private and internal operations of the mind, employing my metaphysical dissecting knife in tracing and laying bare the involutions of motive, and recording the gradually accumulating impulses, which led the personages I had to describe primarily to adopt the particular way of proceeding in which they afterwards embarked.

Early in the writing Godwin decided to switch his narrative from the third to the first person, a device retained in all his subsequent novels, and with that special concern for physical sensation and psychological motive he immerses the reader in his hero's situation, leaving us as anxious for the next development as is Williams himself.

But although *Caleb Williams* is rightly regarded as a pioneer psychological novel, it is its concern with broad patterns of personality and motivation, and the occasional passage of highly subjective writing, at times almost stream-of-consciousness in style, that make it so, not detailed characterization. Godwin's contemporaries may have regarded Falkland as one of the finest creations in literature, to be compared even to Hamlet; Jones too, they found fascinatingly horrible; and even Jane Austen, of all people, admired the characterization of *Caleb Williams*, though she thought the book perverted none the less. But those same figures seem to us flimsy facsimiles, more material for Godwin's metaphysical dissecting knife than real personalities. His concern is not with recognizable individuals but with human embodiments of honour, curiosity, integrity, obsession and fear. The central characters are each of them a tragic hero destroyed by a single flaw, Falkland by his sense of honour and reputation, Williams by his inquisitiveness. It is the blot on his honour when Tyrrel beats him that leads to Falkland's crime; it is his sense of reputation which will not permit him to confess the truth, cankered though he is by guilt and remorse; it is that same misguided sense of reputation which drives him further, in his relentless pursuit of the innocent Williams. But at the same time Williams's pointless curiosity ensures that the fugitive is not entirely the hero, the pursuer not entirely the villain; in his own way Williams torments and destroys Falkland as surely as Falkland torments and destroys him.

Godwin was about three-quarters of the way through his first volume when he sent it to Marshall for comment, and to his horror had it returned

> with a note nearly in these words: – 'If you have the smallest regard for your own reputation or interest, you will immediately put the enclosed papers in the fire' . . . . It is hardly necessary to say that the receipt of this note was the means of disturbing me. It was three days before I fully recovered the elasticity and fervent tone of mind required for the prosecution of my work.[6]

Luckily another adviser, the novelist Elizabeth Inchbald, was more encouraging. 'God bless you' she began, threatening to change it to a 'God damn you' if the rest of the novel were up to the same standard. But then Marshall had seen only the first, least impressive volume, and as Mrs Inchbald later added,

> Your first volume is far inferior to the two last. The second is sublimely horrible – captivatingly frightful. Your third is all a great genius can do to delight a great genius . . . . It is my opinion that fine ladies, milliners, mantua makers and

boarding-school girls will love to tremble over it, and that men
of taste and judgment will admire the superior talents, the
incessant energy of mind you have evinced.[7]

To Godwin's great relief, Mrs Inchbald proved the better
prophet, and *Caleb Williams* became an even greater and more
enduring success than *Political Justice*. The *British Critic*, bitterest
critic of the earlier work, might complain that

> this piece is a striking example of the evil use which may be
> made of considerable talents, connected with such a degree of
> intrepidity as can inspire the author with resolution to attack
> religion, virtue, government, and above all, the desire (hitherto
> accounted laudable) of leaving a good name to posterity,[8]

but most of its readers were satisfied that it was an excitingly
original story. Republished some twenty-eight times in a variety of
languages during Godwin's lifetime, and as often again since, it was
also the inspiration for several plays, most notably George Colman's
Iron Chest, which would provide Tom Cooper with one of his most
celebrated roles. Much later in life Godwin was asked whether he
liked the play. 'Certainly not –', he replied, 'the best parts of the *Iron
Chest* are those that have no relation to *Caleb Williams*.' For Colman
turned psychological suspense into sheerest melodrama, losing all
the depth and strength of the original. The characters based on
Falkland and Williams are deprived of their special motivations
and, as Colman explained, 'I have cautiously avoided all tendency
to that which, vulgarly (and wrongly, in many instances) is termed
Politicks; with which, many have told me, Caleb Williams teems.'[9]
To his chagrin Godwin had even to write to Colman, to get so much
as a complimentary ticket to the performance.

Still, Godwin had not intended his book for an audience of theatre-
goers, nor even – as Mrs Inchbald was doubtless well aware – one of
fine ladies, milliners, mantua makers and boarding-school girls. In
fact he came almost to resent the fact that *Caleb Williams* proved so
eminently readable:

> And, when I had done all, what had I done? Written a book to
> amuse boys and girls in their vacant hours, a story to be hastily
> gobbled up by them, swallowed in a pusillanimous and un-
> animated mood, without chewing and digestion. I was in this
> respect greatly impressed with the confession of one of the most
> accomplished readers and excellent critics that any author
> could have fallen in with (the unfortunate Joseph Gerrald).* He

*Godwin does not mention that Gerrald read the book in Newgate Gaol, see
p. 82 below.

told me that he had received my look late one evening, and had read through the three volumes before he closed his eyes. Thus, what had cost me twelve month's labour, ceaseless heartaches and industry, now sinking in despair, and now raised and sustained in unusual energy, he went over in a few hours, shut the book, laid himself on his pillow, slept and was refreshed, and cried,

Tomorrow to fresh woods and pastures new.[10]

Nor was this just annoyance that what had cost him so much should be so easily enjoyed by others. Godwin had intended his book to have a serious purpose over and above its tale of suspense, beyond even its dissection of personality and motive. As the Preface makes clear, it was intended as a demonstration of moral and political truth, an illustration of the ways in which 'the spirit and character of the government intrudes itself into every rank of society', an account 'as far as the progressive nature of a single story would allow . . . of the modes of domestic and recorded despotism by which man becomes the destroyer of man'. It, too, was a contribution to the Great Debate.

Godwin's insistence that Caleb Williams is a political novel has often puzzled commentators, for its illustration of how a country squire can tyrannize his tenants with virtual impunity, of how those in authority will favour lords and masters against their serfs and servants, hardly amounts to a radical critique of *Things as They Are*, to give the novel its original title. True, Caleb's spell in jail does enable Godwin to describe the prison conditions of the day, and attack a system under which an innocent man can be detained for several months, undergoing hardship even unto death, while awaiting his trial. And this critique goes beyond the prisons to the laws themselves: the upright Hawkins, a truly Godwinian figure, will not take his case to court, 'being of the opinion that law was better adapted for a weapon of tyranny in the hands of the rich, than for a shield to protect the humbler part of the community against their usurpations'; and the honourable Falkland, likewise,

will never lend my assistance to the reforming mankind by axes and gibbets; I am sure things will never be as they ought, till honour and not law be the dictator of mankind, till vice is taught to shrink before the resistless might of inborn dignity, and not before the cold formality of statutes.

More striking still, Godwin illustrates the way in which the law can actually beget crime, through the story of Raymond, leader of the thieves among whom Williams hides when he escapes from prison. Raymond has all the marks of an upright and benevolent man – he

is the noble bandit, a character who is to recur in Godwin's fiction –
but having erred once it is impossible for him ever to return to
legitimate society: he will be judged for what he has done, not by
what he is now. And to prove the point Godwin cites true cases of
murderers executed fourteen and even forty years after their crimes,
regardless of how they have lived in the meantime.

No doubt the impact of all this on an audience unused to any sort
of social conscience in a work of fiction was greater than it is now –
Fanny Burney was annoyed enough to insist that the book was
'Things *as they are not*' – but for Godwin himself this was but a minor
theme, and when the *British Critic* complained of this attack on the
laws of its country, it provoked a letter from the author insisting that
his

> object is of much greater magnitude. It is to expose the evils
> which arise out of the present system of civilized society; and
> having exposed them, to lead the enquiring reader to examine
> whether they are or are not, as has commonly been supposed,
> irremediable; in a word to disengage the minds of men from
> prepossesion, and to launch them upon the sea of moral and
> political enquiry.[11]

Yet politics and government as such seem to figure in the novel not
at all, and if we read *Caleb Williams* with *Political Justice* in mind,
looking for a fictional illustration of its theoretical doctrines, we are
more likely to be struck by differences than by similarities. *Political
Justice*, for example, stresses the importance of independence, the
necessity of each man's thinking and acting, and even living, by
himself; *Caleb Williams* in contrast, dramatizes the unbearable
isolation of its narrator, whose fear of discovery prevents him from
communicating with his fellow men. Even more striking is the
characterization of Falkland, presented from beginning to end as a
man of the greatest nobility and virtue, and accepted as such by
Godwin's readers, no matter how far his character becomes divorced
from his actual conduct. Indeed it is precisely this tension, between
what he is and what he does, that makes Falkland so fascinating a
creation. Yet according to *Political Justice*, virtue is to be judged by
deeds, and deeds are to be judged by their effects, by the good that
they do. The account of Falkland seems a fictional refutation of that.

Or, of course, vice versa. Godwin's narrators do not always speak
for their author, nor are their attitudes necessarily his. The
'virtuous' Falkland will do anything to protect an honourable
reputation: he will commit murder, allow an innocent man to hang
for the crime, and persecute the foolish youth who uncovers the
secret. He has nobility and honour enough, but there is no true

morality, no impartial benevolence, in him. The most outstanding qualities of intellect and imagination are perverted by an overriding concern for personal reputation and social position. This, perhaps, is how the spirit and character of the government, the false values of a corrupt society, intrude themselves into every rank of man, not just the bandits in their forests and the prisoners in their cells, but the squires in their mansions.

Some have wanted to go further than this, and suggest that the political message of *Caleb Williams* is symbolic rather than overt, with Falkland, the embodiment of traditional values, standing for established institutions, the inquisitive Williams standing for Godwin himself, and the secret by which Caleb destroys Falkland being the message of *Political Justice*. But unhappily for this interpretation, he never discovers just what is in that mysterious trunk – 'Surely Mr Falkland would not keep in brandy the gory head of Tyrel?',[12] sneered the novel's most caustic critic, Thomas de Quincey – nor is Caleb's attitude to Falkland, mingled admiration and regret, by any stretch of the imagination Godwin's attitude to political institutions. It is, rather, his attitude to Edmund Burke, and the similarity between Caleb's final farewell to Falkland and the note added to *Political Justice* at Burke's death in July 1797 is too striking to be entirely accidental. Any criticism is not of Burke the man, let alone of Burke the writer, whom Godwin elsewhere ranked with Milton, Shakespeare and Bacon, but of the political system that corrupted so great a talent:

> He has unfortunately left us a memorable example of the power of a corrupt system of government, to undermine and divert from their genuine purposes, the noblest faculties that have yet been exhibited to the observation of the world.[13]

Falkland, clearly, *is* Burke, and *Caleb Williams* the demonstration of how our society and its values can corrupt even such a one as he. (See P. N. Furbank, 'Godwin's Novels', *Essays in Criticism*, 1955. For the more plausible interpretation of Falkland as Burke, see J. T. Boulton, *The Language of Politics* (1963), Chap. 11, sec. iii.)

But the trouble of it is that Godwin's admiration for Burke stands in the way of his story's intentions, for it is Falkland's merit, and not the erroneousness of his values, which dominates his book. The virtue that fascinates the reader is the virtue that Caleb found in his master, the virtue that Godwin found in Burke, not the virtue that *Political Justice* would deny to them both. So far from revealing aristocratic values as a perversion of true morality, *Caleb Williams* seems rather to endorse them, implying that the intrinsic worth of a Falkland can survive even the most malevolent actions. Godwin's moral is one thing; but the tendency of his book, its actual effect on the reader, seems quite another.

But perhaps this is not, after all, the real moral of *Caleb Williams*. Yet another of the apparent conflicts between novel and political treatise concerns the power of truth. For truth, according to *Political Justice*, is omnipotent; there is nothing it cannot do and no one it cannot persuade. Yet although Caleb knows the truth about Falkland and Falkland lies about him, it is Falkland who is believed unquestioningly, while Caleb is despised, reviled, persecuted and imprisoned. Here, perhaps, lies the explanation of the two endings to Godwin's story. The adventures of Caleb Williams come to their climax when he decides, at last, to face his persecutor, and charge him openly with the murder of Tyrrel. In the original version of the Postscript that follows, Caleb once more fails to carry conviction, and is sent to prison where it seems he is being drugged or poisoned, and a second Postscript, written in feverish, disjointed sentences, makes it plain that, having learnt of Falkland's death, Williams is also about to die. It makes an appropriate ending to the tale so far. Caleb's misfortunes deepen as the plot develops, and the only possible resolution is a final confrontation in which both parties stake all. Nor is there any reason to think that things will go better for Caleb this time, that his story will prove any more convincing now than before. But while the broken phrases of that second Postscript, all dashes and uncompleted sentences, provide an apt conclusion to the increasingly excited tempo of the narrative, it is for all that a somewhat downbeat ending. One can sympathize if Godwin felt he needed more of a denouement, some final twist that might give his story a more dramatic climax.

Accordingly, three days later, Godwin scrapped that ending and rewrote his final ten pages. Face to face with Falkland at last, Caleb is horrified at the state to which the man has been reduced. His original admiration combines with pity for his suffering, but it is too late now to pull back. He tells his story as forcefully as he can, though stressing the essential virtue of the man he is accusing. And this time his hearers are moved to agreement, not least Falkland himself, who throws himself into Williams's arms, praising his character and confessing his own guilt. But three days later Falkland is dead, and Caleb is left with the knowledge that he has become in effect a murderer himself, who has destroyed not just the man but also what was of more importance to him, his reputation, his honour. Now it is Williams's turn to live with the evil he has done. Falkland may be dead, but his memory continues to plague and pursue him as inexorably as the man had done alive.

This second ending is in many ways more satisfying than the first, adding a further dimension to the book's dissection of character and motive. Moreover it is only when Williams is prepared to trust unreservedly in truth, instead of trying to keep Falkland's secret, that justice – of a sort – is done. But although more uplifting, it also seems less plausible, more contrived, all too obviously a case of *veritas ex machina*. The point of the story so far seemed to be that, things being as they are – the book's title, after all – truth cannot always be victorious over error. As Godwin remarks of the no-nonsense Mr Forrester, the character based on Thomas Holcroft, 'he had not the skill to carry conviction to an understanding so well fortified in error.' Men corrupted by deception, coercion and the political superintendence of opinion, can scarcely be expected to rely solely on truth, or to recognize when it is presented fearlessly to them. Perhaps that, too, is how the spirit and character of the government intrudes itself into every rank of society.

But what, in that case, is the real moral of *Caleb Williams*: that truth will be victorious over error if we trust in it without qualification, as Godwin belatedly suggests; or that things being as they are, men are unable to rely on or recognize the unqualified truth, as the bulk of the novel seems to demonstrate? There is a fundamental difficulty here, one which breaks through in the novel in spite of itself, and one that would shortly confront Godwin again, and eventually defeat him.

Nevertheless it was not because it seems so perversely to promise what the book fails to deliver that *Caleb Williams*'s Preface did not appear in its first edition. Perhaps it was because the Robinsons had recently been fined for selling the second part of Paine's *Rights of Man* that *Caleb Williams* was originally published, in May 1794, under the imprint of B. Crosby. But also, as Godwin explained when the Robinsons did publish the second edition,

> This preface was withdrawn in the original edition, in compliance with the alarms of booksellers. Caleb Williams made his first appearance in the world, in the same month in which the sanguinary plot broke out against the liberties of Englishmen, which was happily terminated by the acquittal of its first intended victims, in the close of that year. Terror was the order of the day, and it was feared that even the humble novelist might be shown to be constructively a traitor.

Godwin, no less than his hero, now stood in danger of imprisonment, perhaps even of death.

7 ♣ A case of constructive treason

> It is much to be desired, in moments pregnant with so important consequences, that an individual should be found, who could preserve his mind untained with the headlong rage of faction, whether for men in power or against them; could judge, with the sobriety of distant posterity, and the sagacity of an enlightened historian; and could be happy enough to make his voice heard, by all those directly or remotely interested in the event.[1]
>
> *Considerations on Lord Grenville's and Mr Pitt's Bills*, 1795

♣ With the political pamphlets came the political associations. From the first there had been the Revolution Society and the Constitutional Society, founded by John Horne Tooke after a quarrel with Wilkes in 1771, and subsequently revived as the Society for Constitutional Information. But though Tooke himself was no more a believer in natural rights than was Burke or Godwin, his Constitutional Society soon fell under the spell of Paine, and in 1792 the more moderate establishment figures, led by Thomas Brand Hollis and twenty-three MPs, including Sheridan and Grey, set up instead their less radical Society of the Friends of the People. The difference in nature and membership between this and another new body of that year, the London Corresponding Society, is best indicated by their contrasting finances: the Friends of the People set themselves an annual subscription of two and a half guineas; the rate for the Corresponding Society was a penny a week. Organized from his Piccadilly shop by the Scots shoemaker Thomas Hardy, the Corresponding Society was soon in contact with some twenty or thirty similar bodies in different parts of Britain, and joined with the other societies in establishing friendly relations with their French counterparts such as the Jacobin Clubs, at first relatively moderate but soon to become notorious. The Revolution Society, the Constitutional Society, the Friends of the People, the Corresponding Societies, all sent addresses of greeting and goodwill to the French on the inauguration of the republican Convention in September 1792.

But this increasing political agitation met with an equal and equivalent increase in political repression, and 1793 saw a gradual clamp-down on the more radical groups and a rash of minor prosecutions, especially of booksellers who dared distribute the outlawed *Rights of Man*. Among the small fry to escape with a caution was a Dumfriesshire exciseman rash enough to send to France, with his compliments, a cargo of smuggled guns which he had impounded; his name was Robert Burns. In the Commons a petition for parliamentary reform, presented on behalf of the Friends of the People by Charles Grey, was rejected by the crushing margin of 282 to 41, and after a second unsuccessful attempt later in the decade, Grey had to wait until 1832 before he could carry the measure through, this time as prime minister – though by then he had regretted his association with even so moderate a body as the Friends of the People.

By the autumn of 1793 the struggling French republic had fallen into the hands of Robespierre and his Committee of Public Safety, and a campaign of terror was being waged against all figures of authority. Support for the revolution in Britain was beginning to give way to misgiving and outright fear, and the local societies were widely thought to threaten similar violence at home. Indeed the Corresponding Societies could well be regarded as the British equivalent of the Jacobin Clubs, a comparison no longer to their advantage, and when a deliberate attempt to copy French pro-cedures on this side of the channel, a British Convention, assembled in Edinburgh that November with delegates from all parts of the country – the Friends of the People notably abstaining – Pitt's government decided it was time to act. The Convention was broken up and its leaders charged with sedition, though in fact guilty of little more than organizing a political conference. The unfortunate Joseph Gerrald, who had treated *Caleb Williams* as mere light reading, was one of five sentenced to fourteen years' transportation. After being held for more than a year in London prisons, in the hope that he might publicly renounce his principles and earn himself a pardon, he was whisked off to Australia so suddenly that he had not even the chance to say farewell to his daughter who had stayed near him, and he died within the year. Another delegate, Robert Watt, who seems to have been an *agent provocateur* who got rather carried away with the role, was proved to have manufactured arms and plotted the capture of Edinburgh Castle, and was publicly executed, though happily without the gruesome refinements laid down by the law against High Treason.

On 14 April 1794 the London Corresponding Society organized a mass meeting on the green at Chalk Farm to protest against the sentences on Gerrald and the others; three hundred members of the Constitutional Society expressed similar views on 2 May. Plans were circulating for another Convention that might challenge the policy of repression, but this time the government moved first. The secretaries of both societies were arrested, and their papers seized; Habeas Corpus was suspended, and a special parliamentary committee set up to investigate the conspiracy. Soon several prominent democrats, Hardy, Tooke and Thelwall among them, were under arrest, though cross-examination proved futile when others followed Tooke's lead in refusing to answer questions until properly charged and represented. It was not until 2 October that an indictment was drawn up, and a charge presented to the Grand Jury which would decide whether there was a case to be answered.

It says something for the state of public feeling at the time that it could seriously be believed that the Corresponding Society was involved in an absurd 'pop-gun' plot, in which the king was to be assassinated by a poison arrow blown through a hollow walking stick. But with France now in the grip of Robespierre's reign of terror the outlook for the accused was not hopeful, and the dice were laden even more heavily against them when Lord Chief Justice Eyre presented his formal Charge to the Grand Jury. Building on a statute of Edward III which defined High Treason as any overt act that could be shown to 'compass or imagine the Death of the King', Eyre proceeded to argue that any attempt to overthrow the government or remove the monarchy must be 'to design such a horrible Ruin and Devastation which no King could survive',[2] and thus qualified as treason within the meaning of the act. Of course the mere intention to influence parliament would not count as treasonable, but any attempt to change the system other than through the sovereign will of Parliament itself, perhaps any attempt to force Parliament's hand, to 'overawe the Legislative Body, and extort a Parliamentary Reform from it', must do so, for the simple reason that

> it is in the Nature of Things, that the Power should go out of their Hands, and be beyond the Reach of their Controul . . . . In effect, to introduce Anarchy, and that which Anarchy may chance to settle down into; after the King may have been brought to the Scaffold, and after the Country may have suffered all the Miseries, which Discord, and Civil War shall have produced.[3]

Accordingly the Lord Chief Justice had not the slightest doubt that

> a Project to bring the People together in Convention in Imitation of those National Conventions which we have heard of in France in order to usurp the Government of the Country, and any one Step taken towards bringing it about . . . would be a Case of no Difficulty that it would be the clearest High

Treason; it would be compassing and imagining the King's Death, and not only His Death, but the Death and Destruction of all Order, Religion, Laws, all Property, all Security for the Lives and Liberties of the King's Subjects.[4]

And the plain fact of it was that the political societies did hope to replace the unreformed Parliament of their day by a National Convention on the French model, without being under any illusion that Parliament itself might agree to the change. So it was clear that the twelve indicted on 6 October were not the only ones to have committed treason as Lord Eyre had now redefined it, and that they would be lucky to escape, like the organizers of the Edinburgh Convention, with mere transportation. For the charge was High Treason and the penalty was death, accompanied by the peine forte et dure: to be hung by the neck, cut down while still living, the bowels cut out and burnt before your eyes, then to be beheaded and quartered. Rumour had it that 800 arrest warrants, 300 of them already signed, were awaiting the first conviction, when the climate of opinion was dramatically altered by the publication in the *Morning Chronicle* of an anonymous article, the 'Cursory Strictures on the Charge Delivered by Lord Chief Justice Eyre'.

In the circumstances one might have expected a heated, not to say hysterical, attack on this threat to personal liberties, or at least a defence of the policies of the political societies. But the author of the *Cursory Strictures* chose to meet Eyre on his own ground, quoting law, commentary and the Lord Chief Justice himself, not to defend the accused but to destroy the extravagant charge of 'constructive treason'. That statute of Edward III had provided an exact definition of High Treason precisely in order to prevent the arbitrary exercise of power by the monarch against those of his subjects who happened to displease or disagree with him. But now, as Eyre himself conceded, the charge was being extended, in ways not originally envisaged, on the extraordinary ground that 'no law-giver had ever ventured to contemplate it in its whole extent'! By his own admission the Chief Justice was taking on himself what no lawmaker had yet dared do. But if any course of action which might result in the death of a king was now to constitute treason, then there was hardly anything, and hardly any body, which might not be declared treasonable: 'An association for Parliamentary Reform may desert its object and become guilty of High Treason. True: so may a card club, a bench of justices, or even a Cabinet Council.'[5]

The *Cursory Strictures* provided the accused with their only possible defence. It could hardly be shown that they had not advocated the radical reform of Parliament; but whatever a Lord Chief Justice might say, that was no treason. The rebuke struck home, and 'instead of the guilt and conviction of the accused, nothing was heard of, in the streets and places of resort, than the flagrancy of the offences of the charge.'[6] Horne Tooke, as he passed a fellow prisoner in the exercise yard, held up a copy and called 'By God, Joyce, this lays Eyre completely on his back'. The heavily legal tone of the article, its measured citing of statute and authority, led some to suspect the work of the liberal attorney Felix Vaughan, who acted as junior counsel for some of the accused. In fact it was the work of Godwin.

Godwin, we know, had been lucky to escape prosecution over the publication of *Political Justice*, but unlike Holcroft he had soon tired of political meetings. For one thing he preferred to devote his time and his energies to writing; for another his insistence on private judgment, his attack on the ways in which institutions inhibit individual reason, were hardly compatible with membership of any sort of political club. Once he had helped the Revolutionists draft a friendly letter to their sister societies in France, but now *Political Justice* explicitly criticized the radical associations for their 'tremendous apparatus of articles of confederacy and committees of correspondence', their 'fallacious uniformity of opinion . . . which no man espouses from conviction, but which carries all men along with a resistless tide', the ease with which 'the conviviality of a feast may lead to the depredations of a riot'.[7] Accordingly the only organization he belonged to now was the Philomatheans, their membership limited to twenty-one, whose monthly discussions ranged from self-love to soldier versus priest, from incest to the means of reform. Holcroft was another member and the committee was obliged to introduce fifteen-minute time glasses, though the only time they had to be turned was when Godwin or Holcroft held the floor.

But it was by reason and writing that Godwin proposed to change the world, and as soon as *Political Justice* was finished, before it was even published, he had been writing again in the papers under his old pen-name of Mucius. He had attended Paine's trial, doubtless wondering what might lie in store for himself when his own book appeared:

Good God! what species of monster is this Thomas Paine, that all the rules of equity cease to be rules the moment he is the subject of animadversion! . . . We all know by what means a verdict was procured: by repeated proclamations, by all the force, and all the fears of the kingdom being artfully turned against one man.[8]

For as Godwin rightly suspected, this was only a beginning. 'Every man, if we may believe the voice of rumour', he had warned in his Preface,

> is to be prosecuted, who shall appeal to the people by the publication of any unconstitutional paper or pamphlet; and, it is added, that men are to be prosecuted for any unguarded words that may be dropped in the warmth of conversation and debate.[9]

And as the second edition would note, 'the first conviction of this kind, which the author was far from imagining to be so near', actually occurred the day after he wrote those words. Daniel Crichton, an unemployed Scotsman newly arrived in London, had paid a drunken visit to the Tower, where the sight of the regalia had prompted him to snort 'Damn the King; we have no King in Scotland, and we will soon have no King in England.' For that he was sentenced to three months' imprisonment, plus £200 in surety for good behaviour for a further year. Godwin's immediate response was a series of letters to the *Morning Chronicle*, protesting about these savage verdicts against Crichton and Paine, and warning of the scaremongering and witch-hunting that motivated such bodies as John Reeve's answer to the radical clubs, his Association for Preserving Liberty and Property against Republicans and Levellers. True, the constitution was in danger, but the danger came not from men like Paine or Crichton:

> What is the true meaning of this cry in favour of the Constitution? What part of the Constitution is it about which the attention of these new associators is engaged? It is the old, boasted privilege of Englishmen; liberty of speech; but their attention is not engaged to confirm, but to destroy it.[10]

In December 1793 Godwin was writing again, about the deplorable treatment of Muir and Palmer, two Scots radicals convicted of sedition on the flimsiest of evidence. Their judge, Lord Braxfield, had ruled that any criticism of the British constitution was seditious, since the British constitution was perfect, and had urged one juror to 'Come awa', Maaster Horner, come awa', and help us to hang ane of thae damned scoondrels', and now they were awaiting transportation in the hulks at Greenwich, where Godwin visited them, to observe the dreadful conditions for himself. But though ready to protest against injustice and defend freedom of opinion wherever necessary, Godwin resolutely rejected all extremism, to right or to left. He disapproved of the Edinburgh Convention as he disapproved of all assemblies, and wrote to Gerrald to urge moderation and restraint at his forthcoming trial. With his exceptional qualities of character, Gerrald should simply ignore the packed jury and the biased judges, and speak directly to the people, trusting in the power of truth to reveal the reformers as the genuine friends of their country. And that, as it happened, was Gerrald's tactic, only to be told that if he had acted from pure motives, then he was far more dangerous than if he had acted from criminal ones. When Gerrald insisted that Christ too had been a reformer the same Lord Braxfield chuckled to his fellow judges, 'Muckle he made o' that; *he* was hanget.' There was 'not a pretence left', declared Fox, 'for calling Scotland a free country, and a very thin one for calling England so.'

As Gerrald lay festering in Newgate Gaol Godwin visited him regularly, and much of what he saw there found its way into *Caleb Williams*: indeed both of the book's endings, Caleb's sickness in prison and his impressive sincerity at his trial, may have been inspired by the unfortunate Joseph Gerrald. Yet when another close friend, John Thelwall, was among those arrested, Godwin decided against coming to his cell, on the unfortunate grounds that in the present crisis he should not put his own life – 'this treasure which does not belong to me, but to the public' – in danger for some purely personal gratification, but only for the palpable benefit of all. Not that that prevented him from offering Thelwall his advice, chiding him for his 'spirit of resentment and asperity against your prosecutors', and urging him to base his defence not on legal precedent but 'that eternal law which the heart of every man of common-sense recognizes immediately'.[11] Godwin was right to consider himself at risk; perhaps he was right too to preserve himself until the time he could be of most use; certainly he was right to urge restraint on the outspoken Thelwall. But it remains an absurdly patronizing letter to write to a man lying in the Tower under threat of execution.

When those first arrests were made Godwin was still seeing *Caleb Williams* through the press. Then, free for the moment from the obligations of writing, he had gone off to visit family and friends in Norfolk, the first time in twelve years that he had been more than forty miles from London. After that there was an invitation to visit the formidable Dr Parr who had once been Gerrald's tutor, but when the *Morning Post* published a report that Thomas Holcroft would be among those indicted by the Grand Jury, Godwin decided to stay on in London. The testimony of William Sharp, who gave King's Evidence, was that Holcroft was one of 'many who entertained French ideas of Equality . . . he thought that no man should have a coach 'til he was grown old'.[12] But when the expected warrant failed to appear and another paper denied the rumour, Godwin left for Hatton, near Warwick, where Parr had his church.

It was the very next day, 6 October, that the indictment was published, and when he discovered that he was among those charged, Holcroft marched directly into court to stand trial with the rest, a stroke as bold as any in his currently fashionable plays, and thoroughly disconcerting to the authorities, who would have preferred to drag him struggling from some place of hiding. But although he was willing enough to admit that he was Thomas Holcroft he would accept no talk of treason, and the Lord Chief Justice seemed almost to suspect some trick. 'If I understand you rightly', he said, 'you now admit that you are the person standing indicted in the name of Thomas Holcroft?' 'That, indeed, my Lord, is what I cannot affirm – I have it only from report.' The judge was hardly satisfied: 'I do not know you and it is therefore impossible for me to know whether you are the person stated in the indictment.' 'It is equally impossible for me my Lord.' 'Why then, Sir, I think you had better sit still.' But after anxious discussion between Chief Justice and Solicitor-General, Holcroft was duly committed, and taken to Newgate Gaol.

As soon as he heard the news, Godwin wrote to Holcroft's daughter, to say he would come home at once if he could be of assistance and by Monday 13th he was back in London and, throwing caution to the winds, visiting Holcroft in his cell. He knew as well as any that if these trials succeeded he would be a target himself; he knew that someone must speak out against the charge that Eyre had laid. If he could not defend these 'honest and well-intentioned, though mistaken men' and their political associations, at least he could defend the law, and the liberty and happiness of all. So he carefully studied Eyre's *Charge to the Grand Jury*, then shut himself up over the weekend, Friday to Sunday, to compose a reply. That Tuesday, 21 October, it appeared in the *Chronicle* and was immediately republished in pamphlet form. The government did manage to persuade the publisher to withdraw it, but another, Daniel Isaac Eaton, 'was *thereby* induced upon application made to him, not only to sell what remained of the first edition'[13] but to provide a second at half the original cost of one shilling. Eaton also published an anonymous 'Answer to the Cursory Strictures' (believed to be the work of 'Judge Thumb', otherwise Sir Francis Buller, one of the trial judges, who carried this nickname because of his ruling that it was perfectly legitimate for a man to beat his wife with a stick, provided it were not thicker than his thumb) from *The Times* of 25 October, together with Godwin's equally anonymous 'Reply', which the worried *Morning Chronicle* had declined to print.

But more surprisingly, Godwin wrote personally to Eyre, signing himself 'an impartial, honest man', to apologize for the intemperate tone of some remarks in the *Cursory Strictures*. They would have been more moderate, he says, had he had more time for reflection, for 'I cannot believe that truth will ever be injured by a sober and benevolent style.'[14] The path that he trod in the face of extremism to either side was an exceeding narrow one, but he stuck to it unswervingly.

The trials began on 28 October, with Thomas Hardy the first to face the jury and Thomas Erskine, who had previously defended Paine, as his counsel. It was obvious from the start that the *Cursory Strictures* had made their point, for the Attorney-General began by disavowing any charge of 'constructive treason', while Erskine denied any possibility of treason by mere implication. The court was crowded with sympathizers, Godwin and his friends Fawcett, Dyson and Marshall among them, and people all over the country followed the proceedings in a fever of anxious attention. Charles Grey was there too, 'in order to learn how to conduct myself when it comes to my turn. If this man is hanged there is no safety for any man.' It was not until 5 November that the jury retired, returning three hours later with the verdict Not Guilty. A triumphant crowd pulled Hardy through the West End in a coach, but Hardy was in no position to savour his victory. While he had been in prison his house had been broken into and his shop looted. His sick and pregnant wife had been forced to flee; the child was still-born and his wife was dead.

Next to be tried, a fortnight later, was the astringent Horne Tooke, a very different prisoner at the bar from the dour Hardy. It was far from being his first spell in court and, used as he was to defending himself, he persuaded the judges to let him sit beside Erskine, where he enjoyed himself hugely, interrupting constantly, cross-examining the witnesses and provoking the politicians, even offering to hum a song to see if the tune were treasonable. In his defence he called not only Fox and Sheridan but the prime minister himself, to testify somewhat unwillingly to their former collaboration in the cause of parliamentary reform, for Tooke's principles had once also been Pitt's. In any case Tooke was the least revolutionary of the defendants. Holcroft might recall that

> when a member of the Constitutional Society, I have frequently heard him utter sentences, the first part of which would have subjected him to death, by the law, except for the salvo that followed; and the more violent they were, thus contrasted and equivocatory, the greater was his delight,[15]

but as Hazlitt says, Tooke 'would rather be *against* himself than *for* anyone else . . . . Provided he could say a clever or a spiteful thing, he did not care whether it served or injured the cause.'[16] He might approve the execution of Louis, being in favour of kings but also in favour of cutting off the head of one every fifty or a hundred years, but as he put it himself, if his companions were in a coach headed for Windsor, 'I will go with them to Hounslow. But there I will get out: no further will I go, by God.' The trial lasted a week, the jury returned an immediate verdict of Not Guilty, Tooke treated the court to a triumphant harangue, and went off to dinner with his doctor. As he was leaving the room a lady admirer tried to tie her silk scarf around his neck, but he told her to go easy: he was rather ticklish around that part for the moment.

The prosecution now decided to concentrate on its strongest case, against Thelwall, and on 1 December Holcroft and three others were discharged without trial. Annoyed at being cheated of the opportunity to justify himself and his conduct, Holcroft requested permission to address the court, and the judge was at first inclined to humour him. But when he learnt that the speech would last 'only half an hour' he changed his mind, and Holcroft marched down into the court to take his seat beside the waiting Godwin. It was obvious to all that the charges had come to nought, and after only four days, one judge sleeping through the whole seven hours of the opening speech, Thelwall was acquitted too. At dinner that evening Godwin and Holcroft shared in his victory.

Clearly the government had miscalculated in trying for treason and the death penalty, instead of sedition and transportation, but the defendants still had much to thank Godwin for. The *Cursory Strictures* had come to their assistance when they needed it most, and the atmosphere of their trials had been vastly different from that of the absent Paine. Horne Tooke, though he constantly patronized 'little Godwin', knew well enough what his debt was:

He often questioned me with affected earnestness as to the truth of the report that I was the author of the 'Cursory Strictures' . . . of which pamphlet he always declared the highest admiration, and to which he repeatedly professed that he held himself endebted for his life. The question was revived at the dinner I have mentioned. [On 21 May 1795.] I answered carelessly to his enquiry that I believed I was the author of that pamphlet. He insisted on a reply in precise terms to his question, and I complied. He then requested that I would give him my hand. To do this I was obliged to rise from my chair and go to the end of the table where he sat. I had no sooner done this than he suddenly conveyed my hand to his lips, vowing that he could do no less by the hand that had given existence to that production. The suddenness of his action filled me with confusion; yet I must confess that when I looked

D

back on it, this homage thus expressed was more gratifying to me than all the applause I had received from any other quarter.[17]

Godwin regularly visited Tooke at Wimbledon, where he lived with his two illegitimate daughters, and they remained friends, Tooke poking fun and Godwin taking ready offence, for many years thereafter. There is, for example, the splendid story (unhappily too good to be true, for we know from Godwin himself that Tooke commented adversely on *Political Justice* back in March 1793 – see p. 62 above – unless, perhaps, this incident concerns the second or third editions) of Godwin meeting Tooke in Johnson's bookshop one day in 1797 and asking whether he had yet read *Political Justice*, and what he thought of it. Tooke would say only that Godwin had made free use of Helvetius and Rousseau. 'That I never thought of denying, Mr Tooke', replied Godwin huffily, 'but pray, may not I at least claim the merits of elucidation, useful arrangement, and even of the ornaments of composition?' But Tooke was never lost for an answer. 'Though you and I eat good beef and mutton', he said, 'it by no means follows that we should shite good beef and mutton.' 'This is just the character of Parson Horne', is supposed to have been Godwin's crusty comment, 'who was never known to be pleased with any other man's writings or actions, nor any other man with his.' 'Never but once had I full battle with H. Tooke, *tête à tête*', wrote Godwin many years later. 'It ended, after an obstinate contest, with his losing his temper; and then I dropped it.'[18]

8 ♣ The firmament of reputation

There was not a person almost in town or village who had any acquaintance with modern publications that had not heard of the 'Enquiry Concerning Political Justice' or was not acquainted in great or small degree with the contents of that work. I was nowhere a stranger. The doctrines of that work (though if any book ever contained the dictates of an independent mind, mine might pretend to do so) coincided in a great degree with the sentiments then prevailing in English society, and I was everywhere received with curiosity and kindness. If temporary fame ever was an object worthy to be coveted by the human mind, I certainly obtained it in a degree that has seldom been exceeded. I was happy to feel that this circumstance did not in the slightest interrupt the sobriety of my mind.[1]

Account of the visit to Warwickshire in 1794

♣ Godwin was now at the meridian of his sultry and unwholesome reputation, blazing with a confidence and a pride that seemed almost to demand a fall. *Political Justice* had put him at the centre of political controversy; *Caleb Williams* had made him a literary sensation. To have produced in such quick succession two works so striking and original, yet so different in tone and execution, was certain proof of extraordinary genius. He could hardly fail to be the most admired, or at least the most discussed, writer of the day, and even those bemused by his doctrines were eager to make his acquaintance. The Earl of Lauderdale, a founder member of the Friends of the People, began to invite Godwin to his political dinner parties, and in this unaccustomed high society he made the acquaintance of Charles Fox.

To Godwin himself, basking in the warm glow of reputation, the 'delicious delights of self-complacency' to use his own revealing phrase, the celebrity that greeted him in Warwickshire seemed no more than his due. Not vain in any straight-forward sense, his need of acceptance and approval was nonetheless so deep-seated that it took an excess of acclamation to put him at his ease; extravagant praise, so far from interrupting the sobriety of his mind, actually proved necessary for it. Self-complacency, he later wrote, is 'the indispensable condition of all that is honourable in human

87

achievements';[2] without it he lapsed once more into self-doubt. So when a young man called Gurney wrote that the name of Godwin would soon supersede that of Christ, Godwin complimented him on his acuity, and sought his acquaintance. For Godwin's fame lay most among a generation of idealistic writers and thinkers whose eager imaginations he could fire with his vision of reason, truth and justice. Men like Robert Southey, Samuel Coleridge and William Wordsworth.

Southey read *Political Justice* as early as November 1793. 'I am reading such a book!', he wrote ecstatically to a friend, 'Talk of morality in – Pontiphon's wife and Solomon's song! Democracy, real true democracy is but another name for morality – they are like body and soul.' And it was Southey who introduced Coleridge to the book at Oxford the following year, when they developed together their scheme for a Pantisocracy, a Godwinian community of rational equals to be founded in North America. 'Gerrald, Holcroft and Godwin – the three first men in England, perhaps in the world – highly approve our plan',[3] wrote Southey in November 1794, though he had yet to meet Godwin himself. And Coleridge, though 'I think not so highly of him as you do', was sufficiently impressed by *Political Justice* to draft a 'Sonnet to Godwin', which appeared in the *Morning Chronicle* for 10 January 1795 (in 1811 Coleridge claimed to have written this sonnet before he had even read *Political Justice*, but it is clear from his letters of the time that this was a slip of memory. He read the book in October 1794, and wrote the poem that December):

> O form'd t'illumine a sunless world forlorn,
> As o'er the chill and dusky brow of night,
> In Finland's wintry skies the Mimic Morn
> Electric pours a stream of rosy light,
> Pleas'd I have mark'd OPPRESSION, terror-pale,
> Since, through the windings of her dark machine,
> Thy steady eye has shot its glances keen –
> And bade th'All-lovely 'scenes at distance hail'.
> Nor will I not thy holy guidance bless,
> and hymn thee, GODWIN! with an ardent lay;
> For that thy voice, in Passion's stormy day,
> When wild I roam'd the bleak heath of Distress,
> Bade the bright form of Justice meet my way –
> And told me that her name was HAPPINESS.

Coleridge was later to 'confess with much moral and political contrition, that the lines and the subject were equally bad',[4] and even at the time he complained to Southey that 'the mediocrity of the eight first lines is *most miserably magazinish*', quoting only the last six in the hope that Southey might come up with a better beginning. But Southey's attempt, pencilled in the margin of Coleridge's letter, was hardly more successful:

> What tho' Oppression's blood-cemented fame
> Stands proudly threat'ning arrogant in state,
> Not thine his savage priests to immolate
> Or hurl the fabric on the encumber'd plain
> As with a whirlwind's fury. It is thine
> When dark Revenge mask'd in the form ador'd
> Of Justice, lifts on high the murderous sword
> To save the erring victim from her shrine.[5]

In December 1794, two weeks after Thelwall's acquittal, Coleridge had met Godwin at Holcroft's, amid 'talk of self-love and God' to quote from Godwin's diary. For Coleridge, like Godwin, saw governments and private property as the prime causes of injustice and inequality; he too looked forward to a progressive, non-violent improvement in society. But he was utterly opposed to Godwin's atheism and his moral opinions, and after meeting the man his attitude to the book changed dramatically. 'Of this work it may truly be said', he told his audience in May 1795,

> that whatever is just in it, is more forcibly recommended in the Gospel, and whatever is new is absurd. Severe Moralist! that teaches us that filial love is a Folly, Gratitude criminal, Marriage Injustice, and a promiscuous Intercourse of the Sexes our wisdom and our duty.[6]

When this criticism was repeated in his short-lived newspaper *The Watchman* it provoked an angry counter-attack in the *Bristol Gazette* from one 'Caius Gracchus', but Coleridge replied that he now rejected 'Mr Godwin's Principles as vicious; and his book as a Pandar to Sensuality'.[7] He repented of his complimentary sonnet, and promised instead a series of essays, a 'Reply to Godwin' in which, he told Thelwall, he would 'compare the two systems, his and Jesus's.'[8] The intention, in effect, was to Christianize Godwin, but what began as a 6 shilling pamphlet almost ready by December 1796, grew into a general treatise on moral philosophy and never appeared, if it was ever finished.

Southey, who had 'all but worshipped Godwin' as Coleridge never had, came to renounce him almost as quickly, though without as yet the benefit of meeting him personally. According to Coleridge, indeed, Southey had never understood, had scarcely even read, *Political Justice*: he had simply looked into it, found some ideas that coincided with his own, and so took it as a worthy expression of all his opinions without appreciating the half of what was involved, only to be horrified to discover what he had actually committed himself to. And Southey, unlike Coleridge, never again altered his attitude to Godwin, detesting the 'brute materialism, blind necessity and black atheism' of the book, and always speaking of the man himself with a scorn that approached obsession.

In fact it was Wordsworth, least under Godwin's spell personally, who got to know him best. They met first in February 1795, and it was probably on that occasion that, according to Godwin himself, he converted Wordsworth from the theory of self-love to that of benevolence, in the course of an evening, and when later that year Wordsworth was staying with their mutual acquaintance, Basil Montagu, further down Chalton Street at No. 15, they became firm friends. But though he is supposed to have advised a law student to 'throw aside your books of Chemistry and read Godwin on necessity',[9] Wordsworth was never an acolyte, as Coleridge and Southey had been. *Political Justice*'s second edition he dismissed out of hand as 'a piece of barbarous writing' with 'scarce a sentence decently written';[10] like Coleridge he began but never finished a critique of Godwin's moral theories; and if his verse drama *The Borderers* is, as often suggested, his repudiation of Godwinism, it shows only that he did not understand it. Certainly the *Descriptive Sketches*, for example, might seem to contain much that is pure Godwin, with its talk of 'Man, entirely free, alone and wild' who

> Confess'd no law but what is reason taught,
> Did all he wish'd, and wish'd but what he ought.

But the *Descriptive Sketches* and *Political Justice* were published in the self-same month.

In this we have the key to Godwin's sudden and striking success. His faith in the power of reason, the perfectibility of man, the inevitability of the millennium, were shared by many, the poets not least, before they had even read him. It was this which accounted for the unreasoning optimism with which *Political Justice* was greeted, the same enthusiasm that welcomed the revolution in France. What Godwin provided was an impressive statement of principles they already half believed, accompanied by all the trappings of reasoning and proof and backed up with arguments which even those who balked at the conclusions seemed unable to fault. But by the same token those opinions would be discredited and abandoned as the French revolution proceeded on the bloody path that Burke had forseen. A belief in inevitable human progress, once so natural and pervasive, soon came to seem entirely misplaced, unable to survive a Robespierre who could quote reason and Rousseau with the best of them. *Political Justice*, Godwin later lamented, had but four brief years of fame.

Once Godwin had been convinced that truth and freedom were on the march together. Describing a society without wars, crimes, laws or governments he had nevertheless insisted that these things 'are at no great distance; and it is not impossible that some of the present race of men may live to see them in part accomplished.'[11] And it was not simply that the standard of reform, once raised in France, would soon be carried through the rest of the world. Even more to the point,

> ten pages that should contain an absolute demonstration of the true interests of mankind in society could no otherwise be prevented from changing the face of the globe than by the literal destruction of the paper on which they were written.[12]

Godwin, no doubt, had his own text in mind, but that passage too, had to be deleted. The subsequent history of France as well as Britain had shown that truth does not so easily triumph over error, nor virtue over vice. Since 1789 there had been three democratic constitutions, and none had survived; the Rights of Man and of Citizens, so nobly promulgated in the preamble to the first, had never been much in evidence. Now civil war and foreign invasion had been halted only by the desperate expedient of a reign of terror that cost some 40,000 lives. (The majority of these died in the prisons, or were executed for taking part in civil war; less than 3,000 were the victims of Paris's infamous Revolutionary Tribunal. 40,000 also happens to be the estimate of those executed after the liberation of France in 1944.) The experience demonstrated, even to one as idealistic as Godwin, that there was no simple recipe for political justice. What the first edition had taken on trust, now called for demonstration.

The main task for 1795, accordingly, had been a thorough-going revision of *Political Justice* (the second edition, dated 1796, was in fact published on 26 November 1795), and also of *Caleb Williams*, which had arrived at its second edition even more quickly. Always a meticulous, not to say fussy, writer, Godwin never missed an opportunity to refine what he had already written, even to the extent of marking alterations for the next edition in the pages of the one just published. Often enough these changes are minor verbal improvements – the second edition of *Caleb Williams* for example, replaces 'countenance' by 'face' throughout, and the mysterious iron chest becomes a trunk – but he could also, as in the next edition, shift whole chapters about, and even change the names of characters, so that the inexorable Jones takes over the more sinister name of another character, Gines, in a way that must have generated the greatest confusion when readers of the third edition came to discuss the plot with readers of the first.

But the revision of *Political Justice* went far beyond that. We know from the original Preface that Godwin was dissatisfied with his book even before the last pages left his hands, and here was his opportunity to remedy the defects caused by its hand to press composition, to make the text more consistent. But, as Godwin apologizes to purchasers of his first edition, the changes are everywhere: no single chapter emerges unscathed, new ones are added, old ones deleted, and others so thoroughly altered that, of the eight Books, 'the four first and the last may, without impropriety, be said to be rewritten.'[13] Yet, surprisingly, it is the chapters on ethics, not those on politics, that undergo the most substantial changes, with a less extreme defence of sincerity, a more balanced critique of promises, a partial justification of rights and private property, and a more careful examination of the fundamental principles on which these theories depend – almost as if Godwin now realized that the hopes of mankind must lie in personal morality, not public politics.

But generally this second edition is altogether more cautious, more guarded, than the first, suggesting that Godwin had taken to heart the advice of Samuel Newton. This time he explains that by perfectibility he means not the attainment of absolute perfection, an idea 'pregnant with absurdity and contradiction', but rather an unending improvement; the speculation that mind might prove powerful over matter to the extent that man becomes immortal is replaced by the round declaration that the idea of immortality is absurd, and the question therefore meaningless; the attack on 'the established mode of excluding visitors' by announcing oneself not at home, originally delivered with such high-minded moral indignation, is now offered as a consideration which 'may afford an amusement and relief in the midst of discussions of a more comprehensive and abstracted character'; the wholesale critique of the institution of matrimony is directed more specifically towards marriage 'in the form now practised'; the recurring refrain that had once accompanied even the most startling assertions, that 'nothing could be more simple', 'more unquestionable', 'more certain', is largely deleted; and gone too is the constant suggestion the millennium is ready waiting just around the corner.

To some these modifications seemed to turn *Political Justice* into a recantation, at least a parody, of its former self:

In the *quarto* (that is, the original) edition of Political Justice, Mr Godwin advanced against thrones and dominations, powers and principalities, with the air of some Titan slinger or mono-machist from Thebes and Troy, saying – 'Come hither, ye wretches, that I may give your flesh to the fowls of the air'. But in the second or *octavo* edition – and under what motive has never been explained – he recoiled absolutely from the sound he himself had made: everybody else was appalled by the fury of the challenge, and through the strangest of accidents, Mr Godwin also was appalled. The second edition, as regards principles, is not a re-cast, but absolutely a travesty of the first; nay, it is all but a palinode . . . . In relation to the hostility of the world, he was like one who, in some piratical ship, should drop his anchor before Portsmouth – who should defy the navies of England to come out and fight, and then, whilst a thousand vessels were contending for the preference in blowing him out of the seas, should suddenly slip his cables and run.[14]

But de Quincey sees only the trappings, not the arguments that lie behind; he is like a man who admires the daring of a performance because the actors shout obscene words at their audience. The fact of it is that, considered as a work of philosophy, the second edition of *Political Justice* is both more successful and more significant than the first, while still retaining enough to shock and outrage its more sensitive readers. It lacks only that sense of excitement and discovery, of an author being driven by his argument who knows whither, that made the first edition so fascinating a document. But in place of that, *Political Justice* is now for the first time rooted solidly in argument, no longer a flight of intellectual fantasy; and political justice itself, once floating in its realm of pure reason free from all contact with base human reality, is now demonstrated to be inevitable, deducible from the very nature of man.

The theory of perfectibility did not originate with Godwin – the idea came from the French Encyclopedists, the word itself from Rousseau – and anyone who believes in social and political progress believes in human perfectibility in something approaching Godwin's sense. But in his hands the doctrine had taken a fresh and characteristic twist. Even those who recognized a material and scientific progress were nevertheless reluctant to admit any corresponding moral improvement, believing it impossible to change human nature. Indeed for Rousseau '*perfectibilité*' was not necessarily for the good, since he found man at his noblest in his natural, uncivilized, uncorrupted state. But for Godwin there was no need to change human nature. He might have been reared in a Calvinist doctrine of original sin, but that was one piece of Calvinism which did not survive into his mature thought: 'The vices of youth spring not from nature, who is equally the kind and blameless mother of all her children';[15] 'Every child that is born has within him a concealed magazine of excellence.'[16] Original sin lies not in man but in his institutions, 'the opposition they produce between public and private good, the monopoly they create of advantages which reason directs to be left in common'.[17] Left to himself, free from the constraints and distortions of government and law, man will incline towards the good and the true, which for Godwin are much the same. True, *Political Justice* declares that 'we bring into the world with us no innate principles . . . we are neither vicious nor virtuous as we first come into existence.'[18] But man is nevertheless born with a capacity, a predisposition even, to virtue, in that the mechanism of the human mind will itself see to it that, with the steady diffusion of knowledge, error and vice will give way to truth and justice. Progress, perfectibility, political justice, are not merely possible; they are inevitable.

The proof of all this is advanced in five simple steps;

> Sound reasoning and truth, when adequately communicated, must always be victorious over error: Sound reasoning and truth are capable of being so communicated: Truth is omnipotent: The vices and moral weakness of man are not invincible: Man is perfectible, or in other words, susceptible of perpetual improvement.[19]

The first of these was for Godwin a philosophical commonplace, so obvious as hardly to need argument at all; his contemporary Blake held equally that 'Truth can never be told so as to be understood, and not be believed.' No doubt the idea derived originally from Descartes, in his claim that once we perceive some matter clearly and distinctly we cannot be mistaken about it. But for Godwin it came more directly from Locke and Helvetius. 'The knowledge of truth', writes Godwin in words which are almost those of Locke, 'lies in the perceived agreement or disagreement of the terms of a proposition';[20] once our ideas are clear to us we can no more mistake falsity for truth than we can mistake black for white. Ignorance and error rest on confused understanding; once we know what we are saying, and what the evidence is, we cannot be misled.

Of course Godwin is not saying that ignorance and error are impossible. The argument is only that 'truth, when adequately communicated, is, so far as relates to the conviction of the understanding, irresistible.'[21] People fall into error because they accept as true judgments which they do not yet fully understand, or which have not been adequately demonstrated to them. This, as Descartes also urged, is our fundamental mistake, from which springs not only factual but also moral error. This is why we must encourage frankness and sincerity, why we must reject all deception and secrecy; this is why each man must learn to think and judge for himself, trusting not in authority but in the evidence, believing nothing because he has been told to believe it, but only because he can see for himself that it is so.

The next step in the argument again seemed obvious to Godwin. There are, he concedes, truths we do not know, perhaps even truths we cannot know. But once something is known, that discovery can be communicated to others, simply by repeating the argument or evidence that led to the original discovery. Yet quite apart from the practical difficulties of having to have each and every truth confirmed before we can accept it for ourselves, there is surely a fundamental problem here. For are there not some truths which not everyone is capable of grasping, some proofs which not everyone is capable of following? Godwin may reply, as he does, that

> Man is a rational being. If there be any man who is incapable of making inferences for himself, or understanding, when stated to him in the most explicit terms, the inferences of another, him we consider as an abortive production, and not in strictness belonging to the human species. It is absurd therefore to say that sound reasoning and truth cannot be communicated by one man to another. Whenever in any case he fails, it is that he is not sufficiently laborious, patient and clear.[22]

But what he has to establish is not that all men are rational, but that all men are equally rational, so that what can be demonstrated to and understood by one person is, in principle at least, capable of being demonstrated to and understood by any other human being worthy of the name. Here too the argument comes from Locke: 'we bring into the world with us no innate principles'; the mind is at birth as Locke pictured it, a blank tablet or empty box which derives all its content from external impressions. It follows therefore, as Hartley and Helvetius also argued, and as their successors, the behaviourist psychologists, argue still, that there are no natural inherited differences in the intellectual powers of men. It is the three all-powerful Es – experience, environment, education – which make us what we are. And on that assumption Godwin's argument fundamentally depends.

The third step in the argument, that truth is omnipotent, may seem to follow from what has gone before, but in fact it is the crucial move. For the conclusion is not just that 'every truth that is capable of being communicated, is capable of being brought home to the conviction of the mind'; the conclusion is that 'every principle which can be brought home to the conviction of the mind, will infallibly

produce a correspondent effect upon the conduct.'[23] The very title of
the chapter is 'The Voluntary Actions of Men Originate in their
Opinions'. What is a voluntary action? Involuntary action 'takes
place in us, either without foresight on our part, or contrary to the
full bent of our inclinations', as when we burst into tears without
expecting to, or even against our will. By contrast 'voluntary action
is, where the event is forseen previously to its occurrence, and the
ideas of certain consequences to result form the . . . motive belonging
to that event.'[24] Thus voluntary action depends on our beliefs about
what we are doing and what its consequences will be. It follows,
therefore, that once we convince men that something is so, their
voluntary actions will take account of that knowledge; their opinions
will be altered, but so will their deeds. This is what is meant by 'the
omnipotence of truth, or, in other words . . . the connection between
the judgment and the outward behaviour'.[25]

Godwin is here, without quite realizing it, taking issue with Hume
in the famous debate of reason versus the passions. Godwin believes
that reason by itself is sufficient to motivate action, but in Hume's
celebrated argument 'reason alone can never be a motive to any
action of the will', 'reason is, and ought only to be, the slave of the
passions, and can have no other office but to serve and obey them.'
Reason, says Hume, can tell us only how things are; only some
feeling, of desire or fear, hope or anxiety, can actually move us to
action. But if Godwin does not have Hume explicitly in mind, he is
well enough aware of this argument that man is governed by 'sense',
as he calls it, and not by reason. Such thinkers, he says, exaggerate
the power of passion; a change in our beliefs can overcome even the
strongest feelings:

> The better to determine this question, let us suppose a man to
> be engaged in the most progressive voluptuousness of the most
> sensual scene. Here, if ever, we may expect sensation to be
> triumphant. Passion is in this case in its full carreer [sic] . . . .
> Alas, in this situation, nothing is so easy as to extinguish his
> sensuality! Tell him at this moment that his father is dead, that
> he has lost or gained a considerable sum of money, or even
> perhaps that his favorite horse is stolen from the meadow, and
> his whole passion shall be instantly annihilated: So vast is the
> power which a mere proposition possesses over the mind of
> man.[26]

History is full of cases where men have ignored personal desire,
pleasure and pain, and acted instead in accordance with their
convictions.

Of course Hume would reply to all this that while beliefs may be both relevant and effective in shaping our conduct, passion remains necessary. A man will not act voluntarily unless it is an action he wants to perform; he will not be interrupted from his scene of progressive voluptuousness unless he feels strongly about the death of his father or the loss of his horse. Similarly the mere fact that we know that something is the right or rational thing to do will not by itself ensure that we will do it; we will do it only if we want to be right or rational. But as Godwin insists, 'The word passion is a term extremely vague in its signification,'[27] and an argument like Hume's depends on taking it in a wide and exaggerated sense. To say that I must want to perform the action or else I would not bother, is not to say that I must have a passion for doing it. The greater majority of our actions, happily, are unattended by passion in any strict sense of the word. It is only if by 'passion' we mean any preference, however slight and dispassionate, that we can argue that all action pre-supposes passion. And if that is what we mean, then so far from rejecting the claim, Godwin explicitly accepts it:

> In this sense without all doubt passion cannot be eradicated; but in this sense also passion is so far from being incompatible with reason, that it is inseparable from it . . . . If therefore this be the meaning of passion in the above proposition, it is true that passion ought not to be eradicated, but it is equally true that it cannot be eradicated; it is true, that the only way to conquer one passion is by the introduction of another; but it is equally true that, if we employ our rational faculties, we cannot fail of thus conquering our erroneous propensities. The maxims therefore are nugatory.[28]

So when Godwin says, as he subsequently does, that 'voluntary action implies desire', that if a man 'forsee any thing that is not apprehended to be pleasure or pain, or the means of pleasure or pain, this will excite no desire, and lead to no voluntary action,'[29] this is not simple inconsistency, with Godwin trying to have it both ways. For reason and passion – in this wide sense of the term – are one and the same thing: to desire something, in this weak and broad sense, is to judge it desirable, and to believe it desirable is to desire it. Nor is Godwin here committing the error of which Moore accused Mill, of thinking that the fact that some people desire something proves that it is desirable. Rather, he is arguing that 'to perceive a preference is to prefer',[30] that it is precisely in the judgment or opinion that one course of action is preferable to the other that the preference, the so-called 'passion', consists:

> It may be inferred that the contending forces of reason and sense, in the power they exercise over our conduct, at least pass

through the same medium, and assume the same form. It is opinion contending with opinion, and judgment with judgment.[31]

So we are 'no longer at liberty to consider man as divided between two independent principles, or to imagine that his inclinations are in any case inaccessible through the medium of his reason.'[32] Our voluntary actions originate in our opinions, including our opinions as to what is preferable or desirable. This is why 'whatever can be adequately brought home to the conviction of the understanding may be depended upon as affording a secure hold upon the conduct.'[33] This is why truth is omnipotent.

It follows from all this, Godwin believes, that the vices and moral weakness of man are not invincible. 'Vice and weakness are founded upon ignorance and error';[34] so long as we are mistaken about how things really are, about what is genuinely good and desirable, we will desire the wrong things and act accordingly. But if truth can be discovered and communicated we will come to desire what is truly desirable, and our conduct will be just and virtuous. The omnipotence of truth means, therefore, that every man can be made not just to see how he ought to behave, but to behave as he ought. Reason will lead us to truth, and truth will lead us to justice. It follows, in short, that man is perfectible, which is to say, susceptible of perpetual improvement.

Nevertheless the argument is, as it stands, incomplete. For it has yet to be shown that vice is unreasonable, that a man acquainted with truth and acting in accordance with it, will therefore do what is right. In fact many would deny that morality is capable of demonstrative proof. Contemporary moral philosophers almost universally question the assumption that it is possible to establish moral conclusions by sound reasoning and truth; the very point of the celebrated distinction between fact and value is precisely to set morality outside the realm of objective proof, and if that distinction is valid, there will be no secure moral truths to be omnipotent over conduct, to ensure that rational men will act in accordance with eternal and impartial justice. Godwin, however, has an argument, not to demonstrate that value can be derived from fact, but to prove that just action is to be preferred to all others. If that can be established, then a rational man, recognizing that truth, will not only believe that justice is right, but will do as justice demands. It is, therefore, an argument on which the proof of perfectibility depends, and it, too, is an argument added in this second edition. It is an argument to which we shall return.

For the moment, however, it is enough to see Godwin's proof of the omnipotence of truth, and hence of the perfectibility of man, as resting on three basic assumptions, not always explicit and each one debatable: that all men are by nature sufficiently rational to be capable of recognizing the truth, however complex, however abstruse, if only it is presented clearly to them; that our actions are governed by reason not passion, by our opinions not our feelings, or at any rate that there need be no conflict between the two; and that sound reasoning and truth will demonstrate that justice is the most desirable course of action, to be preferred to all others. Grant these propositions, grant, too, the doctrine of necessity, the doctrine that everything happens in accordance with inexorable laws of cause and effect, so that once the conditions are satisfied the result must inevitably follow, and it follows equally that truth will inevitably determine opinion, and opinion will inevitably determine conduct. Thus the steady growth of knowledge and understanding will not merely enable human progress; it will actually ensure it. Political justice is not just imaginable, it is inescapable. Men may be Yahoos now, but one day they will – indeed must – become Houyhnhnms.

9 ♣ Genial and benignant power!

Discussion, reading, enquiry, perpetual communication; these are my favorite methods for the improvement of mankind, but associations, organized societies, I firmly condemn. You may as well tell the adder not to sting . . . as tell organized societies of men, associated to obtain their rights and to extinguish oppression . . . to be innocent, to employ no violence, and calmly to await the progress of truth. I was never at a public dinner, a scene I have now not witnessed for many years, that I did not see how the enthusiasm was lighted up, how the flame caught from man to man, how fast the dictates of reason were obliterated by the gusts of passion, and how near the assembly was, like Alexander's compatores at Persepolis, to go forth and fire the city, or, like the auditors of Anthony's oration over the body of Caesar, to apply the flaming brand to the mansion of each several conspirator.[1]

To P. B. Shelley, 1812

♣ The failure of the 1794 treason trials might mean that democrats went no longer in fear for their lives, but the policy of repression continued unabated. The Constitutional Society had broken up almost at once, destroyed by the loss of its papers and the King's Evidence of Adams, its secretary. The Friends of the People lingered on for a year before voting to withdraw from political activity. Only the Corresponding Society continued to prosper, with Thelwall, who had been giving regular lectures at the Beaufort Buildings in the Strand, addressing enormous open-air rallies, of 150,000 and more, in June and again in October of 1795. But when the royal coach was stoned on the way to the opening of Parliament – 'My Lord – I – I – I've been shot at' gasped the startled king, as a stone shattered a window – the government felt it was time to act again. On 6 October Pitt proposed to the Commons a ban on seditious meetings, while Grenville in the Lords introduced a companion bill to achieve by law what Eyre had failed to do by jury, and extend the crime of treason to cover not just overt acts which threatened the monarch's life, but any incitement to his hatred or contempt.

But if the government could repeat its tactic, so too could Godwin, and no sooner had he completed his revision of *Political Justice*, before it was even published, than he was writing again, with the same deliberate haste as the year before, not to protest against this belated extension of the law against treason – perfectly legitimate after all, so long as it was the work of Parliament and not a judge – but to attack the bills as an unjustified restriction on freedom of speech. They go further than their authors imagine or intend, Godwin suggests, until even 'common speculative and philosophical disquisitions', works which examine the basis of monarchy and aristocracy, might find themselves outside the law. But longer and more diffuse, these *Considerations on Lord Grenville's and Mr Pitt's Bills* lacked both the incisive argument and the popular impact of the *Cursory Strictures*, and only two days later Godwin was sitting disconsolately with his friends Dyson and Mackintosh, watching the two 'Gagging Acts' go through the Commons. The politics of moderation were everywhere in retreat.

For although he charged Pitt and Grenville with over-reacting to the danger, Godwin was none the less convinced that there was a danger to react to: his pamphlet is signed 'A Lover of Order'. 'If the most important duty of those who hold the reigns of government be, at all times, to take care of public security', it warns in tones that resemble more than ever those of Burke, 'it is peculiarly so in the present crisis . . . . The dangers of anarchy and tumult are much greater now than at any ordinary period.'[2] *Political Justice*'s new edition would be even more critical of the political societies, their factionalism, their shibboleths, their demagogy, their restlessness, their rivalry and bickering, their tumult and violence, verbal if not physical. So Godwin is hardly concerned to defend the Corresponding Society and its mass meetings; on the contrary, 'the government of this country would be unpardonable, if it did not yield a very careful and uninterrupted attention to their operations.' And he follows that up with an unflinching attack on that 'impatient and headlong reformer' Thelwall, who stirs up 'all the indignant emotions of the mind' and puts the passions in training for scenes of riot and lynchings, then protects himself with a hypocritical appeal to universal benevolence, like 'Iago adjuring Othello not to dishonour himself by giving harbour to a thought of jealousy'![3]

> True, we must reform . . . . But reform is a delicate and an awful task. No sacrilegious hand must be put forth to this sacred work. It must be carried on by slow, almost insensible steps, and by just degrees . . . . This is the genuine image of reform; this is the lovely and angelic figure that needs only to be shewn, in order to be universally adored. Oh, Reform! Genial and benignant power! how often has thy name been polluted by profane and unhallowed lips! How often has thy

standard been unfurled by demagogues, and by assassins
drenched and disfigured with human gore![4]

Thelwall was aghast at this stab in the back from a man he
thought of as a teacher, an ally and a friend. He knew of Godwin's
qualms at what he had heard in the Beaufort Buildings – 'he has
frequently endeavoured to dissuade me from continuing my lectures,
by arguments strong and convincing I suppose to him, though to me
they appeared visionary and futile'[5] – but he hardly expected a
public attack at so perilous a time. He reproached Godwin privately,
and defended himself publicly in the pages of his *Tribune*, to which
Godwin responded with characteristic complacency, retracting
nothing and allowing only that he may have been misunderstood.
The rumour soon got about, as it had with Burke, that he had been
won over by the traditional bribe of a government pension.

Yet there was no treachery here; Godwin was merely being true to
his principles. For although he might preach the decay of governments, he had never preached their overthrow. *Political Justice* might
look forward to a world where traditional institutions, traditional
authorities, traditional values, traditional habits of mind, are all of
them abolished; but it also rejects any use of force or violence: 'we
shall have many reforms, but no revolutions.'[6] True, Godwin had in
his first edition been prepared to allow that a certain degree of
public disorder – he was thinking of France in 1789, not France in
1793 – might well be justified, if necessary in the name of progress.
But he did not believe, even then, that civil disturbance would prove
either desirable or necessary, and his second edition would be still
more critical of violence in every form. Not that he objects to
bloodshed as such, for 'death is in itself the slightest of human evils'
inasmuch as, unlike pain or tyranny, it can mean nothing to him
who suffers it. But revolutions 'are the produce of passion, not of
sober and tranquil reason'. So far from promoting progress they
actually hinder it, by inhibiting independence of thought and action,
freedom of intellectual enquiry, and the orderly march of truth.
Indeed if violence proves the only way of effecting political change,
that itself shows that we are not yet ready for it. We cannot be forced
into truth; we cannot be made rational against our wills.

But while *Political Justice* presents to us a blueprint of society in its
ideal state, it seems to offer no practical policy, no political
programme, for achieving that ideal. Godwin has proved to his own
satisfaction that the authority of governments lies in the consent of
the government, and it follows accordingly that once that consent is
removed, governments lose their authority. So we are like 'ten
thousand men of sound intellect, shut up in a madhouse, and

superintended by a set of three or four keepers', convinced that their whips and straw and bread and water are in our best interests. But one day truth will prevail:

> The prisoners are collected in their common hall, and the keepers inform them that it is time to return to their cells. They have no longer the power to obey. They look at the impotence of their late masters, and smile at their presumption. They quietly leave the mansion where they were hitherto immured, and partake of the blessings of light and air like other men.[7]

Yet it could hardly be so simple, and it was not until *Political Justice*'s final chapter that Godwin really faced up to 'The Means of Introducing the Genuine System of Property', which is to say the means of achieving political justice. It was, evidently, the doubts and queries of his more practical friend William Nicholson that forced him down from the visionary heights of the immediately preceding pages, to explain precisely how we are supposed to get from here to there. And the answer proved familiar enough.

'Let us imagine to ourselves a number of individuals', Godwin had written earlier,

> who, having first stored their minds with reading and reflection, proceed afterwards in candid and unreserved conversation to compare their ideas, to suggest their doubts, to remove their difficulties, and to cultivate a collected and striking manner of delivering their sentiments. Let us suppose these men, prepared to mutual intercourse, to go forth to the world, to explain with succinctness and simplicity, and in a manner well calculated to arrest attention, the true principles of society. Let us suppose their hearers instigated in their turn to repeat these truths to their companions. We shall then have an idea of knowledge perpetually gaining ground, unaccompanied with peril in the means of its diffusion. Reason will spread itself, and not a brute and unintelligent sympathy.[8]

And in these closing pages of *Political Justice* he returns again to the ability of an educated elite, chosen as our representatives, to lead the mass of mankind into the promised land. We must rely, first of all, on the 'enlightened and wise', those 'persons of some degree of study and reflection', to discover the moral and political truth and proclaim it moderately but fearlessly. Then, more surprisingly, we must rely on 'the rich and the great', individuals with the financial independence and personal integrity to set themselves above temporary personal considerations, and so give guidance to the 'friends of equality in general', men such as you and I.

It hardly needs the footnote of later editions to remind us that chief amongst the rich and great of his own day Godwin ranked Edmund Burke, as he doubtless included himself among the enlightened and wise. Thelwall, no less than the virulent anti-Jacobins who came after, had mistaken his man. The author of *Political Justice* was still the man who had praised Burke so effusively in the *Political Herald*, the man who at Fox's death in 1806 would describe him as 'the most illustrious model of a Parliamentary Leader on the side of liberty that this Country has produced . . . . the great ornament of the Kingdom of England during the latter part of the eighteenth century'.[9] Later in life he had a phrase he liked to repeat to those bemused by the evident contradiction between the man and his doctrines, the end and the means. 'My creed is a short one', he would say. 'I am in principle a Republican, but in practice a Whig.'

To Thelwall, of course, this was mere armchair radicalism, to think that political reform and social progress might be achieved through reading, writing, and the occasional conversation amongst philosophers. But it was difficult to remain enemies with Godwin for long, and it comes as no surprise to discover that in July 1796

> Godwin while at Norwich was reconciled to Thelwall at
> William Taylor's, and I have since seen them walking together
> round our Castle Hill. Of course the former will no longer be
> accused of 'cherishing a feebleness of spirit', nor will the latter
> again be compared to Iago. Like Gog and Magog or the two
> Kings of Brentford they will now go hand in hand in their
> glorious schemes.[10]

In fact, however, their political careers, whether separately or together, were virtually at an end. Thelwall retired, to become a teacher of elocution specializing in the treatment of stammering, an impediment he had himself overcome to be the most powerful orator of his day, and the *Considerations*, likewise, effectively marked the end of Godwin's involvement in practical politics. In October 1795 he had proposed to Robinson a political commentary, but he never again wrote primarily on political theory, and though he followed current affairs with interest he had little to say about them in public. The increasing restriction of freedom of speech and liberty of the press did not rouse him again, and even the imprisonment of Joseph Johnson, who had published the *Considerations*, and, many years later, of Daniel Isaac Eaton, who had made government interference his reason to publish the *Cursory Strictures*, passed entirely without comment from him. The only contemporary event to inspire, once more, a pamphlet reprinted from the *Morning Chronicle*, would be Napoleon's escape from Elba, when we find Godwin writing in defence of the Emperor, urging that he be left alone and in peace, to restore order among the unruly French!

Not that the failure of the *Considerations* to make any impression on either government policy or radical opinion had disillusioned Godwin personally, toying again with the idea Sheridan had put to him a decade before:

> I ought to be in Parliament. My principles of gradual improvement are particularly congenial to such a situation. It is probable that in the course of the next six years circumstances may occur, in which my talents, such as they are, might be of use. I am now forty years of age: the next six years will be six of the most vigorous years of my life. I would be no infrequent speaker. I would adhere to no party. I would vote for no proposition I did not want to see carried. I would be an author of motions; thus endeavouring to call public attention to salutary ideas.

But even at the height of his fame and self-confidence he still had some doubts:

> This is a situation that would excite envy and satire; it would be incumbent by splendour and activity of talent to disperse the cloud. If I were elected to parliament, this would be at first a source of humiliation; I should then be the last of gentlemen, whom am now one of the first of plebians; it must be the task of great energies to enable me to look erect in this situation. It is better, in a personal view, that the man should always appear greater than the situation, rather than the situation should appear greater than the man.[11]

And in any case Godwin could not have been more mistaken about those next six years, personally or politically.

Though intended, no doubt, more as a threat than a promise – no executions were carried out under them – the Gagging Acts nevertheless succeeded where the treason trials had failed, and by the time that the Corresponding Society was formally outlawed in 1799 it had been so undermined by regular prosecution and so thoroughly infiltrated by government spies that it had long ceased to have any effective existence. Public unrest would culminate in the navy mutinies of 1797, but it was directed more against the hardships of war – enforced enlistment, deplorable conditions, increased taxation, the price of bread – than in support of reform, and when Grey renewed his proposal to modernize Parliament it was rejected by an overwhelming margin of four to one, on the grounds that it would be foolish to mend one's roof in a thunderstorm. Those great swelling sentiments of liberty with which Godwin, like so many of his generation, had greeted 1789 subsided now. For them at least, the game was over, the cause was lost.

What, then, of the omnipotence of truth, the necessity of political justice, which Godwin had not merely advocated but demonstrated, in a proof itself intended to carry conviction to the minds of men? Events had conspired against him, as they always conspired against him, but an argument founded in necessity and the nature of things should be impervious to any little local difficulty. The problem lay deeper than that; it lay in the pages of *Caleb Williams*, in the controversy with Thelwall. 'In the midst of the singularities with which that valuable work abounds', Thelwell had complained of *Political Justice*,

> nothing is perhaps more remarkable than that it should at once recommend the most extensive plan of freedom and innovation ever discussed by any writer in the English language, and reprobate every measure from which even the most moderate reform can rationally be expected.[12]

The conflict with Thelwall was the old conflict, the conflict between political theory and political practice, but ultimately the difficulty went deeper, deeper perhaps than either man fully appreciated. For Godwin's arguments, carrying him ever further as they do, carry him finally into a circle from which it seems impossible to escape.

There is on the one hand the critique of political institutions, the belated realization that governments must actually be abolished if men are ever to trust in truth and rely on reason:

> The true reason why the mass of mankind has so often been made the dupe of knaves, has been the mysterious and complicated nature of the social system. Once annihilate the quackery of government, and the most home-bred understanding will be prepared to scorn the shallow artifice of the state juggler that would mislead him.[13]

But there is on the other hand the growing awareness of the dangers of anarchy, the recognition that we cannot expect to attain political justice overnight, by the simple expedient of abolishing political institutions. Men who have never been permitted to think for themselves will not suddenly become rational, just because all restraints have been lifted from their conduct. On the contrary,

> Individuals, freed from the terrors by which they had been accustomed to be restrained, and not yet placed under the happier and more rational restraint of public inspection, or convinced of the wisdom of reciprocal forbearance, would break

out into acts of injustice, while other individuals, who desired only that this irregularity should cease, would find themselves forced to associate for its forcible suppression. We should have all the evils attached to a regular government, at the same time that we were deprived of the tranquillity and leisure which are its only advantages.[14]

Thus the argument against governments is that so long as political institutions exist, individuals will never learn to rely on reason and respect truth. And the argument against their overthrow is that until individuals have learned to rely on reason and respect truth, some form of government remains necessary, to avoid the greater evils of anarchy. But in that case it is difficult to see how political justice can be possible at all, if men have to become fully rational before the state of society can exist which will enable them to become fully rational. Perhaps Godwin was aware of this difficulty. 'It is not . . . by any means necessary', his first edition had insisted,

that mankind should pass through a state of purification, and be freed from the vicious propensities which ill-constituted governments have implanted, before they can be dismissed from the coercion to which they are at present subjected. In that case their state would indeed be hopeless, if it were necessary that the cure should be effected, before we were at liberty to discard those practices to which the disease owes its most alarming symptoms.[15]

But by the second edition he began to have some doubt. 'If the annihilation of blind confidence and implicit opinion can at any time be effected, there will necessarily succeed in their place, an unforced concurrence of all in promoting the general welfare . . .', he proudly declares. Then adds, almost as an afterthought, 'It may be to a certain degree doubtful, whether the human species will ever be emancipated from their present subjection and pupillage.'[16] It is, in effect, the dilemma illustrated by *Caleb Williams* in spite of itself; things being as they are, truth will often fail to be victorious over error; how then can we rely on truth to alter things as they are?

Godwin personally never lost faith in perfectibility through reason and truth, a belief that he continued to endorse, sometimes confidently, sometimes less so, to the end of his life. But the argument by which he had established it was now to be undermined, not by political affairs but by personal experience. Hardly had he formulated his striking demonstration of the omnipotence of truth than he began to question those assumptions on which it was based. Reason, yet again, had convinced him of what subsequent reflection would lead him to deny. He was about to undergo the most profound revolution of his life, more devastating even than that of France.

At forty Godwin was famous and fêted but a bachelor still, eligible enough but hardly handsome, with a short stocky body 'surmounted by a large head that might befit a presentable giant',[17] a head made to seem even more massive by his thinning hair, broad forehead, penetrating eyes and, above all, his nose. 'Oh most abominable nose!', sneered Southey, sensitive enough about the size of his own. 'Language is not vituperatious enough to describe the effect of its downward elongation.'[18] But despite his plainness and his lack of social graces, his sensitivity to criticism and ridicule, his frequent outbursts of angry self-righteousness, Godwin did not lack female company. Success had made him more extrovert, more self-confident, than at any other time. He abandoned his sombre parson's clothes for a blue coat and stockings, a yellow waistcoat and breeches, and for once in his life he was not lost for conversation. Fame, they say, is an aphrodisiac, and there gathered around him a cluster of fashionable left-wing ladies, each flattered by the attentions of so illustrious a figure.

Not that Godwin was by any means the 'Pandar to Sensuality' that Coleridge charged him with being. True, *Political Justice* had some pretty startling things to say about sexual relations:

> The intercourse of the sexes will . . . fall under the same system as any other species of friendship . . . . I shall assiduously cultivate the intercourse of that woman, whose accomplishments shall strike me in the most powerful manner. But 'it may happen, that other men will feel for her the same preference that I do'. This will create no difficulty. We may all enjoy her conversation, and we shall all be wise enough to consider the sexual commerce a very trivial object. This, like every other affair in which two persons are concerned, must be regulated in each successive instance by the unforced consent of either party.[19]

But this apparent endorsement of free love amounts to something less than it seems to. As Godwin's editor remarks, 'it seems unlikely that an author who objects to community of meals is advocating community of wives,'[20] and 'intercourse', in particular, does not suggest to Godwin what it suggests to us. His permissiveness springs not from libertinism but from his Nonconformist background, even if it takes a Godwin to produce from puritan premises such conclusions as these. For duty, not desire, should govern sexual attachment:

Reasonable men now eat and drink not from the love of pleasure, but because eating and drinking are essential to our healthful existence. Reasonable men will then propagate their species, not because a certain sensible pleasure is annexed to this action, but because it is right the species should be propagated; and the manner in which they exercise this function will be regulated by the dictates of reason and duty . . . . It cannot be definitely affirmed whether it will be known in such a state of society who is the father of each individual child. But it may be affirmed that such knowledge will be of no importance.[21]

But for all this disparagement of sexual feeling, part of the critique of emotion that runs right through *Political Justice*, Godwin seems actually to have sought out the company of attractive women, who now numbered among his closest friends. Naturally we know little of his sex life, but we do know that his daughter tells us something less than the truth when she says of her father,

He was in a supreme degree a conscientious man, utterly opposed to anything like vice and libertinism, nor did his sense of duty permit him to indulge in any deviation from the laws of society, which though he might regard as unjust, could not, he felt, be infringed without deception and injury to any woman who should act in opposition to them.[22]

Opposed though he was to vice and libertinism, Godwin's sense of duty precisely obliged him to deviate from the laws of society when he considered them unjust; and his daughter was the living proof.

As it happens Godwin had felt it time to make a judicious approach to the institution of matrimony as far back as 1784, when he was twenty-eight. He had written home to his younger sister Hannah to see if she might know of a suitable partner among her friends, and excited at the prospect of a place for herself in a London household, she had eagerly recommended a certain Miss Gay. But Godwin's reaction can be gauged from another, more distant and more jaundiced letter from his sister about 'poor Miss Gay'. The matter was dropped, and Hannah made her own way to London in 1790, to find employment as a dressmaker and become a member of her brother's circle. But the fact of it was that in the 1780s Godwin, still a struggling journalist, could hardly afford to marry. Things were different now.

First and in most ways foremost in his coterie of lady friends was Elizabeth Inchbald who, like Holcroft, had begun on the stage and then turned to writing. Three years older than Godwin, married at eighteen and widowed at twenty-five, she had had to support herself ever since, a capable, determined, self-centred woman, striking rather than attractive, tall and slender, fair and freckled, her gowns 'always becoming, and very seldom worth so much as eightpence'.[23] But looks and general appearance were irrelevant where Mrs Inchbald was concerned, for she could play upon her feminine charm and forceful personality to the utmost, 'a piquante mixture', as Godwin put it, 'between a lady and a milkmaid'.[24] When she 'came into a room, and sat upon a chair in the middle of it as was her wont, every man gathered round it, and it was vain for any other woman to attempt to gain attention.'[25] She was, in short, a flirt, one of those women, so Godwin complained, who 'put in and out a heart as easily as they put on and take of their clothes'.[26] 'That segment of a *look* at the corner of her eye –', despaired Coleridge. 'O God in Heaven! – It is so cold and cunning – thro' worlds of wilderness I would run away from that heart-picking look!'[27]

Godwin had read the manuscript of Mrs Inchbald's most success-ful novel, *A Simple Story*, for the publishers Robinson towards the end of 1791, and when they met early the following year they became intimate friends, with a lifelong custom of sending each other the text of their latest works for comment Godwin had even celebrated the completion of *Political Justice* by going with Robinson to see Mrs Inchbald's latest comedy, *Every One Has His Fault*, which he then reviewed favourably for the *European Magazine*. 'He saw her fre-quently, he delighted in her manners, her conversation, her loveli-ness,' writes Godwin's daughter Mary, anxious as ever to avoid any hint of scandal; 'yet he was not in love, and, above all, never thought of marrying her.'[28] Yet Godwin's diary records 'talk of marriage' with Mrs Inchbald in September 1793, and the thought was still in the air several years later. Holcroft, too, was fascinated by her, and pursued her when he became a widower. But Mrs Inchbald, a Catholic and clearly reluctant to sacrifice her independence to anyone, never remarried.

By 1794 her special position was to some extent usurped by Maria Reveley, the young and pretty wife of a political acquaintance. Maria became Godwin's willing pupil, eager to be instructed in the art and practice of political justice, and accompanied her dis-tinguished tutor on his visits to Gerrald and Holcroft in Newgate Gaol – only to be thrown into a frenzy of agitation when it was suggested that Holcroft might call her as a witness in his defence. Often enough Godwin began the day with breakfast at the Reveleys', and again daughter Mary tells something less than the truth when she reports that Maria 'was married, and this circumstance was a barrier to every sentiment except friendship, but he certainly experienced for her more of tenderness and preference than for any other among his acquaintance.'[29] Coleridge, writing to Thelwall to sympathize at Godwin's dastardly attack, reports Godwin's 'endeavours to seduce Mrs Reevely [sic]',[30] and Godwin's diary lists a series of confessions and conferences at the Reveleys' in the winter of 1793–4. Nor was the feeling all on his side. The Reveley marriage was not a happy one, and later, when both their circumstances had changed, Godwin would remind Maria of what had once passed between them. 'You said you loved me', he wrote, 'for years loved me! Could you for years be deceived?'[31]

Completing a trio of particular friendships was Amelia Alderson, a noted beauty whom Godwin had met during his 1794 visit to Norwich. To her, as to many another, the famous Godwin was at first a disappointment:

> I found him indeed eloquent, entertaining and luminous in argument, even beyond my conception of his abilities, but my fancy had so long delighted to picture him a man after *his own heart*, that I shrank back almost displeased from a man after the *present state of things*.[32]

Godwin, however, was rather more impressed with her, and when Amelia came up to London later that year, there to attend the treason trials, he sat her down and cross-examined her on her opinions, arriving at the somewhat irrelevant verdict that she 'was more of a *woman*' than when he saw her last. 'Their friendship was purely such as is formed every day in society',[33] daughter Mary doggedly insists, yet when Amelia came back to town the following year Godwin was waiting for her 'with hair *bien poudré*, and in a pair of new, sharp-toed, red morocco slippers, not to mention his green coat and crimson under-waistcoat'.[34] He made a point of dining with her before he left on a second visit to Dr Parr in Warwickshire, and as Amelia wrote gaily home.

> he wished to salute me, but his courage failed him. 'While oft he looked back, and was loth to depart'. 'Will you give me nothing to keep for your sake, and console me during my absence', murmured out the philosopher, 'not even your slipper? I had it in my possession once, and need not have returned it' . . . . You have no idea how gallant he is become; but indeed he is much more amiable than ever he was. Mrs Inchbald says the report of the world is, that Mr Holcroft is in love with her, she with Mr Godwin, Mr Godwin with me, and I am in love with Holcroft . . . . She often says to me, 'Now you are come, Mr Godwin does not come near me'.[35]

(The editor of Amelia's letters dates the first of these quotations 1794, and the second 1796, but 1795 seems a more plausible date for Godwin's outbreak of modishness, and although he visited Parr in 1794 and 1795 he did not do so again until 1797, by which time he was no longer paying court to Miss Alderson.)

For Amelia, too, was something of a flirt. 'I hate you for always throwing Coquette in my teeth' goes one typically flighty letter to Godwin, '– it is a bad habit and you have lately acquired a worse – you called me a bitch the last time I saw you, but no matter'.[36] By July 1796 Godwin had brought himself to the point of making a proposal to Alderson, the father not the daughter, but to both their reliefs, it seems, nothing came of it. 'Mr Holcroft too', Amelia wrote the following year, 'has a mind to me, but he has no chance.'

There were others who fluttered round so great a celebrity, none more persistent than the curious Mary Hays, an intense and enthusiastic little lady, plain to the point of ugliness, who wrote a typically fulsome letter of self-introduction in October 1794:

> Perhaps no apology could be equally proper for a stranger addressing Mr Godwin, and presuming to solicit a favour, as a plain statement of the truth! Disgusted with the present constitutions of civil society, an observance of which the storms which have lately agitated the political hemisphere has forced upon every mind not absolutely sunk in apathy or absorbed in selfishness, the writer of this letter has been roused from a depression of the spirits, at once melancholy and indignant, by an attention to the 'few puissant and heavenly endowed spirits, that are capable of guiding, enlightening and leading the human race onward to felicity!' Among these, fame has given a distinguished place to the Author of 'Political Justice' . . .[37]

Godwin's reply was understandably cautious, anxious to avoid being trapped in a correspondence of this magnitude. 'I always admire your letters', he told her once,

> and when I read them, am sorry that invincible circumstances preclude me from having often the pleasure of seeing you. I am sorry too that the nature of my avocations restrains me from entering into regular discussions in the epistolary mode.

For the eager Miss Hays was an indefatigable correspondent, and her notorious novel *Emma Courtney*, published in 1796, was built around her own love letters, extraordinarily self-revealing though they were. They tell the story of a woman who pursues her chosen man with the insistent demand that he declare his love forthwith or state the reason why, backed up with arguments designed to crush in advance any objections or qualifications he might happen to have, so that they might enter into a union which is 'wholly the triumph of affection', inasmuch as 'the individuality of an affection constitutes its chastity'. It all ends tragically, of course, with Emma lamenting 'the consequences of confused systems of morals'. Hardly the typical delicate lady's novel of the day, its readers thought it shockingly advanced, not just for the heroine's relentless and most unladylike pursuit of her hero, but also for its constant appeal to the opinions, and often enough the writings, of such as Godwin and Wollstone-craft. 'I am convinced you do me justice', Emma writes at one point, *for this I do not thank you*, it is a duty to which I had a claim, and which you owed, not only to me, but, to yourself.' For Mary intended her scandalous story as a moral tale, and the moral is not, as it must surely seem, that reason and truth are inappropriate in matters of love, but that her heroine had used too little reason, not too much. As Emma says of herself, as Mary is saying of *her*self, 'Alas! my boasted reason has been, but too often, the dupe of my imagination.' For all the world a demonstration of the inadequacy of Godwin's moral psychology, of the impossibility of reason's dic-tating to the passions as political justice requires, *Emma Courtney* is actually Mary Hay's confession of her own inadequacy, her inability to live the life of reason that Godwin had prescribed.

The true identity of Mary's hero was still a mystery when her collected correspondence was published in 1925, and some had hoped to cast Godwin himself in the role, concluding that he had once to reject a proposal of marriage – or its equivalent – from the un-shakable Miss Hays. But for those who actually read the novel Godwin was there already, along with Mary's letters to him, in the person of Francis, the philosopher to whom Emma turns for guidance and moral support. In fact her lover, if that is not too active a word, was William Frend, at whose home Godwin first met William Wordsworth. But Mary's aggressive and argumentative letters fared no better in real life than they did in the novel, and by the time that the book was published their relationship, such as it was, had come to an end. Soon after Mary fell into an even more disastrous involvement with Charles Lloyd, a satirist who made Godwin one of his prime targets, and Lloyd, as unlikely to be sympathetic to Mary's opinions as he would be attracted by her looks, treated the whole affair as an enormous joke, reading her letters aloud to his friends and composing mock-serious replies in the style of Rousseau.

Lloyd satirized Mary too, in his novel *Edmund Oliver*, but she lives on most vividly as Bridgetina Botherim, the dwarfish, desiccated, cross-eyed heroine of Elizabeth Hamilton's *Memoirs of Modern Philosophers*. Dreadfully serious, and given to long harangues in which she quotes copiously from both *Political Justice* and the *Enquirer*, Miss Botherim is another who demonstrates by rational argument that the man of her choice must be in love with her – though he suspects nothing of the matter – and then cannot understand how a rational man can fail to accept the proof. She, too, argues from universal principles and the nature of things, appealing so often to General Utility that her mother comes to wish she had never heard of the man. Godwin enters, in the person of Bridgetina's adviser, Dr Myope, whose teachings lead to such calamities that he is in the end converted, though to a Christianity very different from the austere Calvinism from which he began. Nor do his theories fare much better: Miss Botherim, who since she is rather taller sitting than standing cannot properly be said to rise from her chair, is out walking one day when she falls in with Holcroft, in the guise of Mr Glib, who is delighted to see her exerting those energies so praised in *Caleb Williams*. 'That's it!', he cries, 'energies do all. Make your legs grow long in a twinkling. Won't then sweep the streets with your gown. All owing to this d--d good-for-nothing state of civilization. No short legs in an enlightened society.' But as Bridgetina haughtily replies, 'Certainly, if a person of energetic mind chooses to be tall, there is nothing to hinder it; mind, we all know, being despotic over matter; but I see no good in being tall, for my share, and would rather remain as I am.'

Yet this unlikely figure would play cupid for William Godwin. Mary Hay's two chosen oracles were Godwin and Mary Wollstonecraft – she was the latter's 'baldest disciple', according to the *English Review*, though it isn't clear which Mary the pun is directed against (see the verse quoted p. 157 below) – and she was determined to bring them together. So it was Mary Hays, in January 1796, who gave Godwin the chance to meet again, after a gap of almost four years, the noted vindicatress of the rights of both men and women, recently resident in revolutionary France, mistress to the American adventurer Imlay, and mother of his daughter, Fanny.

10 ♣ A salutary and respectable institution

> Now only was it that I tasted of perfect happiness. To judge from my own experience in this situation, I should say, that nature has atoned for all the disasters and miseries she so copiously and incessantly pours upon her sons, by this one gift, the transcendental enjoyment and nameless delights, which, wherever the heart is pure and the soul refined, wait on the attachment of two persons of opposite sexes.
>
> *St Leon*, 1799

♣ They had met originally on 13 November 1791, at dinner at Joseph Johnson's, where Godwin had gone to meet Tom Paine, and he had not been much impressed:

> I had . . . little curiosity to see Mrs Wollstonecraft, and a very great curiosity to see Thomas Paine. Paine, in his general habits is not a great talker; and though he threw in occasionally some shrewd and striking remarks, the conversation lay principally between me and Mary. I, of consequence, heard her, very frequently, when I wished to hear Paine.[1]

She was already the celebrated political writer that he still hoped to become, entitled to the courtesy title of 'Mrs' Wollstonecraft because, it has been said, the production of a book, like that of a child, was considered indelicate if it occurred outside the married state. But Godwin personally thought little of the strident tone, sloppy reasoning and erratic grammar of her emotive response to Burke, *A Vindication of the Rights of Man*, published a year earlier, nor was Mary herself at thirty-two a particularly attractive personality, arrogant and insensitive, more used to managing the lives of others than to controlling her own, and as she was soon to demonstrate, emotionally immature, unable or unwilling to recognize the forces that motivated her conduct. They met again once or twice after that, but generated in each other only a mild mutual dislike.

Two months later, in January 1792, Mary published her *Vindication of the Rights of Women*, a powerfully original work fully deserving of its pioneering place in the canon of Woman's Liberation, for all its extravagant rhetoric and exaggerated romanticism. Mary attacks the educational and social practices of the day, by which women were trained to be nothing but 'the toy of man, his rattle, and it must jingle in his ears whenever, dismissing reason, he chooses to be amused'. She denies any artificial, non-biological, difference between the sexes, and especially the idea that 'man was made to reason, women to feel'. Women share with men the divine gift of reason, and ought therefore to share the same virtues and the same worth. If they will only put aside their false and demeaning femininity, women can become man's equal in reason and dignity as God intended them to be. For Mary's aim is not so much to alter men's attitude to women as to alter women's attitude to themselves, degraded as they are by 'mistaken notions of female excellence' by which men, women and society are all equally the losers. Her main argument, she says herself,

> is built upon this simple principle, that if woman be not pre-
> pared by education to become the companion of man, she will
> stop the progress of knowledge, for truth must be common to
> all, or it will be inefficacious with respect to its influence on
> general practice.

With benefit of hindsight, it is tempting to discover many such points of similarity between the *Rights of Woman* and *Political Justice*. There is the same emphasis on reason, the same faith in the power of private judgment, the same belief in inevitable progress. But in fact the differences are more manifest than the resemblances. Mary is no abstract theorist: this is a critique of existing practices, not a search for fundamental principles from which some ideal state of society might be deduced. She appeals to reason not from any theory of human nature, but because it is the gift of God to all his children. Her tone of exultant piety and inexorable moralism is entirely alien to Godwin, at least at that time; there is in her none of that sense of cutting away the moral cant, of getting down to basics, which is so refreshing in him. Yet equally, where Godwin lists with scholarly precision the demonstrable disadvantages of a state of inequality, Mary burns with ill-controlled indignation at the despair and suffering that injustice can bring. Here, as elsewhere, it is difficult to avoid the ironic conclusion that Godwin was made to reason, Mary to feel. But if Mary was the more emotional, the less reflective of the two, she was also the more practical, seeing the world as it was, not through the distorting spectacles of social theory, and with an acute sense of why society, and in particular the relation between the sexes, should function as it does. Typically her own work on the *Education of Daughters*, published three years after Godwin's *Account of A Seminary*, deals with the actual practice of teaching, how girls can be given the education they both deserve and require, not with its theoretical justification.

At first Mary intended to write a second volume of the *Rights of Women*, which would deal with the political inequalities and civil rights largely ignored in the first. But as her publisher Johnson later told Godwin, 'her exertions were palsied, you know the cause'. For it was in the excited literary circle that gathered regularly at Johnson's that Mary met, and became infatuated with, the Swiss painter Henry Fuseli, who, according to William Blake,

> The only man that e'er I knew
> Who did not make me almost spew

but according to Godwin 'the most frankly and ingenuously conceited man I ever knew'. An ugly, shock-haired gnome of a man, Fuseli was eighteen years older than Mary, intelligent, sensual, extrovert and above all, talkative. His feverish imagination and fire-cracker mind fascinated her, his ready temper made him something of a father figure, and this vitality and passion exerted a strong attraction that she could not recognize for what it was. 'A rational desire', so she called it, 'a strength of feeling unalloyed by passion.' Fuseli, who had recently buried a disreputable past beneath the respectability of marriage, nevertheless enjoyed the company of women and, even more, their enjoyment of his. He later claimed to have carried Mary's letters around unopened for days, but he was also willing to claim that he had transformed 'a philosophical sloven, with lank hair, black stockings and a beaver hat' into a mature and striking woman of some beauty and considerable charm. Mary moved her lodgings closer to his, and demanded 'the satisfaction of seeing and conversing with him daily'. By March even Godwin had heard the 'story of Mrs Wollstencraft'.

Matters came to a head at the end of 1792, when Mary suggested to the Fuselis, husband and wife, that she might come and live with them in a state of 'spiritual concubinage'. Receiving the inevitable reply, she travelled on her own to Paris, hoping, she said, 'to lose in public happiness the sense of private misery', and there fell in with the inconstant and child-like Gilbert Imlay, full of exaggerated stories of his past and grandiose plans for his future. Her intelligence and determination attracted him, his charm and sensuality captivated her, and by summer they were lovers. In September 1793, when the French government ordered the detention of all Britons, Imlay registered Mary at his embassy as his wife and therefore an American, but they had never married. It was hardly the time or place for a ceremony that might call attention to Mary's presence, and if Imlay was glad of a reason not to make their alliance legally binding, Mary too was pleased at 'not having clogged my soul by promising obedience &c &c'. But she regarded herself as wed in spirit, for she was pregnant.

Yet Imlay had not bargained on a family as well as a wife, and too weak to cope for long with Mary's demands and perseverance, he began to lose interest. 'Tickling minnows he had hooked a dolphin', in Virginia Woolf's striking image, 'and the creature rushed him through the waters till he was dizzy and wanted only to escape.' She followed him to Le Havre, where her daughter Fanny was born, and then, in the spring of 1795, to London. Imlay did send her to Scandinavia on his behalf as 'my best friend and wife . . . to take sole management of all my affairs and business', but he had meantime acquired a new mistress. 'I have looked at the sea', Mary wrote before embarking at Hull, 'and at my child, hardly daring to own to myself the secret wish that it might become our tomb.' She had attempted suicide once already.

Returning to London in October Mary discovered that Imlay and his mistress had set up house together. This time she laid her plans more carefully. She went first to Battersea Bridge but there were too many passers-by, so she hired a boat and rowed herself upstream to Putney, where she walked about in the heavy rain for half an hour, that her sodden clothes might carry her down the more quickly. Even then she did not sink but, swallowing water, lost consciousness from the searing pain. Somehow she was rescued.

Mary did not lack friends in these miserable months. There was the ever-dependable Johnson, her patron and adviser, both a father and a brother, she said herself; and there was the eager Miss Hays whom, like Godwin, she had once unsuccessfully tried to fend off. And so it was, with her worst times behind her but the final break with Imlay still to come, that Mary Wollstonecraft found herself invited, on Friday 8 January 1796, to take tea with Thomas Holcroft and William Godwin.

Their positions had reversed since 1791. Now Godwin was the successful author with a reputation far eclipsing hers, and he was prepared to be magnanimous towards a disagreeable woman. 'I shall be happy to meet Mrs Wollstonecraft', he replied to Mary Hay's invitation,

of whom I know not that I ever said a word of harm, and who has frequently amused herself with depreciating me. But I trust you acknowledge in me the reality of a habit on which I pique myself, that I speak of the qualities of others uninfluenced by personal considerations, and am as prompt to do justice to an enemy as a friend.[2]

He was expecting, no doubt, the aggressive philosophical sloven of four years before, and was already on the defensive against her anticipated sarcasm. Instead he found an attractive and alluring woman with a past, and a present, that aroused his sympathy. 'Her person was above the middle height', wrote Mary Hays,

> and well proportioned; her form full; her hair and eyes brown; her features pleasing; her countenance changing and impressive; her voice soft, and, though without great compass, capable of modulation. When unbending in familiar and confidential conversation, her manners had a charm that subdued the heart.[3]

She was probably taller than he and as strong-minded as ever, but she had matured and softened with experience, and Godwin was no longer afraid of her. They met again at dinner a week later.

The following month Mary happened on Imlay at the home of mutual friends. They dined together next morning, but there was no reconciliation, and Mary went to visit friends in Berkshire, there to make her mind once for all. When she returned, in April, she called on Godwin uninvited, a breach of the conventional lady's etiquette that he would later feel obliged to justify. He, meanwhile, had read and admired her published *Letters from Scandinavia*, and offered an invitation to an unprecedented dinner party to be held on the 22nd. Others had entertained Godwin often enough, but apart from regular suppers and breakfasts with the likes of Holcroft, Fawcett, Dyson and Wordsworth, Godwin's deliberately frugal existence had ruled out any entertaining of his own. It was only, as he says, when a group of friends 'good humouredly invited themselves to dine with me' that he felt obligated to return their hospitality, though he had to order both the food and the plates to put it on from a neighbouring coffee shop. The party of twelve in his 'little deserted mansion' that Friday afternoon included Holcroft, James Mackintosh and family, the Dr Parr he had visited in Warwickshire and Parr's two daughters, Mrs Inchbald, and 'Mrs Imlay'.

But other irons were still smouldering in the fire, and though the name 'Imlay' or 'Wollstencraft' is common in the diary for May, it is no more so than Alderson, Reveley, or Inchbald. In June Godwin was reading Mary's new comedy for her, but in April he had read Amelia's, and when he travelled to Norfolk in July, there to be reconciled with Thelwall, it was partly to 'propose to Alderson'. But perhaps he anticipated a refusal, and wanted only to clear the ground. Certainly he later claimed that during this separation 'each furnished to the other the principal topic of solitary and daily contemplation',[4] and only three days after the conference with Dr

Alderson he was writing facetiously to Mary, well aware that a middle-aged philosopher was in danger of appearing ridiculous in this unaccustomed role:

> Shall I write a love letter? May Lucifer fly away with me if I do. No, when I make love it shall be with the eloquent tones of my voice, with dying accents, with speaking glances (through the glass of my spectacles), with all the witching of that irresistible, universal passion. Curse on the mechanical, icy idiom of pen and paper. When I make love, it shall be in a storm, as Jupiter made love to Semele, and turned her at once into a cinder. Do not these menaces terrify you?[5]

But though he warned her 'I expect to arrive on this day sennight at seven o'clock in the morning, to depart no more', in fact his first call, back in town, was on Amelia Alderson, to put that little matter to rest.

After the break with Imlay Mary had been intending to go abroad again, to Italy, to Switzerland, to anywhere so long as it was away. But while Godwin was in Norfolk she moved instead into more permanent accommodation just around the corner from him, on what is now the Euston Road. The entries 'chez moi' and 'chez elle' commence in his diary on 15 August; and then, on 21 August, 'chez moi, toute':

> The partiality we conceived for each other was in that mode which I have always considered as the purest and most refined style of love. It grew with equal advances in the mind of each. It would have been impossible for the most minute observer to have said who was before and who was after. One sex did not take the priority which long established custom has awarded it, nor did the other overstep that delicacy which is so severely imposed. I am not conscious that either party can assume to have been the agent or the patient, the toil spreader or the prey, in the affair. When, in the course of things, the disclosure came, there was nothing, in a manner, for either party to disclose to the other . . . . There was no period of throes and resolute explanation attendant on the tale. It was friendship melting into love.[6]

No doubt the awkward and inexperienced Godwin needed Mary's encouragement, but Mary too was uncertain, fearful of fresh disappointment. Her notes to Godwin clearly reveal her anxiety, regret, even guilt, at what had happened, always on the defensive, always prepared for some rebuff: 'But I mean not to hurt you. Consider what has passed as a fever of your imagination; one of the slight mortal shakes to which you are liable – and I – will become again a *Solitary Walker*. Adieu!'[7] But with Godwin steadfastly reassuring in his patient pedantic way, her mounting relief is obvious. After Imlay he must have seemed dull, plain and clumsy, but he was absolutely reliable, giving Mary the security and unqualified affection that Imlay had been incapable of, and which she needed now more than ever; and she, in her turn, awoke Godwin as Imlay had awoken her. For him it was a new experience indeed: 'I had never loved till now, or, at least', he added with his customary philosopher's exactitude, 'had never nourished a passion to the same growth, or met with an object so consummately worthy.'[8]

For the moment they kept the affair secret from even their closest friends, and though Mary took charge of Godwin's washing and mending, and had her own key to his apartment, they retained their separate establishments. Nor was this simply for decorum's sake. *Political Justice* had declared itself against cohabitation, not only because it carries with it 'some inevitable portion of thwarting, bickering and unhappiness' – shades of Newton, Marshall and Cooper – but also because 'it checks the independent progress of the mind':

> All attachments to individuals, except in proportion to their merits, are plainly unjust. It is therefore desirable, that we should be the friends of man rather than of particular men, and that we should pursue the chain of our own reflections, with no other interruption than information or philanthropy requires.[9]

But if cohabitation interferes with both reason and justice, marriage is contrary to truth as well:

> The evil of marriage, as it is practised in European countries, lies deeper than this. The habit is, for a thoughtless and romantic youth of each sex, to come together, to see each other, for a few times, and under circumstances full of delusion, and then to vow to each other eternal attachment. What is the consequence of this? In almost every instance they find themselves deceived. They are reduced to make the best of an irretrievable mistake. They are presented with the strongest imaginable temptation to become the dupes of falsehood. They are led to conceive it their wisest policy, to shut their eyes upon realities, happy, if by any perversion of intellect, they can persuade themselves that they were right in their first crude opinion of their companion. The system of marriage is a system of fraud; and men who carefully mislead their judgments in the daily affair of

life, must always have a crippled judgment in every other concern. We ought to dismiss our mistake as soon as it is detected; but we are taught to cherish it.[10]

No doubt there is a certain naivety in Godwin's belief that a couple might become personally and sexually intimate, yet retain complete independence of feeling, thought and action merely by living apart. But it was hardly to be expected that the man who dismissed marriage as an 'affair of property', 'a monopoly and the worst of monopolies',[11] should now marry – and marry a woman who had herself called marriage 'legalized prostitution'. But by the end of the year Mary found she was pregnant again, and with the aftermath of her first pregnancy still fresh in her mind, she was understandably apprehensive. 'I am, however, prepared for anything', she wrote defensively to Godwin, when finally there could be no doubt. 'I can abide by the consequence of my own conduct, and I do not wish to involve any one in my difficulties.'[12] But faced with this conflict of duties, to his principles and to his lover, Godwin abandoned the former and on 29 March 1797 they were secretly married at Old St Pancras Church, with Marshall and the parish clerk their only witnesses. (Mary Wollstonecraft thus became the first of three Mary Godwins, two of them Mary Wollstonecraft Godwins. I will continue to call her Mary Wollstonecraft, reserving the name 'Mary Godwin' for her daughter, and referring to Godwin's second wife as Mary Jane.) 'Some persons have found an inconsistency between my practice in this instance and my doctrines. But I cannot see it . . .', Godwin wrote somewhat shamefacedly to Tom Wedgwood, from whom he had had to borrow £50 to settle Mary's debts, without explaining why he needed the money.

Nothing but a regard for the happiness of the individual, which I had no right to injure, could have induced me to submit to an institution which I wish to see abolished, and which I would recommend to my fellow-men, never to practise but with the greatest caution. Having done what I thought necessary for the peace and respectability of the individual, I hold myself no otherwise bound than I was before the ceremony took place.[13]

And he added a final apologetic footnote: 'We do not entirely cohabit.'

At first Godwin kept the news to a select few. He had a 'confidence' with Maria Reveley, and wrote to Holcroft and to 'Mère', the French suggesting that he was not sure how best to explain the situation. To Holcroft, indeed, he did not even name the lady, but Holcroft was not deceived so much as offended. 'I cannot be mistaken concerning the woman you have married', he wrote back. 'It is Mrs W. Your secrecy a little pains me. It tells me you do not yet know me.' But 'From my very heart and soul I give you joy. I think you the most extraordinary married pair in existence.'[14] Godwin's note to their improbable cupid, Mary Hays, was only slightly more forthcoming, with its coy reference to 'my fair neighbour': 'We found that there was no way so obvious for her to drop the name of Imlay, as to assume that of Godwin. Mrs Godwin – who the devil is that? . . . .'[15]

But until *The Times* of 15 April published its garbled report of the marriage of a 'Mr Goodwin, author of a Pamphlet against the institution of Matrimony, to the famous Mrs *Wolstonecroft*, who wrote in support of the *Rights of Women*', few but Hays and Holcroft would have linked the names of Godwin and Mary. They still lived their separate lives, so much so that Godwin once objected to Mary calling on Holcroft, since he was his friend not hers; and a mere month before the wedding Mary had written 'Did I not see you, friend Godwin, at the theatre last night? I thought I met with a smile, but you went out without looking round'[16] – and friend Godwin it was, as we know from his diary. Instead the gossip was that Mary was being courted by John Opie, who had been painting her portrait, while Godwin was still pursuing Mrs Inchbald. 'Mrs Inchbald is said to be on the point of bestowing her hand on Mr Godwin', the *True Briton* had reported on 1 February.

> If there by any truth in this report, it is to be hoped that the Author of *Political Justice* will not think gratitude for such a favour of crime, lest the lady, in the instance of her *marriage vow*, should retaliate on him his other doctrine, that it is not necessary *to keep promises*,

adding a day or two later that her new play is to be called *The Virgin Wife* and 'the critics do not know what to make of it'. But eight months later the *Monthly Visitor* could be more perceptive, when it looked back to an evening when Godwin, Wollstonecraft and Opie had all been present:

> Mr Opie was, as usual, very attentive to Mrs Wollstonecraft. But the philosopher – the lover of Mrs Wollstonecraft, and the great man who contends that men may live without sleeping – was himself fast asleep in the chimney-corner. This insignificant incident might have taught our fashionable lookers-on that Mr Godwin and Mrs Wollstonecraft, possessing, thus eminently, the happy quality of mutual distance, were marked for man and wife!

And Opie, who had the signal distinction of a divorce, obtainable then only at great expense and by special dispensation of Parliament, neatly rounded things off by marrying Amelia Alderson.

That still left Mrs Inchbald. Whether it was annoyance that Godwin, who accompanied her in public more than he did Mary, had kept his secret from her; whether it was disgust at their immorality; whether it was irritation at being so dramatically upstaged; or whether it was disappointment – or pique – at losing so celebrated a suitor, we cannot know. Mary, who cared no more for 'Mrs Perfection' than Mrs Inchbald cared for her, may give a hint when she writes to Godwin 'I do not like her the less, for having spoken of you with great respect, and even affection – so much so that I begin to think you were not out in your conjecture – you know what.'[17] But whatever the cause Mrs Inchbald was prepared to act as a substitute for no woman, and the moment she learnt of the marriage she wrote furiously to Godwin, to cancel their appointment at the theatre next Wednesday. 'Assured that your joyfulness would obliterate from your memory every trifling engagement, I have entreated another person to supply your place . . . . If I have done wrong, when next you marry, I will act differently.'[18] Nothing abashed, Godwin took Mary instead and, with Maria Reveley and Amelia Alderson as embarrassed witnesses, there was a public quarrel between the two ladies.

The others, however, were delighted. Maria may have wept when she heard the news, but Amelia had once declared that of all the famous sights she had seen, the only ones to live up to their reputation were the Lake District and Mrs Imlay, and the two were soon among Mary's closest friends. Godwin's mother, now seventy-five, wrote happily but erratically from Norfolk, chiding him for not mentioning he had become a father as well as a husband – the reference is presumably to Fanny Imlay, not to Mary's pregnancy – and rejoicing that

> your broken resolution in regard to mattrimony incourages me to hope that you will ere long embrace the Gospel . . . . You are certainly transformed in a moral sense, why is it impossable in a spiritual sense, which last will make you shine with the radiance of the sun for ever.[19]

She sends a congratulatory box of eggs, offers a spare feather bed, and warns them against making 'invitations and amusements'. But elsewhere there was polite amusement, or thinly veiled sarcasm, at Godwin's theoretical discomfort. 'A very suitable match', agreed Anna Barbauld, like Mary, a member of Johnson's literary circle.

but numberless are the squibs which are thrown at Mr Godwin on the occasion, and he winces not a little on receiving the usual congratulations. In order to give the connection as little as possible the appearance of such a vulgar and debasing tie as matrimony, the parties have established their separate establishments, and the husband only visits his mistress like a lover, when each is dressed, rooms in order, etc. All this may possibly last till they have a family, then they will probably join in one menage, like other folks.[20]

Godwin moved his own rooms further up Chalton Street, to No. 17 in the Evesham Buildings, while Mary went with Fanny to Clarendon Square right at the top of the road, where a set of thirty-two paired houses, four storeys high and linked by wedge-shaped wings, formed an enclosed shape, gardens in the middle, of sixteen sides. It was known as the 'Polygon', built in 1793 as a resort for French émigrés, and later, for a time, the home of Charles Dickens. It stood on the very edge of town, separated from the villages of Camden Town and Chalk Farm by market gardens and open fields. This pleasant rural setting would be Godwin's base for the next ten years.

His practice was to leave the Polygon immediately on rising, to work in the Evesham Buildings through the morning, and visit friends in the afternoon, not returning home until after dinner. Then the evenings would be their time together, seeming 'to combine, in a considerable degree, the novelty and lively sensation of a visit, with the more delicious and heartfelt pleasures of domestic life.'[21] In the novel *St Leon*, two years later, Godwin recaptured these private moments together:

Separation gave us respectability in each other's eyes, while it prepared us to enter with fresh ardour into society and conversation. In company with each other, hours passed over us, and appeared but minutes . . . . We were both of us well acquainted with the most eminent poets and finest writers of modern times. But when we came to read them together, they presented themselves in a point of view in which they had never been seen by us before . . . . At other times, when not regularly engaged in this species of reading, we would repeat passages to each other, communicate the discoveries of this sort that either of us had made in solitude, and point out unobserved beauties, that perhaps neither of us would have remarked, but for the suggestion of the other . . . . It is difficult to imagine, how prolific this kind of amusement proved of true happiness. We were mutually delighted to remark the accord of our feelings, and still more so, as we perceived that accord to be hourly increasing, and what struck either as a blemish in the other, wearing out and disappearing . . . . Each of us hourly blessed our common lot, while each believed it impracticable elsewhere to have found so much worth blended with so much sweetness.

Mary was writing a novel, *Maria, or the Wrongs of Woman*, intended to play *Caleb Williams* to her *Vindication of the Rights of Women*, and Godwin had just published his volume of essays called *The Enquirer: Reflections of Education, Manners and Literature*. The intention was to present the leading themes of *Political Justice* – the value of sincerity, the necessity for independence, the evils of cohabitation – in a more cautious, more piecemeal and, as Godwin admits, possibly less consistent manner. But the first, and better, part was devoted entirely to education, a topic which the earlier work had largely ignored; the second is more miscellaneous, with essays on the evils of poverty and of wealth, the servitude of servants and the despicability of beggars, the characters that are associated with the various trades and professions, the importance of reputation and of posthumous fame. But most remarkable of all is a final, extremely lengthy, essay 'Of English Style' in which Godwin surveys the major writers of the previous two centuries and charges them one and all with verbosity, poor construction and, especially, faulty grammar, marking out their weaknesses with asterisks until the page comes to resemble an outbreak of measles, a treatment his own writing could scarce survive. But for all his pernicketyness and lack of historical sense, his account of a good prose style is admirable enough and, at the time, admirably true of his own:

> The beauty of a style consists in this, to be free from unnecessary part and excrescencies, and to communicate our ideas with the smallest degree of prolixity and circuitousness. Style should be the transparent envelop of our thoughts; and, like a covering of glass, is defective, if by any knots and ruggedness of surface, it introduces an irregularity and obliquity into the appearances of an object, not proper to the object itself.[22]

Nevertheless the *Enquirer* failed to repeat the success of Godwin's novel and his treatise. He wrote a further essay while the book was in the press, 'under the impression that the favour of the public might have demanded another volume', but the second edition did not appear for another twenty-five years.

That year also saw the major revision of *Caleb Williams*, into whose plot he now introduces a woman of great charm and beauty, henceforth a staple ingredient in all his fiction; and also a third, much less thorough-going revision of *Political Justice*. (*Political Justice*'s third edition, dated 1798, was actually published in December 1797.) The intention, he says, is 'merely to remove a few of the crude and juvenile remarks . . . he thought himself able to detect, in the book as it originally stood'[23]: for example, that 'we are sick and die, generally speaking, because we consent to suffer these accidents';[24] that rational men will 'probably cease to propagate. They will no longer have any motive, either of error or reason, to induce them';[25] that 'in a state of equality it will be a question of no importance, to know who is the parent of each individual child'.[26] Personal experience was changing Godwin's opinions too, and it comes as no surprise to find, in the critique of a practice contrary to reason, truth and justice, that

> all these arguments are calculated to determine our judgment in favour of marriage as a respectable and salutary institution, but not of that species of marriage, in which there is no room for repentance, and to which liberty and hope are equally strangers.[27]

The separation of their daily lives had one especially pleasing aspect, in the stream of messages that flowed between Godwin and Mary, short scrappy notes covering all the trivia of day-to-day existence – their health and their spirits, domestic arrangements, appointments and apologies, requests for books and comments on them – and so providing a delightful glimpse into their private world. (These attractive and moving letters have been collected and edited by Ralph M. Wardle, *Godwin and Mary* (1967).) 'I send you your linen', writes Mary when they are still single.

> I am not sure that I did not feel a sensation of pleasure at thus acting the part of a wife though you have so little respect for the character. There is such a magic in affection that I have been more gratified by your clasping your hands round my arm in company than I could have been by all the admiration in the world.[28]

For as she reminds him 'There are other pleasures in the world, you perceive, beside those known to your philosophy.'[29] But then Mary was always ready to poke fun at his theories, or at her own. 'Women are certainly great fools', she wrote once; 'but nature made them so. I have not time, or paper, else, I could draw an inference, not very illustrative of your chance-medley system.'[30] 'But you have no petticoats to dangle in the snow', she summed up, when she realized she must be pregnant again. 'Poor women, how they are beset with plagues – within – and without.'[31]

Again we note the differences between them, Mary erratic and excitable, with so many sentences broken off in mid-course that she is sometimes barely intelligible; Godwin neat and formal, cloaking his feelings in facetiousness and bad French, a habit she occasionally catches from him. But if Godwin reveals little of himself, Mary's insecurity is manifest, from her agitation when she becomes his mistress, through the anxiety with which she discovers she is pregnant again, to the growing calm of their marriage. For if Godwin sometimes takes her bantering too seriously, he is always stolidly reliable, patiently assessing and answering each doubt and fear that she throws at him, his sympathy and affection no less real for being so carefully expressed.

There were times, even so, when he gave her cause to worry. There was the walking trip into Warwickshire and Staffordshire with Basil Montagu, an illegitimate son of the Earl of Sandwich and, for the moment at least, an enthusiastic Godwinian. When Montagu was introduced to Sheridan as a man who believed gratitude was a vice, Sheridan's reply outdid that of his former ally Burke: 'I always thought *reading* was a vice', he said, 'and now I am convinced of it.' They were off to visit Dr Parr and Tom Wedgwood, and though he assured her it was in both their interests, inasmuch as absence increases affection, Mary grew nervous as the day of Godwin's return was postponed again and yet again, until finally she lost her temper: 'Whatever tenderness you took away with you seems to have evaporated in the journey, and new objects – and the homage of vulgar minds, restored you to your icy Philosophy.'[32] She was six months pregnant and haunted by the fear that this lover, too, might desert his child.

Then there was the crisis of Miss Pinkerton who, to Godwin's manifest enjoyment, was showing him rather too close and marked an attention. She supped with him the night before he left London, and was at tea again the night of his return. With Imlay never far from her thoughts Mary again charged Godwin with succumbing to conceit and flattery, and took it on herself to write to the lady, complaining of this 'strange behaviour' – which Godwin, when the note was submitted for his approval, duly changed to 'incomprehensible conduct'. Miss Pinkerton's reply was brief and to the point: 'At length I am sensible of the impropriety of my conduct. Tears and communication afford me relief.'[33]

But Mary's moodiness and irritability were well known, and a constant source of aggravation with the sensitive yet tactless Godwin – especially in view of his candour, as it seemed to him, his self-righteousness as it often seemed to others. 'Perfect confidence, and sincerity of action is, I am persuaded, incompatible with the present state of reason', Mary told him once.

I am sorry for the bitterness of your expressions when you denominated, what I think a just contempt of a false principle of action, *savage resentment and the worst of vices*, not because I winced under the lash, but as it led me to infer that the conquettish candour of vanity was a much less generous motive.[34]

Still, Mary had reason to feel insecure, and Godwin found within himself an unexpected store of sympathy and tolerance to draw upon. Gradually she learnt to trust him, to rely on him, to depend on him, to be reassured by his dogged refusal to be antagonized by matters of no importance, and their upsets were soon over:

The partner of my life was too quick in her conceiving resentments; but they were dignified and restrained; they left no hateful and humiliating remembrances behind them; and we were as happy as is permitted to human beings.[35]

To Godwin himself it was a revelation. 'The supposition that I must have a companion for life is the result of a complication of vices', he had said in *Political Justice*. 'It is the dictate of cowardice, and not of fortitude. It flows from the desire of being loved and esteemed for something that is not desert.'[36] But his novels revealed how deeply he felt the need of a companion whose affection and faith could sustain him through his adversities, and through the constant démêlés with which, no less than Mary, he tested those closest to him. Indeed the refrain of *Political Justice* that we must each of us be a world unto ourselves, independent of all others, is so incessant that we begin to wonder whether Godwin is not trying to convince himself even more than the reader. Then the narrator of the later novel *Fleetwood* discovers with a shock that 'nature had provided a substitute in the marriage-tie, for this romantic, if not impossible friendship', and that shock was Godwin's too. At last he had found someone who loved and admired him for himself and not for his achievements, someone who supported and strengthened him even as he supported and strengthened her, and from that moment the theme of independence vanishes from his writings. 'Too much independence is not good for a man', says Fleetwood again. 'It conduces neither to his virtue nor his happiness. The discipline which arises out of the domestic charities, has an admirable tendency to make man, individually considered, what man ought to be.'

There is no doubting, either, Godwin's manifest affection for Fanny, who would ask after 'Man' as often as her mother. He had to be warned against spoiling her, and promised to return from his visit to Wedgwood with a present from the Land of Mugs. But understandably his letters refer as often to 'last and least (in stature at least)', little William. 'Salute William in my name', he told Mary. 'Perhaps you know how.' And she shared the thought:

> I was not quite well the day after you left me; but it is past, and I am well and tranquil, excepting the disturbance produced by Master William's joy, who took it into his head to frisk a little at being informed of your remembrance. I begin to love this little creature, and to anticipate his birth as a fresh twist to a knot which I do not wish to untie. Men are spoilt by frankness, I believe, yet I must tell you that I love you better than I supposed I did, when I promised to love you for ever . . . You are a tender, affectionate creature; and I feel it thrilling through my frame giving and promising pleasure.[37]

The baby was expected for the end of August.

Believing as she did that the business of child-bearing was surrounded with altogether too much mystique, and having complained in the *Rights of Women* that even midwifery was being closed to women, Mary was content to be assisted solely by a Mrs Blenkinsop. She had had no problems with Fanny's birth, her health had been good through this pregnancy too, and she was still writing notes to Godwin even when she rightly had 'no doubt of seeing the animal today'. It was born at 11.20 that evening, Wednesday 30 August. But it would have to be named after the mother, and not the father.

Even so Godwin had to wait until two in the morning to get a glimpse of his new daughter, and with Mrs Blenkinsop waiting anxiously for the afterbirth to be expelled, he was sent off to fetch the doctor, Poignard, who reached into the womb and cut the placenta away, piece by piece, without anaesthetics and without antiseptics, but with much loss of blood. Later that day Mary told Godwin 'she had never known what bodily pain was before'. Somewhat to Poignard's annoyance she insisted on being seen by a medical friend, Dr George Fordyce, but Fordyce could see no cause for alarm and the crisis seemed over. None of them could know that the torn shreds of flesh were slowly putrefying inside her.

Yet Godwin must still have been worried, for on Friday he called on Anthony Carlisle, the same Anthony Carlisle who had warned him against overtaxing his brain when he wrote *Political Justice*, and who had also been advising Mary during her pregnancy, and

Carlisle came to see her next morning. That evening Mary took a turn for the worse, a close friend, Eliza Fenwick, was appointed to nurse her, and on Sunday Godwin went in search of yet more medical acquaintances. But they were not home, and he came back late to learn that Mary had already had one fit of feverish shivering, soon to be followed by another. Fordyce was hastily recalled, the baby was sent to join Fanny at the Reveleys', and Mrs Blenkinsop produced puppies with which to draw off the unwanted milk. Poignard, irritated by the interference of the Godwins' friends, whether they were obstetricians or not, discharged himself from a case he was clearly losing, and Fordyce took charge. He had the advice of Dr John Clarke, the acknowledged expert in problems of childbirth. But Clarke was not hopeful either.

Wednesday was for Godwin 'the day of greatest torture in melancholy series.' Carlisle had advised him to feed Mary with wine from a teaspoon, but he had no idea how much to give her or how often, or whether it was doing her good or ill. When he asked the maid how their mistress seemed, she told him that in her judgment, she was going as fast as possible. Desperate now, he sent Basil Montagu, whose own wife had died in childbirth four years before, to fetch Carlisle, and although Carlisle was dining four miles out of town, on the the other side of London, the two were back within three-quarters of an hour. Carlisle did not leave the house again that week, Clarke called every day, but there were no signs of improvement. On Friday Godwin and Mary spoke of death, and there was a 'Solemn communication' between them, but when he went to her again next morning she was unable 'to follow any train of ideas with force or any accuracy or connection'. And through it all Godwin's terse diary recorded every detail, each visit and each visitor, until its unvarying rows of neat handwriting are interrupted, once and once only, by the entry for Sunday 10 September:

Sep. 10. Su   20 minutes before 8 ....
....
....

At twenty to eight on a Sunday morning, twelve days after the birth of her second daughter, Mary Wollstonecraft died, her last words 'He is the kindest, best man in the world.' It would be another thirty-five years before Godwin could describe, however inadequately, what he felt at that moment:

It is impossible to represent in words the total revolution this event made in my existence. It was as if in a single moment 'sun and moon were in the flat sea sunk'. Nature that had been so beautiful, so resplendent, so fascinating, lost at once the soul to which it was indebted for all its charms. The rainbow tints of the globe in which I dwelt, the soft and tender hues, the delicate blendings, the undulating lights, varying for ever, and chasing one another beneath the cope of heaven were gone; and, in place of them, every thing was stained with one melancholy colour, one deadly and unwholesome brown. The air appeared to me murky and thick, an atmosphere that bore pestilence on its wings. I looked around me; the outline of things, though obscure and dim, was the same; but where was now the grace that so lately animated them, the ornament that had tingled in my veins and shot through my soul.[38]

11 ♣ The empire of feeling

> My life has in this respect had a greater variety in it, than that perhaps of most human beings. Every four or five years I gain some new perception, become intimately sensible to some valuable circumstance, that introduces an essential change of many of my preconceived notions and determinations. Every four or five years I look back astonished at the stupidity or folly of which I had a short time before been the dupe. For this reason no man ever stood more in need of the best intellectual society, while perhaps no man ever suffered more from the dearth of it.[1]
>
> Memorandum, early 1800s

♣ On 15 September 1797, at ten in the morning, Mary Wollstonecraft was buried beside old St. Pancras Church, where she had been married but six months before. Godwin could not bring himself to attend the funeral, but sat alone in Marshall's lodgings trying to compose a letter of thanks to Anthony Carlisle. One of his closest, oldest friends, Joseph Fawcett, came to keep him company that evening, but he knew that consolation was useless. 'I know from experience we were formed to make each other happy', he had written to Holcroft the afternoon of Mary's death, with more truth than he yet knew. 'I have not the least expectation that I can now ever know happiness again.'[2] Fanny and Mary came home from the Reveleys', Hannah Godwin's friend Louisa Jones was installed as a housekeeper to care for both them and him, and on 20 September Godwin abandoned his bachelor study in the Evesham Buildings, and made the Polygon his only home.

The best, perhaps for him the only, way to handle his grief and anguish was to throw himself back into writing. The day after the funeral he had picked up again the autobiographical novel *Mary* he had laid aside the morning of her death; two days later he was sorting through her papers and writing to those who had known her well; by 24 September he had begun the story of her life, and by the end of the year it was finished. The outcome of this act of catharsis and remembrance was the frank and tender *Memoirs of the Author of the Vindication of the Rights of Women*, Godwin's most immediately attractive work, elegant, restrained, sensitive, and in Wordsworth's sense true poetry, emotion recollected in tranquillity. For the first time in his writing genuine feeling shows through, feeling analysed and held in check, but feeling unmistakably, without the contrived rhetoric of some of his other books or the mawkish romanticism with which Mary would undoubtedly have written a memoir of him. Despite the depth and the range of emotion that he had so recently and unexpectedly been subjected to, the *Memoirs* are surprisingly distanced, so that we see Mary as she was, and not simply as a distraught husband would like us to see her.

No doubt it was by devoting himself to this measured portrait of his lost wife that Godwin was able to deal with his despair in the way that he knew best, the way of reason and reflection. It was this that enabled him to resume so quickly his old well-ordered existence, writing in the morning, visiting in the afternoon, the theatre in the evening. Yet to some this restraint seemed only to complete the picture of a monster of pure reason, to whom love for a wife, and the fact of her death, were simply truths to be recognized and allotted each its due place in the general scheme of things. Mary's friend through Fuseli, William Roscoe of Liverpool, jotted in his copy of the Wollstonecraft *Memoirs*

> Hard was thy fate in all the scenes of life
> As daughter, sister, mother, friend and wife;
> But harder still, thy fate in death we own,
> Thus mourn'd by Godwin with a heart of stone.

Perhaps there is some truth in this caricature: we can imagine Godwin distraught and confused at Mary's death, but not overwhelmed or losing control. But this is not to say he felt nothing; his feelings could work themselves out in writing and reflection, and be none the less real for that. Knowing Godwin, those three straight lines drawn across the laconic record of his daily doings are far more moving than the most impassioned outburst of grief. They tell us what he felt, as no fine words can do. Not even French would be adequate to the occasion.

The *Memoirs* appeared in January 1798, together with four small volumes of *Posthumous Works*, largely made up of Mary's unfinished novel and her letters to Johnson and Imlay. But though Godwin had arranged and numbered their own correspondence, he did not include it. Perhaps he thought it too personal, or perhaps it reminded him too vividly of his loss; but more probably he considered that those scrappy notes lacked the literary merit and romantic appeal of the tender and desperate correspondence with Imlay which, he says, 'may possibly be found to contain the finest examples of the language of sentiment and passion ever presented to the world.' To his readers, however, it seemed a strange and shocking decision, to publish your wife's love letters to another man.

And although what is most attractive to us about the *Memoirs* themselves is the frank and totally unsensational way in which Godwin tells the troubled and tragic story of his dead wife, to his contemporaries it was a work of unparalleled insensitivity and immorality. Of course Godwin believed that since truth will always prevail over ignorance and prejudice, a clear and convincing statement of Mary's history was all that was needed to defend her character. But as always he was wrong. 'Blushes would suffuse the cheeks of most husbands', declared the *Monthly Review*,

> if they were *forced* to relate those anecdotes of their wives which Mr Godwin voluntarily proclaims to the world. The extreme eccentricity of Mr Godwin's sentiments will account for this conduct. Virtue and vice are weighed by him in a balance of his own. He neither looks to marriage with respect, nor to suicide with horror.[3]

Because it told of Mary's love for Fuseli, a married man, and her affair with Imlay, the novelist Charles Lucas dubbed the book *Godwin's History of the Intrigues of his own Wife*. 'A convenient Manual of speculative debauchery', Thomas Mathias called it,

> with the most select arguments for reducing it into practice; for the amusement, initiation and instruction of young ladies from 16 to 25 years of age, who wish to figure in life, and afterwards in Doctor's Commons, and the King's Bench, or ultimately in the notorious receptacles of patrician prostitution.[4]

And because Godwin made no secret of the fact that he had been intimate with, before marrying, a woman who already had one illegitimate child, the Baptist preacher Robert Hall denounced it in his sermon *Modern Infidelity Considered* as 'a narrative of his licentious amours'. It was said of this same Reverend Hall, that whenever he heard of some cases of 'unnatural depravity or abandoned profligacy' he would exclaim, 'I could not have supposed any man capable of such an action – except Godwin.' Yet many readers were as shocked by the fact that Mary had tried to take her own life, not once but twice, as by her promiscuity: suicide, it seems, was truly the fate worse than death. And behind it all, explaining everything but excusing nothing, was her evident lack of religion.

But there, at least, Godwin was to blame. He had played down Mary's religious convictions, and at the end declared almost triumphantly that 'during her whole illness, not one word of a religious cast fell from her lips'. Yet Mary was always a sincere Christian, and it was a topic on which she and Godwin had often disagreed, good-humouredly enough. 'I would leave you a God bless you – did you care for it,' she joked at the end of one note, repeating a conceit she had once addressed to Imlay; 'but alas! you do not, though Sterne says that it is equivalent to a – kiss –.'[5] Or again, more revealingly, 'how can you blame me for taken [sic] refuge in the idea of a God, when I despair of finding sincerity on earth.'[6] But if Mary needed her faith, Godwin preferred to minimize it. The story got about that as she lay dying she cried out, 'Oh Godwin, I am in heaven'; to which the philosopher patiently replied, 'You mean, my dear, that your physical sensations are somewhat easier.'

But this anecdote was as nothing, compared to the outrage of the reviewers. It was the history of a 'philosophical wanton' seethed the *European Magazine*, to be

> read with disgust by every female who has any pretensions to delicacy; with detestation by everyone attached to the interests of religion and morality; and with indignation by anyone who might feel any regard for the unhappy woman, whose frailties should have been buried in oblivion.[7]

And certainly there were admirers of Mary who thought the book a disgrace to her memory. Southey, who had come to dinner at Mary's invitation in May 1797, lamented that Godwin showed 'a want of all feeling in stripping his dead wife naked'. But then Southey, more than half in love with Mary, was no longer an admirer of her husband. 'I never praised living being yet, except Mary Wollstonecraft,' he once said, conveniently forgetting there had been a time when he 'all but worshipped Godwin' himself. 'The men to whom she attached herself were utterly unworthy of her.'[8] And some have even wanted to blame Mary's posthumous reputation and the consequent rejection of her feminism on the extravagant sincerity of the *Memoirs*, almost as if they feared that *Fraser's Magazine* might be right when it declared at Godwin's own death that 'in writing "The Life of Mary Wollstonecraft", he has done more good unintentionally than it ever could have, intentionally or otherwise, done evil. We shall not have any such lady in our literature again.'[9]

Nevertheless, Godwin's mother managed to find a different moral in his 'genteel present of the Memoirs of yr wife':

> I hope yo are taught by reflection your mistake concerning marriage there might have been two children that had no lawful wright to anything yt was their fathers with a thousand other bad consequences children and wives crying abt ye streets without a protector.[10]

And that, more surprisingly, was the lesson drawn also by Mrs Opie, who, as Amelia Alderson, had once been courted by Godwin, had compared Mrs Imlay to the Cumberland Lakes, and then married the man who had been cast as Mary's suitor. Her *Adeline Mowbray*, published in 1805, was clearly inspired by the life of Mary Wollstonecraft. It tells of a girl reared in the New Philosophy, who falls in love with but refuses to marry a philosophical anarchist named Glenmurray. 'I am entirely out of the question', she tells him: 'you are to be governed by no other law but your desire to promote general utility, and are not to think at all of the interests of an individual.' But though they are thoroughly happy together, the strains, the misunderstandings, the recriminations caused by their unorthodox alliance undermine Glenmurray's health, and he dies urging Adeline to marry his friend and kinsman Berrendale. Reluctantly Adeline succumbs, but Berrendale, the Imlay figure in the story, is unfaithful, deserts her and marries again, while Adeline, dying in the arms of the mother who had once damned her, repents her foolishness and acknowledges the necessity of a legal institution of marriage, if only for the security of her children.

This stirring tale is presented officially as a critique of Godwinian theories of marriage, and was accepted as such by its readers (Harriet Shelley for one: see p. 246 below). Yet the real moral of the story seems very different, for Adeline's unsanctioned liaison with Glenmurray is fulfilling and faithful, while her marriage to Berrendale is miserable and deceitful. The difficulties that Adeline and Glenmurray face come entirely from the prejudice of others, whose admiration and respect turn to distaste and contempt the moment they realize that she is not actually married. Every such detail – the liberties men take when they think Adeline is Berrendale's mistress, their sincere apologies when they discover she is his wife – seems only to support Godwin's opinion that the distinction between married and unmarried love is wholly artificial, that the latter may well be more genuine and certainly more honest, that it is only the attitudes of society that create a difference where by rights no difference should be. How far all this was deliberate on Mrs Opie's part – how far she intended to disguise a Godwinian message in non-Godwinian clothing; how far her original Godwinism escaped in spite of itself – we cannot tell. But the moral ambiguity is fascinating, much more so than the dreadfully turgid tale itself, sagging under the accumulated weight of sentiment and moralism. And if Mary is hardly flattered by the portrait of Adeline, Godwin had little cause for complaint, if he is indeed the model for the noble and trustworthy Glenmurray.

Still, Godwin was clearly shaken by the storm of abuse his tribute unleashed, and in a second edition later in 1798 did his best to undo the harm. He could scarcely delete all reference to Fuseli and Imlay, even had he wanted to, but he did modify those passages that might lend themselves to misconstruction, deliberate or otherwise. In the first edition Mary had never 'believed the doctrine of future punishments'; a lady whose companion she had once been had had on the premises 'one son already adult'; her friendship with Fuseli had 'proved the source of the most memorable events of her subsequent history'; the connection with Imlay had been something 'for which her heart secretly panted'; when Imlay left her in Paris, the Irish patriot Archibald Hamilton Rowan had been 'a person from whose society . . . Mary derived particular gratification'; her *Letters from Scandinavia* were imbued with 'all the romance of unbounded attachment'; and Godwin himself had enjoyed many 'personal pleasures' in her conversation. All this is deleted, the passages involving Fuseli are substantially recast, Godwin defends Mary's calling at his rooms uninvited, and this eloquent defence of their unmarried state –

> Certainly nothing can be so ridiculous upon the face of it, or so contrary to the genuine march of sentiment, as to require the overflowing of the soul to wait upon a ceremony, and that at which, wherever delicacy and imagination exist, is of all things the most sacredly private, to blow a trumpet before it, and to record the moment when it has arrived at its climax[11]

is replaced by a belated admission that

> ideas which I am now willing to denominate prejudices, made me by no means eager to conform to a ceremony as an individual, which coupled with the conditions our laws annex to it, I should undoubtedly, as a citizen, be desirous to abolish. Fuller examination however has since taught me to regard this among those cases, where an accurate morality will direct us to comply with customs and institutions, which if we had had a voice in their introduction, it would have been incumbent on us to negative.[12]

But there is another alteration, no less revealing. What in the first edition has been an acute examination of the intellectual and emotional differences between Godwin and Mary now becomes a discussion of a general difference between the sexes, 'the one . . . more accustomed to the exercise of its reasoning powers, and the other of its feelings'[13] – and this in a tribute to the woman whose enduring achievement was precisely to challenge the idea that 'man was made to reason, woman to feel'! Or again, where Mary had protested against the image of femininity that presents her sex as 'sweet flowers that smile in the walk of man', Godwin's later *Deloraine*, the story of a marriage of unalloyed happiness ended by a death in childbirth, insists that

man is the substantive thing in the terrestial creation; woman is
but the adjective, that cannot stand by itself. A sweet thing she
is; I grant it . . . . But she is a frail flower; she wants a shelter,
a protector, a pioneer. She is all that omniscience, that
principle of divine meditation (so far as we can understand it),
could produce for the best consolation, the entire repose and
the good of the stronger sense, and in forming his happiness,
she forms her own.

Godwin was no admirer of the second *Vindication*, for all its virtues
'undoubtedly a very unequal performance, and eminently deficient
in method and arrangement',[14] and reluctant as he was to grant
rights even to men, he was hardly a believer in the rights of woman.
Instead he preferred the system of chivalry which, 'like those
admirable principles in the order of the material universe',[15] keeps
each sex in its proper place, encouraging mutual deference, mutual
support and mutual respect. 'I cannot be blind enough to credit what
some have maintained, probably more from the love of paradox than
any other cause, that there is any parity between the sexes,' he
would write in *Fleetwood*. 'Till the softer sex has produced a Bacon, a
Newton, a Hume or a Shakespeare, I never will believe it.' Godwin
learnt much from Mary, but her most important teaching eluded him
entirely, and when he came to list his 'four principal oral instructors'
– Joseph Fawcett, Thomas Holcroft, George Dyson and S. T.
Coleridge – it evidently never occurred to him to mention Mary
Wollstonecraft.

Yet Mary changed Godwin philosophically as well as personally.
In September 1798, immediately after the second publication of the
Wollstonecraft *Memoirs*, he drew up a list of the works he would
write as soon as he had finished the play and the novel he had
already begun, and first and foremost would be

a book to be entitled 'First Principles of Morals'. The principal
purpose of this work is to correct certain errors in the earlier
part of my 'Political Justice'. The part to which I allude is
essentially defective, in the circumstance of not yielding a
proper attention to the empire of feeling . . .[16]

Godwin found more than happiness and security with Mary
Wollstonecraft; he also discovered emotion, and neither the man nor
his opinions could ever be the same again. When their friend
Thomas Tuthill excused himself from the funeral on the ground that
it would be dishonest of an unbeliever to partake in a religious
ceremony, Godwin told him 'I honour your character, I respect your
scruples. But I should have thought more highly of you if at such a

moment, it had been impossible for so cold a reflection to have
crossed your mind.'[17] Not long before he would have sided with
Tuthill.

But now the apostle of reason had become 'the new man of
feeling', to quote *Fleetwood*'s mysterious subtitle, and that disease·
infected all his thought. Godwin's theories of politics, of morality, of
education, of man himself had all been erected on one central basis,
the omnipotence of truth and the perfectibility of man. But that, in
turn, rested on three crucial, contentious assumptions: that all men
are by nature sufficiently rational to be capable of recognizing the
truth, however complex, however abstruse, if only it is presented
clearly to them; that our actions are governed by reason not passion,
by our opinions not our feelings, or at any rate that there need be no
conflict between the two; that sound reasoning and truth will
demonstrate that justice is the most desirable course of action, to be
preferred to all others. Remove that foundation and the whole
impressive structure will come crashing down, leaving us to pick
through the pieces and discard most as broken and useless. Yet
calmly, remorselessly, point by point, the memorandum of September 1798 destroys them all:

> I am . . . desirous of retracting the opinions I have given
> favourable to Helvetius' doctrine of the equality of intellectual
> beings as they are born into the world, and of subscribing to
> the received opinion, that, though education is a most powerful
> instrument, yet there exist differences of the highest importance
> between human beings from the period of their birth . . . .
> The voluntary actions of men are under the direction of their
> feelings. . . . Reason, accurately speaking, has not the smallest
> degree of power to put any one limb or articulation of our
> bodies into motion . . . .
> Again, every man will, by a necessity of his nature, be in-
> fluenced by motives peculiar to him as an individual . . . . The
> spring of motion within him will certainly not be a sentiment of
> general utility . . . .
> I am the more anxious to bring forward these alterations and
> modifications, because it would give me an occasion to show
> that none of the conclusions for the sake of which the book on
> 'Political Justice' was written are affected by them . . . .[18]

But Godwin was mistaken there, his change of opinion more
catastrophic than he ever appreciated. He may have been a better
man thanks to Mary Wollstonecraft, kinder, more tolerant, more
human; but he was also a worse, a less original and less interesting,
philosopher.

In fact Godwin's change of mind over the first assumption dated back to *Political Justice*'s second edition. The relevant chapter might be called 'The Characters of Men Originate in their External Circumstances', and open with the bold declaration that it will 'attempt to prove . . . that the actions and dispositions of mankind are the offspring of circumstances and events, and not of any original determination that they bring into the world',[19] But it insists none the less that 'it would be ridiculous to question the real differences that exist between children at the period of their birth,'[20] that 'at the moment of birth each man has really a certain character, and each man a character different from his fellows.'[21] And the third edition had gone even further: 'Children certainly bring into the world with them a part of the character of their parents.'[22]

But it still does not follow, Godwin believes, that men are not equally rational, or at least equally capable of rationality, equally capable of recognizing the truth when once it is presented clearly and convincingly. The question of how far children differ in intelligence at birth is probably impossible to answer; but it is also irrelevant, since any such difference is entirely a matter of capacity or potentiality, and actual attainment may be affected as much, if not more, by education and training. Children are born with physical defects, but this does not mean that those defects cannot be cured or compensated. Similarly the fact that one child has an initial intellectual advantage over another does not mean that they are not both equally educable, that the effects of education might not eliminate any inborn advantage:

> That a man brings a certain character into the world with him, is a point that must readily be conceded. The mistake is to suppose that he brings an immutable character . . . . In what sense can a new-born child be esteemed wise? He may have a certain predisposition for wisdom. But it can scarcely be doubted that every child, not peculiarly defective in his make, is susceptible to the communication of wisdom.[23]

So education is the great equalizer. If one man fails to understand the truths which another attempts to communicate, it is not because he is incapable of appreciating them, but because he has not had the appropriate training, the relevant experience, the necessary education. In abandoning Helvetius Godwin need not yet abandon the perfectibility of man.

The second assumption, however, is more crucial. Once allow that men might be motivated by feeling regardless of reason, by their emotions rather than their understanding of what is the case, and it no longer follows that truth is omnipotent. Yet it is this assumption, of the three, that Godwin now rejects most unambiguously:

> Reason . . . has not the smallest degree of power to put any one limb or articulation of our bodies into motion. Its province, in a practical view, is wholly confined to adjusting the comparison between different objects of desire, and investigating the most successful mode of attaining those objects.[24]

They are almost the words of Hume, and it was, Godwin says, his reading of Hume's *Treatise of Human Nature* in 1795 which destroyed the Sandemanianism of *Political Justice*: 'The second edition . . . was then nearly printed off, but the change in my sentiments may be traced in the later sheets of each of the volumes.'[25] But the impact of Mary cannot be discounted either, and in fact Godwin's change of mind is revealed not in the revision of 1795 but that of 1797. If any edition is the palinode, the recantation, that de Quincey claimed to discover in the second, it is the third.

Yet even there the changes are minor, with talk about truths occasionally replaced by talk about feelings. It is only in an introductory 'Summary of Principles established and reasoned upon in the following work' that Godwin begins to develop a theory which stands in flat contradiction to the text that follows. For if, as he now says, the voluntary actions of men are under the direction of their feelings, if reason is not an independent principle and has no tendency to excite us to action, then he has no longer any grounds for relying on human perfectibility. Ironically, the point is made with absolute clarity in the body of the book that follows:

> If man be, by the very constitution of his nature, the subject of opinion, and if truth and reason, when properly displayed, give us a complete hold upon his choice, then the search of the political enquirer will be much simplified. Then we have only to discover what form of civil society is most comfortable to reason, and we may rest assured that, as soon as men shall be persuaded from conviction to adopt that form, they will have acquired to themselves an invaluable benefit. But, if reason be frequently inadequate to its task, if there be an opposite principle in man resting upon its own ground, and maintaining a separate jurisdiction, the most rational principles of society may be rendered abortive, it may be necessary to call in mere sensible causes to encounter causes of the same nature, folly may be the fittest instrument to effect the purposes of wisdom, and vice to disseminate and establish the public benefit. In that case the salutary prejudices and useful delusions (as they have

been called) of aristocracy, the glittering diadem, the magnificent canopy, the ribbands, stars and titles of an illustrious rank, may at last be found the fittest instruments for guiding and alluring to his proper ends the savage, man.[26]

Godwin was in truth 'viciously persuadable by the arguments of others', dogmatic and opinionated maybe, but never stubborn, always willing to abandon some hardwon conclusion the moment he thought he detected in it some crucial mistake. But a change of mind does not necessarily refute an argument. First opinions may still be best, and for myself I believe that Godwin's original approach was a considerable advance on that of Hume. For what Godwin had argued was not that feelings have no power to move us, a doctrine that hardly needed a Hume or a Wollstonecraft to demonstrate its absurdity. Rather he had rejected the simple opposition – either reason or the passions – that Hume had endorsed. It was not a matter of the one being a slave to the other, as Hume put it; it was a matter of the desire to do something, the 'passion' in that weakest broadest sense, itself being an opinion or judgment, the judgment that all things considered this is the thing to do. That is why 'passion is so far from being incompatible with reason, that it is inseparable from it'.[27] That is why 'we are no longer at liberty to consider man as divided between two independent principles, or to imagine that his inclinations are in any inaccessible through the medium of his reason'.[28] And that is why we should reject the unreal distinction that Hume foisted upon subsequent philosophy – and upon William Godwin.

Yet Godwin's new-found-land of feeling means not only that we can no longer rely on men to be motivated by truth; it means also that we can no longer rely on them to be motivated by justice. The third assumption of the argument had been that sound reasoning and truth will show justice to be the most desirable course of action, so that rational men acquainted with that truth will inevitably choose to do as justice demands. And justice, of course, is pure impartial justice, directed at the benefit of all men equally. But Godwin tells us now that

> as every man will know more of his kindred and intimates than strangers, so he will inevitably think of them oftener, feel for them more acutely and be more anxious about their welfare . . . . It is impossible that we should be continually thinking of the whole world, or not confer a smile or a kindness but as we are prompted to it by an abstract principle of philanthropy.[29]

And with that concession collapses the step from truth to justice, the final link in the proof of perfectibility.

12 ♣ Domestic and private affections

Some readers of my graver productions will perhaps, in perusing these little volumes, accuse me of inconsistency, the affections and charities of private life being everywhere in this publication a topic of the warmest eulogium, while in the Enquiry Concerning Political Justice they seemed to be treated with no degree of indulgence and favour. In answer to this objection all I think it necessary to say on the present occasion, is that, for more than four years, I have been anxious for opportunity and leisure to modify some of the earlier chapters of that work in conformity to the sentiments inculcated in this. Not that I see cause to make any change respecting the principle of justice, or any thing else fundamental to the system there delivered, but that I apprehend domestic and private affections inseparable from the nature of man, and from what may be styled the culture of the heart, and am fully persuaded that they are not incompatible with a profound and active sense of justice in the mind of him that cherishes them.

Preface to *St Leon*, 1799

♣ Looking back on the original *Political Justice* from March 1800, Godwin thought he could detect in it three fundamental errors, each 'connected with the Calvinist system which had been so deeply wrought into my mind from early life, as to enable these errors long to survive the general system of religious opinions of which they formed a part'. One was 'Stoicism, or an inattention to the principle that pleasure and pain are the only bases on which morality can rest', and error 'rooted from my mind principally by the acute arguments of Mr George Dyson, in 1794'. The second was 'Sandemanianism, or an inattention to the principle that feeling, not judgment, is the source of human actions', an error detected under the influence of Hume, but also, no doubt, of Mary Wollstonecraft. The third was 'an unqualified condemnation of the private affections',[1] and here the impact of Mary was most obvious of all. Of all the doctrines of *Political Justice*, this was the one Godwin was now most anxious to renounce.

It was a doctrine that derived ultimately from the American Calvinist Johnathan Edwards. But Godwin had not been much impressed when Samuel Newton tried to make him read Edwards as

a boy, and he had acquired it instead from the first of his four
principal oral instructors Joseph Fawcett, 'a declared enemy of the
private and domestic affections; and his opinions on this head, well-
adapted to the austerity and perfection which Calvinism recom-
mends, had undoubtedly great influence on my mind'.[2] It was a
doctrine that Fawcett had continued to preach into the 1790s, in his
highly fashionable sermons at London's Old Jewry Meeting House,
where the congregation included not only such Godwinians as
Montagu, Nicholson and Hazlitt, but Wordsworth, John Kemble
and Sarah Siddons. But it was a doctrine that Godwin was
characteristically prepared to take further, beyond the point where
its original author dared go. For neither Edwards nor Fawcett had
dismissed these 'limited affections' out of hand. They might not
partake of true virtue, they might even interfere with it, but they
share some of its excellence, and in any case are better than nothing.
Edwards's point was rather the good Calvinist one, that the
effectiveness of the domestic affections reveals our human weakness,
our inability to live up to the requirements of *true* virtue. But
Godwin, inevitably, believes that man both can and should be
virtuous in even this strict sense. If I assist those closest to me just
because they are close to me, when I might have been of more
assistance to someone else, a stranger or even an enemy, then
personal attachments have led me to commit an injustice against my
fellow men. If the private affections interfere with true virtue then
they must be vicious, a force for evil not for good, nor merely an
obstacle to morality but positively immoral, something of which the
genuinely moral man will take no account.

Or so Godwin believed when he wrote *Political Justice*. But life with
Mary had changed his mind about that too, about that more than
anything, and appropriately it was the revised edition of the
Wollstonecraft *Memoirs* that first announced the fact. Indeed so
important did Godwin consider the passage that he quoted it again in
the Preface to *St Leon* the following year, and then for a third time in
the *Reply to Parr* two years after that:

A sound morality requires that 'nothing human should be
regarded by us as indifferent; but it is impossible we should not
feel the strongest interest for those persons we know most
intimately, and whose welfare and sympathies are united to our
own. True wisdom will recommend to us individual attach-
ments; for with them our minds are more thoroughly maintained
in activity and life than they can be under the privation of
them, and it is better that man should be a living being, than a
stock or a stone. True virtue will sanction this recommendation;

since it is the object of virtue to produce happiness; and since
the man who lives in the midst of domestic relations, will have
many opportunities of conferring pleasure, minute in the detail,
yet not trivial in the amount, without interfering with the
purposes of general benevolence. Nay, by kindling his sensibilities, and harmonising his soul, they may be expected, if he
is endowed with a liberal and manly spirit, to render him more
prompt in the service of strangers and the public.[3]

It would be a year or two yet before he could properly amplify the
point, but in the meantime there was the novel he was writing
precisely to illustrate it, a novel which began as his 'Opus Magnum',
then became 'Natural Magic' and later 'The Adept', then finally *St
Leon*.

Once again Godwin built his story round an idea that has since
become hackneyed, the idea of a man who possesses both the elixir
of life and the philosophers' stone, and so holds the twin secrets of
eternal youth and unlimited wealth. His hero, it appears, is a
case-book manic-depressive, veering between bouts of insane grief at
the loss of his fortune at the gaming tables, and outbursts of overwhelming joy at the happiness of the simple domestic existence to
which those losses have reduced him and his family. There comes,
however, a mysterious stranger who bequeaths St Leon the two
fateful secrets, on condition that he reveal them neither to his wife
nor to us. Secrecy and deception throw up an inevitable barrier
between husband and wife, and talk of black magic leads to their
persecution. The wife dies in childbirth, the family is broken up, and
St Leon escapes to Spain, there to be arraigned by the Inquisition on
suspicion of alchemy. After twelve years' imprisonment he is about
to be burnt at the stake when, at the last possible moment, he
manages to escape and, rejuvenated in the most literal sense, travels
to Hungary, intending this time to put his limitless wealth at the
service of all mankind. But here too he arouses only suspicion and
resentment, and is thrown into the uncomfortable company of
another victim of man's injustice to man, the ferociously forbidding
Bethlem Gabor. Gabor, indeed, is so riddled with misanthropy that,
rather than allow St Leon to do good unto others, he throws him into
a dungeon, and so uncovers the secret of his wealth. But at just that
moment Gabor's castle is captured and Gabor himself slain by
French troops under the command of St Leon's own son, Charles.
Yet St Leon's exertions on behalf of the Hungarians, then subjects of
the Turk, have made him the enemy of all mankind, according to the
French, and he has to keep his identity secret, hoping to put his
powers to the particular benefit of his son, by providing a dowry for

the woman he wishes to marry. Unhappily, the father now appears so much younger than the son that he is mistaken as a rival for the lady's affections, and when Charles discovers that this is also the man they have been seeking, he unwittingly challenges his own father to a duel. Once more St Leon is forced to flee, and observe from hiding his son's happiness, his own blackened reputation.

After the comparative failure of the *Enquirer* and the reception of the *Memoirs*, Godwin was more than usually apprehensive about this new book, especially when those he showed it to seemed not much impressed, considering it vastly inferior to *Caleb Williams*. Even a week after its publication on 2 December 1799 Godwin was still so tormented with uncertainty that, though 'desirous of calling on someone, to learn more exactly the character of the book, I had not the courage . . . to look an acquaintance in the face'.[4] But he need not have worried: Opie approved; Mary Hays gave 'full applause'; Horne Tooke told him 'you write better each time than the time before'; and Mrs Inchbald responded with a long and detailed critique, generally favourable, but suggesting that he should not have apologized for his change of opinion over the domestic feelings, but left it to the reader to discover for himself this conflict between 'Godwin's Head' and 'Godwin's Heart'. In fact *St Leon*, the most romantic in the literary sense of all Godwin's novels, appealed powerfully to the reading public of its day – a time when the trifling tales of a Jane Austen were rejected as unpublishable – and a second edition duly followed, only a month after the first.

To most it was, in Coleridge's phrase, 'the furiously misanthropic Bethlem Gabor', an actual historical figure, who dominated the book, just as Falkland had dominated *Caleb Williams*. But to us Gabor is hopelessly melodramatic, all ugliness and malevolence, a somewhat irrelevant piece of Gothic padding. Instead it is St Leon's wife, Marguerite de Damville, who most captures our interest, the one half-way realistic heroine in Godwin's fiction. When Mary Wollstonecraft complained at the contemporary caricature of women as creatures of sweetness and light to be worshipped, not treated as human beings, her complaint applies as clearly to Godwin's novels as it continued to do to those of Scott and Dickens. His leading ladies are as virtuous as they are beautiful, as boring as they are improbable. But Marguerite, appropriately, is the one partial exception. Though still a paragon, some degree of individuality comes through. For St Leon's lyrical description of his marriage is Godwin's fictional recreation of his happiness with Mary. Even their daughters bear an uncanny resemblance to Fanny and Mary, only five and two at the time of writing.

But if Godwin's contemporaries ranked *St Leon* with *Caleb Williams* as 'two of the most splendid and impressive works of the imagination that have appeared in our times',[5] it also has its all-too-obvious weaknesses of ponderous prose, a contrived plot, and the frequent failure to suspend disbelief. Nowhere are these illustrated more tellingly, or more amusingly, than in a curious sequel to Godwin's *Adventures of St Leon, A Tale of the Sixteenth Century*, in the form of the *Adventures of St Godwin, A Tale of the Sixteenth, Seventeenth and Eighteenth Centuries*, by none other than Count Reginald de St Leon himself, otherwise Robert Dubois. This was no vicious political satire such as Godwin had begun to grow used to, but a comparatively gentle parody which at first follows the original plot closely and quotes large hunks from the text, if only to poke fun at the story, its pompous prose and self-conscious displays of erudition. While looking for the mysterious stranger, for example, St Leon hears a low cry which, in Godwin's words, 'arrested my attention, and caused me to assume an attitude of listening'. 'Now, I say, that is a picture', continues Dubois's hero, 'you see the man standing in a cunning posture and listening . . .'. Or when Charles St Leon makes to accompany his father, ' "upon this I put a peremptory prohibition". Hey, do not you think that is a good round period? Not quite so simple as the case required perhaps, but the last two words are thumpers, that is enough for me'!

And Dubois carries the story on from where its first author left it, so that we find Guillaume de St Godwin involved in a series of duels – usually over the alleged seduction of assorted wives by this externally handsome youth – and surviving them all in virtue of his invulnerable life. When things get out of hand he is consigned to the Bastille for a period of 177 years and 2 days, which brings him to 14 July 1789. Then, fearing he might lose his head – though not of course his life – under Robespierre, he sets sail for America. The ship sinks under him but 'you might as well attempt to drown a cork as an immortal', and the waves wash him into Portsmouth harbour. In England he finds at last a place where no suspicion attaches to a man who lives in great wealth without any visible means of support, but he soon tires of the fashionable whirl and devotes himself instead to radical politics and a great two-volume treatise on the necessity of nature, the perfectibility of man, and the power of truth – all this by a man whose life has been one long lie!

Yet *St Leon* itself was no mere work of science fantasy or science fiction. It may have its moments of fashionable Gothic horror, stolen from Mrs Radcliffe, but there are no loving scenes of the mixing of mysteriously smoking chemicals or the startling transformation of dross into gold, greybeard into youth. At times, indeed, it is the sheerest magic, with St Leon producing gold apparently out of thin air, or turning it into negotiable tender as easily as he manufactured the raw material. But Godwin has no interest in the mechanics of magic; *St Leon*, like *Caleb Williams*, is a novel with a moral, and this time the moral can hardly escape the most inattentive reader. St Leon is prepared to sacrifice everything in the pursuit of unlimited wealth and eternal life, yet 'a common degree of penetration might have shown me, that secrets of this character cut off their possessor from the dearest ties of human existence, and render him a solitary, cold, self-centred individual'. In the end he finds himself, as sooner or later all Godwin's heroes find themselves,

> utterly alone in the world, separated from every being of my species. No man could understand me; no man could sympathise with me; no man could form the remotest guess of what was passing in my breast . . . . This, and not the dungeon of Bethlem Gabor, is the true solitude. Let no man, after me, pant for the acquisition of the philosophers' stone.

Happiness and security lie not in powers and possessions but in a life of simplicity, the fulfilment of marriage, those private and domestic affections that St Leon had and lost with Marguerite de Damville, that Godwin had had and lost with Mary Wollstonecraft.

It was hardly surprising that the author of *Political Justice* should now write so persuasively in support of marriage; understandable, too, that *St Leon* should defend re-marriage as an equally salutary and respectable institution (see the epigraph to Chapter 17 below). But Godwin was no longer the eligible bachelor flattered by the flutterings of the left-wing ladies. At forty-three he was a widower, ageing fast, his celebrity ebbing away, and for all his experience in the theory and practice of education, scarcely suited to the task of raising two small daughters single-handed. 'The poor children', he had written despondently to one of Mary's friends,

> I am myself totally unfitted to educate them. The scepticism which perhaps sometimes leads me right in matters of specula-tion is torment to me when I would attempt to direct the infant mind. I am the most unfit person for this office; she was the best qualified in the world. What a change. The loss of the children is less remediless than mine. You can understand the difference.[6]

For a moment, perhaps unsubconsciously, Godwin may even have thought he could now resume his stately pursuit of Mrs Inchbald. It is difficult, otherwise, to explain his writing to her the very day that Mary died, to regret the breach that had separated his two closest lady friends. 'I always thought you used her ill', he wrote, 'but I forgive you. You told me that you did not know her. You have a thousand good and great qualities. She had a very deep-rooted admiration for you.'[7] And Mrs Inchbald had replied that same day, with an equal lack of tact:

> You have shocked me beyond expression, yet, I bless God, without exciting the smallest portion of remorse . . . . I did not know her. I never wished to know her: as I avoid every female acquaintance, who has no husband, I avoided her. Against my desire you made us acquainted. With what justice I shunned her, your present note evinces, for she judged me harshly . . . . Still I feel for you at present. Write to me again. Say what you please at such a time as this; I will excuse and pity you.[8]

Of course Godwin did write again, to defend his dead wife, only to have Mrs Inchbald, less offensive but hardly more compassionate, belittle his loss of the day before by comparison with the death of her own husband some eighteen years previously, in 'circumstances so much more dreadful than those that have occurred to you, as the want of warning increases all our calamities'.[9] Perhaps it was meant also as a protest against Godwin's secret wedding, when all the town knew him as *her* escort. And so the bitter correspondence went on: Godwin describing Mrs Inchbald's treatment of Mary as 'base, cruel and insulting'; she replying that 'I could refute every charge you allege against me . . .; but I revere a man either in deep love or in deep grief: and as it is impossible to convince, I would at least say nothing to irritate him,'[10] a sentence sufficiently irritating in itself. Finally she wrote to put 'an end to our acquaintance *for ever*. I respect *your prejudices*,' she told him, 'but I also respect *my own*.'[11]

But it was in March 1798 that Godwin's pursuit of a mother for his children began in real earnest. It had become his habit to take an annual vacation away from London, and this time he went to Bath to stay with sisters of his housekeeper, Louisa Jones. There he met the sisters Lee, local schoolmistresses and joint authors of a successful series of contemporary *Canterbury Tales*. At supper with them Godwin was at his most pleasant and entertaining, 'concerning the power of attending to a trifle (such as working men) while engaged in an affair more serious', and the younger and more able sister, Harriet, 'lively and sensible' and 'with a little of coxcomb in her manners', caught his eye. He may have thought 'Miss Harriet had talents but was too constantly acting a part',[12] but he settled on her as a suitable companion.

Back in London Godwin wrote meaningly that when Miss Lee had said 'you *supposed* you should hear *of* me, I am determined to understand that you *expected* to hear *from* me',[13] and invited her to come to stay with him, with Miss Jones their chaperone to protect her from idle tongues. But he received no answer, and when he found that she had actually been to town and gone again without so much as calling on him, he wrote to complain of this thoughtless treatment – and to mention that he just happened to be going to Bristol the following week. Harriet replied politely enough, explaining that she had never received his first letter, but in the margin of this one she wrote

> The tone of this letter appears to me to betray vanity disappointed by the scantiness of the homage it has received, rather than mortified by any apprehension of discouragement . . . . This journey to Bristol has no reference to me; as far as that is concerned he visits me simply as an acquaintance; but his title to be received as such has been lost by the forwardness to employ the privileges, and claim the rights of a more endeared relation.[14]

Godwin, clearly, saw himself as a marvellous catch for this provincial spinster; but Miss Lee, ever the proper lady, thought him altogether too presumptuous.

Their 'conference' in Bristol on 9 June proved inconclusive, but when Harriet and her sister came back to London later in the month – though not to stay with Godwin – he accompanied them both to the theatre, and held several more conferences. Intrigued at the prospect of matrimony and seeing some mutual advantage in their alliance, Miss Lee was none the less a little apprehensive at taking so notorious a husband as the irreligious Mr Godwin. So he set about winning his lady in the way that came easiest to him, marshalling careful arguments in his favour and refuting one by one the various objections she might raise against him. 'In the situation in which our conversation left the subject to which it related', he would write, 'I feel it incumbent upon me to trouble you once more upon paper with some ideas that rose in the course of it, for your more careful consideration.'[15] These are surely the least emotional love letters in existence; they might as well concern some third party. The most that Godwin will permit himself in the way of romance is the considered plea, 'Do not go out of life, without ever having known what life is. Celibacy contracts and palsies the mind, and shuts us out from the most valuable topics of experience.'[16]

But Harriet Lee would not be persuaded – religion, what Godwin was unwise enough to call bigotry, was the barrier between them – and she wrote to insist that the matter be closed. It is hard to tell which upset Godwin most, the failure of his suit or the failure of his arguments, but he drafted reply after reply, ranging from the contrite – 'You have humbled my pride; you have given a severe blow to the self-complacency of my heart';[17] – through the anguished – 'I cannot bear, after what has passed between us, to part thus'[18] – to the downright reproachful: 'What you have done is in the genuine style of the eleventh and twelfth centuries. You have put out of sight the man, and asked only what he believed.'[19] But in the end he had to admit defeat:

> But I have done. I entertain no hopes of a good effect from what I now write, and merely give vent to the sentiments your determination was calculated to excite. I have made no progress with you . . . . If ever you be prevailed on to listen to the addresses of any other man, may his success be decided on more equitable principles than mine have been.[20]

By July of the following year Godwin was in pursuit again, and with rather more feeling. Willey Reveley, whose wife Maria had always been something more than a friend and pupil, had died suddenly of a cerebral haemorrhage. It had not been a successful marriage, and Godwin knew of Maria's feelings for him, as she knew of his for her, so he lost no time in writing. (Godwin's daughter reports that after Mary's death Godwin's 'visits and attentions had excited Mr Reveley's jealousy, and they became to a great degree discontinued. His uprightness and candour of character made him disdain the suspicion, but he withdrew, unwilling to be the cause of the domestic feud.'[21] She must be confusing this with the incidents before Godwin's marriage.) It was a terrible mistake. Whatever the past difficulties Maria could not so promptly turn her back on fifteen years of marriage; the horror of watching her husband's senses weaken and fail, one by one, before her very eyes had left her in a state of total shock the whole week following; she was in no position to contemplate a proposal before even a month had passed; and she wrote to tell him so. But Godwin, of course, could see no rational need for a period of mourning, and he had no fear of scandal. 'How my soul disdains and tramples on these cowardly ceremonies,' he replied. 'Is woman always to be a slave?'[22] But no matter how he pressed her, Maria refused to see him. 'You have it in your power to give me new life,' he wrote,

> a new interest in existence, to raise me from the grave in which my heart lies buried. You are invited to form the sole happiness of one of the most known men of the age . . . . When all obstacles interposed between us, when I had a wife, when you had a husband, you said you loved me, for years loved me!

Could you for years be deceived? Now that calamity on the one hand, and no unpropitious fortune on the other, have removed these obstacles, it seems your thoughts are changed, you have entered into new thoughts and reasonings . . . .[23]

No doubt Maria was worried that Godwin would prove too demanding, too dominating, a husband, but she made the mistake of telling him she feared she was not sufficiently intelligent to make him a worthy wife. Of course Godwin was only too willing to refute these arguments, and it had, inevitably, quite the wrong effect, with Maria more and more convinced he would crush her in person as he crushed her objections in writing, and Godwin more and more annoyed that she would not listen to the voice of reason. This time there is no doubting the feeling, on his side at least – 'There is nothing upon earth that I desire so ardently, so fervently, so much with every sentiment and every pulse of my heart, as to call you mine'[24] – but whatever hope he had of capturing the pretty young widow, still only twenty-nine, he lost through his thoughtlessness and insensitivity:

In one of your first intimations to me since your widowhood you said you could not see me, or any unmarried man, *for some time* . . . . I think however, you pay too little attention to my feelings. Two months of etiquette have now nearly elapsed, and no elucidation of this *some time* has yet reached my ears.[25]

When finally they met, at the end of 1799, Maria was already in the company of John Gisborne, whose intellect stood in no danger of dominating hers. The following May they were secretly married, and Godwin, who had still not entirely lost hope, was pained as much by the secrecy as by the wedding. But on that score, at least, he was in no position to complain.

The horror of loneliness, the misery of human isolation, this is the eternal refrain of all Godwin's mature novels. But nowhere is it expressed more powerfully, or more bitterly, than in *St Leon*:

Friendship is a necessity of our nature, the stimulating and restless want of every susceptible heart. How wretched an imposture in this point of view does human life for the most part appear! With boyish eyes, full of sanguine spirits and hope, we look round us for a friend; we sink into the grave, broken down with years and infirmities, and still have not found the object of our search. We talk to one man, and he does not understand us; we address ourselves to another, and we find him the unreal similitude only of what we believed him to be. We ally ourselves to a man of intellect and of worth; upon further experience we cannot deny him either of these qualities; but the more we know each other, the less we find of resemblance; he is cold, where we are warm; he is harsh, where we are melted into the tenderest sympathy; what fills us with rapture is regarded by him with indifference; we finish with a distant respect, where we looked for a commingling soul; this is not friendship. We know of other men, we have viewed their countenances, we have occasionally sat in their society: we believe it impossible we should not find in them the object we sought. But the disparity of situation and dissimilitude of connection prove as effectual a barrier to intimacy, as if we were inhabitants of different planets.

It is in part the cry of a distraught widower, uncertain how to reorganize his life or care for his children, but there was more to Godwin's isolation than that. Lost in his private happiness with Mary Wollstonecraft, he had not noticed how admiration had given way to abhorrence, how his former reputation had become a liability. He had changed but so had the world, and now he was more truly alone than he had ever been when he had preached the doctrine of self-sufficiency in all things. Like St Leon he too would be forced into hiding, the maligned and persecuted victim of an honest but misguided attempt to promote the welfare of his fellow men.

13 ♣ Apostasy and calumny

Two centuries perhaps after Philip the Second shall be gathered to his ancestors [he died in 1598], men shall learn over again to persecute each other for conscience sake; other anabaptists or levellers shall furnish pretexts for new persecutions; other inquisitors shall arise in the most enlightened tracts of Europe; and professors from their chair, sheltering their intolerance under the great names of Aristotle and Cicero, shall instruct their scholars, that a heterodox doctrine is the worst of crimes, and that the philanthropy and purity of heart in which it is maintained, only render its defenders the more worthy to be extirpated.

St Leon, 1799

♣ The death of Mary Wollstonecraft marks a watershed in Godwin's life in almost every respect. It would be overly romantic to suggest that he never recovered from the shock of losing in childbirth his wife of a mere six months, the woman who had woken in him depths of feeling he had never before suspected. A man can hardly live almost as long again, remarry, acquire new friends, new children, new opinions, new projects, new problems, without that sudden catastrophe losing much of its sting. Nevertheless, the independent bachelor devoted to the benefit of all mankind had become, in the space of a year, a middle-aged widower with special responsibility for two infant girls. The severe moralist prepared to judge friend and foe alike by the eternal dictates of impartial justice, a man patronizing and petulant by turn, had been transformed into a new man of feeling, well-meaning and tolerant, though soon to become petty and inconsequential. Startling doctrines based on the power of truth and man's essential rationality were replaced, under Mary's influence, by a more commonplace appeal to human emotion. But more corrosive still, the writer who thrived, depended even, on praise and reputation now found himself an object of fear and hatred, despised and rejected even by some who had been his fervent admirers. No sooner had he discovered what he stood to gain from a close emotional attachment than he found himself alone again, cut off from his fellows at just the time he was most in need of private affection and public support.

No one could now look to France for a model, however tarnished, of a just and rational society. In place of the noble people's democracy anticipated a decade before, she had become a corrupt and exhausted imperialist state, held together by the success of her forces under the Corsican general Bonaparte. In Britain the spirit of reform was dead, destroyed as much by fear of French-style anarchy as by the 1795 Gagging Acts, and when Napoleon was appointed Commander-in-Chief of the Army of Britain, with the aim of establishing an English Directory that could include Paine, Tooke and Thelwall, such admiration for the revolution as lingered on gave way at last to an old-fashioned patriotism. Nothing remained of the prestigious group of liberals and democrats with whom Godwin had once identified himself. The parliamentary faction headed by Fox, Sheridan and Burke had disintegrated at Burke's defection; more radical figures like Paine and Priestley had long since had to flee the country; others, like Tooke and Thelwall, were now in retirement; and many who had greeted the revolution with such fervour now preferred to forget or conceal their earlier enthusiasm, or attempted to atone for their sins by the vehemence with which they attacked their former friends. Those few, like Godwin or Holcroft, who attempted to hold true to their principles found themselves solitary and friendless indeed, while the anti-radicals, and especially the *Anti-Jacobins*, scourge of the defeated left, lost no opportunity to press home their advantage, growing more vindictive with every month that passed. The 1790s had begun in a fever of political debate, but they closed in a fury of political abuse. The intention was no longer to out-argue your opponent, but to ridicule and vilify him. These were the years of the scurrilous journals and the satirical novels, the years of mockery and treachery, of apostasy and calumny. And in the general rout of radical opinion Godwin, once most radical of all, would suffer most of all. In vain did he protest that he had from the first criticized the French and the wantonness with which they appeared ready to proceed to extremities, just as he had gone on to criticize radical extremism in Britain. In the atmosphere that now prevailed, that was of little account.

An undated note looks back to this wretched period, and wonders what had gone wrong:

> It was at that time my purpose to live and die a bachelor. I resolutely applied myself to the producing the mature fruits of my intellect unshackled by any supererogatory impediments to the attainment of my object. That done, I had leisure to feel the burthen of a solitary life and I married. What was the moral offence I committed in this, I know not; nor do I know how

much less of evil would have attended the decline of my life, if I had not married.[1]

What had gone wrong was that Godwin's faith in social and moral progress had come to seem worse than a blind and foolish optimism. Our security and happiness seemed to depend not on political change but on political stability, precisely as Burke had argued. It was no longer enough to concede that 'a long period of time must probably elapse' before political justice was attained; it now seemed obvious that all progress must be illusion, that instead of appealing to man's reason we must guard against his passions. An idealism that had once seemed ennobling, even if misguided, now came to seem positively dangerous, and none more so than the extravagant idealism of a Godwin. 'Most people', said de Quincey with a nice touch of anachronism, 'felt of Mr Godwin with the same alienation and horror as of a ghoul, or a bloodless vampire, or the monster created by Frankenstein.'[2]

Godwin later dated the reaction against himself and his theories from the spring of 1797, from the time of his marriage, and certainly it was the reception of the *Memoirs* that gave him his first inkling of what lay in store. They may even have precipitated the attack, giving the more general reading public its first horrified glimpse of what had so far lain hidden in a weighty work of philosophy, for the outrage was directed as much against the author as against his dead wife:

> Fierce passion's slave, she veer'd with every gust,
> Love, Rights, and Wrongs, Philosophy and Lust:
> But some more wise in metaphysic air,
> Weigh the man's wits against the lady's hair.[3]

And if Mary was an easy target how much easier was Godwin, with his plough without a ploughman and his people who will not sleep, fall ill or die; his rejection of gratitude and promises, of matrimony, family and personal property; his arguments against law, punishment and responsibility; his absurd faith in human reason and perfectibility. Godwin was made for satire, and again and again he appears in the most celebrated comic novels of the day: as Mr Vapour in Elizabeth Hamilton's *Letters of a Hindoo Rajah* (1796); as Mr Subtile in Isaac D'Israeli's *Vaurien* (1797); as Stupeo in George Walker's *Vagabond* (1799); as Mr Subtlewould in Robert Bisset's *Douglas, or the Highlander* (1800); as Dr Myope in Elizabeth Hamilton's *Memoirs of Modern Philosophers* (1800), friend and confidant of Miss Bridgetina Botherim.

How fitting, too, that Godwin, should breach his own principles in taking Mary for his wife:

The motives (alas! tis too plain)
Which me to Maria would draw,
Are stronger than those which restrain, –
I submit to Necessity's law . . . .

Do not grieve if hereafter I flee
Your caresses, nor deem me capricious:
I fane would be grateful to thee;
But alas! to be grateful is vicious . . . .

As for me, I will never confine
Your beauties alone to these arms,
Nor yet will you hear me repine,
Though multitudes taste of your charms.

You will vow at the altar indeed
To your husband alone to adhere,
But you're from that prejudice freed
Which would make you perform what you swear.[4]

But as always it was the *Anti-Jacobin* that published the most scurrilous attack on the marriage of Wollstonecraft and Godwin, in its derisive 'Vision of Liberty' of August 1801:

Then saw I mounted on a braying ass
William and Mary, sooth, a couple jolly;
Who married, note ye how it came to pass,
Although each held that marriage was but folly?
And she of curses would discharge a volley
If the ass stumbled, leaping pales or ditches:
Her husband, sans-culottes, was melancholy,
For Mary verily would wear the breeches –
God help poor silly men from such usurping b———s.

Whilom his dame the *Rights of Women* writ,
That is the title to her book she places,
Exorting bashful womankind to quit
All foolish modesty and coy grimaces;
And name their backsides as it were their faces;
Such license loose-tongued liberty adores,
Which adds to female speech exceeding graces;
Lucky the maid that on her volume pours,
A scripture, archly framed for propagating w———s

William hath penn'd a wagon-load of stuff,
And Mary's life at last he needs must write,
Thinking her whoredoms were not known enough,

> Till fairly printed off in black and white. –
> With wondrous glee and pride, this simple wight
> Her brothel feats of wantonness sets down.
> Being her spouse, he tells, with huge delight,
> How oft she cuckolded the silly clown,
> And lent, O lovely piece! herself to half the town.

Yet if Godwin and his theories were easily ridiculed, there were also those who regarded them as more pernicious than absurd. Novels like Mrs Opie's *Adeline Mowbray* (1805), the anonymous *Dorothea, or a Ray of the New Light* (1801), or Charles Lloyd's *Edmund Oliver* (1798), were intended to warn their readers of the dangers of Godwinian principles put into practice. Most bitter of all, Charles Lucas's *Infernal Quixote* (1800) presents Godwin and his ilk as Diabolists, sent to us by the very Devil to pervert us with the New Philosophy. And just what this New Philosophy was believed to represent in the way of moral instruction is perhaps best exhibited in the story of one Timothy Newlight, as told in Bisset's *Historical, Biographical, Literary and Scientific Magazine* for 1799. Educated at a Dissenting Academy, Newlight is accordingly well instructed in the principle that 'Whatever has been established is bad'. He meets a beautiful seventeen-year-old and gratefully remembers that 'philosophy had taught me that it was lawful to gratify natural appetite that tended to the propagation of the species.' But since the girl stubbornly holds to

> the old absurd notions about marriage, I thought it best, *upon the whole*, to promise to submit to that contemptuous ceremony. She was so little acquainted with philosophy, that she believed a promise to imply an intention of performance; not having learned from Godwin that all promises are in themselves bad, and to be performed no farther than suits the convenience and inclination of the promiser.

Before that, however, he manages to get the girl pregnant, and when her mother dies of shame discovers that

> the daughter had not sufficiently studied philosophy to expel, as she ought to have done, all private affections. In vain I endeavoured to convince her that her mother would now be resolved into the great mass of matter, and might probably, in some form or other, produce equal good to the whole.

So Newlight turns for relief to the wife of a man who has saved him from drowning, for it is clear that she will find more happiness with him than with her elderly husband. His first mistress begs him in the name of Heaven – 'fool that she was to suppose that a disciple of Godwin minded Heaven' – to stay with her and her child, but he reminds her that 'I continued constant to her as long as inclination prompted me, and that longer was totally unphilosophical to expect.' Even when he finds his new mistress in the arms of an Irish adventurer, Newlight is nothing abashed, insisting that 'there was no evil in her conduct until she intended to conceal it. For as my favorite and adored philosopher says, in the commerce between the sexes, there is no harm in inconstancy, unless you make a secret of it.' So the two share the lady's charms between them.

But the husband sues Timothy for seduction, the judge refuses to listen to his disgusting Godwinian arguments, and he finds himself fined damages of £3000 which he cannot pay, because his mother, fired by the Dissenting doctrine of the equalization of property, had 'made great practical advances in the levelling scheme', and given it all away. When 'a friend, to use the old language of absurdity, assisted me', Timothy repays the debt by seducing his daughter too, 'it being lawful to deceive a woman to gratify a natural appetite, and propagate the species'. Soon he is driven to theft, gambling, and attempted murder, before turning highwayman and making his own contribution to the equalization of property by forcing his own uncle to stand and deliver – for 'what is an uncle, or what even would a father be, to a disciple of the new philosophy?'

Nor was the most brilliant and most savage cartoonist of the day, James Gillray, to be left out of the fun, though he did not know Godwin well enough to attempt a caricature. An etching in the *Anti-Jacobin* for August 1798 shows the leading radicals worshipping at the shrine of 'The New Morality': Southey and Coleridge are twin asses flanking a Cornucopia of Ignorance, from which spill such works as the *Enquirer*, the *Wrongs of Woman*, and the Wollstonecraft *Memoirs*; Paine is a crocodile wearing a set of lady's stays, Holcroft an 'acquitted felon' in leg irons, Charles Lamb and Charles Lloyd a frog and a toad reading from their recent publication *Blank Verse*; also on hand are Priestley, Thelwall, Horne Tooke, Fox and Erskine; Godwin is a jackass, standing on his hind legs and braying aloud from a copy of *Political Justice*. Another print, from 1800, 'The Apples and the Horse-Turds', shows Napoleon, as First Horse Turd, swimming out to join the floating Golden Pippins – the various crowned heads of Europe – under the illusion that he can be one of their number. Among the turds waiting in a pile on the bank are those labelled Price, Priestley, Holcroft and Godwin.

Godwin was hardly the man to reply in kind to this 'flood of ribaldry, invective and intolerance which has been poured out against me and my writings',[5] even had he known how. But there were others more deserving of his attention, critics prepared to argue against him in a way that he could if not always respect, at least respond to. Coleridge, we know, had planned a *Reply to Godwin* back in 1796, but it never materialized, and so it was not until 1798 that, as Godwin says, 'a forlorn hope of two little skirmishing pamphlets began the war':[6] Thomas Green's *Examination of the Leading Principles of the New System of Morals,** and W. C. Proby's *Modern Philosophy and Barbarism.* They were, as it happens, two of the most interesting responses to *Political Justice,* one an acute criticism of extreme Utilitarianism, the other a revealing comparison of Godwin's ideal state with that of ancient Sparta. But later that year they were joined by the book which would prove the most enduring of all replies to Godwin, a work whose reputation would soon obliterate that of its original inspiration; Thomas Malthus's *Essay on the Principles of Population.* Godwin himself regarded it as the best, perhaps the only, reasoned critique of his theories, and he went out of his way to make Malthus's acquaintance and invite him to breakfast at the Polygon, the better to discuss the differences between them.

But Malthus was the exception. Godwin had grown used to criticism where once he had attracted praise. Indeed the leading light of the *Anti-Jacobin* itself was the George Canning who had once pressed himself on Godwin, at Sheridan's back in the 1880s. According to Walter Scott, Canning had changed sides only when Godwin had come to announce that in the event of a revolution they intended to make Canning their leader, a story that has scarcely the ring of truth. But Canning was only a minor acquaintance from the past; this was no personal treachery. James Mackintosh was a close personal friend, one of the select few to be invited to that unique dinner party in April 1796. And Mackintosh was that professor from his chair, sheltering under the great names of Aristotle and Cicero, that St Leon had foretold, when he had added the ability to read the future to his other magical powers.

Mackintosh's *Vindiciae Gallicae* had been the most scholarly of the replies to Burke, but its author had since confessed his error, and there had been an emotional reconciliation not long before Burke's death in 1797. Half an hour with Burke, Mackintosh said later, had upturned the reflections of a lifetime, and never again could he think of revolution without a shudder. Now he planned a series of lectures on the *Law of Nature and of Nations* whose *Introductory Discourse,*

*Godwin also calls Green's 'the first pamphlet . . . which ushered in the tremendous war against philanthropy'. In fact the first published statement of objections which were to become standard seems to have been in an anonymous article called 'Is Private Affection Inconsistent with Universal Benevolence?' in the *American Universal Magazine* for April 1797.

published by way of advertisement and preamble, made it clear that Godwinism would be a prime target. Godwin wrote to protest, and received a polite and dignified reply: he intended no personal disrespect, Mackintosh insisted, and hoped they might remain friends, though literary adversaries. But the lectures which followed, commencing in February 1799 and continuing once or twice weekly through to June, poured ceaseless ridicule and scorn on 'such fanciful chimeras as the golden mountain or the perfect man'.[7] The hall was packed with everyone who had ever had any social or intellectual pretension to liberal opinions, the same public which five years before had read *Political Justice* with such enthusiasm, but eager now to discover a more cautious, more orthodox truth. Mackintosh treated them to a virtuoso display of learning, rhetoric and sophistry, though to the one or two, like Fawcett and Hazlitt, who looked for some argument behind the oratory, some answer to the questions that Mackintosh ceaselessly heaped upon his audience, the lectures were disappointing as well as distasteful.

Godwin had missed the first lecture but he attended the next two, and then felt he must stay away, because the references to himself 'were so continual, and had so little moderation, as made it utterly improper for me to be the silent spectator and witness of an attack, to which from its nature and circumstances I could not reply.'[8] What irritated him most was Mackintosh's steadfast refusal to name any names, restricting himself to innuendo and generalities and avoiding any specific reference that might give Godwin the chance to defend himself. But his audience knew well enough who he had in mind, and Mackintosh became the prince of the apostates, his reward a government appointment in India and a consequent knighthood, and the satirical verses of both Coleridge and Lamb:

> Though thou'rt like Judas, an apostate black
> In the resemblance one thing thou dost lack;
> When he had gotten his ill purchas'd pelf,
> He went away and wisely hanged himself;
> This thou may do at last, yet much I doubt,
> If thou hast any bowels to gush out.[9]

Originally Mackintosh had had difficulty in obtaining permission to use Lincoln's Inn for his lectures; the following year he was invited to repeat all thirty-nine.

Worse was to come. Godwin was under attack from the pulpit as well as the lectern, and towards the end of 1799 Robert Hall, another former admirer of events in France, preached his sermon on *Modern Infidelity Considered* – 'infidelity' meaning lack of religious faith, not unfaithfulness – in which, Godwin said, 'every notion of toleration or decorum was treated with infuriated contempt.'[10] In fact Hall's tone was relatively moderate by comparison with Mackintosh's, but it was, at least by implication, an attack on the Godless morality of Godwin and Hume, and the following year another published sermon, C. Findlater's *Liberty and Equality*, would include an appendix devoted specifically to Godwin's absurd opinions. Then it was the turn of Dr Parr.

It was Mackintosh, in January 1794, who had first introduced Godwin to Parr, known as 'the Whig Dr Johnson' partly for his physical appearance, partly for his enormous erudition; and Parr had been so delighted with this new acquaintance that he said 'Jemmy, I was very angry with you yesterday, but now you have brought Godwin to me I cannot help forgiving you.'[11] Parr had insisted that Godwin visit him in Warwickshire, and when Godwin had hurriedly left to go to Holcroft's assistance, had let him go only on the assurance that he would return the following year. Parr, in his turn, had also been a guest, with his two daughters, at the 1796 dinner party, and Godwin had visited him for a third time with Basil Montagu, on their 1797 trip into Staffordshire. True, Montagu had warned Godwin of 'some unfortunate misunderstanding' when Parr came up to London the following year, but Godwin had sought him out at once 'and with my customary frankness related to you what I had heard',[12] and that, evidently, had been the end of that. So when Godwin sent Parr a gift copy of *St Leon*, knowing that Parr must surely approve his change of heart about the domestic affections, he also took the opportunity to complain of Mackintosh's treachery. Clearly he hoped for Parr's sympathy and support. But Parr did not reply.

The answer, when it came, was shattering. Parr had been invited to give the annual Spital Sermon, delivered on Easter Tuesday before the Lord Mayor of London, on 15 April 1800, and now he too took the opportunity to strike out at the New Philosophy, and at Godwin in particular. But though it was this that finally provoked Godwin to defend himself, in fact Parr's was the weakest critique of all, a sermon in the worst sense, packed with empty rhetoric and continual appeals to authority, but with no attempt at reasoned argument. In its published version the notes – which as Parr modestly says, he has ventured to make very copious – run to full 135 pages, against the 24, in much larger type, taken up by the sermon proper; and one note, in particular, is almost twice the length of the original text. Yet they consist of almost nothing but quotation piled upon quotation, authority heaped on authority, until in the jaundiced opinion of the *Edinburgh Review* the pamphlet seemed 'to concern every learned thing, every learned man, and almost every unlearned man since the beginning of the world'.[13] In sum, an extraordinary display of pointless erudition by a man who boasted a library of more than 10,000 volumes. A contemporary caricature shows half of Parr's audience sound asleep, the rest suffocating in the smoke from his pipe.

But what upset Godwin was not Parr's criticisms, such as they were, but the tone of 'gall, intolerance and contempt' with which he presented them. For some, indeed, it was the 'Spiteall Sermon'. Parr may be prepared to call Godwin 'a writer of great celebrity and acuteness', and to praise the 'sagacity and candour' with which the *St Leon* Preface admits his earlier errors. But he speaks also of 'a man to be smiled at as dealing in groundless and unauthorised hypotheses' in this 'age in which so much has been said to so little purpose about perfectibility'. And he offers this warning to those misguided young men who might 'suppose that any one man, by any series of reasonings, can lay open the laws of the moral world, with the clearness and fulness of Newton, when he unfolded those of the natural':

> Let me, further, inform him, that superstition is not the *only* venom which pollutes and cankers the natural sentiments of the heart, that philosophy, no less than religion, may be disgraced by pharisiacal votaries; and that in the drudgeries which may be necessary to uphold the cause of metaphysical, as well as theological mysticism, self-delusion is often the vassal of zeal, hypocrisy and pride.

'Let us beware of those proud cosmopolites', Parr quoted Rousseau, 'who deduce from books the far-fetched obligations of universal benevolence, while they neglect their actual duties to those around them!'

Godwin was completely at a loss to understand this betrayal. He and Parr had differed often enough on matters of religion and politics, but their disagreements had never been personal. Godwin told him once that 'he understood everything except my system of Political Justice; and he replied that was exactly the case with me.'[14] Parr had told Montagu that he considered Godwin 'more skilful in moral science than any man now living'. But now Parr, too, had attacked him, behind his back and at just the moment when he stood most in need of someone to defend his integrity and his motives, if not his opinions; and had attacked him on the one topic where Godwin thought they were most in agreement, morals.

Godwin had not attended Parr's sermon, but he learnt of its contents soon enough, and tried to contact Parr before he left London. But Parr managed to elude him, and wrote instead a long pompous rebuttal of Godwin's complaints, padded out with a defence of his noble and upright friend Mackintosh. He had not, Parr explained, previously seen the offensive remarks about Christ in the *Enquirer*, which too closely resembled 'the impious effusions of Mr Voltaire'; he had 'been shocked, in common with all wise and good men', by the *Memoirs* of Mary Wollstonecraft; and he had now 'discovered the dreadful effects of your opinions upon the conduct, the peace, and the welfare of two or three young men, whose talents I esteemed, and whose virtues I loved.'[15] (This particular complaint mystified Godwin. The reference is presumably not to Joseph Gerrald, who had been sentenced to transportation before Godwin and Parr even met, but to another of Parr's ex-pupils, John Twedall, whom Godwin met through Wordsworth in 1795. Twedall subsequently suffered a nervous breakdown, left England in despair, and had recently died in Athens. But Godwin knew nothing of that, and would hardly have regarded it as his responsibility even if he did.) Yet Parr had said nothing of this when they had met two years before, nor was the *Enquirer* noticeably more anti-Christian than *Political Justice*. In all likelihood what had actually offended him was its account of the character typical of a clergyman:

> He will be timid in enquiry, prejudiced in opinion, cold, formal, the slave of what other men may think of him, rude, dictatorial, impatient of contradiction, harsh in his censures and illiberal in his judgments. Every man may remark in him study rendered abortive, artificial manners, infantine prejudices, and a sort of arrogant infallibility.[16]

Not that Godwin had intended this personally, any more than he expected his various clerical friends – Fawcett, Kippis, Parr – to take offence. It was a deduction from first principles, an examination of the essential nature of the profession they happened to practice, not a generalization from personal experience. But in Parr's case, perhaps, the portrait was too true for comfort.

> So good, so bad, so foolish and so wise,
> By turns I love thee, and by turns despise

was the verdict of another friend, the aptly-named Philip Homer, a master at Rugby School. Parr wrote to Godwin again in October, to return the presentation copy of *St Leon*, and to make it clear that while his wife and daughter had read the novel, he himself had been careful not to. It was obviously intended to end their acquaintance. And so it did.

This, then, was the result of Godwin's plan to devote himself to 'the usefulness and service of my fellow creatures . . . to increase, as far as lies in my power, the quantity of their knowledge and goodness and happiness'. Even Holcroft, his closest friend the past fifteen years and perhaps that 'man of intellect and worth' mourned in *St Leon*, had had to desert him, unable to withstand the strains of life as an 'acquitted felon' as he was often called, despite the fact that he had been discharged without trial. Now that his dramas could no longer count on a favourable reception from fashionable London audiences, Holcroft had left England for Hamburg in July 1799, with a new, his fourth and final, wife, no older than his own daughter. As well as negotiating a German edition of *St Leon*, he also planned to buy up some of the hordes of looted paintings circulating on the continent and ship them back to England twenty or thirty at a time, to be sold at a handsome profit. But Holcroft was no art-expert, and this ill-considered venture only increased the tensions between himself and Godwin, who was expected to handle the British end of the business. From Hamburg he moved to Paris, where visiting Britons would be warned by *The Times* to beware 'one of the "*soidisant*" twelve Apostles of Liberty . . . who though once in the *road to ruin* seems now is in the highway to fortune'[17] as a paid informer for the French government. Embittered, morbid, more inflexible than ever, Holcroft did not return to England until September 1802, during the short-lived Peace of Amiens. Godwin, meanwhile, would have to face his enemies, and his critics, alone.

14 ♣ The famous fire cause

It must be confessed that in all these exaggerations there is a noble and gallant spirit, which leads us to admire the speaker. But when we consider him as laying down an everlasting code of morals, what he says under these heads is worthy of a distinct and unhesitating censure.*[1]

Posthumous *Essays*, 1873 (written 1834–6)

♣ Mackintosh and Proby had been chiefly concerned with Godwin's political doctrines, Malthus with the economic consequences of his ideal of rational equality. But it was the moral theories that had most aroused the wrath of Godwin's critics, both serious and satirical:

> We nobly take the high priori road
> And reason downward, till we doubt of God.
> Tho' men of no minds call me madman and oaf
> Yet my friends all declare me un grand philosophe . . . .
>
> Religion I hate – for I hate all restraint,
> And whatever I've been, I'm no longer a saint;
> Each volume of Ethics may rest on the shelf
> For the main spring of action is centred in Self . . . .
>
> The rogue or adulterer should not, when taken,
> A penalty pay, for the man was mistaken
> In seeking his pleasure; but who is so nice
> To blame such an error, and call it a vice . . . .
>
> Should my liberal notions e'er meet with a stop,
> And my lungs be cleared up by that sophist – a *drop*,
> I still would maintain that my exit, forsooth,
> Was 'Political Justice' contending with Truth.[2]

To Thomas Green, indeed, Godwin had performed a public service in stating his principles clearly and drawing the consequences unflinchingly, so that everyone could see, once and for all, the true content, the full horror, of the New System of Morals. For it was Godwin, not Bentham – then scarcely a name, despite the publication in 1789 of his now classic *Introduction to the Principles of Morals and*

*Godwin is referring to Christ's Sermon on the Mount!

Legislation – who was seen by his contemporaries as the most prominent disciple in the school of Hume, the leading advocate of what was variously termed the New Morality, the Modern Philosophy, the system of expedience, the philanthropic system, or even Modern Infidelity, meaning by that a morality without God, a morality therefore without authority, a selfish self-centred morality of 'vanity, ferocity and unbridled sensuality'.[3]

Yet to Godwin himself it was all perfectly obvious – 'Nothing can be less exposed to reasonable exception than these principles'[4] – so obvious that originally, in his first edition, he had not even bothered to explain those principles before proceeding to an illustration that was as self-evident to himself as it was monstrous to his critics. The opening pages of *Political Justice* make for relatively plain sailing, with little to startle or outrage the moderately sympathetic reader, until suddenly, at the start of Book II, he is plunged without warning into the extraordinary, fascinating example where Godwin appears, in Charles Lamb's delightful phrase, as 'counsel for the Archbishop Fénelon versus my own mother, in the famous fire cause':[5]

> The illustrious archbishop of Cambray was of more worth than his chambermaid, and there are few of us that would hesitate to pronounce, if his palace were in flames, and the life of only one of them could be preserved, which of the two ought to be preferred . . . . Suppose I had been myself the chambermaid; I ought to have chosen to die, rather than that Fénelon should have died . . . . Supposing the chambermaid had been my wife, my mother or my benefactor. That would not alter the truth of the proposition. The life of Fénelon would still be more valuable than that of the chambermaid; and justice, pure, unadulterated justice, would still have preferred that which was most valuable . . . . What magic is there in the pronoun 'my', to overturn the decisions of everlasting truth? My wife or my mother may be a fool or a prostitute, malicious, lying or dishonest. If they be, of what consequence is it that they are mine?[6]

It was yet another sparkling opportunity for satire. In George Walker's *Vagabond* the hero, Fenton, finds that the girl he has made pregnant is trapped with her father in their burning farmhouse. While he stands debating with himself which of the two justice requires him to save ('Let go the ladder', cried several; 'why do you keep it useless?') both are destroyed and the unfortunate Fenton is accused of contriving the girl's death. But satire aside, what sort of morality, what sort of justice is this, that requires us to prefer an archbishop to a mere chambermaid, even though she be our mother, our wife or our benefactor?

Justice, we have seen, is merely 'a general appellation for all moral duty',[7] another name for utility, 'or more periphrastically, the production of the greatest general good, the greatest public sum of pleasurable sensation'.[8] But equally, to benefit one man, no matter who he may be, at the expense of others, is injustice unless a greater general good is ensured thereby. True morality, true justice, as Godwin reminds us, is no respecter of persons. Yet men may differ, perhaps in their capacity for happiness, certainly in their ability to provide happiness for others. 'By justice', says Godwin, when his second edition at last provides us with the necessary explanation, 'I understand the impartial treatment of every man in matters that relate to his happiness, which is measured solely by a consideration of the properties of the receiver, and the capacity of him that bestows.'[9] But justice itself may sometimes require that we discriminate, and favour one man against another, not for any purely personal reason, but because one man is capable of 'a more refined and genuine happiness', or, more crucially, more capable of spreading that happiness to others. 'Of consequence that life ought to be preferred which will be most conducive to the general good.'[10]

Fénelon, then, was a moralist and educationalist whose epic poem *Telemachus* preached the brotherhood of man, the corruption of absolute power, the evils of luxury, the virtues of simplicity, and the pleasures of disinterested benevolence. Well-nigh unreadable now, it was a favourite text in the Dissenting Academies and had on its public – including Bentham as well as Godwin – something of the same dramatic effect that *Political Justice* would have on its. So

> in saving the life of Fénelon, suppose at the moment he con-
> ceived the project of the immortal Telemachus, I should be
> promoting the benefit of thousands, who have been cured by the
> perusal of it, of some error, vice and consequent unhappiness.
> Nay, my benefit would extend further than this; for every
> individual, thus cured, has become a better member of society,
> and has contributed in his turn to the happiness, the infor-
> mation and improvement of others.[11]

In the strictness of impartial justice I must save a notable benefactor such as Fénelon in preference to a nonentity like his chambermaid, no matter who that chambermaid might be. So far from its being a son's duty to save his mother if he can, that would actually be immoral, unjust, if Fénelon's life were truly the more valuable: 'What magic is there in the pronoun "my" to overturn the decisions of impartial truth?'

Godwin himself came to regret he had chosen so extreme an example, and in the second edition the chambermaid who might be your mother becomes a valet who might be your father, presumably because that is a less offensive illustration. Later still he wished he had cited some man of action, a Brutus or Napoleon, instead of a mere writer, since 'the benefit to accrue from the writing of books is too remote an idea to strike and fill the imagination'.[12] But if a parent who ensures that a son gets a post to which someone else is better fitted is regarded as biased and acting unfairly, why not also a son who saves a parent, and leaves to perish someone more worthy? The fact that I feel differently about my mother has nothing to do with the morality of the situation: 'Justice requires that I should put myself in the place of an impartial spectator of human concerns, and divest myself of retrospect to my own predilections.'[13] Justice, pure unadulterated justice, is no respecter of persons.

It is easy enough to see the rationale of this position; it is more difficult to find it in any way attractive or sympathetic. It seems a morality of remote cold-blooded intellect in which normal human feelings are allowed no place; at the very least it suggests someone who thinks only in abstract principles, with no understanding of the flesh and blood of human relationships on which any workable morality must be based. We remember, too, that Godwin rejected companionship and marriage along with gratitude and the domestic affections, and it seems significant that, for him, 'disinterest' is a synonym for benevolence. And so we come back to the caricature of him as some monster of intellect, a desiccated calculating machine all uncomprehending among his theories, 'his great head full of cold brains',[14] with no conception of what people are really like or what actually motivates their behaviour towards one another. Then we remember that after his brief happiness with Mary Wollstonecraft he had changed his mind about the domestic affections, and planned a new work 'which would correct certain errors in the earlier part of Political Justice', this being 'essentially defective, in the circumstance of not yielding a proper attention to the empire of feeling'. Now, perhaps, he knew what life and morals were all about.

This is a natural judgment, but not an entirely fair one. As a philosopher, Godwin was bound to seem detached from everyday human problems, and the cool control of his theoretical writings contributes to an appearance of remoteness. Later in life, in the Preface to his *History of the Commonwealth* he would apologize for this scholarly detachment in terms that were probably intended more widely: 'I have no desire to be regarded as having no sentiments or emotions when anything singularly good or singularly evil passes under my review. I wish to be considered as feeling as well as thinking.' Yet his novels were widely regarded as over-emotional, with their sensational plots and themes of passion, and the man himself was all too liable to outbursts of irrational feeling. Even before Mary Wollstonecraft he had been no monster of intellect, and neither was his morality. It too had to be considered as feeling as well as thinking. Indeed it was his insistence on the superior joy that can come only from doing good to others which, as much as anything else, so captivated Godwin's eager literary disciples. 'No book ever made me feel more generously', reported the diarist Crabb Robinson. 'I have never before, nor I am afraid, have I ever since, felt so strongly the duty of not living to one's self, but of having for one's sole object the good of the community.'[15] Godwin saw himself merely as taking seriously, more seriously than the Christians ever had, Christ's teaching that we should love our neighbour as ourselves, and that all men are our neighbours, not just those who live nearby. It was a morality of the best of emotions and the highest of human pleasures, a morality of benevolence, a morality of happiness.

According to Saint-Just, Robespierre's disciple who shared the scaffold with his master, the eighteenth century had 'discovered happiness'. Certainly Godwin had discovered it in the writings of the French *philosophes* that he read as a young preacher at Stowmarket, and remained convinced ever after that morality consisted in the pursuit of happiness for all. That was itself a radical enough idea, more familiar to us than to his contemporaries, as the climax to Coleridge's complimentary sonnet reminds us. It was Godwin, he says, who

> Bade the bright form of Justice meet my way –
> And told me that her name was HAPPINESS.

The orthodox position was rather that morality called for a stern, thankless and unrelenting struggle against evil, against original sin, against human nature itself. Indeed to a Calvinist such as Godwin had been almost from birth, happiness seemed incompatible with virtue rather than essential to it. But Helvetius – and Fénelon – had convinced him otherwise, and as the character of Falkland in *Caleb Williams* was intended to demonstrate, morality is nothing without a concern for the welfare of others. Men and their actions are to be judged not by their inherent piety or purity, but by the good, which is to say the happiness, that they produce. 'Morality is that system of conduct which is determined by a consideration of the greatest good.'[16] 'And what is the greatest good?', responds a character in the *Vagabond*. 'A term without meaning, a cant phrase to avoid a duty. The greatest good is, to be upright and sincere before God.' For a traditional moralist a duty was some specific requirement that must always be observed, the duties of a son, a citizen, a Christian. Man's conduct is governed by such rules and regulations; their infringement constitutes sin. But for the New Philosophy of Hume and Godwin, a man may do anything – indeed he *ought* to do it – so long as it produces happiness.

It was scandalous enough that Godwin should teach that the moral man pursues happiness. But in his second edition he went further and identified that happiness, not as one might expect with philosophical understanding or the apprehension of truth, but with pleasure, pure and simple. 'Stoicism, or an inattention to the principle that pleasure and pain are the only bases on which morality can rest' was one of the three Calvinist blemishes that Godwin later detected in the original *Political Justice*, an error 'rooted from my mind, principally by the acute arguments of Mr George Dyson, in 1794. It has been corrected with some care in the subsequent edition.'[17] And that was something of an understatement, for although the second edition was officially his opportunity to correct the various 'inaccuracies of language and reasoning . . . respecting the properties and utilities of government', in fact it is the chapters on ethics that underwent the most radical revision. All but one were completely rewritten, arguments were added every bit as crucial to Godwin's conclusions as his attempted demonstration of the omnipotence of truth, and Dyson thus became the third, the youngest, and the most mysterious, of Godwin's four principal oral instructors.

So it was Dyson, not Bentham – whom Godwin had read and ignored while writing *Political Justice*'s first edition – who convinced Godwin that pleasure is the only value, the supreme good: 'That which will give pleasure neither to ourselves nor others, and from which the fruits of joy can be reaped in no stage, and at no period, is necessarily good for nothing.'[18] To his more conservative readers it smacked of the utmost depravity and unbridled sensuality. The familiar commandments of morality were to be replaced by the single maxim, to seek out pleasure: 'Morality is nothing more than a calculation of pleasures; nothing therefore which is connected with pleasurable sensation, can be foreign to, or ought to be despised in a question of morality.'[19] No wonder Lamb's friend Lloyd complained that the modern philosophy 'rejects the doctrine of obedience', worse still 'rejects all restraints upon the passions . . . and considers the indulgence of them a natural right';[20] no wonder Jane Austen was delighted to find some new acquaintance 'as raffish in his appearance as I would wish every Disciple of Godwin to be'.[21] Yet to us Godwin reveals himself merely as a classic Utilitarian, at one

with Bentham and with Mill in judging an action by its consequences, in identifying goodness with happiness, and happiness
with pleasure:

> Utility . . . is the only basis of moral and political truth . . . .[22]

> Morality is nothing else but a calculation of consequences, and
> an adoption of that mode of conduct which, upon the most
> comprehensive view, appears to be attended with a balance of
> general pleasure and happiness . . . .[23]

> Good is a general name, including pleasure, and the means by
> which pleasure is produced. Evil is a general name, including
> pain, and the means by which pain is produced.[24]

It is this Utilitarianism, of course, which leads Godwin to his
uncompromising conclusions, to his verdict in the famous fire cause.
But that seems precisely to be the trouble. Utilitarianism is
eminently plausible as moral theories go, and has greatly influenced
social and moral attitudes for a century or more. Yet cases can easily
be devised where a Utilitarian will conclude that we should do
something which for most of us goes against what we might call our
moral instincts. The famous fire cause itself is just the sort of example
often invoked as providing an exception to, perhaps even a
refutation of, Utilitarian principles. Not, of course, that Godwin
would be at all disconcerted to find his conclusions leading him into
conflict with commonsense morality: so much the worse for common
sense. But behind this difficulty lies another, more fundamental, and
for Godwin more crucial. We may agree that there is more to be
gained, more value even, in rescuing Fénelon and leaving some
parent to perish, but people just are not like that. We are motivated
not by rational considerations of what might be best for all, all
things considered, but by particular emotions of love and pity. No
man of feeling will be able to do what Godwin and the Principle of
Utility tell him he ought to do. It is, you might say – as Jonathan
Edwards in effect did say – a morality that we ought to adopt if only
we could. But we cannot. So we do not.

That, as it happens, was precisely the criticism that Godwin had
to answer, when Parr's Spital Sermon provoked him finally to a
defence of his doctrines. Yet it was also a criticism he had already
answered, for *Political Justice* had contained arguments to demonstrate that pure impartial justice is more valuable, indeed more
desirable, than any other course of action. A rational man acquainted
with that proof will accordingly desire to do as justice demands; a
rational man will prefer to save Fénelon instead of his chambermaid,

no matter who that chambermaid might be. Rational men – as we are all, in essence, rational men – will be capable of justice, of acting not simply for their own good, or even for the good of particular individuals, but for the good of all.

It is benevolence that holds the key to justice. All his life, from his earliest writings until his last, Godwin rejected 'the grovelling principle, born in France, and which is the curse of modern times, that all human motives are ultimately resolvable into self-love',[25] and advocated instead what he regarded as the traditional British doctrine of Shaftesbury, Butler, Hutcheson and Hume, 'that self-love is not the source of all our passions, but that disinterested benevolence has its seat in the human heart.'[26] As it happens, that grovelling principle was born in England, in the writings of Hobbes, but its return home in Bentham's care was for Godwin the great disaster of contemporary thought. Here, for once, he disagreed with the *philosophes* of France: in replacing benevolence with self-love, they replaced virtue with mere prudence; without benevolence there can be no morality at all.

Benevolence is, first of all, the only truly moral motive: if the aim of morality is to do good unto others, then the desire to do good unto others must be the best of all desires. But more than that, virtue itself requires benevolence. A man might do something that benefits others by mistake, or from some purely selfish motive; his action may be good, but he is not virtuous, not unless he does it *because* it will benefit others: 'The most beneficient action that ever was performed, if it did not spring from the intention of doing good to others, is not of the nature of virtue.'[27] So virtue is impossible without benevolence; if men are ever to be capable of virtue, they must first be capable of benevolence.

At first Godwin had been content to insist that man is not wholly self-interested, that we can and often do act solely for the good of others. The doctrine of self-love treats all action as mere reflex, away from pain and towards pleasure, but once we recognize that voluntary action depends on deliberation and foresight, we can see that there is no reason why our actions might not be based on a concern for others, as they often are. But then Dyson convinced him not just that morality consists in the production of human pleasure, but that men are motivated solely by the prospect of pleasure and the fear of pain. The doctrines are commonly linked, as they are in Bentham and Mill as well as Godwin, because together they mean that no morality which does not appeal to considerations of pleasure can have any appeal, or indeed any relevance, to us, while a morality which promises pleasure and happiness will give us every reason, indeed the only reason, to be moral. But there is, notoriously a problem here. Each man is supposed to be motivated solely by what gives him personally pleasure; but morality is supposed to aim at the pleasure of all men equally. How, then, are we to bridge this gap between the pleasures of one and the pleasures of all? Mill, for one, failed, offering the fallacious argument that 'each man's happiness is a good to that person, and the general happiness, therefore is a good to the aggregate of all persons,' when all too clearly each man may desire his own happiness without anyone desiring the happiness of all. But Godwin succeeded, by the simple expedient of recognizing that among the pleasures which contribute to individual happiness are the pleasures of benevolence, pleasure in the happiness of others.

The argument that Godwin provides in support of this, in *Political Justice*'s second edition, is striking both in itself and as an anticipation of Mill some seventy years later, though both derive ultimately from David Hartley. 'It is', Godwin says, 'merely one case of the phenomena of habit.' 'It is the nature of the passions, speedily to convert what at first were means into ends.'[28] We start out desiring something – money, the happiness of someone else – for the sake of the pleasure it will bring us, but we end up desiring it for its own sake, 'without retrospect to ourselves . . . and willingly submit to torture and death, rather than see injury committed upon the object of our affections.'[29] Benevolence may begin in self-love, the pursuit of pleasure and the avoidance of pain, but it does not always arise out of self-love. It may even come to replace it.

Admittedly, by the end of his life Godwin was no longer prepared to accept this argument, which seemed to concede altogether too much to the doctrine of self-love. For no one could plausibly deny that men act benevolently, sometimes even against their own interests. The argument is rather that if they do, then it is only because it pleases them to. Even the benevolent man is acting from self-love, except that he gets his pleasures from helping others whereas another man gets his from wine or good food. In the last analysis both are equally selfish, though their selfishness takes different forms, one more socially desirable than the other. But Godwin now sees through to the fundamental error on which the whole doctrine rests. Certainly the benevolent man is benevolent because he wants to be, because he will be dissatisfied with himself if he fails to help those whom he can. But this does not mean that he helps them solely to avoid this dissatisfaction, that his reason for benevolence is simply to avoid uneasiness for himself. We have to distinguish between a man's doing as he wants, which is what we mean by acting voluntarily, and his doing it solely for what it will bring him personally, which is what it is to act from self-love.

The advocates of self-love have, very inartificially and unjustly, substituted the abstract definition of a voluntary agent, and made that stand for the motive by which he is prompted to act. It is true that we cannot act without the impulse of desire or uneasiness; but we do not think of that desire and uneasiness; and it is the thing upon which the mind is fixed that constitutes our motive.[30]

Nevertheless, it is not enough to show that man is capable of benevolence. If Godwin is to establish that disinterested justice is possible he has to show, not that benevolence exists, but that benevolence is superior to, stronger than, self-interest or any other desire. The first edition, once again, had been content to argue that benevolence provides an abundant source of happiness, not only because it makes us happy ourselves, but also because it brings in its train friendship, esteem, affection, even prosperity and success: in short, Benevolence Always Pays. But the trouble with this rather too slick and implausible argument is that it seems to mean that we should be benevolent because it is in our interest to be so, and though this may give us some reason to promote the happiness of others, it will do so only so long as their happiness does not conflict with our own. Benevolence will give us reason to be moral only when morality is in our interests, but in Godwin's eyes, to be moral only because it suits us is not to be moral at all.

The second edition, therefore, has a different argument, altogether more impressive and original. It turns on another key point of difference between Godwin and Bentham. For while Bentham regards all pleasures as equally valuable, Godwin, like Mill, sees some as more worthy, or as he puts it, 'more exquisite', than others. This obviously creates a problem, for if pleasure is to be the sole criterion of value, how can one pleasure be judged superior to another? That was why Bentham insisted that pleasures can be assessed only in such terms as how strong they are, how long they last, how quickly they can be attained, or how many people can share in them; any one pleasure will be interchangeable with any other pleasure of the same strength, duration, and the rest. Thus it does not matter, so far as the pleasure goes, what cause excites it, so long as we feel it; what matters is only the 'interesting perception' produced in us. The pleasures of the sadist are not for that reason worse than the pleasures of the saint; they can only be stronger or weaker, longer or shorter. In a celebrated phrase, 'Pleasure for pleasure, pushpin is as good as poetry.'

Yet all this is plausible only so long as we think of pleasure as a sensation distinct from whatever excites it, so that what matters is what we feel, not why we feel it. But it is now well recognized that pleasure is not itself a sensation like a tickle or pins and needles, or even a feeling like feeling drowsy or feeling sick. There are pleasant sensations, but pleasure itself is not a sensation that we might feel, like a pain, in our teeth or neck. Pleasure, in short, is more a state of mind than a state of body. And this means that pleasures cannot be divorced from their objects or causes as pains can: I cannot separate my pleasure that my friend has finally got the job he wanted from the fact that, as I believe, he has got that job. As the object differs, so will the pleasure; pleasures with different objects may be different types of pleasure; and pleasures with very different objects may not be comparable at all, no more than the novels of Tolstoy and the fugues of Bach. There are, then, different sorts of pleasure, different forms that pleasure can take, and once we recognize that fact we can see that even if pleasure alone is good, one kind of pleasure may still be preferable to another.

So Godwin believed, and he attempted to demonstrate that the pleasures of benevolence are not only different from, but superior to, all other pleasures. There is, he suggests, a scale of pleasures, a hierachy of happinesses, and the fact that a man is entirely content at one level need not mean that there is not greater happiness awaiting him at another:

> The man who has once performed an act of exalted generosity, knows that there is no sensation of corporeal or intellectual taste to be compared with this . . . . He ascends to the highest of human pleasures, the pleasures of disinterestedness. He enjoys all the good that mankind possess, and all the good that he perceives to be in reserve for them. No man so truly promotes his own interest as he that forgets it. No man reaps so copious a harvest of pleasure, as he who thinks only of the pleasures of other men.[31]

At first it may seem that Godwin is arguing here that the pleasures of disinterest or benevolence are superior to other pleasures because they carry with them a greater quantity or intensity of enjoyment, and if that were so it would be just the sort of argument that Bentham could accept, if only it were true. Yet I doubt whether Godwin means to claim anything so implausible as that we get more pleasure from contemplating the happiness of others than from anything else; he must surely have heard of envy. Rather the suggestion is that when we do get pleasure from the happiness of others, it is a pleasure of a different sort from the pleasure we get from, say, literature and music, as different as aesthetic pleasure is from the pleasure of eating and drinking. It is, moreover, a pleasure which consists in sharing the joys of others. It is in this sense that the benevolent man 'enjoys all the good that mankind possess, and all the good that he perceives to be in reserve for them . . . . No man reaps so copious a harvest of pleasure as he who thinks only of the pleasures of other men.' It is in this sense that pleasures of benevolence are superior to, more exquisite than, other pleasures, not because they are necessarily more intense or more enduring, but because they are pleasures which incorporate the pleasures of others. They are, we might say, double pleasures, or pleasures twice over.

True, we may also take pleasure in our own pleasure, and for Godwin the delights of self-esteem were also among the highest pleasures. 'The love of fame', he once said, 'is the ape of the best of passions.'[32] But it is benevolence which is truly the best of passions. The pleasures of benevolence are superior to all other pleasures, even those of self-esteem, because they incorporate the pleasure not of one but of many, indeed of everyone. For pleasure is pleasure no matter who enjoys it, and the more who enjoy it the more there is for all to share. There is, therefore, no rational reason for preferring the pleasure of one man to that of another, even when that man is ourself. There is, after all, such a thing as a disinterested pleasure in the happiness of others, and it and it alone can provide us with a motive for genuinely moral conduct, a motive for justice itself:

> The system of disinterested benevolence proves to us that it is possible to be virtuous, and nor merely to talk of virtue; that all which has been said by philosophers and moralists respecting impartial justice is not an unmeaning rant; and that when we call upon mankind to divest themselves of selfish and personal considerations, we call upon them for something which they are able to practice.[33]

It is probable that Godwin himself did not realize just how important this argument was. For it is not simply a proof that men are capable of the disinterested benevolence that justice requires; it is a proof that justice is preferable to, because more desirable than, any other course of action. If that proof can be brought home to the conviction of the understanding, it will infallibly produce a corresponding effect upon the conduct, and men will be capable not merely of justice but of political justice, that ideal state of affairs where every man lives for the good of his fellows, and for that alone. Here, then, is the argument left hanging in our discussion of the omnipotence of truth, an argument on which that proof of perfectibility itself depends.

Suppose, for instance, that the life of Fénelon will be the means of

more happiness to more people than will the life of his chambermaid. The argument has been that saving Fénelon will therefore be
the means of greater pleasure not only to others but also to myself, in
so far as I can take pleasure in their pleasure. A rational man,
uncorrupted by the insidious effects of society and government, will
accordingly recognize that it is more desirable to save Fénelon than to
save his chambermaid, no matter who that chambermaid might be.
If, as a rational man, he accepts that truth then he will also desire it,
for to believe it desirable and to desire it are one and the same thing;
and if he desires it then he will do it, in so far as he is free to do as he
desires. Thus sound reasoning and truth will lead us to save Fénelon
and not the chambermaid. Men reared on truth and reason, as we
all too evidently are not, will be men capable of disinterested
benevolence, of living the life of justice that *Political Justice* describes.

So this is how truth will lead us to justice. Yet it, too, is an
argument undermined by the crucial memorandum of September
1798 –

> It is impossible that we should be continually thinking of the
> whole world, or not confer a smile or a kindness but as we are
> prompted to it by an abstract principle of philanthropy. The
> series of actions of a virtuous man will be the spontaneous
> result of a disposition naturally kind and well-attempered. The
> spring of motion within him will certainly not be a sentiment of
> general utility.[34]

– an argument that would finally collapse three years later, in
Godwin's *Reply to Parr*.

15 ♣ Antonio, a tragedy

> For myself I am almost glad that you have not (if you have not) dramatic talent. How many mortifications and heart aches would that entail on you. Managers to be consulted; players to be humoured; the best pieces that were ever written negatived, and returned to the author's hands. If these are all got over, then you have to encounter the caprice of a noisy, insolent and vulgar-minded audience, whose senseless *non-fiat* shall in a moment turn the labour of a year into nothing.[1]
>
> To Mary Shelley, 1824

♣ If old friendships seemed to die with the century, the new one brought new acquaintances more satisfying and more enduring than any since Mary's death. From time to time Godwin would visit Joseph Fawcett in retirement at Edgware, writing his nondescript pacificist poetry, or he would walk across to Wimbledon to see Horne Tooke, shortly to be elected to parliament by the rottenest borough of them all, Old Sarum – a deserted hillside with an electorate of seven voters – only to have the House decide he was ineligible to sit because he had once, most reluctantly, been a clergyman. But there were much-needed new companions too, like the artist James Northcote, a pupil of Reynolds and painter of the most impressive, least plausible, portrait of Godwin himself, or the ugly silver-tongued Irish advocate John Philpott Curran, a witty and vivid conversationalist and one of the warmest, most spontaneous people that Godwin ever knew, 'dashing, *étourdi*, coarse, vulgar, impatient, fierce, kittenish'.[2] It was Curran who urged Godwin to visit Ireland as soon as he could find the time; it was Curran who patched up the rift with Mrs Inchbald; and it was Curran whom Godwin called 'the sincerest friend I ever had',[3] perhaps because, for all Curran's fine instinct for the telling phrase, the two seem never to have quarrelled. But more significantly still, there were Coleridge, Lamb and Hazlitt.

Coleridge had met Godwin only once before, back in 1794, and had taken an instant dislike, to the man as much as his opinions:

> He appeared to me to possess neither the strength of intellect that discovers truth, or the powers of imagination that decorate falsehood – he talked futile sophisms in jejune language – I like

180

Holcroft a thousand times better, and think him a man of much greater ability.[4]

But with *St Leon* safely at the printers Godwin had gone off for a few days' visit to Berkshire, there to call on Charles Fox living in semi-retirement at St Anne's Hill, and had come home on 30 November 1799, to find that Coleridge had been waiting for him. Four days later Coleridge called again, bringing with him his Bristol friend Humphry Davy, famous now as the inventor of the miners' safety lamp, though Godwin thought it 'a pity such a man should degrade his vast talents to Chemistry'.[5] Coleridge found Godwin more sympathetic now, more amiable, 'no great thing in intellect, but all the better for having been the husband of Mary Wollstonecraft'.[6] At first 'the cadaverous silence of Godwin's children was . . . quite catacombish',[7] especially by comparison with his own 'somewhat too round and boisterous' son Hartley, who dealt old 'Gobwin' a painful rap on the shins with a ninepin. But the two families were so friendly so quickly that they took Christmas dinner together in Godwin's house in the Polygon.

It was, Coleridge later explained, Mackintosh's treachery that had occasioned 'the first turn of my mind towards you, the first movements' of a juster appreciation of your merits',[8] and, bemused like many another by the contrast between Godwin's extreme opinions and reserved personality, he summed his new friend up with a Latin tag from Hobbes: 'Rationem defectus esse defectum rationis': the reason for the flaw, is the flaw in his reason.[9] Still, he found in Godwin a warmth and steadfastness which he too, sinking slowly into drug addiction, was much in need of, and even more satisfying, an unquenchable willingness to listen to him talk. Godwin himself said he preferred Wordsworth for his poetry and Coleridge for his conversation, and it was Coleridge, deep in Spinoza and a religion which identified God with Nature itself, who thus became the last of Godwin's four principal oral instructors, conquering his atheism and teaching him to find a divinity in all things.

In my fourty-fourth year I ceased to regard the name of Atheist with the same complacency I had done for several preceeding years, at the same time retaining the utmost repugnance of understanding for the idea of an intelligent Creator and Governor of the universe, which strikes my mind as the most irrational and ridiculous anthropomorphism. My theism, if such I may be permitted to call it, consists in a reverent and soothing contemplation of all that is beautiful, grand, or mysterious in the system of the universe, and in a certain conscious intercourse and correspondence with the principles of these attributes, without attempting the idle task of developing and defining it – into this train of thinking I was first led by the conversations of S. T. Coleridge.[10]

Once, said Coleridge, Godwin had exclaimed 'God bless him – to use a vulgar phrase', and 'the pedantry of atheism tickled me hugely'.[11] But in September 1800 Godwin would end a letter to him altogether more reverently, with a 'God (the God of Coleridge and Spinoza) bless you both.'

To Godwin's intense disappointment Coleridge left London for Keswick that spring, but they maintained their friendship through regular, affectionate letters, rehearsing all the details of their projects and their families. 'Kisses for Mary and Fanny. God love them!' writes Coleridge in one postscript. 'I wish you would come and look out a house for yourself here. You know "I wish" is privileged to have something silly follow it.'[12] More flattering still, he invited Godwin to be godfather to his new son Derwent, though he probably meant it as something of a joke, for he must have known that Godwin would not support that mode of imposture and coercion practised on children by their parents, which the Christians know as baptism. Nor was Coleridge himself a believer in the custom, and permitted his son to be baptized only when they feared he would die.

It was Coleridge who introduced Godwin also to his childhood friend Charles Lamb. Once Lamb had written his own relatively modest attack on the infamous republican and atheist, and when Coleridge's promised refutation had failed to appear, had written to demand 'Why sleep the Watchman's answers to that *Godwin*?'[13] But when he met the man in February 1800 he, too, was astonished to discover

a well-behaved decent man . . . . quite another guess sort of gentleman from what your Anti-Jacobin Christians imagine him . . . . he has neither horns nor claws, quite a tame creature I assure you. A middle-sized man, both in stature and intellect.[14]

'Pray Mr Lamb', Godwin said to him, referring to the famous caricature in which he himself appeared as a jackass, 'are you Toad or Frog?', and when Coleridge called on Lamb next morning he found Godwin there before him, enjoying breakfast with this effervescent new acquaintance. They seem an improbable pair, the lively and witty Lamb, the pompous and humourless Godwin, yet perhaps that was part of the attraction, for Lamb clearly enjoyed pulling the leg – and once, as Godwin dozed off in the evening, picking the pockets – of his staid but goodhearted crony, 'The Professor' as he liked to call him, who had read more books that were not worth reading than any man in England. Soon they were the closest of friends, as close as Godwin and Holcroft had once been, and though they would sometimes quarrel, Godwin taking offence at Lamb's gentle mockery, Lamb irritated by 'Godwin's way of telling a man he is a fool to his face', Lamb could always win him back with a characteristic mixture of humility and whimsy:

> I repent. Can that God whom they votaries say that thou hast demolished expect more? I did indite a splenetic letter, but did the black Hypocondria never grip *thy* heart, till thou hast take a friend for an enemy? The foul fiend Flibbertigibbet leads me over four inched bridges, to course my own shadow for a traitor. There are certain positions of the moon, under which I counsel thee not to take anything written from this domicile as serious.[15]

Whist was their favourite occupation together, with Lamb – but not Godwin – sometimes drinking himself silly in the process. 'As I was coming to town from the Professor's inspired with rum', he reports quite matter-of-factly, 'I tumbled down and broke my nose.'[16]

It was Godwin in his turn who introduced Lamb to William Hazlitt, to make one more of the formidable group of writers and talkers who centred around the hospitable Elia. Godwin and Hazlitt had first met in September 1794, and the Hazlitt brothers had been among the party which celebrated Thelwall's acquittal at the end of that year. To Godwin, indeed, the sixteen-year-old boy must have seemed almost a ghost of his own youth: son of a Dissenting preacher who had served for a time at Wisbech, Godwin's birthplace; a student at the Dissenting Academy at Hackney which, like that at Hoxton, would soon be closed for being too radical; pupil and protégé of Godwin's own tutor, Andrew Kippis; and shortly to abandon the ministry for a career of writing. And the parallelism would continue, for they were in their way two of a kind, equally devoted to their principles – 'I would give up anything sooner than an abstract proposition', Hazlitt said once – equally awkward in company, equally lacking in small talk, equally opinionated, equally given to stormy outbursts. But if Godwin had grown benign and somewhat stuffy, the more temperamental Hazlitt seemed to his friends more than a little crazed, attacking each topic with a vehemence and intensity that Godwin entirely lacked. 'He is ready only on reflection: dangerous only at the rebound . . . .' complained Hazlitt of Godwin. 'He must make a career before he flings himself, armed, upon the enemy, or he is sure to be unhorsed. Or he resembles an eight-day clock that must be wound up long before it can strike.'[17]

Among the subjects to which Hazlitt regularly devoted his talents was Godwin himself. He had called at the Polygon in August 1799 with his friend Crabb Robinson, who would leave a very different portrait of 'the worn-out philosopher who had survived his philosophy', and within a year Hazlitt had become something of an acolyte, Godwin something of a patron. It was Godwin who persuaded Joseph Johnson to publish Hazlitt's first book, a philosophical essay on benevolence called *The First Principles of Human Action*, and it was Hazlitt who would give us our most striking account of Godwin and his fame, his strengths and his weaknesses, his successes and his failures. Yet it was always a stiff and slightly distant acquaintance, with Hazlitt both fascinated and disconcerted by the extraordinary contradictions of the man, the famous writer he read with such exhilaration, the dreary pedant he actually spoke to. 'He is shocking on paper and tame in reality . . .' was Hazlitt's verdict on this armchair radical.

He is naturally a cold and speculative character, and indulges in certain metaphysical extravagances as an agreeable exercise for the imagination, which alarms persons of grosser temperament, but to which he attaches no political consequences whatever.

And the contradictions run deeper still:

He writes against himself. He has written against matrimony and been twice married. He has scouted all the common-place duties, and yet he is a good husband and a kind father. He is a strange composition of contrary qualities. He is a cold formalist, and full of ardour and enthusiasm of mind, dealing in magnificent projects and petty cavils; naturally dull, and brilliant by dint of study; pedantic and playful; a dry logician, and a writer of romances.[18]

It was an ambivalence that would find its most fulsome, most ambiguous expression some five-and-twenty years later, in Hazlitt's glowing tribute in *The Spirit of the Age*.

With *St Leon* out of the way Godwin was concentrating on a new venture, not as yet the promised *First Principles of Morals*, but that was not the only work projected in the memorandum of September 1798. There would also be *Two Dissertations on the Reasons and Tendency of Religious Opinion*; a novel 'in which I should try the effect of my particular style of writing upon common incidents and the embarrassments of lovers'; and finally, 'five or six tragedies'.[19] As it happened Godwin never wrote a *First Principles of Morals*; its place was taken by the *Reply to Parr* of 1801. Nor did he write the *Dissertations on Religions Opinion*; their place was taken, perhaps, by the posthumous *Essays*. The novel was hardly *St Leon*, which he was already writing, but probably the 1805 *Fleetwood*. But alas, there were tragedies.

Godwin had started one back in 1790, and he had been working on another, called 'Alonzo', when Mary died. In September 1798 he had sought out his former acquaintance Sheridan, proprietor of the theatre at Drury Lane, and the following month 'Alonzo' became *Antonio*, a task that would carry him through 1799 and into the new century. The theme of 'Alonzo' had been the betrayal of friendship, but as Godwin painstakingly wrote and rewrote his play its content changed, and it became instead the story of an essentially noble figure destroyed, like Falkland in *Caleb Williams*, by an erroneous sense of honour without which, Antonio says, 'no kindred, no affection can survive'. Antonio, a hero home from the wars, discovers that his sister Helena, who had been betrothed by their dying father to his friend and captured comrade Roderigo, has meanwhile fallen in love with, and married, one Don Gussman. But Antonio regards her as married in spirit to Roderigo and therefore an adultress, and when he fails to persuade the King to annul the marriage he has Helena imprisoned in a convent. Gussman challenges Antonio, but Helena is rescued by another brother and in the final confrontation declares herself prepared to return to the convent, rather than cause bloodshed amongst those she loves. But the King, infuriated by Antonio's continual arrogance, orders him into exile instead, whereupon he bursts through his guards and slays his sister, who dies rejoicing at this solution to all their problems.

Not the most promising material, but Godwin had reason to feel confident. Perhaps *Political Justice* had scorned that 'absurd and vicious cooperation' in which men come forward 'formally to repeat words and ideas that are not their own', but the Sandemanians had been sufficiently un-Calvinist to approve of the stage, and Godwin was always a regular theatre-goer. He had tried his hand at a work of philosophy, a novel, a book of essays, a biography, then another novel, and only the *Enquirer* had been anything less than a sensation. His novels, indeed, were famous for their dramatic plots, their scenes of confrontation, their dialogue: *Caleb Williams* had already been the source of two plays and would inspire a third; *St Leon* would provide the basis for two more. And he was used enough to vetting the scripts of others: Holcroft, Mrs Inchbald, Amelia Alderson, Mary Wollstonecraft. How could a play of his own fail to be a triumph – unless, perhaps, in these altered times the author's name alone would be enough to damn it?

Still, the going proved slow and arduous, and *Antonio* cost Godwin as much effort as anything he ever wrote. His tendency was always to expand on what he had already written, to add further explanation and detail, and each time he revised the text it grew longer, and had to be revised again. But Godwin also lacked any ear for poetry, all sense of stage-craft. Such action as there is, the final confrontation apart, takes place in the wings, leaving the stage free for philosophical debate between the principal characters, carried on in the blankest of blank verse. His prose, once lean and elegant, grew ever more verbose as he grew older, and the pomposity never far away in the novels took over completely when he turned to tragic declamation. But he trusted in his ideas to pull him through, as they had done before.

In October 1799, dining with Godwin, Curran and Mrs Inchbald at the home of his actor-manager John Kemble, Sheridan had announced that he was prepared to accept the piece as it stood. But Godwin, as ever, thought he could make some small improvements here and there, and he was making them still the following summer, when he broke off to pay the visit to Ireland that Curran had been urging on him ever since they met, the one and only trip he ever took outside the mainland of Britain. In Dublin as Curran's guest Godwin found himself surrounded by remembrances of his late wife: her two sisters, Eliza and Everina, who ran a respectable school for all that they were Socinians, as he had once been, and denied the divinity of Christ; Hugh Skeys, who had been husband to Fanny Blood, the childhood friend after whom Mary named her first daughter; and, most remarkably of all, the formidable Lady Mountcashell who, as Margaret Kingsborough, had once had Mary Wollstonecraft for a governess. Always flattered by an invitation to dine with the aristocracy, Godwin struck up a ready friendship with the eccentric Countess, and they wrote to each other regularly about the rearing of their children. Later they would become closer still, bound together by memories of Mary.

Godwin was enjoying himself hugely, grateful to find himself still a celebrity somewhere, but he was anxious to get back to his tragedy, and worried for the children he had left behind in the care of Marshall and his housekeeper, Louisa Jones. There was a problem about Louisa too, for somehow she had become entangled with Godwin's tempestuous young friend George Dyson, the most shadowy of Godwin's four principal oral instructors. Their friendship, dating back to 1788, had been stormy even by his standards, their regular discussions interspersed with equally regular disagreements: 'Dyson sups, talk of happiness'; 'Dyson calls, talk of insult'. 'I know you now', Godwin had written to him once, 'and detest your

venom-fraught vices, almost as much as I love your talents;'[20] or
again

> You have been one of my prime favorites, and whatever may be
> the vicissitudes of your character, the deviousness of your
> conduct, or the fermentations of your uncontrollable passions,
> they will be watched over by me with affectionate anxiety;[21]

and yet again

> My hours too are precious to me. These are the last you will
> ever rob me of. My esteem and affection pale if not supported
> by the esteem and affection of others. Of your sentiments I no
> longer entertain any doubt. Farewel then. Send me a peniten-
> tiary letter if you have not destroyed it that in a too warm
> moment I addresst to you and forget my existence.[22]

At dinner on 29 June, just before Godwin caught the Holyhead
coach for the first leg of his journey to Ireland, there has been 'talk of
Dyson' between himself, Marshall, Louisa and Hannah Godwin.
Four nights later Dyson broke into the Polygon and sat himself
down to write a jumbled, maudlin, ill-tempered note, addressed 'To
the World' but clearly directed more immediately at Miss Jones, its
only coherent passage a complaint that 'I have been from a
superfluous regard to others frustrated of a plan that I shall never be
ashamed of but ever please myself in.' Dyson later wrote Godwin a
mortified apology, barely recognizable as the work of the same man,
insisting that this 'lawless and disgraceful behaviour', 'the insane
procedure you have a right to deem so offensive and injurious,
originated in a tumult of intoxication.' But when we hear of him
next, a year later, he is living at Bath, and living with Louisa Jones,
'I have felt for a very long time that I ought to have told you my
feelings', she wrote to Godwin, 'but I have lived in the hope of
overcoming them the struggle I have had with myself has been very
severe indeed and it would be impossible to convey to you the
emotions that have by turn oppressed and agitated me.'[23] (I can see
no reason to suspect, as some have suggested, that these feelings
were directed at Godwin himself. But there is no mistaking Louisa's
anguish when he told her she could no longer see the children.)
Louisa had been, in effect, the mother of his daughters, the only
mother Mary had ever known, but Godwin angrily forbade her any
further contact with the children. With Dyson, too, it was an end to
their acquaintance. 'Dyson I have known long,' Godwin wrote to
Coleridge. 'I have derived from his intercourse many advantages,
and many painful experiences; he has a mind uncommonly endowed, though distorted and unnatural; if I know any human being
I know that man; but I have done with him.'[24]

It was on 19 August that Papa came back again as he had promised, to 'see the Polygon across two fields from the trunks of the trees at Camden Town. Will Mary and Fanny come to meet me?'[25] *Antonio* was submitted again to Sheridan, who instructed Kemble to include it in the winter season. But Kemble was far from happy. He began to despair whether he would ever receive a final version of the script, the parts that he had seen made him despair even more, and when he excused himself from playing the title role – because the part was too long and 'altogether unsuitable for the state of his lungs', and 'the actions of the character . . . not justifiable upon any principle of ethics or personal prudence'[26] – Godwin went over his head and protested to Sheridan. This rank-pulling succeeded, and Kemble wrote resignedly 'I wish you success with all my Heart, and I will undertake Antonio – I fear the Event, but you shall not want the assistance, you are so good as to say I might render you.'[27] He meant not a word of it.

So, coming ready or not, *Antonio, or the Soldier's Return* made its debut at 6.15 on the evening of 13 December 1800, with the reluctant Kemble in the main part, his sister, Sarah Siddons, as Helena, and a Prologue and Epilogue by Charles Lamb, after Coleridge had declined the honour. Godwin had thought it politic to keep his own involvement secret, and a playwright friend of Coleridge, John Tobin, had attended rehearsals in the hope that the play would be thought to be his. In fact the Drury Lane playbill carried no author's name at all, but one copy has survived, with the words 'by Godwin . . . damned with Universal Consent' scrawled across it. The writing is Lamb's, and it is Lamb who tells the tale best, in his essay 'The Old Actors':[28]

> G. satiate with visions of political justice (possibly not to be realised in our time), or willing to let the sceptical worldlings see, that his anticipations of the future did not preclude a warm sympathy for men as they are and have been – wrote a tragedy . . . . Great expectations were formed. A philosopher's first play was a new era. The night arrived. I was favoured with a seat in an advantageous box between the author and his friends M. [Marshall]. G. sate cheerful and confident. In his friend M's looks, who had perused the manuscript, I read some terror . . . . The first act swept by, solemn and silent. It went off, as G. assured M., exactly as the opening of a piece – the protasis – should do. The cue of the spectators was to be mute . . . . Applause hitherto would be impertinent. Silent attention was the effect all-desirable. Poor M. acquiesced – but in his honest friendly face I could discern a working which told how much

more acceptable the plaudit of a single hand (however misplaced) would have been than all this reasoning. The second
act (as in duty bound) rose a little in interest . . . and the
audience was most complacently attentive. The protasis, in fact,
was scarcely unfolded. The interest would warm in the next
act, against which a special event was provided. M. wiped his
cheek, flushed with a friendly perspiration . . . He had once or
twice during this act joined his palms in a feeble endeavour to
elicit a sound – they emitted a solitary noise without an echo –
there was no deep to answer to his deep. G. repeatedly begged
him to be quiet. The third act at length brought on the scene
which was to warm the piece progressively to the final flaming
forth of the catastrophe. A philosophic calm settled upon the
clear brow of G. as it approached. The lips of M. quivered. A
challenge was held forth upon the stage, and there was promise
of a fight. The pit roused themselves on this extraordinary
occasion, and, as their manner is, seemed disposed to make a
ring – when suddenly Antonio . . . baulks his humour, and the
pit's reasonable expectation at the same time, with some
speeches out of the new philosophy against duelling. The
audience was here fairly caught – their courage was up, and on
the alert – a few blows, *ding dong*, as R . . . s [Frederick
Reynolds, whose son of the same name was a close friend of
Godwin's at the end of his life] the dramatist afterwards
expressed it to me, might have done the business – when their
most exquisite moral sense was suddenly called in to assist the
mortifying negation of their own pleasure. They could not
applaud for disappointment; they would not condemn for
morality's sake. The interest stood stone still . . . . It was
Christmas time, and the atmosphere furnished some pretext for
asthmatic affections. One began to cough – his neighbour
sympathised with him – till a cough became epidemical. But
when from being half-artificial in the pit, the cough got fright-
fully naturalised among the fictitious persons of the drama; and
Antonio himself (albeit it was not set down in the stage
directions) seemed more intent upon relieving his own lungs
than the distresses of the author and his friends, – then G. 'first
knew fear'; and mildly turning to M., intimated that he had not
been aware that Mr K. laboured under a cold; and that the
performance might possibly have been postponed with advantage for some nights further – still keeping the same serene
countenance, while M. sweat like a bull . . .

In fact it was Kemble, 'starched out in a ruff which no one could dispute, and in most irreproachable mustachios', who had put 'the deadly extinguisher on the play', just as he had once done, equally deliberately, with the first performances of Colman's *Iron Chest*. He had never welcomed Godwin's tragedy; as a manager he knew where the fault lay, in its unrelieved verbiage; and as an actor he knew how to emphasize it, by an equally unrelieved delivery:

> In vain the action was accelerated, while the acting stood still. From the beginning John had taken his stand; had wound himself up to an even tenor of stately declamation, from which no exigence of dialogue or person would make him swerve for an instance. To dream of his rising with the scene (a common trick of tragedians) was preposterous; for from the outset he had planted himelf, as upon a terrace, or an eminence vastly above the audience, and kept that sublime level to the end . . . . The procession of verbiage stalked on through four or five acts, no one venturing to predict what would come of it, when towards the winding up of the latter, Antonio, with an irrelevancy that seemed to stagger Helena herself – for she had been coolly arguing the point of honour with him – suddenly whips out a poignard, and stabs his sister to the heart. The effect was, as if a murder had been committed in cold blood. The whole house rose up in clamorous indignation demanding justice. The feeling rose far above hisses. I believe at that instant, if they could have got him, they would have torn the unfortunate author to pieces. Not that the act itself was so exorbitant, or of a complexion different from what they themselves would have applauded upon another occasion in a Brutus or an Appius – but for want of attending to Antonio's *words*, which palpably led to the expectation of no less dire an event, instead of being sedeuced by his *manner*, which seemed to promise a sleep of a less alarming nature than it was his due to inflict upon Helena, they found themselves betrayed into an accompliceship of murder.

And *Antonio*, a tragedy, was never performed again.

For all his recent troubles Godwin had grown accustomed to success. *Antonio* was his first out-and-out failure since embarking on *Political Justice* ten years before. But why had he abandoned the novel, where he had proved so spectacular, and tried his hand so disastrously on the stage?

> Are poets so *few* in this age that He must write poetry? Is morals a subject so exhausted that he must quit that line? Is

the metaphysic well (without a bottom) drained dry? If I can guess at the wicked pride of the Professor's heart, I should take a shrewd wager that he disdains ever again to dip his pen into Prose.[29]

But the real answer was very different, the answer to so many of the questions that vex Godwin's later years: not pride, money. Writing for the theatre was the most rewarding writing of all: when Coleridge's *Remorse* ran for twenty nights in 1813 it made him, he said, almost three times as much as all his previous work put together. What Godwin sought from *Antonio* was not fame as a dramatist – the work was anonymous after all – but cash in hand, with which to meet his ever-more-pressing debts.

Once he had been able to live frugally but comfortably enough by the produce of his pen, sharing what little surplus he had with Marshall or his family in Norfolk. But Mary Wollstonecraft had changed that too, as she had changed everything. First there had been two homes to keep up, and her debts to settle; then there were her children to support, and the household that they generated. Now Godwin was living as a man of independent means, without either the means or the independence. More and more he came to rely on his wealthy friend Tom Wedgwood, for loans and outright subsidies. In July of 1797 Wedgwood had suggested to Godwin a school for gifted children, using special teaching techniques designed for their distinctive needs and abilities. The advisers would be himself and Godwin, Holcroft, Horne Tooke, a medical friend called Beddoes, and anyone else Godwin might care to suggest; for teachers they could try George Dyson, and perhaps Wordsworth and Coleridge, whom Wedgwood had heard well of but had never met. Whatever interest Godwin had had in the scheme had died with Mary Wollstonecraft, but when Wedgwood met Coleridge the following year they discovered a common interest in laudanum and other more exotic drugs. So it fell to Wedgwood, in association with his younger brother Josiah, to rescue Coleridge just as he seemed forced to enter the ministry, by providing him with a lifetime annuity of £150 so that he might devote himself to philosophy. Ironically it was a subsidy that Godwin had deserved, and would need, even more than Coleridge, but pride and over-confidence had cost him the opportunity. Nevertheless, Godwin knew that Wedgwood would always help in any way he could, by cashing the advances on *St Leon* or advancing still more on the prospects of *Antonio*. And if he borrowed from Wedgwood, nervously promising repayment the moment his tragedy appeared, he was still as generous as ever with his own. His attitude, no less than Wedgwood's, was that of *Political*

Justice, that personal wealth must always be at the disposal of he who has most need, or can benefit most.

Godwin's other friends knew well enough the significance of *Antonio*'s failure. In Keswick Coleridge

> received the newspaper with a beating heart, and laid it down with a heavy one. But cheerily friend! it is worth something to have learnt what will not please . . . . There is a paint, the first coating of which, put on paper, becomes a dingy black, but the second time turns to a bright gold colour. So I say – Put on a second coating, friend![30]

Holcroft, in Germany, remembering his own recent disappointments, was sure it was not the play 'but William Godwin who was brought to the bar, and not to be tried, but to be condemned'.[31] But Lamb, closer at hand, recognized that they were damned. He discovered that Godwin had planned a celebration dinner, and had made a list of books he hoped to buy but which 'thy untragedy-favoured purse could never answer':

> The Professor is £500 ideal money out of pocket by this failure, besides £200 he would have got for the copyright, and the Professor is never much beforehand with the world; what he gets is all by the sweat of his brow and the dint of his brain, for the Professor, though a sure man is also a slow.[32]

At supper after the performance Lamb had tried to salvage something from the wreck, and agreed to suggest some improvements, but he later 'joined his true friends in advising him to give it up'.[33] But Godwin, with 'a kind of *blue sickness* about the eyelids', would not, could not, and in January published the text of his tragedy, under his own name.

His enemies, of course, had as much fun with the publication as they had had with the performance. 'The most worthless production, we think, that ever came before us in our critical capacity,'[34] sneered the *British Critic*, discovering no evidence of human perfectibility in Godwin's literary progress, and wondering whether his verse might not be the work of the famous mechanical plough. But the *Anti-Jacobin* was closer to the mark: the play, it said, was 'completely coughed down'; its publication could be attributed only 'to the vanity or poverty of its author'.[35] And as if that were not enough, Godwin made the mistake of following old habit, and sent a copy to Mrs Inchbald. 'I most sincerely wish you joy', she responded with ill-disguised enjoyment,

> of having produced a work which will protect you from being classed with the successful dramatists of the present day, but which will hand you down to posterity among the honoured few

who, during the past century, have totally failed in writing for the stage.[36]

His first impulse, even so, was 'to sit down and write another, in which I should carefully avoid all the errors which contributed with certain external causes to decide the fate of my piece.'[37] Coleridge, attempting to paint a bright colour over *Antonio*'s fate, had suggested an Arabian theme as a suitably 'glowing subject', and within two months Godwin had finished a draft of 'Mizza', later renamed 'Abbas, King of Persia', for Coleridge's approval. But Coleridge dared not send all his criticisms, and those that he did send elicited a hurt reply from the author. Torn between the need to keep his identity secret, and the need to let the anonymous 'two men in buckram' who read scripts for the theatre know that this was the work not of some mere novice but a writer of reputation. Godwin sent the text twice to Drury Lane in 1801. It is 'not quite as complete as I would wish' he told Kemble; 'it is too long',[38] but he needed some encouragement before attempting a revision. But though Kemble offered to look at a second draft, Godwin had lost all heart. Clearly he wanted somebody, anybody, to tell him it was worth proceeding with. But no one would.

16 ♣ The best qualities of a reply

I had heard a thousand times, and I believed, that whoever gave his speculations on general questions to the public with fairness and temper, was a public benefactor; and I must add, that I have never yet heard the fairness or temper of my publication called into doubt. If my doctrines were formed to abide the test of scrutiny, it was well: if they were refuted, I should still have occasion to rejoice, in having procured to the public the benefit of that refutation, of so much additional disquisition and knowledge. Unprophetic as I was, I rested in perfect tranquillity, and suspected not that I should be dragged to public odium, and made an example to deter all future enquirers from the practice of unshackled speculation.[1]

Reply to Parr, 1801

♣ It says something for Godwin's determination, or his desperation, that he should turn so rapidly from one disastrous tragedy to another – and then, three years later, to yet another. But more surprising still, his next publication would be one of his finest achievements, rivalling the *Memoirs* in elegance, second in importance only to *Political Justice*. At first, secure in the conviction that he had spoken the plain truth and that truth, when plainly spoken, must ultimately be victorious, he had thought he could ignore the mounting attacks on his person and his principles. As soon as he had finished *St Leon* and *Antonio* and set his finances in order he could go back to his true vocation, to philosophy and the projected *First Principles of Morals* which would explain and defend the change in his opinions. But reeling under the double impact of the Spital Sermon and the failure of *Antonio*, Godwin changed his mind. For a time he thought of writing to Parr and answering his charges point by point, as Parr had answered him, and perhaps publishing their correspondence. But once over the initial shock Godwin decided instead to produce a pamphlet of his own, an answer to all his critics, personal and philosophical, and an account of the changes in his theories since *Political Justice*. These *Thoughts Occasioned by a Perusal of Dr Parr's Spital Sermon*, known more briefly as the *Reply to Parr*, appeared in June 1801. It was not quite the *First Principles of Morals*, but it was the nearest there would be.

With almost one accord Godwin's critics – Coleridge, Green,

Proby, Hall, Parr – had fastened on his rejection of the domestic affections as the crucial flaw in the entire system, as subversive of genuine morality as Godwin, on his side, regarded those same affections. Disinterested benevolence, impartial justice, are noble ideals, but for mere men impossible ones; their duties must be more specific, more limited. 'The welfare of the whole system of being must be allowed to be *in itself*, the object of all others the most worthy of being pursued,' agreed Robert Hall, but

> to weak, short-sighted mortals Providence has assigned a
> sphere of agency, less grand and extensive indeed, but better
> suited to their limited powers, by implanting certain *affections*
> which it is their duty to cultivate, and suggesting particular
> rules to which they are bound to conform.[2]

For Proby too, 'It appertains to the Deity alone, to act for the general good of mankind; it is he alone who can know what is capable of best administering to that end.' Man with his limited intelligence, limited abilities and limited sympathies must confine his behaviour to that small area 'where he is sure of being able to do some good',[3] the area of those he knows and understands best. The very text of Parr's sermon had been 'As we have, therefore, opportunity, let us do good unto all men, especially unto them who are of the household of faith', the point being that we have most opportunity to do good, not unto all men generally, but unto those who are of the household of faith.

Moreover the objection was not, as Sydney Smith summarized it, that Godwin thought that 'all the crew ought to have the *general* welfare of the ship so much at heart, that no sailor should ever pull any *particular* rope, or hand any *individual* sail';[4] that had never been Godwin's opinion. Rather, the objection was that without a concern for specific individuals there could never be a concern for people in general: the limited, the private and domestic affections, are in fact the means by which we arrive at a concern for all mankind. That, it seems, was to have been the nub of Coleridge's unwritten 'Reply to Godwin'. 'Let us beware of that proud philosophy', he had warned his audience within a month of his complimentary sonnet,

> which affects to inculcate Philanthropy while it denounces every
> home-born feeling by which it is produced and nurtured. The
> parental and filial duties discipline the Heart and prepare it for
> the love of all Mankind. The intensity of private attachments
> encourages, not prevents universal Benevolence.[5]

The physiologist and pioneer psychologist Hartley, whom Coleridge so admired that he gave the name to his eldest son, had argued, like the stimulus-response theorists after him, that all conduct is built up from a series of associations based on immediate experience. And so, Coleridge concluded, the love of mankind must also be built up, step by associative step, from the love of particular individuals. *Political Justice*, he said later in 1795, is therefore

> a book which builds without a foundation, proposes an end without establishing the means, and discovers a total ignorance of that obvious Fact in human nature, that in virtue and in knowledge we must be infants and be nourished with milk in order that we may be men and eat strong meat.[6]

'Extended benevolence is the last and most perfect fruit of the private affections,' said Robert Hall; 'so that to reap the former from the extinction of the latter is to oppose the means to the end', a form of mental (did he mean to say moral?) parricide. But it was a point that Thomas Green made most elegantly of all, with the aid of a quotation from the close of Pope's *Essay on Man*:

> God loves from whole to parts: but human soul
> Must rise from individual to the whole.
> Self love but serves the virtuous mind to wake,
> As the small pebble stirs the peaceful lake;
> The centre moved, a circle strait succeeds,
> Another still, and still another spreads;
> Friend, parent, neighbour first it will embrace;
> His country next; and next all human race.

Where, then, had Godwin gone wrong? 'From a mistaken pursuit of simplicity', suggested Hall;

> from a wish to construct a moral system without leaving sufficient scope for the infinite variety of moral phenomena and mental combination; in consequence of which its advocates were induced to place virtue *exclusively* in some *one disposition* of mind; and since the passion for the general good is undoubtedly the *noblest* and most extensive of all others, when once it is resolved to place virtue in any *one thing*, there remained little room to hesitate which should be preferred.

But Thomas Green, the most acute of Godwin's critics, saw more deeply into the matter. Godwin's mistake, he suggests, is to confuse the effect of morality with its cause, to think that because virtuous conduct will result in the general good, virtuous conduct must therefore consist in acting for the general good: 'The end of parental affection is the preservation of helpless infancy. But do we love our children on that account? The ultimate end here too is the general good, but does it form any part of the incitement?'[7] And behind that error, continues Green, lies another, still more fundamental, the mistake of trying to ground morality in reason:

> Our moral sentiments are original principles of action; and cannot, therefore, as such, be derived from reason. We do not merely *believe* an action to be of a certain description called moral or immoral; we *approve* or *disapprove* it as such; and this sentiment of approbation and disapprobation has a positive influence on human conduct. But approbation and disapprobation are emotions of the mind; and cannot, consequently, originate from reason.

That was indeed the crux, the essential difference between Godwin and his critics. They believed that man is governed by his feelings, and that moral conduct must therefore be grounded in emotion, in the domestic affections in particular. But he believed that truth and only truth has an indisputable hold over conduct, and that morality must therefore be grounded in reason. Indeed *Political Justice* had arguments to demonstrate that that was so: an argument to show that men are motivated by their opinions not their feelings, by reason not by passion; and argument to show that rational men will value impartial benevolence over all other things, even a concern for themselves and their families. They were arguments to which Godwin's critics did not ever address themselves, but perhaps they had no need. For they were arguments that Godwin, under the influence of Hume and Mary Wollstonecraft, had himself abandoned.

The *Reply to Parr*, accordingly, is not concerned to rebut these criticisms; it is, if anything, concerned to accept them, to draw out the implications of Godwin's discovery of the domestic affections, and show that the principles of justice are unaffected. It was a change of heart for which Thomas Green even claimed some credit. 'I flatter myself with having been instrumental in a little humanizing him', he wrote after reading *St Leon*; 'but the volcanic and blasphemous spirit still peeps, occasionally, through a flimsy disguise.'[8] For what Green could not understand was how Godwin could think that the conclusions of *Political Justice* might survive the destruction of its premises. That was what Godwin had still to explain.

So consider, once again, the case of Fénelon and his chambermaid, or less sensationally, his valet. There are, Godwin says, three points that need to be emphasized more than they had been originally. One is that it is a mistake to think that

> if the father is saved, this will be the effort of passion, but if Fénelon is saved, the act will arise only from cool, phlegmatic,

arithmetical calculation. No great and honourable deed can be atchieved, but from passion. If I save the life of Fénelon, unprompted to do so by an ardent love of the wondrous excellence of the man, and a sublime eagerness to atchieve and secure the welfare and improvement of millions, I am a monster, unworthy of the appellation of a man . . .[9]

Another is that even if I do infringe the principle of utility and save my father instead, 'few persons even upon that supposition will be disposed severely to blame my conduct', springing as it does from 'a feeling pregnant with a thousand good and commendable actions'.[10] But the remaining point is most important of all, for a 'consideration of the domestic affections . . . does essentially modify the question of utility, and affect the application of the criterion of virtue'.[11]

Here, too, the ground had been laid in the unpublished memorandum of 1798:

The benefits we can confer upon the world are few, at the same time that they are in their nature, either petty in their moment, or questionable in their results. The benefits we can confer upon those with whom we are closely connected are of great magnitude, or continual occurrence.[12]

That in itself is enough to ensure that justice requires us to pay more attention to those closest to us than to strangers. But Godwin is now prepared to carry the point further, by distinguishing between the good to come from a particular action and the good to come from action of some general type. It may be that on this occasion more good will come from not saving my father, but in general more good results from protecting our families than from rushing to the assistance of strangers. So it might be better, all things considered, to save my father, and so help establish a habit which in the long run will do more good:

The action, viz. the saving of the life of Fénelon, is to be set against the habit, and it will come to be seriously considered, whether . . . it will contribute most to the mass of human happiness, that I should act upon the utility of the case separately taken, or should refuse to proceed in violation of a habit, which is fraught with a series of successive utilities.[13]

But if Godwin has changed his mind about the domestic affections, he has not changed his mind about justice. Even if I can usually do more good to those I know best, even if I can be surer of doing good to my father than to a stranger, it may nevertheless be clear, all things considered, that on this occasion more good will come from saving Fénelon and leaving my parent to perish. In that case the right thing to do will be to save Fénelon after all, even if we would not blame someone who prefers to save his father. The genuinely moral man must temper his concern for particular individuals with an equal concern for all mankind; he must bear in mind the good of all as well as the good of those dearest to him:

> I would desire to love my children; yet I would not desire so to love them, as to forget that I have what we were accustomed to call, before the hoarse and savage cry of Jacobinism! had frightened all moral language from its propriety, *higher duties*.[14]

The famous fire cause might be more complex than Godwin had first presented it, but utility, the benefit of all, is still the ultimate test of morality; and justice, utility, the benefit of all, may still require that Fénelon be saved.

Nevertheless the question is not whether I ought to save Fénelon, but whether I will. The proof of perfectibility, and of political justice itself, had depended on the claim that people can be brought to do as justice demands, whether it be to save my father or to save Fénelon. This is where the argument for disinterested benevolence is crucial, to convince rational men that the most desirable course of action will always be to do as justice requires. But that argument, too, had been swept away by the memorandum of 1798: if man is motivated not by 'an abstract principles of philanthropy' or 'a sentiment of general utility', but by 'motives peculiar to him as an individual', then there is no longer any guarantee that he will act in accordance with justice. Instead of relying on sound reasoning and truth we will have to rely on personal feeling, and as the famous fire cause itself demonstrates, these may sometimes conflict with justice.

Not that Godwin here rejects, or so much as mentions, his argument that the pleasures of disinterested benevolence are the highest of human pleasures; in all probability he would have accepted that argument still. But in its place he introduces a distinction, directed at Parr in particular, 'between the motive from which a virtuous action is to arise, and the criterion by which it is to be determined to be virtuous',[15] between the reason I perform an action and the reason it is right. This, he says, is his only difference with Parr, that he as a philosopher has stressed the criterion, while Parr as a preacher has stressed the motive, though

> this is not the first time in which the well-known maxim has been illustrated, that 'the smaller is the space by which a man is divided from you in opinion, with the more fury and intemperance will he often contend about it.'[16]

Yet Godwin was wrong to believe that this distinction did not affect the system of *Political Justice*: it was, in effect, the very distinction that Green had invoked against him, between the effects of moral conduct and its causes. Once he had argued that to get a man to do something it was enough to demonstrate that it is right; but now he concedes that what gets a man to do something may be different from what makes it right. Justice or utility is what determines whether my action is moral; but something else is needed, some feeling or emotion, to ensure that the action is performed. And to concede that is, for the author of *Political Justice*, to concede everything; it is to concede that truth will not lead us to justice. Justice may demand that we save Fénelon but a mere man might recognize that fact, and still prefer to save his father.

So, humanly speaking we may be incapable of justice, and therefore of political justice. When Dr Parr had pointed out in his scholarly way that Johnathan Edwards had not denied that the private affections were virtuous, only that they embodied *true* virtue, Godwin could only mock such pedantry: 'If any person is either amused or instructed by Dr Parr's distinction between virtue and true virtue . . . I confess I have too much humanity to be willing to disturb his enjoyments.'[17] Yet he was himself conceding the point that a morality of true virtue and absolute justice may be a morality too pure and too perfect for mere human beings. A gap has opened between what justice demands and what men will do, and into that gap tumble all the conclusions, both moral and political, of *Political Justice*. In the end Coleridge was right, when he protested that Godwin had proclaimed an end without establishing the means.

The *Reply to Parr* stands, even so, as one of Godwin's most impressive works, not so much for its reply to Parr, nor even for the much more satisfying and successful reply to Malthus, which we have yet to consider, as for its tone of noble detachment. It was the derision of Mackintosh and Parr that most got under his skin, but for all their provocation Godwin refuses to reply in kind, disdaining to 'dwell on the rabble of scurrilities', all those 'novels of buffoonery and scandal'. Instead he meets the objections to his opinions with measured counter-argument and an honest reappraisal of his original doctrines; he rebuts the personal attacks with dignity, and without a trace of the petulance and self-pity that so often marred his quarrels with his friends. Carefully, impassively, he describes how the tide of reaction had risen until it engulfed both himself and his works, despite the fact that 'I sought no overt effects; I abhorred all tumult; I entered my protest againt revolutions.' He had advanced arguments which in his innocence he had expected to be judged as arguments, and instead had found himself represented 'as a wretch, who only wanted the power, in order to prove himself as infernal as Robespierre'.[18]

Nor was this mistreatment simply a result of the excesses in France. For his enemies had waited until the crises had passed, until 1797, when the radical movement in England had disintegrated and France seemed headed for a form of government not too different from that found elsewhere in Europe, before mounting their attack on the New Philosophy and 'its chief (or shall I say its most voluminous?) English adherent'. And why? Because some who had expected the bursting of a glorious sunshine but found only a sky growing darker and more unpromising had then been anxious to make their peace with institutions and practices they had once rejected, 'nor would they chaffer too obstinately, though it should be necessary to make a sacrifice or two at the shrine of the divinity against whose worship they had too irreverently railed.'[19] But Godwin reserved his deepest complaint for him who of all people had waited until the last, the safest moment 'to muster his troups, and sound the trumpet of war': 'I do then accuse Dr Parr that, instead of attempting to give the tone to his contemporaries, as his abilities well entitle him to do, he has condescended to join a cry, after it had already become loud and numerous.'[20] There is even, Godwin suggests, a touch of dishonesty as well as malice in Parr's critique. For Parr accepted the principle of utility no less than Godwin; his own publication shows that he knew of Godwin's change of heart about the domestic affections; and he was well aware of the distinction between the criterion of morality and the motive for moral conduct.

The rebuke was mild enough, self-denying almost, in view of what Godwin had suffered, but its justice struck home. 'I remember few passages in ancient or modern authors that contain more just philosophy in appropriate, chaste and beautiful diction . . .,' wrote Coleridge in the margin of his personal copy. 'They reflect great honour on Godwin's Head and Heart. Tho' I did it only in the Zenith of his Reputation, yet I feel remorse *ever* to have spoken unkindly of such a man.'[21] Mackintosh, too, was to repent of his treatment of a man who had once been a friend. 'If I ever committed any fault which approaches immorality,' he wrote from Bombay without any apparent twinge of modesty, 'I think it was towards Mr Godwin.'[22] It was only pride, he said, that had prevented him from apologizing in person, though when Godwin learnt of his regret that was, for him, apology enough, and the time would come when Mackintosh could repay that debt of honour. Even Southey declared himself much pleased with Godwin's reply to the Spital Sermon: '. . . yet is the man a good creature – brimful of benevolence – as kind hearted as a child would wish. It should be known to his credit that he is a father to Imlay's child.'[23] But before long he was back to his old opinion:

> I never liked the man and he never liked me. I *did* like his wife –
> I did like and do like what is good in his first book, but in
> proportion as I value what is true there, do I abominate the
> cursed mingle-mangle of metaphysics and concubinage and
> atheism with which he polluted it.[24]

In 1804 he was savaging Godwin again, in the *Critical Review*, and Godwin had, in effect, to repeat the restrained protests of the *Reply to Parr*. And for once Mrs Inchbald was prepared to be polite: 'I think it both severe and well-bred,' she wrote. 'Two of the best qualities of a reply.'[25] Only Dr Parr showed no sign of shame or remorse. His 1809 anthology of *Characters of Fox* would include one by Godwin, and he was heard to remark that Godwin was a man who, with a proper academic education – a Dissenting Academy, of course, could not compare with Harrow and Cambridge – might have become the first of his age. Not until 1825 did he relent sufficiently to write to Godwin, and invite him to visit him again at Hatton. But it was too late: Samuel Parr died on 6 March.

The *Reply to Parr* deserved to stand with the successes of the 1790s, not the failures of the 1800s, and for a moment it did seem to mark a turning point. Coleridge was always convinced that the tide would soon flow back to Godwin, though he expected Mackintosh to provide the stimulus:

> You may well exclaim with Job, 'O that my adversary would
> write a book!' When he publishes, it will be all over with him,
> and then the minds of men will incline strongly to those who
> would point out in intellectual perceptions a source of moral
> progressiveness. Every man in his heart is in favour of your
> general principles.[26]

Godwin, too, was confident that under the 'auspicious and beneficent genius' Bonaparte 'every thing promises that the future government of France will be popular, and her people free'.[27] Now that the war had reached stalemate, and peace negotiations were beginning, the way in Britain, too, seemed clear for a gradual restoration of political liberties and freedom of speech, for some movement back to the principles of reform, when the ideas of a Godwin might be read again with interest and approval, if with rather more scepticism than before. But in 1803 the war began again on very different terms, with England defending the cause of liberty, equality and fraternity against the imperialist First Consul of France, soon to become the Emperor Napoleon I. Even Fox endorsed a war he had previously opposed, and Sheridan joined the government, declaring 'Jacobinism is killed and gone. And by whom? By him who can no longer be called the child and champion of Jacobinism; by Buonaparte'. No one would bother now, nor was there need, to attack theories which belonged to a time of delusory optimism vanished beyond all tracing. Soon *Political Justice* would be changing hands at two shillings the copy.

Public humiliation and private loneliness, the sneers of satirists and the treachery of friends, the lack of a wife for himself and a mother for his children, the failure of his play and the neglect of his writings, all combined to force Godwin in on himself. The effect was not only to crush his dignity and kill his spirit, but to turn him into a caricature of himself: a prophet who could not face the future, an impartial reasoner who could think only of his own immediate needs, a self-sufficient altruist who had increasingly to rely on the assistance of others. He had always been introspective, but now more than ever he felt the need to analyse his strengths and probe his weaknesses in page after page of critical self-examination, penetrating, accurate, and increasingly depressive – 'Such as I am, the world is welcome to me' – until one note ends in a sorrowing list of *amis perdus*: Dyson, Montagu, Parr, Pinkerton, Inchbald, Mackintosh, M. Gisborne, H. Godwin, A. Opie . . .

But Godwin had not soured as Holcroft did. The intensely argumentative young man of the 1780s, the opinionated celebrity of the 1790s, both gave way to kind, mild, fatherly figure, more likely to be patronized than feared, passive and tolerant almost to a fault. He was still in his 40s, but noticeably aged by the dreadful experiences of the past few years, and his old-fashioned clothes, his pedantic manner, his awkwardness, his sheer spiritual weariness – not to mention that 'trick of always falling asleep for some *hour* after supper'[28] – all made him seem older than he was, in appearance as in principles a figure from a bygone age. 'Imagine to yourself a man of short stature, who has just passed the prime of life', wrote an American visitor in 1803,

> whose broad high forehead is fast retreating to baldness, but whose ruddy, thoughtful yet open countenance discovers both the temperature of health and philosophy; of manners remarkably mild, unassuming, rather reserved; in conversation cautious, argumentative, frequently doubtful, yet modestly courting reply, more from a desire of truth, than a love of contending; in his family, affectionate, cordial, accommodating; to his friends confidential, ready to make any sacrifice; to his

enemies – you would never know from Mr Godwin that he had an enemy.[29]

'In short', concluded another American the following year, plainly disappointed by the comparison with the mercurial Fuseli, 'Mr Godwin is a plain, decent, modest, smiling and agreeable little man.'[30]

But if he had lost something of his tendency to preach and moralize, he was as touchy as ever. 'I am extremely modest,' he wrote of himself, and so in a sense he was, neither arrogant nor vain, but his need of admiration and approval, his old sensitivity to criticism, made him seem conceited. Certainly he accepted praise and demanded homage wherever he could, with a self-importance that could be amusing when it was not irritating. But he was grasping at straws and he knew it. Nothing remained of the spirit of excitement in which he had written *Caleb Williams*; the delicious delights of self-complacency had deserted him now. He began an autobiography 'with the intention of being nearly as explicit as Rousseau in the composition of his Confessions',[31] but wisely he abandoned the project before he had taken it properly into his teens. Perhaps he found little of value to report; perhaps he was no longer prepared to trust in truth's inevitable victory over prejudice; but perhaps no one, now, would be sufficiently interested in William Godwin. The renewed war, and especially Napoleon's blockade of Continental ports against British trade, would bring economic depression and public unrest that culminated in the Luddite campaigns of 1811 and 1812. But that was a movement that had no appeal to a Godwin, nor would the ideas of a Godwin have any appeal to it. Bruised, bowed, finally broken, he would conceal his very existence so effectively that the waning tempest passed over-head, leaving him battered, but leaving him alone.

17 ♣ The immortal Godwin, I presume

I never gave credit to that axiom of sickly sensibility, that is a sacrilege, in him who has been engaged in one cordial and happy union, ever to turn his thought to another. Much more reasonable than this is the Indian doctrine, that the survivor ought to leap into the flames, and perish upon the funeral pyre of the deceased . . . . I should hold that in many cases he who entered into a second marriage, by that action yielded a pure and honourable homage to the manes of the first.

St Leon, 1799

♣ It was a Tuesday in May 1801, just before he began to compose his *Reply to Parr*. Godwin was sitting reading on his balcony at the Polygon when a maturely handsome woman appeared at a neighbouring window. 'Is it possible', she exclaimed, 'that I behold the immortal Godwin?' (I have been unable to trace the origin of this celebrated story, but it is too familiar – and too plausible – to omit. But I draw the line at Lady Jane Shelley's tale of Mrs Clairmont throwing notes over Godwin's wall, and generally pestering him, until he had to give in.) And Godwin's diary marked the occasion with one of its rare emphases: '*Meet Mrs Clairmont.*'

Mrs Clairmont, it emerged, was a widow, with a talent for cookery as well as flattery, and two children, Charles and Jane, roughly the age of his own. Strong-willed and intelligent, she had had to make her own way in the world from the age of eleven. Now she eked out a living as a writer and translator, as anxious for remarriage as Godwin himself. This time there was a toil spreader, he was the willing prey, and before long he was helplessly entangled. 'The Professor is COURTING,' marvelled Lamb that September.

The lady is a widow (a disgusting woman) with green spectacles . . . and the Professor is grown quite juvenile. He bows when he is spoke to, and smiles without occasion, and wriggles as fantastically as Malvolio, and has more affectation than a canary bird pluming its feathers when he thinks somebody looks at him. He lays down his spectacles, as if in scorn, and takes 'em up again from necessity, and winks that she mayn't see he gets sleepy about eleven o'Clock. You never saw such a philosophic coxcomb, nor anyone play Romeo so unnaturally.[1]

Godwin had been intending to visit Dublin again, staying at Keswick with Coleridge on the way. Then he thought he might take advantage of the peace negotiations with the French to pay a call on Holcroft in Paris, but the passport application from so notorious a democrat was rejected by the authorities. So instead he stayed home and married Mrs Clairmont, as secretly as he had once wed Mary Wollstonecraft, with Marshall and the parish clerk again the only witnesses. But this time the scandalous details are more obscure. The rumour later was that 'Mrs' Clairmont had never been married, which may explain why she and Godwin partook in two ceremonies that 21 December, one at Shoreditch where the bride signed the register as Mary Clairmont, widow, and another at Whitechapel – in Marshall's absence – where she signed as Mary Vials, spinster. To compound the confusion, a birth certificate issued for her son the following year gives her own father not as Vials but as a Mr Devereux, so it is possible that she, too, was illegitimate. The identity of the father, or fathers of her children is an equal mystery. That same birth certificate gives the father of Charles Gaulis Clairmont as another Charles Clairmont, yet Charles junior was obviously named after Charles Gaulis, a Swiss merchant who met Mary Jane Vials in Spain, and later lived in England. Certainly Mrs Clairmont's daughter Jane was always convinced she came of Swiss stock, seems to have thought she might have been illegitimate, and on one celebrated occasion adopted the name of one of Gaulis's sisters, Trefusis. Yet Charles Gaulis had died two years before Jane was born! Nor does speculation end there, for Godwin's diary has 'William I, ½ after 11 . . . . fetch Mary, Jane' on 4 April 1802 – a miscarriage, it seems, or perhaps a still-birth, less than five months after the wedding. Was his second marriage, too, a matter of necessity as much as convenience?

But this was not the blending of minds, the blossoming of personalities, that had augured so well, so tragically, for Godwin's first marriage. It was more of a partnership, hitting occasional snags as partnerships will, but arranged to the mutual benefit of both parties. For Mrs Clairmont was talented but devious, capable but scheming, relentlessly inquisitive, totally self-centred and notoriously short-tempered. James Marshall, in a position to know her better than most, described her fairly as 'a clever, bustling, second-rate woman, glib of tongue and pen, with a temper undisciplined and uncontrolled; not bad-hearted, but with a complete absence of all the finer sensibilities'. And it was the temper, above all, that caused the trouble. 'My dear love, take care of yourself', Godwin wrote once, before they were married.

Manage and economize your temper. It is at bottom most excellent: do not let it be soured and spoiled. It is capable of being recovered to its primaeval goodness, and even raised to something better. Do not however get rid of all your faults. I love some of them. I love what is human, what gives softness, and an agreeable air of frailty and pliability to the whole. Farewell, a thousand times.[2]

Sometimes there was even talk of a separation, 'a source of great misery to me . . .' said Godwin. 'You part from the best of husbands, the most anxious to console you, the best qualified to bear and be patient towards one of the worst of tempers. I have every qualification and every wish to make you happy . . . .'[3] And if that row blew over, there were others to come. 'I know not what the state of *your* mind is at this moment,' Mrs Godwin had occasion to write, when they had been married almost ten years,

> but mine will be that to which 10,000 daggers are mild, till I hear you accept the reconciliation I now send to offer. Perhaps I was irrational; but it is not a trifling wound to my heart to see myself put by, and thought of as a burden that the law will not let you be free from, because in the hardest struggle that ever fell to the lot of woman, I have lost my youth and beauty before the natural time. However I will try to reconcile myself to what I have long forseen.

And then, a fortnight later, 'Your dear, balmy letter, brought stump-a-stump upstairs at ½-past 9, has set my heart at ease.'[4]

For in his undramatic way, and somewhat to the surprise of his friends and family, Godwin was genuinely happy in his marriage, and more than merely fond of his wife. When she was away from home he would write to her frequently, anxious about her health and her spirits; when it was his turn to travel, it was often wishing that she could join him. Most of all, perhaps, they fed each other's vanity and need of support. 'Be assured . . . that I admire you not less than I love you,' wrote Godwin, resolving another quarrel.

> We are both of us, depend upon it, persons of no common stamp, and we should accustom ourselves perpetually so to regard each other, and to persuade ourselves, without hesitation, without jealousy, and with undoubted confidence, that we are so regarded by each other. God bless you! Good night.[5]

For all that she has been cast as the villain in the tragedy of Godwin's later years, there is no question that Godwin both needed and relied on her. 'You shall now be my mother,' he wrote from his mother's funeral in 1809, 'you have in many instances been my protector and my guide, and I fondly trust will be more so, as I shall come to stand more in need of assistance.'[6] 'Certainly towards him a meritorious wife,' summed up Henry Crabb Robinson, 'though towards others I doubt her sincerity and her integrity.'[7]

To others, in fact, it seemed a disastrous choice. 'Poor Godwin is a terrific example for all conjugal biography,' wrote one widowed old flame to another, Mrs Inchbald to Mrs Opie, 'but he has marked that path which may be avoided, and so is himself a sacrifice to the good of others.'[8] Close friends found they simply had to avoid this terrible woman, even if it meant avoiding Godwin too. 'The Professor's Rib has come out to be a damn'd disagreeable woman,' complained Lamb, 'so much as to drive me and some more old cronies from his house. If a man will keep snakes in his house, he must now wonder if people are shy of coming to see him because of the *snakes*.'[9] And again,

> Godwin (with a pitiful artificial wife) continues a steady friend, though the same facility does not remain of visiting him often. That Bitch has detached Marshall from his house, Marshall the man who went to sleep when the 'Ancient Mariner' was reading: the old, steady, unalterable friend of the Professor.[10]

Yet it is not surprising that the new wife should want the bachelor friend to find other lodgings and Mary Jane knew well enough that the distinguished visitors who still came occasionally to admire the portrait in Godwin's study ('to take another wife with the picture of Mary Wollstonecraft in his house', protested Southey. 'Agh!'[11]) must regard her as a thoroughly unworthy successor, that the Mary Godwin they were most anxious to set eyes upon was the daughter, not the wife.

But whether from jealousy or some more basic streak of spitefulness, Mrs Godwin was only too willing to spread trouble among his friends, passing on rumour and tittle-tattle, and always ready to repeat to one man's face what others had said behind his back. On one famous occasion in February 1804 there was a stand-up row at Lamb's, when Godwin attacked some scheme of Coleridge's, and Coleridge's friend Southey in particular, in the most direct and personal terms. Coleridge made some sarcastic reply and left the matter there, but Godwin went out, asking Coleridge to wait for his return. When he got back an hour later it was with a group of ladies, Mrs Godwin prominent among them, and he at once resumed the argument. Coleridge, 'disgusted at Heart with the grossness and vulgar Insaneocity of this dim-headed Prig of a Philosophocide' (his phrase), 'thundered and lightened with frenzied Eloquence' (Lamb's phrase) for going on two hours. The next morning he sent Godwin a note of abject apology, blaming the incident on an excess of alcohol, only to learn from Lamb that Godwin had confessed he would not have 'persisted in irritating me but that Mrs Godwin had twitted him for his prostration before me – as if he was afraid to say his life was his own in my presence'.[12] On another occasion Mrs Godwin got rid of some unwanted callers – the Baxters, with whom her step-daughter later lived in Dundee – by telling them her husband had just scalded himself and taken the skin from his legs; the next morning they met Godwin himself in the street, clearly none the worse for wear. Not for nothing did Lamb call her 'the liar par excellence'.

By the simple expedient of marrying Mrs Clairmont, Godwin had doubled his family, to which a William junior was added at last, on 28 March 1803. It was more than ever necessary that he earn a living from his pen, and he drove himself as hard as he could. Even before the marriage he had decided to try his hand at a biography, of Lord Bolingbroke perhaps, who in the corrupt time of Walpole had tried to set himself above party, uniting both conservatives and radicals in a programme of rational reform, only to be reviled and attacked by both sides, a man to set beside the classic figures of Greece and Rome, and also a man with whom Godwin found it easy to identify. But his new publisher Phillips could not be persuaded, and Godwin opted instead for a life of Chaucer.

It was another new departure, but one well suited to his talents, and what began as a money-spinner ended up a labour of love. Godwin quickly developed a passion for research, consulting expert friends like Horne Tooke and Joseph Ritson, hunting down forgotten documents in libraries and record offices – a task more difficult then that it is now – and even visiting Woodstock with Phillips, to see where Chaucer had retired. Even so, information about Chaucer himself remained meagre, and rather than abandon his hard-won material Godwin added such a mass of background detail to the story that, as he says himself, Chaucer ends up merely the central figure in a large miscellaneous painting. Indeed these 'Sketches of the Manners, Opinions, Art and Literature of England in the 14th Century', to give the book its subtitle, are more social history than biography, a genuinely pioneering attempt to get beyond the mere chronicle of dates and events into an imaginative reconstruction of the period. But there is no question but that Godwin carried the technique to extremes: the first ten chapters tell us much about the entertainments, culture, education, architecture of the times, but precious little about the poet; there is later a long digression on the contemporary legal system, on the pretext that

Chaucer might possibly have contemplated becoming a lawyer; and so it goes on, until the account of Chaucer's last fifteen years, and hence of the *Canterbury Tales*, had to be truncated drastically to fit into the two volumes that were all that Phillips would allow. 'The incidents of Chaucer's life bear the same proportion to the book that the alphabet does to the encyclopedia', complained Walter Scott in the *Edinburgh Review*, implying that collectors had been reluctant to lend documents to someone with Godwin's views on private property; it 'has no more title to be called a Life of Chaucer than a life of Petrach'.[13] Indeed Scott was so surprised to learn that 1,000 copies had been sold that he could only think that 'as the heaviest material to be come at, they have been sent on a secret expedition, for blocking up the mouths of our enemy's harbours!'[14]

Southey in the *Annual Review* was merely patronizing – 'taking it for granted that all those who read his book were to be as ignorant as he was himself when he began to write it, he has therefore told them all he knows'[15] – but in private he was more scathing, admitting that because of some lingering acquaintance with old Godwin his comments on the 'most despicable and most catchpenny "Chaucer" did spare the lash when it ought to have been more, yea most heavily laid on'.[16] But against all the odds the *Anti-Jacobin* praised this 'very ingenious and able work, which will transmit Godwin to future ages, when his metaphysical and sceptical eccentricities, for the honour of the author, shall be sunk in oblivion',[17] and the *Life of Chaucer* went into a second edition so rapidly and in print so similar to the first that some readers rightly suspected that Phillips had printed the more expensive quarto version and the cheaper octavo one at the same time!

With this moderate success behind him Godwin resolved to try the stage once more. The obstructive Kemble had recently retired from Drury Lane and been replaced by none other than that star of the American stage, Thomas Abthorpe Cooper! When Cooper opened in *Hamlet* in March 1803, Godwin, Holcroft and a heavily-pregnant Mary Jane were there to share in his triumph. But unhappily either the Drury Lane did not take to Cooper, or he did not take to them, and the next year he returned to New York. By then, however, Godwin had already written his 'Camilla', as he first called it. He showed it to Coleridge, who found it dreadfully hard going; he showed it to Lamb, who suggested so many alterations that he signed the letter 'WILLIAM GODWIN!!' and gave his address as the Polygon; he showed it to Holcroft, who took it upon himself to rewrite the whole thing. Nevertheless, Cooper's successor at Drury Lane, Wroughton, seemed to think the play might do as it stood, even if it could do with a stronger climax, and for much of

1804 he and Godwin were in regular correspondence about it. But Wroughton would never come to a decision about when, exactly, the play would be performed. For three years more Godwin would live in the constant expectation that his tragedy would appear next season, always next season.

Instead he went back to the one area where he still felt sure of success, to a novel originally called 'Lambert' but published in February 1805 as *Fleetwood, or the New Man of Feeling*, a subtitle that quite mystified its readers. (Henry Mackenzie's *Man of Feeling* (1771) was the archetypal Novel of Sentiment, where plot and characterization take second place to the detailed description of mawkish emotion. It was extremely popular, and its tale of a moral innocent abroad in a corrupt world might possibly have appealed to Godwin. But there are no discernible similarities with *Fleetwood*, though curiously there are likenesses in both plot and Rousseauesque background between *Fleetwood* and a later Mackenzie novel, *Julia de Roubigné* (1777).) This, evidently, was the story of 'common incidents and the embarassments of lovers' promised in the memorandum of 1798, for, as Godwin explained, he had given up his usual sensational plots for 'such adventures, as for the most part have occurred to at least one half of the Englishmen now existing, who are of the same rank of life as my hero'. The central theme is the old theme, the necessity of friendship, the horrors of loneliness: like *St Leon* it is the story of the unthinking ruin of a perfect marriage, the story of a man who marries late in life only to be tricked by a wicked companion into believing his wife has been unfaithful – a plot which owes more than just that to Shakespeare's *Othello*. But this time the treatment is more morbid, more pessimistic, less satisfying; *Fleetwood* is the fruit of Godwin's second marriage as surely as *St Leon* was the fruit of the first. 'God knows all marriage is a risk', says his hero with feeling, '– is the deepest game that can be played in this sublunary scene'.

Stendhal thought the book a masterpiece and others have ranked it in parts with *Caleb Williams*, yet it is surely one of Godwin's worst. The writing is pompous and long-winded, the story artificial, the characters cardboard, and the development tedious, relieved only by an occasional moment of implausible high drama, as when Fleetwood celebrates the 'marriage' of his wife and her suspected lover by means of life-sized models which he then destroys, and the room along with them, in a fit of insane rage. Yet Godwin still has his moments, two in particular. One is the Dickensian story, far more entertaining than the main plot on which it has no bearing whatsoever, of a boy who escapes the drudgery of a silk factory in Lyons and journeys to Versailles, to reveal his true identity to Louis

XIV. The other is a deliciously mock-heroic verse drama on the adventures of Hercules –

> Ah, no! those godlike fingers ne'er were made
> To ply the nightman's trade

– whose delicate wit is so far removed from anything else Godwin ever wrote, and from the rest of *Fleetwood* in particular, that it is impossible not to suspect the influence, if not the very hand, of the man who was now his best and closest friend, Charles Lamb. But it would take more than a facetious poem and a moral fable for children to save the main text, and *Fleetwood* remained at a single edition. It was evident that the family could no longer live by Godwin's pen alone. They would have to think of something else.

Mrs Godwin was, as she said herself, 'a managing woman'. After translating Voltaire's *Pensées* and the African journals of the French explorer Sylvain Golberry for the Robinsons, she had been editing a three-volume *Collection of Short Stories for the Nursery* for the eccentric publisher Benjamin Tabart. (Because the Juvenile Library's adaptation of Jauffret's *Dramas for Children* is given as by 'The Editor of Tabart's Popular Tales', and an advertisement at the end of the volume ascribes the French version of 'Baldwin's' (i.e. Godwin's) *Fables* to the same author, Godwin has been credited with all these works. In fact the French translation of the *Fables*, and hence presumably also the *Dramas for Children* and the Tabart anthologies, were the work of his wife.) Godwin looked it over, as he looked over all her work, and the idea suggested itself – perhaps she put it to him – why not set themselves up as children's booksellers? He could write the books, their children could sample them, and she could run the business with the help of a professional manager. 'Libraries are soon stocked', as Godwin explained to one prospective backer: 'but the children to be instructed are innumerable, and the demands of one year for their sale scarcely diminishes the demand of the next.'[18] And so in the summer of 1805 they acquired a small shop in Hanway Stret, the back alley that runs from Oxford Street through to the Tottenham Court Road, installed Thomas Hodgkins as their manager, and embarked on the Juvenile Library, to supply the public with 'a choice collection of School Books, also Cyphering Books, Copy Books, Copper-plate Copies, Quills, Pens, Inkstands, Slates, Black-lead Pencils, Maps and Stationery of all kinds'.[19]

Of course it would have been commercial suicide to offer books to children, let alone to schools, that bore the notorious name of Godwin, so the first publication, coinciding with the Battle of Trafalgar on 21 October, was by one 'Edward Baldwin': a collection of *Fables, Ancient and Modern*, clearly inspired by the Tabart *Stories*.

I Exterior of Guestwick Meeting House where John Godwin was minister (*National Monuments Record*)

II Interior of Guestwick Meeting House (*National Monuments Record*)

Godwin remembered how, aged nine or ten, he would steal the key so that he could preach from his father's pulpit at 'a poor lad of the village, whose name was Steele . . . of sin and damnation, and draw tears from his eyes'.

III Thomas Holcroft by
John Opie (*National
Portrait Gallery*)

IV Elizabeth Inchbald by
G. Dance (*National
Portrait Gallery*)

v Godwin and Holcroft at the 1794 Treason Trials (*Royal Academy of Arts, owned by Kenneth Garlick*)

'Holcroft . . . on being liberated, left the dock, and, crossing the court, took his seat beside Godwin. Sir Thomas Lawrence, struck by the happy combination and contrast exhibited in the attitude and expression of the two friends, made a spirited sketch of them in profile . . . the bending meditative figure of Godwin contrasting most happily with the upright, stern and "knock me down" attitude and expression of his friend' (Mary Shelley).

VI John Thelwall, attributed to William Hazlitt (*National Portrait Gallery*)

VII Godwin, aged thirty-nine, about the time of his dispute with Thelwall, by Sir Thomas Lawrence (*British Museum*). Original in the possession of Christoph Clairmont

Engraved by Ridley from a Drawing by Lawrence in the Possession of Dr Baty.

VIII (*left*) Mary
Wollstonecraft in 1791,
by John Opie (*Walker Art
Gallery*)

IX (*below*) Mary
Wollstonecraft in 1797,
by John Opie (*National
Portrait Gallery*)

Mary Wollstonecraft
before and after her love
affairs (the later portrait
was painted when she
was seven or eight
months pregnant): 'In
the champion of her sex,
who was described as
endeavouring to invest
them with all the rights
of men, those whom
curiosity prompted to
seek the occasion of
beholding her, expected
to find a sturdy,
muscular, raw-boned
virago; and they were
not a little surprised,
when, instead of all this,
they found a woman,
lovely in her person, and
in the best and most
engaging senses,
feminine in her manners'
(Godwin's *Memoirs of
Mary Wollstonecraft*).

x Gilray's *New Morality* (1798) (*British Museum*)

Holcroft is the felon in leg irons. Paine the crocodile wearing lady's stays, and Godwin the jackass braying aloud from *Political Justice*. The Frog and Toad are Charles Lamb and Charles Lloyd reading their recently published Blank Verse; Coleridge and Southey are the asses on either side of the Cornucopia of Ignorance, from which spill the *Enquirer*, *The Wrongs of Woman*, and the *Memoirs*, among other books. Priestley, a co-discoverer of oxygen, stands behind with a text called 'Inflam(mable) Air' in his pocket. Thelwall sits on the shoulders of Leviathan (the Duke of Bedford), with Fox immediately behind him. Erskine, who defended Paine and those accused in the 1794 Treason Trials, is the first merman, Horne Tooke the lowest of the flying birds.

xi Dr Parr delivering the Spital Sermon (*British Museum*)

Two contrasting portraits of Godwin in 1801, the Hero and the Man.

XII Portrait by Sir James Northcote (*National Portrait Gallery*)

'Is it national partiality to fancy that such a head could have belonged only to an Englishman?' (*London Literary Gazette*).

XIII Portrait by James Sharples (*Bristol City Art Gallery*)

'He has much less the appearance of a man of genius, than anyone who has given such decided and ample proofs of it' (William Hazlitt).

XIV ?Mary Jane Clairmont (*Clairmont Archive*)

XV ?Mary Godwin (from R. G. Grylls, *Mary Shelley*)

The old lady is believed to be Mrs Clairmont. The young girl was once believed to be Mary, aged sixteen, but this is now disputed. But although Mary was described as fair, not dark, the resemblance to Godwin, especially as a young man, is striking.

XVI Godwin, aged sixty, as he appears in G. S. Mackenzie's *Illustrations of Phrenology* (1820), based on the portrait painted by William Nicholson in Edinburgh.

An anonymous 'skilled phrenologist' provided this striking analysis of the head, allegedly without knowing the identity of his subject:

'In this portrait we discover the indications of very powerful talents: a man of deep thought; such a one as might be an able lawyer, speaker and reasoner; and the development of imitation might assist to render his eloquence powerful, by giving it expression. Benevolence is strong; but there is very little veneration, and very little hope. Cautiousness is large, and so is destructiveness; ideality also is full. It is probable that this person is regular, or a man of order and method; but his reflections must have a gloomy taint; and his dissatisfaction with the world considerable. He is a philanthropist, at least more so than a worshipper; though he believes probably in natural religion. If this portrait be correctly drawn, the right side does not quite agree with the left in the region of ideality, and where Dr Spurzheim places the organ, which he has called in French *Surnaturalité*, or *Sens de Merveilleux*, a disposition to believe in what is marvellous and improbable. This dissimilarity may have produced something contradictory in his feelings, which he may have felt extremely annoying. This person may be respected for his talents, but is not to be envied for his whole development.'

XVII New Palace Yard, sketched around 1831 by Joseph Rickman's daughter Ann (*Archives Department, Westminster City Libraries*)

The doorway in the left-hand corner is the entrance to the Office of the Receipt of the Exchequer, where Godwin had his office. The opening is the Speaker's Gateway, which Godwin lived 'hard by'.

xvⅢ Godwin aged seventy-six, by Sophia Ghent (*Christoph Clairmont*)

'A bald, bushy-browed, thick, hoary, hale little figure . . . he wears spectacles, has full grey eyes, a very blunt characterless nose, and ditto chin' (Thomas Carlyle).

XIX Godwin aged seventy-eight, as drawn by Daniel Maclise for *Fraser's Magazine*.

'His fine head was striking, and his countenance remarkable. It must not be judged of by the pretended likeness put forth in Fraser's Magazine . . . The high Tory favourites of the Magazine were exhibited to the best advantage; while Liberals were represented as Godwin was. Because the finest thing about him was his noble head, they put on a hat, and they presented him in profile because he has lost his teeth and his lips fell in. No notion of Godwin's face could be formed from that caricature' (Harriet Martineau).

This was followed by two books by a 'Theophilius Marcliffe': *The Looking Glass*, or 'A True History of the Early Years of an ARTIST' based on Godwin's enthralled conversations with their nineteen-year-old illustrator, William Mulready; and a *Life of Lady Jane Grey*. A *History of England* already contracted to Phillips as a work that might rival Hume's was easily turned into one for children, followed by a comprehensive guide to classical mythology called *The Pantheon*, and the possibly unpublished *Rural Walks, or First Impressions of Religion*, based, as it seems, on a conversation during a country walk with one of his daughters.

Godwin tried his books out on his own family first, and he knew well the limits of their attention, what would most stimulate their curiosity. But he also had an unexpected knack of writing for children at their own level without being in the slightest patronizing, and his own contributions were among the Library's most successful volumes, republished again and again well into the second half of the century. Perhaps he is never vivid or exciting – certainly he lacks the charm and warmth of his colleague Lamb – but the writing is always simple and direct, if occasionally pedantic, the information both interesting and easily digested. But being Godwin he saw himself as presenting lessons that were moral as well as educational. So the *Fables* have each their explicit moral, even if that to be drawn from the tale of Astrologer who fell into the Pit seems to be that the disaster would never have occurred had he been an astronomer instead. Equally the later *History of Rome* was written because 'it contains the finest examples of elevated and disinterested virtue, that are to be met with in the history of any country on earth'; the *Pantheon* is intended not only to teach classical mythology, but to acquaint children with the manners of other peoples; the hero of *The Looking Glass* provides an example of industry and dedication that all young people should follow; Lady Jane Grey is 'the most perfect model of a meritorious young creature of the female sex to be found in history', and even at the end, when Lady Jane, her father and her husband have all been brought to the scaffold, the author is still careful to warn his readers against unnecessary prejudice:

> Before we conclude this little history, it is proper that you should be told, that all Papists (or, as they are now more usually called, Roman Catholics) are not of the opinion that all Protestants should be burned alive. A person may believe in transubstantiation, and say his prayers with a little ivory image standing before him, and yet be a very worthy man.

But behind his pseudonyms Godwin still had to be careful. He realized that many would think it highly dangerous to make Greek

H

mythology, with its twin infections of paganism and immorality, attractive to children but, he said, 'I confidently trust that nothing will be found in it, to administer libertinism to the fancy of the stripling, or to sully the whiteness of mind of the purest virgin.' But the *Eclectic Review*, though praising Mr Baldwin's style, was still

> dissatisfied with the principle of his performance. It is a principle which no writer, duly sensible of the moral end of man, and aware of how important it is to excite the earliest abhorrence of vice in the youthful mind, would ever have adopted. To palliate the atrocities of classical divinities may do much harm, by weakening this abhorrence.[20]

Even worse, the *Pantheon* was provided with 'engravings of the principal Gods, chiefly taken from the remains of ancient statuary', and so revealing them in various states of careful undress. They are, the *Eclectic* admits, 'as decent as naked figures can be' – a nude Venus turns demurely to one side – but they were still not decent enough, and in the third edition of 1810 the illustrations were altered. 'I am happy to inform you', Godwin wrote to the Reverend Charles Burney, headmaster of the school at Greenwich where William junior would later be a pupil, 'that I have been able to clothe four of the gods for the precise sum of twelve guineas, which, considering the high price of all sorts of apparel at present, I hope you will allow to be a good bargain.'[21]

After this initial burst of activity in 1805 and 1806, to get the enterprise off the ground, Godwin personally wrote only spasmodically for the Library. But he did not expect to be its sole contributor, and friends were drafted in to help. Lady Mountcashell, who had left her husband and eight children to live in London as 'Mrs Mason', the name with which Mary Wollstonecraft had disguised herself in one of her own early works, contributed her *Stories of Old Daniel*, later followed by a *Continuation of the Stories*, and some *Stories for Little Girls and Boys in Words of One Syllable*. Eliza Fenwick, who had nursed Mary as she died, provided both a *Lessons for Children: or Rudiments of Good Manners*, which features such notables as Greedy George, Patient Emma, Merry Agnes, Generous Susan, Lying Lucy and Selfish Sarah, and *Rays from the Rainbow*, 'being an Easy Method for perfecting Children in the FIRST PRINCIPLES OF GRAMMAR without Trouble to the Instructor'. Sheridan's niece, Alice Lefanu, an acquaintance from both Bath and Dublin, wrote a poem called *Rosara's Chain*. But the Godwins' most distinguished contributors would be Charles and Mary Lamb. Charles's little poem on the *King and Queen of Hearts*, published in November 1805 as the first in the Copper Plate Series, a shilling plain and eighteen-pence coloured, was his first attempt at writing specifically for children, and, encouraged, he went on to attempt a series of children's versions of the most famous plays in the language. But it was Mary Jane Godwin, who herself translated several library volumes into French and adapted into English L. F. Jauffret's popular *Dramas for Children*, who persuaded Charles's unstable sister Mary to write for them as well. Without Mrs Godwin's help and management there might have been no *Lambs' Tales from Shakespeare*, no *Mrs Leicester's School*, no *Poetry for Children*, the first and last joint efforts by both Lambs. Nor was she the only Mary Godwin to play her part. Number 6 in the Copper Plate Series was a new version of the old story *Mounseer Nongtongpaw*, published on the first day of 1808. On the second Godwin sent a copy off as the work of his ten-year-old daughter: it was Mary Shelley's first publication.

These first volumes sold well enough, but the shop was faring worse, too much in a back street to attract the passing trade. So the Godwins began to look around for somewhere else, where they could also store their stock and live on the premises. But Hanway Street cost a mere £40 per annum, of which full £35 came back from subletting, and the lease on a suitable property could cost anything up to 1,000 guineas. There was, however, one exception. Over in Holborn a street of impressive-looking, poorly-constructed commercial buildings had recently been punched through the teeming tenements and back alleys, along the line of what is now Holborn Viaduct, to improve access into the City of London. This piece of Georgian property speculation, named Skinner Street after a worthy alderman, had been a failure, not just because of the substandard workmanship, but also because it lay too close both to the Smithfield Markets and the Newgate and Fleet Street prisons, not to mention the Old Bailey, still the site of public executions. When no one would buy the properties they were offered instead as prizes in a public lottery, though even then the drawing had to be postponed twice, and some still needed to be auctioned off in 1809. Premises intended as shops and offices ended up as light factories and warehouses, if they were ever occupied at all, and Skinner Street, 'a declining neighbourhood almost before it could be called new',[22] was prepared to take almost any tenant on almost any terms. Godwin liked the look of No. 41 on the corner of Snow Hill, with a long curving frontage and large windows, ideal for the display of books. It would not come up for lottery for another eighteen months. In the meantime he could have it at the very moderate rent of £150 a year, and so have time to discover whether the site was suitable, and whether his business could support it, before the question of a long-term lease came up. It was too good an opportunity to miss.

So in April 1807 Godwin paid his two quarters rent in advance and the bookshop moved from Hanway Street, followed six months later by the whole family. It would be their home for fifteen years, longer than Godwin lived anywhere else. Almost immediately Hodgkins, the manager, was detected in some fraud and dismissed. Eliza Fenwick was installed in his place, but found it impossible to work under Mrs Godwin, 'of all human beings the subject of my sincerest detestations',[23] and at the beginning of 1808 Mary Jane took charge herself. Outside she placed a carving of Aesop telling his fables to an enthralled group of children, and a sign that would shelter her notorious husband under the thinnest of disguises: M. J. Godwin and Co.

18 ♣ M. J. Godwin and Co.

> Trade was the Alps and Pyrrenees to me. I had to ascend one
> rock after another, and I thought I should never be at the top. I
> was wholly unaccustomed to climb these hills of gold, and felt
> as if my breath would fail me at every turn. Five years ago
> however I set out, and now, like Hannibal in the Roman
> History, or Moses on top of Mount Pisgah, I have a glimpse of
> the promised land. I see its rich vallies, its meandering
> streams, its towering cities, and its fertile fields. I am proud I
> am here; but I wish I was there.[1]
>
> To an unidentified correspondent, around 1810

♣ They were a strangely variegated family, five children who could
claim between them at least as many parents, who moved into the
rickety five-storeyed building next to the boot- and shoe-makers,
across Snow Hill from the Church of St Sepulchre. Godwin had
found it easy to express his obvious affection when his daughters
were small, but as they all grew older together he became remote
and awkward, more dutiful than sensitive, unable to show what he
really felt for them. They, too, had to be fitted into his methodical
timetable, with periods allotted when they might interrupt his
writing or listen to his latest story. He would take them with him
sometimes, to a lecture or the theatre or some other public occasion,
but they were all very much in awe of him, a famous figure so they
were told, though they could see little enough sign of it for
themselves.

At thirteen, Fanny Imlay, as she was still occasionally known, was
the eldest, in appearance more like her father than her mother. As a
baby she had been so lively and boisterous that the *Monthly Visitor*
had seen in her a warning to anyone who might be tempted by the
ingenious but misguided theories of Mary Wollstonecraft: 'Her
philosophy was not the most happy; especially for a female. Miss
Imlay has been spoilt by it. This girl . . . is a sufficient antidote to the
mistaken speculations of her mother.'[2] But somewhere along the
way that playful little girl had been turned into a quiet, serious,
somewhat repressed teenager. The loss of a father before she was
two, the loss of a mother when only three, separation from one
substitute at the age of six, the acquisition of another, formidable
and unsympathetic, when she was seven, all left their mark, and
Fanny revealed her mother's streak of depression and morbid

anxiety without Mary Wollstonecraft's compensating strength of
personality. On the surface she was polite, mild-mannered, dutiful,
the 'sweetness of her disposition' compensating for the plainness of
her face. But that calm exterior concealed a torment of doubts and
fears. She was, surely, St Leon's eldest daughter Julia,

> uncommonly mild and affectionate, alive to the slightest
> variations of treatment, profoundly depressed by every mark of
> unkindness, but exquisitely sensible to demonstrations of
> sympathy and attachment. She appeared little formed to
> struggle with the difficulties of life and frowns of the world; but
> in periods of quietness and tranquillity nothing could exceed
> the sweetness of her character and the fascination of her
> manners.

Fanny was only five when Godwin wrote these words.

In 1805 the two Wollstonecraft sisters had offered to have Fanny
join them in Dublin, but Godwin had already come to rely heavily
on her, partly because she was the eldest child, partly because that
was her nature and his. He was always especially affectionate
towards her, as if he went out of his way to demonstrate that she, the
orphan in the family, was no less his daughter, and as the eldest, the
most reliable and most sensible, the only one who never broke
openly with Mrs Godwin, it fell to Fanny to smooth over the
domestic upsets, to help out in both shop and home. And that, too,
took its toll.

Charles Clairmont was a year younger, and his mother was
anxious that he should receive a fitting education. Godwin exerted
such little influence as he had, in 1802 and again the following year,
to have him accepted at Christ's Hospital, where Lamb and
Coleridge had been pupils, though he urged that his personal
connection be kept quiet, lest the boy suffer from the notoriety of the
step-father. But in 1804 Charles went instead to the Charterhouse,
not far from Skinner Street, where he stayed the next seven years.
Old enough to see him as 'Mr Godwin' rather than a father, Charles
was cordial but slightly distant, his attitude grounded in respect
rather than affection. Still, he could not help acquiring some of
Godwin's traits, mingled as they were with characteristics of his
mother. When later in life the Austrian secret police were ordered to
investigate this relative of the infamous Godwin, they reported him
'arrogant and argumentative about everything, contradicting all
that does not fit in which his ideas'.[3]

Mary Godwin, ten years old at the time of the move to Skinner
Street, was another more like her father than her mother, with the
same fair hair, pale complexion, high forehead, striking eyes and

prominent nose. Godwin had had her character assessed at only nineteen days old by his friend William Nicholson, an amateur phrenologist, though the analysis understandably resembles the mother more than the daughter, except perhaps in the telling detail that when displeased – 'the mouth was too much employed to be well observed'![4] – she displayed neither scorn nor rage, only a resigned vexation. Godwin himself described the differences between her and her sister:

> My own daughter is considerably superior in capacity to the one her mother had before. Fanny, the eldest, is of a quiet, modest, unshowy disposition, somewhat given to indolence, which is her greatest fault, but sober, observing, peculiarly clear and distinct in the faculty of memory, and disposed to exercise her own thoughts and follow her own judgment. Mary, my daughter, is the reverse of her in many particulars. She is singularly bold, somewhat imperious, and active of mind. Her desire for knowledge is great, and her perseverance in every-thing she undertakes is almost invincible. My own daughter is, I believe, very pretty; Fanny is by no means handsome, but in general prepossessing.[5]

Where Fanny was nervous and anxious, always convinced she was somehow at fault, Mary had her father's need to win approval through great works and good deeds. She grew up sad and sickly, always at odds with Mrs Godwin who clearly resented the interest their visitors took in her, and resented in turn the preference given her step-sister Jane. For health and happiness's sake she had often to be sent away from home and, solitary, sensitive, disliking her step-mother with increasing intensity as she grew older, Mary developed what she herself came to see as an 'excessive and romantic attach-ment' to her distant and unresponsive father, a fixation that would dominate both her life and her literature. The theme of an intense but unsatisfying relationship between father and daughter – amounting in one case even to incest – was as central and as common in her novels as was the theme of loneliness in his.

The third girl, named after her mother but known as Jane, was almost a year younger than Mary but, more outgoing and more self-confident, probably seemed the elder of the two. She was her mother's daughter, equally domineering and equally fond of her own way, so much so that when she was but five Godwin was chiding his wife on 'the excess of that baby-sullenness, for every trifle, and to be brought out every day (the attributes of the mother of Jane)'![6] She was also the most attractive of the three girls, a sultry Latin beauty, so dark that the irises of her eyes merged with the pupils. Mrs Godwin had high hopes of her and sent her off to boarding school to acquire French, and a schoolgirl love of intrigue and sensation she would soon have opportunity to indulge to the full. If Fanny was the dutiful daughter and Mary the lonely dreamer, Jane was the romantic, eventually dropping that excessively plain name for the more dramatic Claire.

William junior was the youngest by five years, and as Godwin's one son was confidently expected to achieve great things. He proved bright enough, but so spoilt, so mettlesome and so excessively noisy that when Mary was taken to the seaside on doctor's orders in 1811, she was forced to sleep apart from the rest of the family because young William kept her awake at nights. Even so he could rival his father's achievements as a kitchen orator:

> In the evening, William, the only *son* of W. Godwin, a lad
> about nine years old, gave his weekly lecture; having heard how
> Coleridge and others lectured, he would also lecture; and one of
> his sisters (Mary, I think) writes a lecture, which he reads from
> a little pulpit which they have erected for him. He went
> though it all with great gravity and decorum. The subject was
> 'The Influence of Governments on the Character of the
> People'.[7]

Evidently Mary, who had been to Coleridge's lectures with her father, knew her *Political Justice* too, but it was not a practice she would revive for her own son. When she planned to send Percy to Harrow it was suggested he should rather go somewhere where he might learn to think for himself. 'To think for himself!', she cried out. 'Oh my God, teach him to think like other people!' And her prayer was answered.

Upstairs Godwin had his study, shaped in a quarter-circle where Skinner Street curved round into Snow Hill. 'In the arc there were windows; in one radius a fire-place, and in the other a door, and shelves with many old books';[8] and above the fire the two celebrated portraits, Godwin by Northcote, Wollstonecraft by Opie. And there he worked away, among his books, his papers and his memories, while 'the inglorious transactions of the shop below-stairs furnish me with food, clothing and habitation, and enable me to proceed'.[9] It was 'the most remarkable shop', recalled one young passer-by, who knew nothing of Godwin or his works.

> It boasted an immense extent of window front extending from
> the entrance into Snow Hill and towards Fleet Market. Many a
> time have I lingered with loving eyes over those fascinating
> story-books, so rich in gaily-coloured prints; such careful
> editions of the marvelous old histories; 'Puss in Boots', 'Cock

Robin', 'Cinderella' and the like. Fortunately the front was kept low, so as exactly to suit the capacity of a childish admirer.[10]

But another childish admirer probably remembered it more accurately, when he recalled 'a poor shop, poorly furnished; its contents consisting chiefly of children's books with the old coloured prints that would contrast strangely with the art illustrations of today.'[11]

The drawback, of course, was the location, so close to the prisons that the crowds witnessing the executions sometimes spilled back to the front door, though the gallows themselves were just out of sight round the corner. Only a month before Godwin inspected the property 28 people had been suffocated or trampled to death, and another 60 injured, in the crush of almost 40,000 that gathered to watch the hanging of Haggerty and Holloway for the sensational murder of a lavender merchant. May 1812 would see an equally celebrated occasion, when James Bellingham, a deranged timber merchant who followed the familiar course of blaming all his troubles on the government, but took the less familiar step of gunning the Prime Minister down in the lobby of the House of Commons, was 'launched into eternity'. Lord Byron was among those who sat up all night to witness the event. But Godwin personally had little taste for such diversions. *Political Justice* had been typically dispassionate on the topic of capital punishment:

> To deprive an offender of his life in any manner will appear to be unjust, as it seems always sufficiently practicable, without this, to prevent him from further offence. Privation of life, though by no means the greatest injury that can be inflicted, must always be considered a very serious injury; since it puts a perpetual close upon the prospects of the sufferer, as to all the enjoyments, the virtues and the excellence of a human being.[12]

But fifteen years in Skinner Street would make him more emphatic. 'For myself', he wrote in his *History of the Commonwealth*, 'I entertain an almost invincible abhorrence to the taking away of the life of a man, after a set form, and in cool blood, in any case whatsoever' – while allowing that if any man ever deserved that fate, it was Charles I.

Still, it was not just executions that Godwin avoided. In January 1806 he had been one of the unprecedented crowd that watched Lord Nelson's body borne in state up the Thames from Greenwich to Whitehall, to be buried in St Pauls, and he was at Westminster Abbey ten months later when Fox was laid to rest beside his rival Pitt, who had died earlier that same year. But that was as close to contemporary affairs as he cared to approach; all too willingly he buried himself in the obscurity of Skinner Street. 'Having laid myself bare to the darts of sport or malice to so considerable an extent,' he wrote somewhere about this time, 'I do not feel disposed by any acts or exertions of mine to present myself in any other point to the attacks of the world.'[13] Fêted, feared, ridiculed by turn, now he was simply forgotten.

'Poor Godwin is going to the Dogs, I fear,'[14] wrote Coleridge in December 1807. Their friendship survived, more intermittently now, and Lamb and Hazlitt came less often to Skinner Street than they had to the Polygon. But the connection with Holcroft, worn to a thread by the rows and recriminations of a decade, had finally snapped through the accident of a passage in *Fleetwood*. Mrs Holcroft had written to complain at the story of a Mr Scarborough, whose severity brings about the death of his son. Godwin, mystified at first, replied that the incident was based not on Holcroft and the suicide of his son, but on himself and Tom Cooper. But Holcroft, more embittered than ever, did not believe him. Still, there came a few to seek Godwin out even now, Americans often enough, to whom Jacobinism had been no threat and 'democrat' still a term of praise, men like the ebullient Aaron Burr, an ex-Vice-President, who had tied with Thomas Jefferson for the presidency itself, had killed a political rival in a duel, and had tried to foment revolution in Mexico, only to be tried for treason to his own country for his pains. He was in England in 1808-9 and again in 1811-12, and the Godwins were among his closest friends. The air of dejection that hung over Skinner Street seemed not to bother him at all, nor did he object to the 'sensible amiable woman' who was Godwin's second wife. He listened respectfully while young William gave his weekly lecture; he bought stockings for the three girls to wear to a ball; and when the time came to return home, it was the Godwins who helped him find the fare.

But the truth of it was that Godwin was too busy scaling those unfamiliar Alps and Pyrenees of trade, an activity for which he had neither inclination nor ability, to have much time for politics, friendships, or even for serious writing. Apart from the enthusiastic Memoir of Fox published in the *London Chronicle* in November 1806, there were only two works through the entire decade from 1805 to 1815 which he could properly call his own, and one of those he had written in 1804. That was his new tragedy, finally scheduled for performance at the end of 1807 under the new title of *Faulkener*. The cause of the delay had been not so much the theatre as its leading actor, William Betty, a boy of merely thirteen. Tragic declamation from the mouth of a child had proved a public sensation in an age that thrived on sensations – parliamentary debates were postponed to enable members to attend the performances of this Young Roscius – and Godwin had been content to hitch his fortune to that star. But Betty seemed reluctant to play the part, even after Godwin went over it personally with him. 'It has now been so long before my eyes', Godwin wrote resignedly, 'that I can almost look upon it with the impartiality of a mere bystander.'[15] But by 1807 Bettymania was over, Betty's contract was not renewed, and *Faulkener* could go ahead, on 16 December, with a meaty part for Sarah Siddons, and a Prologue and an Epilogue which were again the work of Lamb.

'A tragedy in five acts', summed up the *Satirist or Monthly Meteor*, 'interspersed with country dances, masquerades, deaths, trials, faintings, &c, &c, &c, &c; written and *founded on fact* by Political Justice Godwin, Esq – and oh what a tragedy it was!' 'I began my composition in verse', Godwin explained in the published version, 'but soon grew discouraged. A perfect facility in writing verse must be the fruit of practice.' So the first act breaks into disconcerting bursts of blank verse before reverting to the prose which, as one critic said, was what it might as well have been. Yet when the curtain fell – so close to one corpse that 'he drew up his arm with an alacrity dead men seldom possess'[16] – and the audience was asked, as customary, whether the piece should be repeated, 'there was a very loud outcry against it, not unmixed, however with some applause; the *Ayes*, we believe, had it; but we cannot suppose that it will last long.'[17] Perhaps Godwin had followed that other custom which Kemble, for his own good reasons, had advised against in the case of *Antonio*: the custom of paying members of the audience to provide the necessary Ayes. The next morning he was up at five, shortening the text, and *Faulkener* scraped by for a few nights more. By comparison with previous disasters it was almost a success. But though he had salvaged some pride, Godwin was never tempted to try the stage again.

The other publication to carry Godwin's name was the curious little *Essay on Sepulchres*, written at the turn of 1808 and published at his own expense early the next year. Mary Lamb describes it best, as a

> great work which Godwin is going to publish to enlighten the world once more . . . . To propose a subscription to all well disposed people, to raise a certain sum of money, to be expended in the care of a cheap monument for the former and future great dead men, – the monument to be a white cross, with a wooden slab at the end, telling their names and qualifications. This wooden slab and white cross to be per-

petuated to the end of time. To survive the fall of empires and
the destruction of cities by means of a map, which was, in the
case of an insurrection among the people, or any other cause by
which a city or a country may be destroyed, to be carefully
preserved; and then, when things got again into their usual
order, the white-cross-wooden-slab-makers were to go to work
again, and set them up in their former places . . . . The proposal (which seems to me very like throwing salt on a sparrow's
tail to catch him) occupies but half a page, which is followed
by very fine writing on the benefits he conjectures would follow
if it were done. Very excellent thoughts on death, and on our
feelings concerning our dead friends, and the advantages an old
country has over a new one even in the slender memorials we
have of great men who once flourished.[18]

In fact the great charm of this little pamphlet is the deadly seriousness with which Godwin approaches his modest, not to say silly,
little suggestion. But no doubt he numbered himself among those
former and future great dead men who could thus be remembered
down all the ages. Once he had suggested men might be able to
conquer death by reason alone, but now he preferred to put his trust
in a cross of wood and a mark on a map. He might be neglected now,
but someday, sooner or later, the inevitable march of truth would
resume, and he would be recognized as the prophet that he was.
Then the white-cross-wooden-slab-makers could go to work, and set
him up in his rightful place. It was, perhaps, a somewhat morbid
thought for a man of only fifty-two, even one as dejected and world-
weary as he, but it came to occupy him more and more, and the
following year he began another essay, unfinished but more to the
point, 'On Death'. It was not simply regret for vanished glories, or
anxiety whether his reputation would survive him. He was more and
more certain he had not much longer to live.

He had been a sickly child until a crisis of smallpox at Newton's
when he was twelve, but he had been robust enough thereafter,
apart from an almost fatal fever on leaving Hoxton Academy. Then,
at twenty-eight, he had suffered several weeks of fainting fits, and
these had recurred in Ireland in 1800, and again three years later,
always in hot summers, never lasting much longer than a minute,
always finding and leaving him in perfect health, and very possibly
connected with his uncontrollable tendency to doze off of an
evening:

If seized standing, I have fallen to the ground, and I have
repeatedly had fits in bed . . . . The approach of the fit is not
painful, but is rather entitled to the name of pleasure, a gentle

fading away of the senses; nor is the recovery painful, unless I am teazed in it by persons about me.[19]

Yet by 1808 these fits had become so regular and so debilitating that Godwin had to take medical advice. The doctors were 'completely puzzled about it; they say it is neither epilepsy nor apoplexy, but partakes of both',[20] these regular 'deliquia', as he lists them in his diary, continued to intensify, turning him into something of a hypochondriac. Time and again, across three more decades, he was convinced that each year would be his last.

Nevertheless, the *Essay on Sepulchres* did mark the beginning of a particularly morbid year. On 23 March 1809 Thomas Holcroft died. When he learnt he had only three weeks to live he called for his daughter, paper, pen and ink, and began to dictate his memoirs, but as his strength gave out he asked to see his old friend once more. They had not met for several years, but Holcroft could do no more than press Godwin's hand to his heart and murmur 'My dear, dear friend'. Godwin called again, but by the third visit Holcroft was too ill to see him, and he died the following day. 'One of the most candid, most upright, and single-meaning men, I ever knew', wrote Lamb in a letter of Elia to the renegade Southey, 'was the late Thomas Holcroft. I believe he never said one thing and meant another in his life.'[21]

The task of completing Holcroft's Memoirs fell to William Hazlitt, all the more urgently because Holcroft left his wife and six children, ranging in age from nine to a few months, virtually penniless. Yet when Godwin, who had been so recklessly personal in his life of Mary Wollstonecraft and had published her letters to a former lover, saw Hazlitt's text he was horrified to discover it included passages from Holcroft's private diary. Thus had the New Man of Feeling decayed into an Old Man of Desiccation, and an expurgated version of Hazlitt's *Life of Holcroft* did not appear until 1816. Lamb dubbed it 'the Life Everlasting'.

The death of Godwin's mother in August seemed to affect him even more deeply, more deeply than one might have expected. She had survived into her eighties, her pious, amiably rambling letters growing ever more disjointed, ever more plaintive, as she watched her family forsake her God. She had done her best for them all, she said,

> but fear most if not all are so deep in debt as not to be ye better for anything I could do for them, am afraid London streets will be fill'd with begging Godwins when I am gone but that's not ye worst Idleness is the mother of all Vice forger's pickpockets or Players wch I take to be very little better. Do you know of

any of them yt are following the precepts of ye precious redeemer of lost mankind who suffered Ignominious death on ye Cross to save sinners from eternal death . . .[22]

Four years earlier she had suffered a stroke that left her conscious and active but totally oblivious of her surroundings, and when Godwin had tried to speak to her she had mumbled her prayers without recognizing him at all. Now she was dead.

But in a practical sense it was Joseph Johnson's death in December that left Godwin most alone of all. Johnson had been Mary Wollstonecraft's employer and patron, and had sometimes been Godwin's publisher too. But he had also been the Juvenile Library's main source of advice, encouragement and professional contacts. From now on they would have to fend for themselves.

It was three years since Godwin had written for the Library himself, and in 1809 he returned to the chore with a *History of Rome* to accompany that of England, and began a *History of Greece*. There was also his *New Guide to the English Tounge*, an essay on word forms inspired by the *School Dictionary* which one of Godwin's regular contributors, W. F. Mylius, Master at the Boy's Academy in Red Lion Square, had compiled for him. 'I think I have made an entirely new discovery as to the way of teaching ye Eng. lange', noted Godwin in his diary, virtually the only personal remark in all its thirty-two volumes, and so proud was he of this attempt to construe English as if it were Latin that he included it not only in subsequent editions of Mylius's *Dictionary*, but also in the *New and Improved Grammar of The English Tongue* which he published for Hazlitt when no one else would take it. Hazlitt personally disliked the book, but the more pedantic Godwin admired it enormously, perhaps because he had revised it extensively in the light of his own knowledge, and to Hazlitt's mild annoyance he brought out an abridged and simplified version of his own, an *Outline of English Grammar*, at the end of 1810.

In fact Godwin was constitutionally incapable of leaving other people's work, or even his own, alone: Mylius's *School Dictionary* was another to be so extensively revised that he came to look on it too as one of the works of 'Edward Baldwin'. But Charles Lamb proved less amenable to Godwin's meddling. After the success of the *Tales from Shakespeare* he had prepared a prose adaptation of Chapman's Homer under the title of *The Voyages of Ulysses*, but Godwin was worried lest certain passages in it prove too strong, if not for the children who would read it, at least for the parents who would have to buy it:

We live in squeamish days. Amid the beauties of your manuscript, of which no man can think more highly than I do, what will the squeamish say to such expressions as these, – 'devoured their limbs, yet warm and trembling, lapping the blood', p. 10. Or to the giant's vomit, p. 14; or to the minute and shocking description of the extinguishing of the giant's eye in the page following. You, I daresay, have no formed plan of excluding the female sex from among your readers, and I, as a book-seller, must consider that if you have you exclude one half of the human species.[23]

Lamb was only partially apologetic. 'The giant's vomit was perfectly nauseous, and I am glad you pointed it out. I have removed the objection.' But the other passages must stay as they were:

As an author I say to you an author, Touch not my work. As to a book-seller I say, Take the work such as it is, or refuse it. You are as free to refuse it as when we first talked of it. As to a friend I say, Don't plague yourself and me with nonsensical objections. I assure you I will not alter one more word.[24]

Not that that prevented Godwin from writing again, to suggest that younger readers would need some explanation of who Homer was, and why they should bother to read him. Lamb exploded, and scrawled his angry reply across the bottom of Godwin's note,

I have read your letter and am fully of the opinion that such a drawling biography as you have chalk'd out is not my forte to write. I totally disagree with you; and prefer my own preface (as I am always likely to do) to any preface a man tells me to write. You must take that, or none. I am *sick* absolutely sick of that spirit of objection which you constantly shew, as if it were only to teaze one, or to warn me against having any more dealings with you in the way of trade. My preface is just a one as I approve, and there is enough of it, but I had quite as lieve have *no preface* if you prefer it. I shall remember Ulysses as long as I live to write.
Yours in the way of friendship still. Ever C.L.[25]

(This note appears to have escaped the attention of anthologizers of Lamb's correspondence.)

Godwin next approached William Wordsworth, to see if he would like to try his hand at verse for children, but Wordsworth declined, politely but firmly, insisting he had neither the ability nor the interest. And so it fell to Lamb again, to have the honour of introducing *Beauty and the Beast* to a British audience. Coleridge, meanwhile, had offered a nursery poem of his own to fill the gap left by Wordsworth's refusal, followed perhaps by a three volume set of

Lives from Moses to Napoleon, after the fashion of Plutarch. But though Godwin was enthusiastic about the former, at least, both projects came to nothing. 'If love and a crust would tempt you to cooperate in my little scheme for refining and elevating the circle of juvenile studies, it is well,' Godwin warned him; 'but

> If these motives be weak, break off betimes.'[26]

And Coleridge took the hint.

The Juvenile Library amounted in all to more than twenty volumes, together with eight booklets in the Copper Plate Series and several individual works and translations into French. But apart from the unfinished *History of Greece* and two volumes of *Scripture Histories* 'given in the words of the original' which have since disappeared, if they were ever published, Godwin had written himself out. The works of Baldwin and Marcliffe continued to be published, revised and abridged again and again, but his own family was outgrowing children's readers, and he could find nothing else to interest him. From 1811 onwards the Library was virtually at a standstill, the one notable exception being the 1814 *Family Robinson Crusoe*, a version of the *Swiss Family Robinson* translated and abridged by Mary Jane Godwin with an even more oppressive moralism than the original. It was another impressive first for the Godwins, and the full version, with the more familiar title, followed two years later. But for the most part Godwin was too busy raising new cash to contemplate new contributions, too nervously paying off the cost of past publications to contemplate fresh ones. And the promised land lay as far away as ever.

19 ♣ The monster with the maw

Let us suppose however that the debtor is clearly in the wrong
. . . Let us suppose that these are vices that will admit of no
explanation. Yet how great and eminent virtues may exist in
this man's bosom. He may be the most generous and phil-
anthropical of mortals. He may be the greatest benefactor the
human species ever knew. Every man probably is inconsistent.
Every man probably, be he in whatever degree virtuous, has
some point to which unaccountably he has not applied those
principles by which he is ordinarily governed . . . . In judging
the past conduct, particularly of others, he that is not liberal
and indulgent, is not just.[1]

Enquirer, 1797

♣ By this time Godwin's finances were in an appalling condition. As
Lamb had said, 'The Professor is never much beforehand with the
world,' but *Antonio* had marked a turning point. Until then he had
lived on credit, in the form of advances against work in progress;
from then on he would live in debt, in the form of promissory notes
which delayed payment as long as the creditor would permit, though
always on terms that eventually cost him more. For a time he trusted
that some new success would set him up again, and in an emergency
there was always Tom Wedgwood, who had been supplying what
amounted to an annual subsidy of £100. Then in July 1905, barely a
week after the Juvenile Library's first advertisements, Wedgwood,
aged thirty-four had died. He did leave a trust fund from which to
continue the annuity to Coleridge and the assistance to the 'several
persons' he had been supporting while alive. But he left it in the care
of his younger brother Josiah, altogether more brisk and businesslike,
and certainly not prepared to let Godwin rely on it forever.

So Godwin had cast around for someone to take Wedgwood's
place, and hit upon the most prominent radical politician of the day,
Sir Francis Burdett, whom he had met at the home of Burdett's
neighbour and principal inspiration, John Horne Took. Burdett had
been elected by Wilkes's old constituency of Middlesex in 1802, but
that result had been overturned in the courts and in the extraordinary by-election that followed the voting had lain neck-and-neck
for a fortnight amidst mounting hysteria, until the polls closed with
Burdett apparently ahead by a single vote – only to be defeated

again on a technicality. Even more to Godwin's point, Burdett had married a fortune when he married a Miss Coutts. But fighting elections, then fighting their results through the courts, was costing him more than enough already, and Burdett declined the offer to become Godwin's patron. So, convinced that someone who worked as devotedly as he must someday reap a just reward for his labours, Godwin had appealed to anyone who might provide temporary assistance: to Joseph Johnson, always willing to help in any way he could; to Richard Phillips, who was reluctantly persuaded not to recall advances made against books never written; to William Nicholson, a businessman himself, who advised that the enterprise could never succeed without proper capital; to the Whig Lords, Lauderdale and Holland, at whose houses Godwin had occasionally dined, once finding himself, back in March 1802, in the august presence of the Prince of Wales; to William Wordsworth; to the Wedgwood bequest. But not everyone who had once been friendly now claimed that offer, and one contact replied in terms that compared Godwin with a bankrupt who has run off with another man's wife!

The move to Skinner Street brought matters to a head. It was on the expectation of *Faulkener*, so Mrs Godwin told Crabb Robinson, that they had taken on the new shop, and instead they had lost full £800, though Robinson commented that 'This could have been meant only in a figurative sense, for he had not £800 to lose.'[2] Yet by the time they had contributed towards the cost of producing, advertising and publishing the play – and, who knows, the hire of an audience to provide them with 'Ayes' – they would be lucky not to have lost real money, too. So at Christmas 1807, when *Faulkener*'s brief run came to an end, Godwin began his 'preparations for subscribing'. The idea – it had been Johnson's of course – was that Godwin's various wealthy acquaintances might contribute a sizeable sum which would then attract the subscriptions of others, and so set the business properly on its feet. Godwin and Marshall drew up an impressive list headed by 'Fox's men': Grey, the Duke of Bedford, Samuel Whitbread, MP. Lauderdale, Holland, Johnson, Phillips and Curran were the main subscribers at £100 each. And by mid-1808 the total stood at well over £1000, and may even have reached £1500. Godwin took a deep breath, gave up his major literary activity of the past two years, the composition of begging letters, and went back to his writing, to the *Essay on Sepulchres* and books by Baldwin.

But this respite was short-lived and Johnson's death, followed in 1810 by Phillips's bankruptcy that Godwin had been nervously attending at London's Guildhall, precipitated another crisis.

Godwin owed both men money, but they had known he could not pay and he had known they would not demand payment, and there the matter had always rested. But now these debts were transferred to other, less easily satisfied creditors, and the few hundred pounds he received in legacies from Johnson and his mother were not enough to cover the £900 or so now demanded of him. For a time there was the hope that he might raise £500 on the estate of a Scots admirer Hepburn, but at first no one would accept the mortgage, then Hepburn withdrew the offer. Instead Godwin raised the money from Wedgwood, with a bond guaranteed by five of his friends, a debt that had still not been repaid, neither capital nor interest, ten years later.

From now on business and life would be one unending struggle from hand to mouth, the restless shifting of burdens from one pair of shoulders to another, until even the largest sums could provide only temporary relief. When Godwin received payment of one bill he thanked the sender kindly but reported that 'the monster with the great maw has opened her mouth and swallowed it up';[3] and even when things seemed to be going well he could never be free of the fear that at any moment another debt would fall due and he would be unable to meet it. Once, casting hopefully around for a way to delay payment on one bill for £100 he came across another for £140 which

> I had utterly forgotten about. Perhaps I never felt a more
> terrible sensation in my life, than when it thus returned to me
> .... I felt a cold swelling in the inside of my throat, a sen-
> sation I am subject to in terrible situations, and my head ached
> in the most uncomfortable manner .... If Turner had not
> come in just then, I think I should have gone mad; as it was,
> the morsel of meat I put in my mouth at supper, stuck in my
> throat.[4]

In the circumstances it is not surprising that friends came to expect a slight touch on their wallet whenever they met, especially if they were younger and cast by Godwin in the role of acolyte. Henry Crabb Robinson, who as a youth had read *Political Justice* with such enthusiasm, was now with the author frequently, 'though his acquaintance was of the least agreeable kind. He made me feel my inferiority unpleasantly, and also in another way disagreeably by demands on my purse for small sums, and trying to make use of me with others.'[5] Godwin's irritating demands were no less irritating for being too petty to justify an outright confrontation, so it is with some enjoyment that Robinson reports how he once introduced Godwin to William Rough, an equally notorious sponger. Next morning each called within an hour of the other, to ask if this fascinating new acquaintance might perhaps be good for a loan!

But if Robinson reports Godwin 'disputatious' as usual, or 'most ungracious in demanding and receiving favours',[6] he nevertheless 'agreed in ascribing his irregularities to distress and not want of principle',[7] and others found his approaches almost flattering. Lamb's biographer Talfourd tells how Godwin

> asked his friends for aid without scruple, considering that their means were justly the reward of one who toiled in thought for their inward life, and had little time to provide for his own out-ward existence; and took their excuses, when offered, without doubt or offence. The very next day after I had been honoured and delighted by an introduction to him at Lamb's chambers, I was made still more proud and happy by his appearance at my own on such an errand – which my poverty, not my will rendered abortive . . . . 'Oh dear,' said the philosopher, 'I thought you were a young gentleman of fortune – don't mention it – don't mention it; I shall do very well elsewhere'; – and then, in the most gracious manner, reverted to our former topics; and sat in my small room for half an hour as if to convince me that my want of fortune made no difference in his esteem.[8]

For if Godwin had learned to ask for assistance almost as a matter of right, not favour, it was from principle as much as from practice. 'Give me that, and that only', *Political Justice* had said, 'which without injustice you cannot refuse. More than justice it would be disgraceful for me to ask, and for you to bestow.'[9]

> My neighbour is in want of ten pounds that I can spare. There is no law of political institution that has been made to reach this case, and to transfer this property from me to him. But in the eye of simple justice, unless it can be shown that the money can be more beneficially employed, his claim is as complete, as if he had my bond in his possession, or had supplied me with goods to the amount.[10]

And though circumstances seldom gave him opportunity, Godwin had always tried to live by that doctrine. With time and energy, which he did have, he was unstinting, and those many who wrote to him for advice and encouragement always found him willing to reply at length and in detail, for as long as they were prepared to write to him. When, occasionally, he did have cash in hand he was sur-prisingly ready to lend it where it might do good, without too much thought for his own future needs. In 1809 he and Marshall helped raise £1,000 for Holcroft's penniless widow and family. In 1810 he took over the finances of a struggling student, Patrick Patrickson, and raised an allowance to see him through college. In 1811 he helped Aaron Burr find his fare back to America, refused to accept the few pounds that Burr owed him personally, lent small sums to Coleridge without a moment's hesitation, and paid for the advertising of Coleridge's London lectures, leaving Coleridge to repay him when he could. And several years later, when his own needs were even more pressing, he raised a few hundred pounds for James Marshall, when he too fell disastrously into debt.

Still, there is no disguising the fact that the decade from 1810 to 1820 was Godwin's most disgraceful and most demeaning. He had long since lost all trace of the pride that had once restrained him from accepting gifts, the dignity with which he had written his first letters of supplication. Borrowing had become second nature, as each day was spent in the restless search for new sources of finance with which to settle old debts. No occasion was too inopportune, no acquaintance too slight, if he thought there might be money in it somewhere. In May 1811 he was at the Haymarket Theatre for a new one-actor called *Trial by Jury*, when his attention was caught by the bizarre behaviour of an eccentric couple in a side box: 'I looked often on these very singular neighbours. I had difficulty to confine my observations within the bounds of decorum. Once or twice I said to myself, Is it possible this should be a man to lend me money?'[11]

By this time it was obvious, if there had ever been any doubt, that Godwin had no head for business. The scale of debt involved in printing and storing whole libraries of volumes meant nothing to him, just as he cared nothing for future debts so long as he could meet, at whatever cost, a present one: if he had to borrow, it was always in the unquestioning faith that whatever went into the firm must sooner or later come out again, and then all would be well. Yet even he recognized the need of someone to advise him properly, now that Johnson was dead, and in 1811 he turned to Francis Place, the Charing Cross tailor who combined a devotion to radical politics with a sound sense of free enterprise, and a reputation for salvaging ailing firms. Place had joined the Corresponding Society in its darkest moments, even as its leaders were arrested in 1794; a year later he became its chairman; a year after that he resigned, disillusioned. He had been one of the organizers when Burdett was finally elected at Westminster in 1807, just as he would skilfully manipulate public pressure during the Reform Bill crisis of 1832. Once such men had sought Godwin out, but it was Godwin who sought out Place.

So Godwin produced his accounts and Place went over them with his wealthy associate John Lambert and a fervent young admirer of Godwin called Elton, or Eltus, Hammond. What they found seemed encouraging enough: Godwin's assets, standing around £7,700, exceeded his debts by a full £3,000; the business was growing and would grow faster still if backed with adequate capital; £2,000 was needed to keep it afloat, £2,500 would keep it going, £3,000 would guarantee success. The intention, moreover, was that Charles Clairmont, now sixteen, should be apprenticed to one of the premier firms in the field, Constables of Edinburgh, and so be able to take over the management from his ailing parents. By the following summer, with £3,000 raised by Place's endeavours, and encouraging reports coming out of Edinburgh, it seemed that their troubles would soon be over.

> But our efforts were useless. In a little time Godwin was as much embarrassed as ever, we had also embarrassed ourselves and been the means of risking the property of others without having done any permanent service to Mr Godwin. Mr Godwin was at length obliged to repay some of the money we had caused several to advance, this he did, not from the proceeds of his business as he ought to have done, but by inducing his own particular friends to increase the amount of the sums they had advanced. A Mr Hume, a private friend of Godwin's, one or two others, and Mr Taylor of Norwich, with whom we were not connected lost considerable sums, and full £2,500 were wholly wasted.[12]

Perhaps the only one to get his money back was Hammond, who had borrowed £500 from his sisters; Place and Lambert, who had originally contributed £250 each, ended up losing £365 in the attempt to protect their friends; and the unhappy results of the affair would haunt Godwin for years to come.

Irritated by this failure, Place was convinced there must be dishonesty in it somewhere. He had done his sums correctly, and raised the amount needed to set things right,

> and to this hour I am satisfied that it might and ought to have been so notwithstanding the accounts laid before us were not correct accounts, and did not contain a true statement but had been fabricated to induce us to procure the money.

Once he 'had never heard anything alleged against his moral character. I had heard much in his praise and I have benefitted in no small degree by his writings. I was therefore pleased to have him for a friend.' But now he thought he knew his man better:

> As respects his own purposes Godwin was one of the most heartless, the most callous of men. He was perfectly regardless

of the mischief he might bring upon any one, and quite as regardless of the feelings of others, when his own ends could be best and most promptly answered by inflicting unhappiness on them. These matters annoyed him so little that I have sometimes doubted, whether they did not afford him satisfaction, when they fell upon those who had not readily conformed to his wishes. He was ingenious, plausible, argumentative, persuasive and persevering to an enormous extent. He could easily turn any man to account who reposed the least confidence in him and he never failed to do so. But in all this he was unwise.

With only a moderate share of prudence and honesty, half the efforts he made to procure money and make enemies would have made him a flourishing man, had these efforts been diverted as they ought to have been, and surrounded him with a multitude of friends . . . . Mr Godwin had however many good points, and no man could keep company with him without being benefitted. This was the case with Mr Hammond, Mr Lambert and myself. Mr Hammond almost adored him, and Mr Lambert admired him excessively. But Godwin compelled us all three to give him up, as he had done many others. Had Godwin been placed in other circumstances, or had he had a more prudent woman for a wife, instead of the infernal devil to whom he was married [someone has drawn a blue pencil through this phrase], his good qualities would have preponderated and he would have been a man of extensive influence as well personally as by his writings and would have lived in ease and comfort and been a happy man.[13]

Yet Godwin's accounts were more likely to be muddled than deliberately falsified – unless, perhaps, they were the work of his wife. Certainly he was capable of concealing one business arrangement from the parties to another, or pretending that negotiations were more advanced than they actually were. But if Godwin deceived others about the true state of his finances he also deceived himself. The plain fact of it was that no one, not even Godwin himself, ever knew exactly what his debts were, or where they lay. Nevertheless, when Place and Hammond went back over the accounts they came to the startling conclusion that for ten years past Godwin had been borrowing some £400 a year from personal friends alone, so that his annual expenses must have exceeded £1,500, despite living in Skinner Street rent free. As Shelley was later to demand in utter perplexity, and with even more justice, where on earth had the money gone?

It is hard to know where to look for an answer. A parsimonious

man himself, Place preferred to represent Godwin as an idle
spendthrift, yet the promissory notes that he cashed from day to day
were always for basic necessities – food, clothing, household sup-
plies – never luxuries, and as Horace Smith, another to be drawn
into the morass of Godwin's finances, commented, though his debts
were unending yet 'he lived in an almost primitive simplicity, and
had no expensive habits'.[14] Was it, then, the fault of the infernal
devil to whom he was married? She was, we know, scheming,
ambitious and selfish; it had not taken more than a touch of flattery
and some domestic comforts to capture her willing husband. But
there, perhaps, she had come unstuck, for the Godwin that she
married was no longer the immortal figure she had addressed from
her window, and certainly not someone in a position to keep her in
the style to which she intended to grow accustomed. The business
had scarcely begun before Godwin was reporting that 'her health
and strength have somewhat given way, I really believe for want of
those relaxations and excursions to sea-bathings and watering
places, which are the usual lot of women in the class of life in which
she was born',[15] though he was well aware it was not the class of life
in which she had lived until now. It was more a case of her being
determined to have, at last, the respectable middle-class existence to
which she felt entitled. Doubtless she lived beyond their means, with
servants for the house, schools for the children – *her* children, that is
– and almost annual seaside vacations for her own peace of mind,
with Godwin travelling down the Thames on a new-fangled river
steamer, to join her for an occasional weekend.

Even so it is rather too easy to blame everything on Mrs Godwin.
She worked as hard as he did, and Godwin himself believed he owed
these things to her, both for what she put into shop and library, and
for the misery and ill-health that his difficulties inflicted on her. It
was in 1812 that he wrote her a curiously apologetic appreciation,
more character reference than love letter, to thank her for her efforts
on behalf of them all:

> I have long wished for the opportunity of writing to you a letter
> on the subject of the following, and am not without a sanguine
> hope that it will afford you satisfaction. You have often
> reproached me with not doing justice to your character, your
> qualifications and your exertions . . . . You were perhaps
> destined by your intrinsic nature for something much better
> than my wife. Most deeply do I grieve that you should have
> been involved in any straits of mine, or that you should
> experience any privations arising out of my circumstances.[16]

It was a letter that Jane Clairmont carefully preserved, because her step-sister 'was ever speaking with contempt of my mother', and to show that 'the father did not share the same intemperate prejudice of his daughter'.

Perhaps, then, it was simply impossible to live the self-sufficient life that Godwin intended, without a private income. There was nothing distinctive about being in debt: Dr Johnson was arrested for it twice, and Wordworth, Coleridge and Southey all needed their patrons or pensions or public positions. What was distinctive was that Godwin had tried to support himself, and instead of diminishing his burdens had increased them. It is possible, indeed, that for most or all of its nineteen years the Juvenile Library actually ran at a loss. Certainly it seems a bottomless well into which Godwin would pour the funds of anyone ill-advised enough to let him. But perhaps that too is an illusion, for the debts that plagued him so constantly, tended to be the same debts, postponed for the moment and with the utmost difficulty, then returning to plague him again. Godwin himself was constantly insisting that with just a bit more help he could clear £1,000 a year, and those who advised him – and they were many and experienced – seem to have agreed. Some of his volumes – especially the Baldwin *Fables*, the Lamb *Tales*, and the Mylius *Dictionary* – were extremely successful, and by the end of the decade, when the Library itself was at a standstill, there is no doubt that the business was bringing in more than it was paying out.

There is, moreover, one further answer to the question of where the money went: 'I have from time to time,' said Godwin, 'a paroxysm of discounting.' The business, as he was quickly to regret, was begun almost haphazardly, without capital or income, but with debts totalling almost £1,000. It was only by obtaining some promise to pay at a future date, then selling it off immediately at a discount, or by issuing some promise of his own, that Godwin contrived to keep going. But when those bills fell due he would be liable in full for the original amount, which he could raise only by another discount on a larger sum. The loss each time might be a mere 5 or 7 per cent, but repeat the process at intervals of, say, sixty-five days, and the annual rate of interest begins to mount. The sheer quantity of his promissory notes proves that Godwin's credit was good, but once in debt, as he was even before he began, it was virtually impossible ever to get out again. It might have been a different story, had some of that capital been there from the start.

So why did he not simply give it up, when all the efforts of himself, his wife and his friends came so signally to nought? Because he could see no alternative, no other way of supporting his family and providing for them when he was gone, as he was sure he soon would be. Nor, ironically, would he contemplate letting his friends and backers down, after all that they had done for him. 'He is in some respects a poor creature – ', Place had written, fairer and more sympathetic than he would soon become,

> he fears poverty, not I think much on his own account, but for his family – this I think very silly – he fears shame this I think quite as silly in a man who does nothing in itself shameful – he fears he shall not succeed in obtaining the loan which has for its object to repay the advances of friends . . . some of whom will be ruined if he fail – and this distracts him, a more miserable creature than he seems to be hardly exists, he is not a man of the world in the sense he ought to be to obtain a living by business.[17]

And whatever else is mysterious, that surely was the case.

It was indeed an ironic situation. There was Godwin, evidently prepared to commit any sort of personal injustice in order to avoid bankruptcy, an evil created solely by the pernicious institutions of law and private property. And there was Place, who claimed that it was *Political Justice* that persuaded him a businessman could still be an honest man, since there was no injustice in relying on the wealth of others! But in September of 1814 Godwin had to report that he could no longer meet his obligations, and Place angrily accused him of distortion and deception that stopped just short of downright dishonesty: once, for example, he had on Place's instruction made a bill payable at his bankers, but omitted to mention that he had no banker! Godwin, of course, was always ready with some explanation or excuse, sometimes a word of apology or regret, though never a hint of shame, but Place was no less self-righteous, no less anxious to justify his every action. And so it went on, accusation and counter-accusation, until Place was provoked into quoting Godwin against himself, to the man's understandable fury:

> Your chapter on 'Sincerity' teaches me to avoid this, and leads me to say, that the highmindedness of which you there speak is sadly lowered by endeavouring to obtain money by the means you have unhappily resorted to. Men of rank – of power – of riches – of high reputations – shun you, so I have found, because you are willing to be dependent.[18]

Yet Godwin had, in effect, already countered Place with another doctrine drawn from the pages of *Political Justice*. 'All promises have this in their nature,' he had explained,

> 'I cannot command events; but if events happen which I have a right to expect, then I will do so.' The promise of an honest man is merely the expression of his earnest desire, and his

resolute purpose to do a thing. If I promise to be in America next year, does that imply that I can command the waves or the tides? But because the thing I cannot master thwarts you, I am to be treated as the refuse of all mankind.

It was the opportunity for a noble debate, Place on sincerity and independence, Godwin on promises and property. But neither man was in the mood for that now.

Political Justice, of course, had insisted that property must belong to him who has most need of it, or can benefit most from it. True, Place might reply that the money had been advanced only on the understanding that Godwin would repay it, in due amounts at due intervals. But *Political Justice* had also denied that there was any obligation to keep a promise, as such, at all: the question is only which course of action is of most benefit to all. True, I ought not disappoint others when they are relying on me, but that obligation arises whether I have promised or not; and if letting them down will actually increase the general welfare, then that is what I ought to do.

Yet this must seem rather too easy, too patently self-serving, if it means that Godwin is under an obligation to repay only in the unlikely event that the money would be of greater benefit to Place than to himself. It is surely important – not just socially convenient but morally desirable – that sometimes we should be able to rely implicitly on others, no matter who stands to benefit what. That, presumably, is why we have promises at all, and formal contracts, to ensure as best we can that people will act in a specified way, without changing their minds whenever some other course of action strikes them as better. If there were no special obligation to keep a promise we could never put a special trust in others doing as they have said, and we would be worse, not better, off than before. And nowhere would this be more obvious more quickly than in the reluctance of one man of business to lend money to another, if he could not be reasonably certain of getting it back as agreed. A world without promises would, to Godwin's greater distress, be a world without loans!

The discussion of promising, however, was one of those completely rewritten for *Political Justice*'s second edition. Godwin is now prepared to concede what he calls passive or negative rights, not a right positively to do something but a right not to be interfered with by others: 'Every man has a certain sphere of discretion, which he has a right to expect shall not be infringed by his neighbours,'[19] a 'sphere of discretion which another may not, unless under the most imperious circumstances, infringe.'[20] So justice may demand that my neighbour supply me with some of his wealth or possessions, but his sphere of discretion also means that it is not for me, or anyone else, to force him to do so. And it emerges that the obligation to keep a promise is like the obligation not to invade another's property. For the distinctive feature of a promise is not that other people rely on my doing something, but that by promising I encourage them to rely on me, so that they base their conduct on my assurance. To take an example that comes easily to Godwin, if someone promises me £500 on completion of a book over which I then spend several months, he can hardly argue that he need not pay me after all, because he has found some better use for the money. That would be more than letting me down, disappointing my expectations. It would be inveigling me into doing something I would not otherwise have done, and therefore an interference with my sphere of discretion, my right – my duty, rather – to decide my own conduct for myself. And Place, similarly, would surely not have raised the money that Godwin needed, if he had not believed that Godwin would eventually pay it back.

But if there are times when promises ought to be kept, there are also times when they ought to be broken, and for Godwin the test is straightforward enough. It may be a fine judgment whether the good to come from breaking my word will outweigh the evil of interfering in someone else's sphere of discretion. But sometimes it will. A starving man is entitled to take another's food by force if necessary, and similarly I may be entitled to keep for myself the money I have promised to another:

> It is in vain that the whole multitude of moralists assures us, that the sum I owe to another man, is as little to be infringed, as the wealth of which he is in possession. Every one feels the fallacy of this maxim . . . . The means of payment, particularly with a man of slender resources, must necessarily be fluctuating, and he must employ his discretion, as to the proportion between his necessary and his gratuitous disbursements . . . . In fine, it is a law resulting from the necessity of nature, that he who has any species of property in trust, must have a discretion, sometimes less, and sometimes greater, as to the disposal of it. [21]

Justice, impartial justice, was on Godwin's side after all.

But unhappily the argument does not end there. Justice may sometimes demand that we keep our promises, and sometimes that we break them. But it also demands that we should not make promises in the first place. For one thing, I ought to do something because it is just, not because of a promise; the practice of making and keeping promises teaches me to do something from a precarious and temporary motive which ought to be done for its intrinsic recommendations. If therefore right motives and a pure intention are constituent parts of virtue, promises are clearly at variance with virtue.[22]

And for another, men must learn to rely on their own exertions, not on the promises of others. Place was right, after all, to preach independence to William Godwin.

Yet if justice requires that we make no promises, it also requires that we help others not because they have asked us, much less because we or they have promised, but simply because they have need of us. In a world of justice Godwin would not have asked for Place's assistance in the first place, and would not have promised to repay. But in a world of justice Place would have come to his assistance without the asking, and without the promise.

20 ♣ A young gentleman of fortune

The system of domestic life is so delicate a structure, and it is so impossible for a bystander truly to appreciate the interior events, the discussions and mutual unfitnesses that may occur in the conjugal state, that every human being must be permitted to be in a considerable degree his own judge and jury in that trial. The exercise of these functions imposes on him an awful duty. A severe moralist . . . will task himself to bear as much as patiently and philosophically can be born in that engagement, from respect for the universally received institutions of his contemporaries, and in some measure, of all civilized life; and especially where there are children, from a regard to what the welfare of their rising minds may require.*

Lives of the Phillipses, 1815

♣ Perhaps it would have been best had Godwin remained in the decent obscurity – decent only because obscure – of Skinner Street, an obscurity best captured in a cartoon from December 1812 which portrays him as a top hat floating on the waters of Lethe, a pair of hands clutching at a passing copy of *Political Justice*. So successfully had he concealed his very existence that the *Horace in London* satires of the following year would describe him as 'slumbering in St Paul's churchyard':

> Our Temple youth, a lawless train,
> Blockading Johnson's window pane,
> No longer laud they solemn strain,
>   'My Godwin!
>
> Chaucer's a mighty tedious elf,
> Fleetwood lives only for himself,
> And Caleb Williams loves the shelf,
>   My Godwin!

It was only in that same year, 1813, that a government spy proudly cracked the secret of M. J. Godwin and Co.

The proprietor, he announced, was not a Mr. J. Godwin (the anonymous spy was not the only one to misread the – deliberately

*Godwin, writing in 1814, is discussing John Phillips's desertion of his wife and family.

misleading? – sign 'M. J. Godwin and Co.', see p. 247 below) at all, but *Political Justice* Godwin who had used a pseudonym to smuggle his works into respectable institutions like Christ's Hospital and then advertised the fact in *The Times*, all as part of 'a regular system to supersede all other elementary Books and to make his Library the resort of Preparatory Schools that in time the principles of democracy and Theophilanthropy may take universally'. More sinister still, 'in order to allure schools of a moderate and lower class, he holds out the temptation of allowance of threepence in every shilling for such books as are published by him.' And such books! There is a Mythology, 'an insidious and dangerous publication', which professes to exalt Christianity over paganism but instead 'hints the wisdom of the morality of the heathen world.' There are histories of England, Rome and Greece (here too the spy was misled by the Godwins' publicity: the *History of Greece*, though begun in 1809 and advertised for several years after that, was not completed and published until 1821) in which 'every democratical sentiment is printed in Italics that they may not fail to present themselves to a Child's Notice': the *History of Rome*, for example, 'leaves off at the reign of Augustus and in *Italics* remarks that . . . when it ceased to be a Republic it ceased to deserve the name of History.' But worst of all there is

> a pocket dictionary the Danger of which consists in giving only *one* meaning to words which have several and omitting all such words as philosophers of the present day do not like to explain – for example take the word 'Revolution' the meaning given is Things returning to their first state.

Another entry even suggests that the Mohammedans have a Bible of their own, which they call the Sheran: 'By such means did Voltaire and his brethren for twenty years before the revolution in France spread infidelity and disloyalty through the remotest provinces of that country and we know too well how they succeeded.'[1]

Of course the spy had taken care to distort the facts. What the *History of Rome* actually says, in italics that mark the end of the text, is that 'the quarrels of the tyrants make no proper part of the history of the Roman Republic', that 'Rome scarcely retained any feature of that illustrious, high-minded and independent nation it had hitherto been.' The dictionary, moreover, was actually the work of Mylius, and the spy had coalesced two innocuous definitions – 'a returning motion; a great change in a state or nation' – into a single more damaging one. Even so, a correspondent in the *Christian Remembrancer* eight years later chanced to be on safer ground when he too protested the partiality of such school texts as those by 'the notorious Godwin', with his tendentious definitions of 'church', 'King' and 'liberty'. Mylius had defined these as 'a place where Christians worship God', 'a monarch', and 'freedom'. But Godwin, never able to leave well alone, had subsequently changed them to 'a body of Christians professing the same rule', 'a single person in a state, to whom extraordinary power is confided for life', and 'permission to anyone to judge of his own duties, and act accordingly'.

Still it would be difficult to read serious sedition into any of this, and across the back of the anonymous report the authorities wrote their verdict in a single word, 'Nil'. That weary, burdened old man, fast approaching sixty, seemed unlikely to foment any revolutions now. Yet at the same time there was growing up a new generation of eager idealists to whom Jacobinism was as remote as Cromwellism. They, too, were beginning to discover *Political Justice*, and recreate in their imaginations the heady delights of a world founded in reason, truth and justice. Even as Place and his associates were casting around for the £3,000 that might carry Godwin into a secure old age, events were conspiring to throw a new light on him, even harsher and more enduring than before.

Right from the time he first made a name for himself Godwin had grown used to receiving letters from unknown young men, asking his advice and assistance in the lonely and arduous business of educating themselves. Invariably he would reply at length and in detail, recommending his own rotary pattern of reading and study, and supplying an exhaustive list of books that they might read with profit. Eventually the exercise became so routine and so repetitive that Godwin had his reply printed, so as to 'have the Paper always at hand, to give away to any person to whom I judged it might be desirable'.[2] This was his *Letter of Advice to a Young American*, originally published in the *Edinburgh Magazine* for March 1818 then privately distributed by Godwin himself, and reprinted again and again, especially in North America, where it became one of his most widely circulated works.

Sometimes these youths became protégés, like Patrick Patrickson, the penniless student who had broken with his family over his decision to study law at Cambridge, and for whom Godwin raised an allowance among his wealthier acquaintances such as Basil Montagu, now a Bankruptcy Commissioner, or Matthew Raine, the Master at Charterhouse School where both Charles and young William were pupils. Some even became benefactors, like Elton Hammond, who was working with Place and Lambert to raise Godwin's £3,000. Indeed Hammond, so impressive in physique and feature that, according to Place, 'had an accurate portrait been taken of him, it might have stood for a more perfect head of Christ according to the ideal notion of artists than any portrait I have ever seen on canvas, or any head I have ever seen in real life,'[3] made a practice of pursuing the great men of his age, Bentham and James Mill as well as Godwin, among whom he confidently expected to number. But his exaggerated devotion to the progress of mankind tipped slowly into madness, and it came as no surprise to his friend Crabb Robinson when Hammond shot himself on the very eve of 1820. To Godwin's intense disappointment Hammond left all his papers to Robert Southey, to whom he had written but never actually met; and, as Southey told Crabb Robinson, he was glad they had not been left to anyone who shared Hammond's dreadful opinions, and especially not to Godwin,

> who I hear has been very inquisitive concerning them . . . for in spite of the dreadful insanity of which they contain the most decided proofs, a publication might have been made from them, which would have done infinite mischief and would, I verily believe, have occasioned as many acts of suicide as Goethe has to answer for.[4]

Perhaps Southey knew of Patrickson's fate also.

It was Southey who was responsible, half accidentally, for the most famous, most significant, disciple of all. It was back in January 1812 that Godwin had received that first grandiloquent letter of introduction, soaked in flattery that even he might have thought excessive:

> The name of Godwin has been used to excite in me feelings of reverence and admiration. I have been accustomed to consider him as a luminary too dazzling for the darkness which surrounds him, and from the earliest period of my knowledge of his principles, I have ardently desired to share on the footing of intimacy that intellect which I have delighted to contemplate in its emanations. Considering, then, these feelings, you will not be surprised at the inconceivable emotions with which I learned of your existence and your dwelling. I had enrolled your name on the list of the honourable dead. I had felt regret that the glory of your being had passed from this earth of ours. It is not so. You still live, and I firmly believe are still planning the welfare of human kind. I have but just entered on the scene of human operations, yet my feelings and my reasonings correspond with what yours were. My course has been short, but eventful. I have seen much of human prejudice, suffered much from human persecution, yet I see no reason hence inferable which should alter my wishes for their renova-

tion . . . . I am young: you have gone before me, I doubt not a veteran to me in the years of persecution. Is it strange that, defying persecution as I have done, I should outstep the limits of custom's prescription, and endeavour to make my desire useful by friendship with William Godwin? I pray you to answer this letter. Imperfect as it may be, my capacity, my desire, is ardent, and unintermitted. Half-an-hour would be at least humanity employed in the experiment.[5]

It was signed Percy B. Shelley.

There was no reason why Godwin should have heard of Shelley, yet Shelley's boast that his course, though short, had been eventful was nothing less than the truth. Though not yet twenty, he had already published two juvenile novels and co-authored two books of poetry, had engaged himself to one Harriet, been expelled from Oxford, and then eloped with a second Harriet. He would live barely ten years more, yet become one of the handful of poets whose names are household words. Perhaps it was more of an exaggeration to claim that the prejudice and persecution he had suffered came from an adherence to Godwin's principles, but Shelley, an indulged child, had sufficient intelligence, or sufficient imagination, to represent the petty restrictions of boarding school, the taunts of his fellow pupils, the rigid incomprehension of his father, as all of a piece with the social tyrannies and political impositions attacked in *Political Justice*. He had read the book at Eton, and would read it again and again, at least six times more, between 1810 and 1820, its influence evident already in the pamphlet for which he had been expelled from Oxford, his *Necessity of Atheism*, more exactly an argument against the possibility of proving God's existence, closing with the Godwinian declaration: 'Truth has always been found to promote the best interests of mankind, – Every reflecting mind must allow that there is no proof of the existence of a Deity. Q.E.D.'

But Shelley's interest also lay in what he called the 'Godwinian anti-matrimonial system'. Marriage, he told his friend Hogg, 'is hateful, detestable – a kind of ineffable sickening disgust seizes my mind, when I think of this most despotic, most unrequired fetter.'[6] He was writing, as it happened, from the home of the Westbrooks, and he had, no doubt, been elaborating the same opinions to their handsome daughter Harriet. But if Harriet loved Shelley, as she certainly seemed to, it was the strictly married kind she had in mind, and to stress the point she presented him with a novel which dramatized the evils that flow from an illicit connection. It was, of all things, *Adeline Mowbray*! Shelley was not in a position to appreciate the irony behind this story by a woman for whom Godwin himself had once made a formal proposal, but he was probably astute enough to recognize that its moral was not what Mrs Opie, or at any rate Harriet, intended. Nevertheless, Harriet won the argument, and in August of 1811 they had eloped to Edinburgh, in a fashion so casual to suggest that the Westbrooks were not at all unwilling to see their daughter married into the aristocracy.

From Edinburgh Shelley had gone to Keswick to seek out Coleridge, but found Southey instead, and so discovered that Godwin was not after all to be enrolled among the honourable dead. He had heard that a Mr John Godwin sold books in Holborn, his informant misreading the sign just as the government spy had done, but the moment he discovered that it was actually *the* Godwin, his Godwin, he sat down and wrote his extraordinary letter of self-introduction. Perhaps Southey had told him too of the old man's notorious susceptibility to flattery, for it was a letter well-calculated to excite Godwin's interest. A reply came almost by return, and at once they were involved in a weekly correspondence whose intensity took Godwin somewhat aback. This exuberant youth seemed as certain as he had once been that the millennium could be quickly achieved through sheer strength of conviction. But Godwin? 'I think he is old', wrote Shelley, 'but age with *Godwin*, must be but the perfecting of his abilities.'[7] Soon he would know his man better.

In fact age had made Godwin more Burkean than ever, but the impetuous Shelley was prepared to set the world on its head if it would give him half the chance, and for the moment his career was providing a curious echo of Godwin's own. Once, in the *Political Herald* for 1786, Godwin had written 'To the People of Ireland', advising them to follow a course of moderation and react only if provoked. But Shelley, equally characteristically, wanted to deliver his inflammatory 'Address to the Irish People' in person. In a letter of enormous length and philosophic calm Godwin, repeating arguments he had once addressed to Thelwall, tried to persuade him from this foolishness, but to Shelley, no less than Thelwall, those arguments 'strong and convincing I suppose to him . . . appeared visionary and futile'. He would not be moved, not even when Godwin warned 'you are preparing a scene of blood', and urged him 'to save yourself and the Irish people from the calamities with which I see your mode of proceeding to be fraught' and return at once to London:

I have a friend* who has contrived a tube to convey passengers

*This anticipator of the Northern line, who proposed whisking carriages from London to Brighton by means of compressed air, was Maria Reveley's son Henry, who later became a friend and protégé of Shelley himself.

sixty miles an hour: be youth your tube. I have a thousand things I could say, really more than I could say in a letter on this important subject. You cannot imagine how much all the females of my family, Mrs Godwin and the three daughters, are interested in your letters and your history.[8]

Before long Shelley had stirred up such feelings, and had attracted to himself such a crowd of beggars and informers, that he was forced to abandon Ireland and move to Lynmouth on the North Devon coast. There he made his next cause that of Daniel Isaac Eaton, the man who had once made government pressure his reason to publish the *Cursory Strictures*. Eaton had recently been sentenced to imprisonment, with an hour in the public pillory, for the 'blasphemous libel' of publishing Paine's *Age of Reason*, though the crowd, instead of pelting him with rotten eggs, over-ripe tomatoes and animal guts from the nearby markets, as they were supposed to do, had brought him biscuits and glasses of wine, flowers and flags of triumph. Godwin, living a block away, preferred to ignore the event, but Shelley produced an open letter to the trial judge, his 'Letter to Lord Ellenborough', of which the alarmed printer burnt almost all thousand copies. What Godwin thought of it we do not know. Had gratitude been a virtue, it was a letter he might have written himself.

But just as Godwin had been urging Shelley to visit him in London, so Shelley had been urging him – or if not Godwin, then his daughter Fanny – to visit them at Lynmouth, so in September 1812 Godwin set out to meet the author of these extraordinary letters. 'And now for the sea', he wrote happily home from Bristol. 'The sun shines; the weather is fine; and the waiter, a wise man, tells me, the wind is favourable.'[9] But instead they met dreadful storms, a voyage of some seventy miles lasted fifty-one hours, with Godwin half-dead from sea-sickness and fainting fits – and he arrived to find the Shelleys gone, gone these three weeks, gone without warning and without explanation, gone no one knew why and no one knew whither! Disconsolate, Godwin returned to London, by land.

It seems, in retrospect, a curious thing to do, to embark on a long journey in poor health to visit someone you do not know, and who cannot even be relied on to be there when you arrive. Yet Godwin was in the habit of taking a summer vacation away from London, Devon seemed as good a place as any, and after their long and revealing correspondence Shelley was not entirely a stranger. But there was also another reason, the old reason. In response to a request for some personal details Shelley had happened to mention that he was 'heir by entail to an estate of some £6,000 per annum'. He had gone on to apologize for the undemocratic fact that he stood to inherit a fortune he had neither earned nor deserved. But to Godwin, alas, no apology was needed.

The only consolation Godwin could snatch from his exhausting journey was that Shelley would soon be in London, so it was there that they met after all, on 4 October 1812. To others, to Shelley's friend Hogg for example, the sage of Skinner Street proved a remarkably dull, almost comic old gentleman, drinking enthusiastically from his cup of green tea – 'gunpowder tea, intensely strong' – then slapping it down on the table with an old-fashioned gesture and promptly falling into a deep, soundly snoring sleep, still sitting bolt upright in his chair and threatening to topple out of it at any moment, but somehow managing to stay just where he was. But Shelley, in his excitement, saw nothing of that, and while he sat talking eagerly with Godwin of matter and spirit, utility and truth, atheism and clergymen, church and government, to name but a few, Harriet took careful note of this fascinating household. There was Godwin, so like a bust of Socrates, with 'manners soft and pleasing', 'much taken with Percy', and to her surprise 'quite a family man'. There was his wife – always able to impress at first meeting – with 'a great sweetness marked in her countenance', 'great fortitude and unyielding temper of mind', and 'very great magnanimity and independence of character'. There was Fanny, 'very plain but very sensible. The beauty of her mind fully overbalances the plainness of her countenance'. And there was young William, who is 'extremely clever, and will, I have no doubt, follow the same enlightened path that Godwin has before him.'[10] The others were all away from home: Charles with Constable's in Edinburgh; Jane at boarding school at Walham Green, but meeting the Shelleys on her occasional weekends home; and Mary in Dundee for her health, returning just in time to set eyes on Shelley once, on 11 November.

But the idyll was not to last. No doubt Shelley expected Godwin to snatch back the torch of liberty from the fire of his enthusiasm, but Godwin expected Shelley to sit at his feet and listen quietly to the cool lessons he had to teach him, and soon Shelley could sit still no longer. On 13 November the Godwins came to dine at the Shelleys' hotel, to find that they had left town that morning, without a word of explanation or apology. Fanny's letter of polite complaint received a teasing, flirtatious reply, rebuking her temerity at thus daring to address 'one of those formidable and long-clawed animals called a *Man*',[11] but Godwin himself seemed unruffled, continuing in letters the detailed advice for reading and study that he had been giving in person. Yet to Shelley it was little short of a disaster that his idol should prove not just 'old and unimpassioned' but prejudiced and excessively demanding of homage and attention. Once, to his amazed disbelief, Godwin had coloured with irritation at receiving a letter addressed, not as was proper to 'William Godwin, Esq', but to plain 'Mr W. Godwin'!

But if Shelley was disappointed in Godwin, Godwin was equally disappointed in his protégé. He had soon discovered that Shelley was in receipt of a bare £400 a year, scarcely enough for a man of his tastes and habits. But that had not prevented Godwin informing Place that, in an emergency, he would 'firmly call on my young friend to assist me'. For, as someone who stood to inherit a large fortune one day, Shelley would always be able to find people ready to pay cash now for the promise of a much greater sum when eventually he did inherit; though also, as a young man whose father and grandfather were both still living, he could hardly hope for favourable terms, and would be lucky to get away with three or even four to one. As he had told Godwin, before they even met,

> I might, it is true, raise money on my prospects, but the percentage is so enormous that it is with extreme unwillingness I should have recourse to such a step, which I might then be induced to repeat, even to a ruinous frequency and extent.[12]

So perhaps that was why, when Shelley returned to London the following spring, he carefully avoided the old man, who did not discover his presence there for a full month. The excuse was that Harriet now found Mrs Godwin 'so dreadfully disagreeable that I could not bear the idea of seeing her',[13] but Godwin was not the only friend they had been ignoring. Shelley's one concern was to print and publish *Queen Mab*, the long philosophical poem he had discussed with Godwin the previous year, then finished off in the seclusion of North Wales, a lyrical investigation of the tyrannies of positive institution, the supremacy of private reason, and the eventual perfectibility of man, complete with detailed explanatory notes discussing all manner of issues raised, however fleetingly, in the poem itself, from the distance of the stars to the true nature of wealth, and culminating in an impassioned defence of vegetarianism. There are quotations from the *Enquirer*, references to *Political Justice*, long passages – especially on necessity, and on the despotism of marriage – which read as if they had been lifted straight from Godwin's own pages, and even the atheism is one that he could endorse: 'There is no God', says the poem; but the notes explain, 'This negation must be understood solely to affect a creative Deity. The hypothesis of a pervading Spirit co-eternal with the universe remains unshaken.'

Reading Shelley without knowing Godwin, it has been said, is like reading Milton without knowing the Bible, and these themes would recur again and again, most notably in the verse drama of 1820, *Prometheus Unbound*. Yet Godwin was not overly impressed, nor noticeably flattered. Like others of the day he found Shelley's poetry almost unreadable, and much preferred his prose. '*You* have what appears to me a false taste in poetry,' he told him once. 'You love a perpetual sparkle and glittering, such as are to be found in Darwin and Southey, and Scott and Campbell.'[14] He could not bring himself to read *Prometheus Unbound* right through, 'for he hates to read books that are full of obscurities and puzzles; and then S. never writes with a calm and proper tone, but rather with anger, and bitterness, and violence.'[15] But there was more to Godwin's dislike than a distaste for fancy and fantasy, an incomprehension in the face of poetic imagery. In Shelley's verse Godwin's theories undergo a slight but devastating alteration: where Godwin intellectualized, Shelley romanticized; what appealed to him was the moral vision, not the logical argument; and his poetry presents us with a world of political justice without the proofs of *Political Justice*. To know Godwin only through Shelley, is not to know him at all.

Godwin, however, had other things on his mind. In August 1813 Shelley turned twenty-one, and two months later he was persuaded to his first perilous step, selling for £500 a post-obit bond that would be worth £2,000, when finally he inherited. And, as he had feared, having taken that first step it was that much easier to take a second, and early in 1814 he and Godwin were discussing a further bond, to a value of £8,000, which they might sell at auction for as much as £3,000, to be divided evenly between them. Not that Shelley himself took much interest in the negotiations, leaving the sale that March in Godwin's hands, and coming to London only when his signature was needed on the relevant documents. But it was such transactions as these, not philosophy, that kept him at Skinner Street through the early summer, hiding from his own creditors in his Fleet Street lodgings but taking his meals with the Godwins, while Harriet waited in Bath with their new daughter, named Ianthe after the heroine of *Queen Mab*. And it was not until 6 July that Shelley could come to Godwin with the news that his share, after costs, would be £1,120 – and that he was utterly, unshakably, eternally, in love with Godwin's daughter Mary, and she with him, and that they intended to devote their lives to one another.

Godwin was amazed and appalled in equal measure. Bustling around the city arranging the loan on Shelley and postponing payments on the loan to Place he had noticed nothing of what was going on. To his lasting regret Fanny, reliable, sensible, dutiful Fanny, was holidaying in Wales with her aunts; if she had been at home things would never have reached this pass. But it was only now that he learnt how Mary, to escape the strains of Skinner Street and the company of her step-mother, had fallen into the habit of taking a book to Old St Pancras Cemetery, there to sit and muse beside her mother's grave; how with Jane their discreet but intrigued chaperone, Shelley had begun to follow her there, to talk of Mary's unhappiness at home and his growing disenchantment with Harriet; how ten days before, beneath the willow tree, they had at last blurted out their feelings for one another.

Not for nothing was Shelley fond of a quotation from St Augustine, 'I was not yet in love, but I was in love with love itself; and I sought for something to love, since I loved loving.' All his life he liked to surround himself with an entourage of lady admirers, with whom he would fall in and out of love as the fancy took him. He had been intrigued enough by the plain but presentable Fanny, but now there was her sister, gentle and delicate, golden-haired and fair-skinned, with her father's striking eyes shining out of an oval face, still the age that Harriet had been when he eloped with her, and with a name – Mary Wollstonecraft Godwin – that alone was enough to ensure his devotion. 'Who was that pray?' asked Hogg, when Mary rushed up to them one day in the Skinner Street shop, 'a daughter?' 'Yes', replied Shelley tautly. 'The daughter of Godwin?' 'The daughter of Godwin and Mary.'[16]

> They say thou wert lovely from thy birth,
> Of glorious parents, thou aspiring Child.
> I wonder not – for One then left this earth
>   Whose life was like a setting planet mild,
>   Which clothed thee in the radiance undefiled
> Of its departing glory; still her fame
>   Shines on thee, through the tempests dark and wild
>   Which shakes these latter days; and thou canst claim
> The shelter, from thy Sire, of an immortal name.[17]

For the past three years Mary had been away more often than she had been home, and until that summer Shelley had met her only once. But for all that Harriet was pregnant again, and that they had gone through a second marriage ceremony on 24 March lest their Edinburgh wedding prove invalid and so disinherit their children, Shelley was beginning to regret his hasty elopement, an act of romance as much as desire. The doll-like Harriet saw herself too much as a fine lady, no fit soul-mate for an unworldly man of letters and philosophy – she had even refused to nurse her daughter, for fear of what it might do to her figure. It is possible, too, that Shelley told Mary that Harriet had been unfaithful to him. Certainly that was the story put about later, and if Shelley told it to Mary he was notoriously capable of convincing himself it was true. But without doubt it was false.

But now all that lay behind him, and trusting in the Godwinian power of truth and reason, plus a totally unGodwinian element of naked passion, Shelley 'had the madness to disclose his plans to me, and to ask my consent. I expostulated with him with all the energy of which I was master; and with so much effect that for the moment he promised to give up his licentious love, and return to virtue.'[18] Or so he told Godwin, but within the week he had summoned Harriet from Bath to announce his intention that the three of them should live together, his wife as his sister and his soul-sister as his wife. Harriet went weeping to the Godwins, to beg them to keep Mary and Shelley apart. Mary assured her she would do nothing to encourage Shelley's love, and promised her father she would not run off with him. But in her copy of *Queen Mab*, with its dedication to Harriet at the front, she wrote

> This book is sacred to me and as no other creature shall ever look into it I may write in it what I please – yet what shall I write – that I love the author beyond all powers of expression and that I am parted from him dearest and only love – by that love we have promised to each other although I may not be yours I can never be another's. But I am thine, exclusively thine.

She was no more capable of sticking to her resolution than was Shelley.

Shelley now began to behave with all the high drama of which he was capable. He presented himself at Skinner Street doubly armed, with laudanum for Mary and he to drink together, and a gun with which to shoot them both. A day or two later he actually took a dose of the drug but, predictably, was discovered in time and saved. All this was kept from Godwin, still trying to arrange for Mary to go into hiding until Shelley had recovered his senses, but in the end 'they both deceived me'. On Thursday 28 July he woke to find a note from Mary on his dressing table: they had left together at five that morning. Mary was still sixteen, Shelley twenty-one; they had known each other for two months.

To the Godwins' astonishment, to everyone's astonishment, Jane had gone too. Her presence on that stolen honeymoon would have been superfluous had she and Mary been the best of friends, and they were very far from that: 'Do not leave me alone with her,' cried Mary at the end of her life, when her daughter-in-law thought the two old ladies might like to chat together on their own. 'She has been

the bane of my life since I was three years old.' True, Shelley liked
Jane more than Mary did, but he had already suffered enough from
the presence of Harriet's sister to be on his guard against admitting
relatives into his domestic circle. Yet Jane went too, and every time
that Shelley and Mary returned to Europe, she was with them still.
The domineering personality and managing ability that she inherited from her mother perhaps made her indispensable to them.
With her schoolgirl imagination inflamed by the whole intrigue, she
had been a key figure from the start, promoting their meetings and
stage-managing their escape. Without her the deed might never have
been done and the infatuated couple, leaving in a fever of apprehension, could not bring themselves to leave her behind at the last, even
had she been willing. And she could speak French.

Of course Mrs Godwin was more worried for her own daughter
than for Godwin's; but then so was he. There was no saving Mary
now, but Jane had got herself into a thoughtless scrape from which
she must be rescued at once: 'Jane has been guilty of an indiscretion
only . . . Mary has been guilty of a crime.' From a nearby stables
they discovered that the runaways had gone to Dover, and Mrs
Godwin set off in pursuit, though Godwin, worried about Shelley's
violence – or his wife's temper? – warned her not to confront Shelley
personally. She did not overtake them until Calais, announcing to
the startled inn-keeper that the young man had run off with her
daughter, *her* daughter. 'I am not the least in love with her', Shelley is
supposed to have said to Mrs Godwin, 'but she is a nice little girl
and her mother is such a vulgar, commonplace woman, without an
idea of philosophy, I do not think she is a proper person to form the
mind of a young girl.'[19] Jane spent that night with her mother, but
next morning announced that she would stay with Shelley and Mary
after all. Mrs Godwin returned to London without uttering another
word. When the Masons – the former Lady Mountcashell and her *de
facto* husband, 'Tatty' Tighe – set out for Pisa the following month
they were asked to do what they could to detach Jane, should they
ever come across the fugitives. There was no knowing whether they
would see any of them again.

21 ♣ The venerable horseleech

Let no man build on the expected gratitude of those he spends his strength to serve! Let him be beneficent if he will; but let him not depend for his happiness on the conviction of his rectitude and virtue that is to be impressed on the minds of others! There is a principle in the human breast, that easily induces them to regard everything that can be done for them, as no more than their due, and speedily discharges them from the oppressive consciousness of obligation.

St Leon, 1799

♣ 'I cannot conceive', Godwin wrote to the most dependable of his financiers, John Taylor of Norwich, 'of an event of more accumulated horror.'[1] The disciple who claimed to owe everything to his teachings, the young gentleman of fortune who might have rescued him from his incessant embarrassments, had tricked and betrayed him, had seduced one daughter and corrupted another. The most promising of his children, the daughter who inherited the talents of both Godwin and Wollstonecraft, whose very name was a portent, had broken her word to him and disgraced herself. And the horrors had only begun.

Two weeks later Patrick Patrickson came to dinner, before returning to Cambridge for his final term as a law student. He had done well and was expected to be placed as high as 8th or 9th Wrangler in his January examinations. But it had been an unhappy four years, and Patrickson felt he could hardly face even one more term: he felt his poverty keenly, and was made to feel it more keenly still by the jeers of his fellow students; after university he could see only the same uncertainty and misery that he had had to suffer there. Godwin had supported him throughout and tried to encourage him again, but at this time his own spirits were unequal to the task. Patrickson returned to Cambridge next day and the following morning was found dead in his rooms, a farewell note to Godwin by his side. 'Flather is the real assassin [not a misprint for 'Father' but the name of Patrickson's closest college companion, and a family friend of the Godwins since 1808],' wrote Mary, when at length she heard the news. And it was on that very same day, 10 August, that young William Godwin, always a ready source of bother, decided to try his own hand at running away because, he said, as a dayboy at Charterhouse, where he had been for the past three years, he suffered from the ridicule of the boarders. It was two nights before he could be located and brought home again. To Godwin's intense relief it was only a few days more before Fanny came home, on 16 August.

Even that was not all. Godwin's share of Shelley's post-obit had been intended only to settle his immediate debts, and they both had known that there would be others to see to before the end of the year. But he could hardly look to Shelley now, wherever he was, and when the quarterly repayment to Place fell due at the end of August Godwin had to write and confess himself at his wits end how to meet it. And so the angry recriminations began. Place had always disapproved of Godwin's reliance on Shelley – no way to run a business – and he was prepared to tolerate these twistings and turnings no longer:

> My mind was so well made up to the necessity of ceasing to have any intercourse with him, that I absolutely refused to continue our acquaintance. I treated him kindly, I said every thing, which I thought ought to be said, and here our intercourse ended.[2]

But if Place preferred to write the debt off, others were less easily satisfied. Repayments of capital and interest, at something like £200 the time were coming round like clockwork, and Godwin could see no possible way of meeting them. For a moment there was the hope that two brothers named Stone might buy a share in the business for £3,000, but as soon as they discovered the true state of affairs they pulled out. In the circumstances it was hard to know whether news of Shelley's return was good news, or bad.

Godwin sent his wife and Fanny to investigate, under strict instructions that they must not communicate with the runaways in any way, and when Shelley saw them and went out to them in the street, they bustled nervously away. So Shelley wrote to Godwin direct, but there was no forgiveness there, only accusation and reproach. There could be no contact until Shelley had returned the daughters and gone back to his wife; and when Shelley's friend Peacock tried to mediate, Godwin told him he would speak about Shelley only to an attorney. 'Oh! philosophy!', lamented Mary in her journal, and Shelley confessed himself equally 'shocked and staggered by Godwin's cold injustice.'[3] To compensate they buried themselves, Jane too, in *Caleb Williams*, *St Leon*, and *Political Justice*.

Just as Mrs Godwin blamed Jane's disgrace on Mary, so Mary blamed everything on Mrs Godwin, 'a woman I shudder to think of.

My poor father! If ——— but it will not do.'[4] Her deep-seated, unsatisfied love for her father – 'Until I met Shelley I justly say that he was my God, and I remember many childish instances of the excess of attachment I bore for him' – had culminated in her running away with his image, younger and more romantic. It was inconceivable that their estrangement could be her doing or his responsibility; the step-mother, always disliked, made an easy scapegoat. Yet Godwin's attitude was hardly the work of his wife; it was not to be expected that he could accept or excuse a married man's running off with his only daughter, the only daughter that was his. Whatever he may have written once about the system of matrimony, he had never endorsed such conduct as this, and at his age was hardly likely to change his mind. No doubt Shelley saw himself as acting by the precepts of *Political Justice* – sincerity, independence, a refusal to allow his preferences or actions to be constrained by the conventions of established institutions – just as Mary saw herself as behaving as her mother would have in those circumstances. And did not *Political Justice*'s first edition, the one that Shelley preferred, dismiss sexual exclusiveness as 'the most odious of all monopolies'?

But Godwin, of course, had not meant that passage quite as Shelley interpreted it:

> True love in this differs from gold and clay,
> That to divide is not to take away.

The mere sexual commerce, he had written, was 'a very trivial object' compared with an open honesty in all personal relationships. It was, after all, the simple truth that they had deceived him, both deceived him. What other reaction could they expect. Yet ironically, it was not the deception, nor the carnality, that seemed to rankle most with Godwin. It was the sense of betrayal, that he who owed him so much had stolen not just his daughter, but what remained of his self-respect and his chance of security for the future. With Mary his willing accomplice, Shelley was not only a seducer, but ungrateful, and a thief – three notions which, in a world of political justice, would have no place at all!

Nevertheless, the Godwins' immediate concern was to save Jane from her foolishness, to get her away from Shelley's dangerous influence and into a convent. 'To Mary I shall always be forward to extend every degree of consideration in my power, whenever she wants it,' Godwin wrote again, not quite truthfully, to Taylor of Norwich. 'But with Jane it is altogether different. She from no motive but frivolity, and a childish love of new things, has thrown herself into a most improper and dangerous situation.' Yet it was not until mid-November that they managed to entice her home, by sending Fanny with the transparent tale that Mrs Godwin was on the point of death. Mary had had to keep out of sight upstairs – 'Papa tells Fanny if she sees me he will never speak to her again; a blessed degree of liberty this!'[5] – and Jane was unable to leave the house until Fanny returned with some decent clothes to wear. But once home she would have none of the suggestion that if she did not care to live with the Godwins, at least she might like to go somewhere else, as a governess perhaps. She would agree to be separated from 'her present friends', in Godwin's dismissive phrase, only on two conditions:

> first, that she should in all situations openly proclaim, and earnestly support, a total contempt for the laws and institutions of society, – and secondly, that no restraint should be imposed upon her correspondence and intercourse with those from whom she was separated. With these condition (sic) we have not complied.[6]

Jane was well aware that the author of *Political Justice* would now jib at the outrageous teachings of a Shelley. Two days later she quit Skinner Street again; from now on she preferred the more romantic name of Claire.

By this time Godwin had got himself into a situation humiliating even by his standards. 'Lambert is worth £300,000', Claire complained,

> and he oppresses and insults Godwin for the paltry sum of a hundred and fifty – pretending at the same time to admire his energy and talent – And it is for these people that Godwin has sacrificed his happiness and well-being – that he refuses to see his daughter and Shelley – the two people he loves best in the world.[7]

For Lambert was threatening him with arrest, and Godwin could see no alternative but to sell off most of his stock in one last desperate, and probably suicidal, attempt to stay in business. Incredibly, it was Shelley to the rescue. Hiding from his own creditors, he still knew all about Godwin's, thanks to secret contacts with Charles Clairmont, who had returned from Edinburgh in January 1814 to take charge of the family firm. Lambert, Place and Taylor were all sent post-obit bonds to cover Godwin's debts to them. (Because Shelley died before his father, these debts were never paid. Of course the commercial money-lenders who paid hard cash for Shelley's bonds took care to protect their investments with a life-insurance policy, but when John Taylor wrote to Place in 1822, not wanting to bother Godwin personally, but wondering whether he would now get back his £300, Place found no difficulty in disillusioning him.) With Clairmont their go-between, Shelley and Godwin began to arrange the sale of another, worth £10,000, that might bring them £1,800 and £1,200 respectively.

Godwin himself was understandably reluctant to accept these peace-offerings. He would not send Shelley his thanks, but told his wife she might do so if she liked; and though Charles had Christmas dinner with the Shelleys, poor Fanny was sent to bed without her meal, only a week before, for accepting a lock of hair in remembrance of her separated sister. She behaved, of course, slavishly on the occasion, grumbled Mary, feeling more and more isolated as pregnancy kept her indoors while Shelley rushed gaily round the town with Claire. It was only when Mary had her baby, on 22 February 1815, that Fanny was allowed to visit her, while Charles arrived with a gift of linen from his hated mother. But though Mrs Godwin could sometimes be seen passing outside, hoping to catch some glimpse through the windows of the *ménage* within, Godwin still kept his distance. Once he came face to face with Shelley and Mary in the street, but pretended he had not seen them and turned aside, muttering that Shelley was so beautiful it was a pity he was so wicked.

The baby, two months premature, was not at first expected to survive, but she seemed to prosper until a disapproving landlady, preferring reliable payers to unmarried mothers forced them to move. Four days later Mary woke to find her daughter, less than two weeks old, dead beside her. Soon after she had a dream, 'that my little baby came to life again; that it had only been cold, and that we rubbed it before the fire, and it lived. Awake and find no baby. I think about the little thing all day. Not in good spirits.' It was the first onset of the depression that would dog the rest of her life with Shelley, and again and again the pattern would repeat itself: Mary ill and depressed, losing a child, separated from her family, worried about her father and nervous for Shelley who, entirely incapable of the support that she needed, would be out in eager pursuit of some new feminine ideal. More than ever Mary needed to be rid of Claire, but though they discussed it often enough, somehow they never reached a decision.

Meanwhile their situation had been altered dramatically by the death of Shelley's grandfather on 6 January, leaving a complex will specifically designed to prevent the irresponsible grandson making further inroads into the family fortune. Shelley's father was eager to see the main inheritance pass to a more reliable younger brother, and Shelley himself was more concerned to guarantee a regular income for the present than to inherit great wealth at some in-determinate date in the future. It was in everyone's interest to buy him out, and Godwin hovered nervously in the background, anxious to offer Shelley advice but still refusing to approach him directly. He was still counting on the £1,200 that Shelley had promised him, the more especially because another creditor, Hogan, was now threaten-ing him with imprisonment. But the tortuous negotiations dragged on, and it was not until May that the Shelleys, father and son, came to a first provisional agreement. Among the various creditors that Sir Timothy agreed to pay off was one W. Godwin, but though the sum mentioned was £1,200, Shelley kept back £200 for himself. That, he insisted, was the arrangement they had made through Charles Clairmont, and the other £200 would follow by November, as soon as father and son had completed their arrangements.

Mary heaved a sigh of relief. They had money at last, her father had been saved yet again, and that same day – 13 May – Claire had gone off for a holiday in Devon. 'I begin a new Journal with our regeneration', she wrote in the back of the old one, almost as if she knew she was pregnant again.

It might have been Godwin's regeneration too. Two days before he had published his first work of any substance since *Fleetwood*, the first writing under his own name for almost a decade; two weeks later he would be provoked into his first public pronouncement on current affairs since 1795. It was almost as if the saga of Shelley and Mary was shaking him from the lethargy into which he had fallen, since the *Reply to Parr* and the yes to Mrs Clairmont.

For several years past Godwin had been amassing a collection of miscellaneous information and publication concerning the two nephews of John Milton, educated by him almost as his own sons, John and Edward Phillips. Ideally he would have liked to write a biography of Milton himself, but instead he published a *Lives of the Phillipses*, since an examination of the pupils must surely throw a revealing light on their illustrious master. Indeed 'Helvetius himself could scarcely have chosen a more qualified tutor, upon whose experiments to have tried the truth of his theories', and unhappily, as Godwin is now quite willing to concede, the experiments refute the theory. For Milton's nephews turned out almost entirely for the bad, allying themselves with the Royalists and contributing to that stream of ribald satires – none of which Godwin can bring himself to quote – whose purpose 'was to debauch the nation and bring back the King'. The elder brother, Edward, eventually mended his ways, but 'John continued through life a shameless, unfeeling buffoon' who specialized in satirical pornography, deserted his wife and children, changed political sides as it suited him, became involved in the conspiracy of Titus Oates, sneered at *Paradise Lost* for possessing 'neither rhyme nor reason', and when his uncle was buried 'did not, I trust, pollute the sad solemnity with his unhallowed presence'. Yet there is much more to the *Lives of the Phillipses* than the lives of the Phillipses and, published in May 1815 at Godwin's own expense, for fear that the information might perish with him, it comes to rival the *Chaucer* as a miscellaneous anthology, for all that it bears the marks of a man who has spent too long writing for children; shorter and more avowedly miscellaneous, it is also the more readable and more interesting of the two.

Godwin's next venture was also characteristic, in a different way. With Napoleon escaped from exile on Elba and back at the head of the armies of France, all Europe was in ferment again. But even now, when Napoleon was to many a traitor to the cause, to others a bloody tyrant, and to some the devil incarnate, Godwin still saw him as an important stabilizing influence, infinitely preferable to the return of Bourbon despotism. It was an unpopular opinion, shared with Hazlitt and Thelwall, but it was one he held strongly, and with Wellington preparing to crush the Corsican again, Godwin found himself writing as of old to the *Morning Chronicle*, to warn against reviving a war that had already lasted more than twenty years. In view of the enthusiasm with which the French had welcomed him back, Napoleon should be recognized as their legitimate ruler, on condition only that he keep the peace with his neighbours. It was the sensible, considered plea of an old man who preferred peace to war, and self-determination to external interference. But his timing was as unhappy as ever.

The first of these letters of 'Verax' appeared on 25 May, and when the *Chronicle* declined to publish another, twice as long and twice as repetitive, Godwin decided to have the two printed together as a pamphlet that would bear his own name. 'I am now drawing to the close of human existence', he wrote in the Preface.

> I can forsee the time, when I shall no longer be a spectator, or a party, however small, to this mortal scene; but I cannot see the termination of the war which seems now ready to burst upon us. It will not improbably last longer than I shall . . .

But the *Letters of Verax* did not appear until 22 June, four days after the Battle of Waterloo and the same day that Napoleon abdicated for the second and final time. Godwin, on the other hand, would last another twenty years.

In actual fact, it was hard to say whose health was the worse, Godwin's or his wife's. 'I seldom call, but they have some tale of affliction to relate,' despaired Crabb Robinson, finding Godwin's conduct now more disturbing than demanding:

> Godwin was in high spirits, but hardly in good spirits. He laughs long and loud without occasion, and mingles with this causeless hilarity great irritability. He is vehement and intolerant . . . . I fear every day hearing something painful of poor Godwin.[8]

Yet for all the depressions and the debts, the misjudgments and misfortunes, there were still a few old friends to keep him company: Lamb, Hazlitt, Curran, James Northcote the artist who had once painted his portrait, James Kenney the dramatist who had married Holcroft's widow, even John Thelwall, re-emerging from an obscurity that rivalled Godwin's own. Only Coleridge, stricken with debts and opium, seemed to have disappeared from everyone's ken to emerge two years later in Highgate, living in retirement and struggling to keep his addiction under control, talking incessantly but doing nothing, until even Lamb found a visit 'so unattractively – repulsing – from any temptation to call again that I stay away as naturally as a lover visits'.[9] They exchanged occasional pleasantries, but Godwin and Coleridge were never again the close friends they once had been. In his place there was Mackintosh, now Sir James Mackintosh, come back from India to make his amends. And there was Robert Owen.

It makes a strange contrast, the anarchist and the socialist, the philosopher and the philanthropist, the thinker and the man of action, the hopeless debtor and the successful entrepreneur, so alike in principles yet in practice a whole Industrial Revolution apart. For although Owen never acknowledged a direct debt to *Political Justice* – perhaps because he never properly read it – he was in effect the Godwin of the new century, with the same basic faith in man's natural goodness and inevitable perfectibility through reason and truth, the same naive optimism that allowed him to dedicate his books to princes and bishops in the confident conviction that they could not fail to be persuaded by a rational demonstration of their own dispensability. Yet while he was no less a businessman than Place, and somewhat more of a humanitarian, Owen somehow avoided the trap of the Skinner Street finances. Instead it fell to Shelley to subsidize the household from his own pocket, all pretence gone that he was raising capital for the business. His extraordinary relationship with Godwin was about to enter a new and even more bitter phase.

'Riches seem to fly from genius', Claire had written to Fanny when Godwin got the £1,000 Shelley had tricked his father into

making available. 'I suppose for a month or two you will be easy –
pray be cheerful.'[10] And so it proved. Godwin had not bothered
about the missing £200 so long as no one was bothering him, but by
October Hogan was threatening again, and £200 was precisely the
sum at issue. Reluctantly, angrily, he broke his dignified silence of
the past few months and wrote again 'in a certain style of haughtiness
and incroachment which', Shelley said, 'neither awes nor impresses
me.'[11] Yet for a moment it seemed that Godwin might be rescued by
another poet, far more prominent and far more wealthy than a mere
Shelley. Mackintosh, eager to recompense the man he had so
injured, got wind of the extraordinary news that John Murray had
offered Lord Byron 1,000 guineas for the poems 'Parisiana' and 'The
Seige of Corinth', and Byron had declined the offer. He thought it
slightly vulgar to make money from his scribblings; it was certainly
more than the verses were worth; but if Murray wanted to include
them in an anthology, rather than publishing them separately, he
could have them for nothing. So Mackintosh put it to a mutual
friend, Samuel Rogers, that Byron might prefer to award this
unclaimed prize to Godwin, 'a man of genius, likely, for his
independence of thinking, to starve at the age of 60 for want of a few
hundred pounds necessary to carry on his laborious occupation'.[12]
And Byron approved the idea: he had met Godwin once; he admired
St Leon enormously; he had even threatened his wife to do by her
'just as Falkland did by Caleb'. So he instructed Murray to give
£600 to Godwin and divide the rest between Coleridge and another
impecunious poet, C. R. Maturin. But Murray, recognizing he had
made a bad bargain of it, balked, whereupon Byron angrily
demanded the return of his manuscripts:

> Had I taken you at your word, that is, taken your money, I
> might have used it as I pleased; and it could be in no respect
> different to you whether I paid it to a whore, or a hospital, or
> assisted a man of talent in distress . . . . The things in question
> shall not be published at all, and there's an end of the matter.[13]

Later he would change his mind again: the 1,000 guineas would
come in handy for settling debts of his own.

So it was back to Shelley after all, and through the first months of
1816 he and Godwin were writing every two or three days, Godwin
demanding the £200 he had been promised, Shelley defending his
failure to pay it originally and justifying his inability to pay it now.
Godwin kept urging the post-obit they had planned more than a
year before, but Shelley would not consider it, knowing it would
surely wreck the delicate negotiations with his father. For all his
extravagance and his own haphazard finances he had a shrewdness

that Godwin totally lacked. Godwin, who had once contemplated a future so remote as to be beyond most men's reckonings, was nevertheless more concerned with cash in hand than with what it might eventually cost; Shelley, the romantic dreamer, had no interest in future wealth provided he could guarantee an income sufficient unto his present needs. But Godwin, unable or unwilling to understand Shelley's situation, tried to wear him down through sheer persistence; and when Shelley did finally scrape something together, he got only an infuriated, infuriating note for his pains:

> I return your cheque because no consideration can induce me to utter a cheque drawn by you and containing my name. To what purpose make a disclosure of this kind to your banker. I hope you will send me a duplicate by the post which will reach me on Saturday morning. You may make it payable to Joseph Hume or James Martin, or any other name in the whole directory.[14]

But then the rumour had got around that the avaricious old republican had sold his daughters to the wealthy young aristocrat for £1,000 each, or £1,500 the pair. It would make anyone reluctant to cash a cheque bearing those particular names. (I have been unable to trace the origin of this celebrated note. Shelley did make a cheque for £200 payable to Hume in December 1815, but if it was actually meant for Godwin it is hard to explain why Godwin was still demanding the missing £200, and Shelley defending his failure to pay it, through the next few months. This letter probably dates from early 1816, or perhaps from late 1814, when the rumour was already about that Godwin had sold off his daughters.)

What hurt and angered Shelley most was that it should be the author of *Political Justice* who so misused and misconstrued him. When Mary produced a son on 24 January 1816 he wrote pointedly that 'Fanny and Mrs Godwin will probably be glad to hear that Mary has safely recovered from a favourable confinement, and that her child is well,'[15] yet they called the boy William, after his implacable grandfather. And when Shelley agreed, a month later, that a meeting would be undesirable – 'on me it would inflict deep dejection' – he nevertheless continued 'But I would not refuse anything which I can do, so that I may benefit a man whom, in spite of his wrongs to me, I respect and love.'[16] Sometimes his patience would snap under the strain:

> Do not talk of *forgiveness* again to me, for my blood boils in my veins, and my gall rises against all that bears the human form, when I think of what I, their benefactor and ardent lover, have

endured of enmity and contempt from you and from all
mankind.[17]

But the very next day he would be half-apologetic again: 'I must
appear the reverse of what I really am, haughty and hard, if I am
not to see myself and all that I love trampled upon and outraged.'[18] In
March exasperation drove Shelley to Skinner Street, several times,
but Godwin still refused to see him.

It was a bizarre situation, with Shelley's role ever less understandable, Godwin's ever less excusable. Even Crabb Robinson, who had
ample evidence of Godwin's shamelessness when it came to money,
refused to believe that he was still borrowing from Shelley. But
perhaps his attitude came as much from guilt as from desperation: it
was only by casting Shelley in the role of a protégé who owed him
respect as well as support – a role that Shelley was anxious enough
to adopt – that Godwin was able to live with the situation he had
fallen into, by accident he thought, and ill-luck. Nor did he think of
his incessant demands as involving any personal inconvenience to
Shelley. He saw the family fortune as a vast pool of unutilized
resource into which they all might dip whenever the need arose, the
more especially because Shelley, no less than he, disapproved in
principle of inherited wealth, which should rather be disbursed to
the greater benefit of all. Godwin's unending importuning, his angry
denunciations when Shelley refused him, his reluctance to accept
any apology or explanation, all sprang from a conviction that it
could only be callousness or insincerity which prevented Shelley
from doing what was so easy for the one, so necessary for the other.

But why on earth did Shelley put up with these insolent demands,
which must surely have disillusioned him completely about the man
with whom he had to deal? In part, perhaps, he was living by the
same doctrine, that the principle of distribution should be merit and
need, not inheritance and possession. As someone with a claim to
enormous wealth he had done nothing to earn or deserve, Shelley
saw it as his personal contribution to the welfare of mankind to
preserve and protect one of their noblest benefactors, no matter how
nasty that benefactor might turn in the process. Godwin, after all,
was a famous philosopher, Shelley a rich nobody. He had his own
hopes and ambitions, but there was as yet no sign of their ever being
realized, and both men were equally convinced that Godwin was the
more important of the two. It is only later, with their roles reversed,
that Shelley emerges as the harassed genius, and Godwin as 'the
venerable horseleech'. (The entry in *The Dictionary of National
Biography*, which thus sets the tone for most subsequent comment on

Godwin, was the work of Sir Leslie Stephen, who had his own reputation for extreme stinginess.)

Yet even now, looking back, pure impartial justice may still be on Godwin's side. Shelley's history is one of reckless extravagance, worlds removed from Godwin's carefully frugal existence. Shelley had his moments of dire poverty, but he brought them on himself; Godwin had no alternative. Godwin's 'foreign' travels were restricted to Ireland, Wales and Scotland, on one occasion each, while Shelley hurtled round Britain and the Continent like a thing possessed. What would Shelley's story have been had he had to live on Godwin's income, or the scanty receipts of his own writing? And what might Godwin's have been had he been born with Shelley's inheritance?

Yet Shelley was driven by more than considerations of justice; he also felt his share of guilt and shame. Godwin he admired extravagantly, for what he had been, and could be, if not for what he was; and later, when he had even more cause to be bitter at the old man's treatment of Mary and himself, he still managed to insist that 'although I believe he is the only sincere enemy I have in the world . . . added years only add to my admiration of his intellectual powers, and even the moral resources of his character.'[19] It seems almost perverse, as if Shelley could not permit himself to see Godwin as he was, and in truth that awkward, austere, remote figure bulked as large in his thoughts as it did in Mary's. He liked to portray his own bewildered father as a tyrant and persecutor, and any contact there was likewise only through an attorney. In Godwin he had someone to admire and pattern himself on; there was no one to whom he felt more indebted, no one whose approval he valued more. And then, when Godwin was suffering most from the injustices of a hostile world, Shelley had increased them, had deceived and injured him, and made him once more an object of scurrility and scorn. In his heart he felt the truth of Godwin's charges, as Godwin felt the truth of his, and if Godwin became, in consequence, ever more unyielding, ever more outrageous in his demands, Shelley on his side believed he owed Godwin all that he could provide. Psychologically, the scurrilous rumour came true: Godwin felt justified in his demands because of what Shelley had done to him; and Shelley paid up, because he had stolen the daughters.

22 ♣ A pauper's grave

The power of terminating our own lives, is one of the faculties
with which we are endowed; and therefore, like every other
faculty, is a subject of moral discipline. In common with every
branch of morality, it is a topic of calculation, as to the balance
of good and evil to result, from its employment in any
individual instance. We should however be scrupulously on
our guard, against the deceptions that melancholy and im-
patience are well calculated to impose. We should consider
that, though the pain to be suffered by ourselves is by no
means to be overlooked, we are but one, and the persons
nearly or remotely interested in our possible usefulness
innumerable.[1]

Political Justice, 1798

♣ Godwin and Shelley still had not met, Shelley and his father still
had not reached a final settlement, when Godwin set out jauntily for
Scotland in April 1816. Byron, that afternoon at Murray's three
years before, had demanded to know why Godwin did not write
another novel. Because it would kill him, he had replied. 'And what
matter?', exclaimed Byron. 'We shall have another *St Leon*!' In fact
Godwin, bored by books of Baldwin, had already made the attempt
in 1811, with a story inspired by the tale of the sleeping beauty, at
once recalling *St Leon* and anticipating *Rip Van Winkle*, the story of a
man who would fall asleep for twenty, thirty or a hundred years at a
time, and wake conveniently at periods of the author's choosing.
But he had got no further than a handful of pages – and an advance
of £150 – before he gave it up in despair. Now, however, after the
Lives of the Phillipses and the *Letters of Verax*, and a vain attempt to
reap some reward from past labours by republishing *Caleb Williams*
and *St Leon* on his own behalf, Godwin was ready to try again. In
December he had gingerly approached another from his list of
publishers, the Archibald Constable to whom Charles Clairmont
had been apprenticed, suggesting that if he were to publish a new
novel anonymously, like that current sensation, the Waverley novels,
perhaps he could attract a new readership who would not dismiss
him out of hand as some relic from the past. Constable had proved
encouraging, and now he was off to discuss the terms.

Godwin could hardly expect the ecstatic welcome which had once awaited him in Warwickshire, or even the interest that had survived in Ireland, but as he wrote happily home 'my reception in Edinburgh has been, as I knew it would be, kind and flattering in the extreme . . . . I cannot well disappoint all the good people that have a desire to see the monster.'[2] There were fruitful meetings with Constable, and with his editors, Francis Jeffrey and McVey Napier; there were flattering invitations from the Earl of Buchan, Dugald Stewart 'the crack metaphysician of Great Britain', and Walter Scott; there was even a William Nicholson – not Godwin's old friend, who had died the previous year – to paint his portrait. The only thing to mar the month's excursion, as pleasant and relaxing as Godwin ever had, was a stormy argument with William Wordsworth when he stayed overnight at Rydal Mount on his way home. Wordsworth's egotism was as legendary as Godwin's pride, their capacity for quarrelling was much the same, and Wordsworth hated Bonaparte as much as Godwin admired him. But like many a démêlé it did not last, and their distant acquaintance survived to the end of their lives. And so Godwin came home, 'quite well and quite a new man', with enough money to pay off the reprint of *Caleb Williams*, and 'all on fire to resume my novel' – and found Shelley gone.

It was presumably no coincidence that the day Godwin returned to Skinner Street was the day that Shelley left England again, and this time, he hoped, for good. He wrote, none the less, from Dover, a letter of apology and farewell intended to put behind them the disagreements that had kept them apart:

> I respect you, I think well of you, better perhaps than of any other person whom England contains; you were the philosopher who first awakened, and who still as a philosopher to a very great degree regulates my understanding . . . . But I have been too indignant. I have been unjust to you. – Forgive me – burn those letters which contain the records of my violence.[3]

The man who had told Godwin never to talk of forgiveness again 'for my blood boils in my veins', had evidently learnt nothing, not even caution. They had barely ceased quarrelling over the promised £200; this time Shelley promises £300.

He and Mary were headed for Geneva with Claire, in pursuit of Lord Byron. Eager to rival her sister with a more celebrated poet of her own Claire had originally approached Byron using the name of Trefusis, under the pretext that she was seeking an appointment at Drury Lane where he was a committee member. Byron, in the throes of a separation from the wife he had married only a year before, had tried to put her off – he boasted once that he had never *seduced* any

woman – but Claire had pursued him with all her mother's determination, until he had done what was expected of him. Almost at
once the spreading scandal involving his half-sister had forced him
out of the country, but Claire, having exhibited her catch to Mary,
was determined to show him off to Shelley too, while Byron, the
most celebrated writer of the day, had his own curiosity to meet this
little-known Percy Shelley, author of the obscure but admirable
Queen Mab and the more recent *Alastor*. Byron's attitude to Claire, an
admittedly attractive but unbearably persistent seventeen-year-old
was never other than contempt, but as he complained 'I could not
exactly play the stoic with a woman who has scrambled eight
hundred miles to unphilosophize me.'[4] Probably none of them yet
knew that Claire was pregnant.

Exaggerated rumours of this *ménage à quatre*, this 'league of incest',
began to filter back to England, and one old sparring partner could
not resist the opportunity for a further poke at Godwin's dignity. 'I
have some curiosity to know', wrote Elizabeth Inchbald, fairly
dripping with innocence, 'whether you have a daughter, or an
adopted daughter, or neither the one nor the other in Switzerland at
present.'[5] Many years before, Mrs Inchbald had written four
volumes of *Memoirs*, but though they had been accepted for publication more than once, they had never yet appeared. Now Constable
expressed an interest, and Godwin was assigned the task of getting
them from her, even bringing the intrigued publisher to meet the
authoress at the end of 1817. 'Mr Constable is a widower, of
amorous complexion,' Godwin warned her, in a remark worthy of
the lady herself, 'and I am not sure that he has not been guilty of the
indelicacy of having endeavoured to prevail on the book to come to
bed with him.'[6] But Mrs Inchbald was careful to preserve the
acidulous distance she had built up over the years, and Godwin was
still to complain at being turned rudely from her door, on more than
one occasion. Her *Memoirs*, alas, were never published. On her
confessor's advice Mrs Inchbald ordered them burnt at her death in
1821 because, so she said, she did not want to be the cause of pain.
So we will never know what they said, about Godwin for one; or
even more enjoyably, just how they said it.

Charles Clairmont, meanwhile, had fallen into a disgrace that
seemed to rival his sisters'. No doubt the Skinner Street business
suffered by comparison with Constable's, where the job was to
publish books not chase after finance, and he had often talked to
Shelley and Mary about emigrating to the West Indies or the United
States or some other 'rather wild project in the Clairmont style.'
But sometime in that same spring of 1816 Charles, then aged
twenty, abruptly left England. What had happened we do not know,

though Godwin later remarked that, for all his other faults, young
William 'has hitherto escaped the low profligacy into which poor
Charles fell'.[7] Crabb Robinson faithfully reports that rumour that
'Godwin has behaved with great cruelty to his son-in-law, young
Clairmont',[8] but Charles's own letters to Shelley make it clear that
he felt guilty at having so deserted his parents, and even more
embarrassed lest he might have to return and face them. And
whatever the cause of the break, it did not lie with his step-father:

> It is true my feelings for my Mother are cold and inactive, but
> my attachment and respect for Godwin are unalterable, and
> will remain so to the last moment of my existence. The un-
> worthy occupations to which I see him forced to lend himself
> have cost me more bitter pangs than I can describe to you. His
> gentleness and rational treatment made an early and deep
> impression on me; I admire and love him infinitely; the news of
> his death would be to me a stroke of the severest affliction; that
> of my own Mother would be no more than the sorrow
> occasioned by the loss of a common acquaintance. Tell me how
> I can serve them both, and I shall not hesitate for a moment;
> but I fear that all connection is cut off as regards this subject.[9]

Even young William, now thirteen, had learnt how to quarrel
with his mother, 'a being of eminent worth, but of much danger,
who is in some respects worthy of universal applause, but in others
to be regarded as an untamed outlaw'.[10] (This undated note, signed
W. Godwin Jnr but in style and script extraordinarily like his father,
refers to his going to the theatre the previous Saturday, to see
Kemble in the *Iron Chest*, without telling Mrs Godwin. In fact the last
appearance of a Kemble in the play had been in May 1801, so the
reference is presumably to Kean, who performed it on Saturday, 30
November 1816.) More and more the burdens fell on Fanny,
sensible sensitive Fanny, so tender and so impressionable that Claire
thought that the sentimental hero of Mackenzie's sickly *Man of
Feeling* would suit her perfectly for a husband. It was Fanny who had
to write secretly to her father in Edinburgh about Mrs Godwin's
health, though under instructions not to alarm him unnecessarily. It
was Fanny who kept Shelley and Mary up to date with the
increasingly bleak news from Skinner Street. How Godwin, so sick
with worry that he could scarcely sleep at night, had been lent £300
which actually belonged to the government and would therefore have
to be repaid the moment it was needed. How when Sheridan, the
last survivor of that glittering political faction to which Godwin had
once allied himself, one of the rich and great on whom he had pinned
his hopes of peaceful reform and democratic progress, had died,

bitter, forgotten and in debt, that July, Godwin had gone day after day to Westminster Abbey, to stand beside the grave and mourn the hopes and aspirations that had once been theirs. How 'I wish Papa had not begun this letter, it is so cold when I can assure you, he speaks of you with great kindness and interest. I hope the day will not be long before you are reconciled.'[11] How ill-health and over-work were making Mrs Godwin more demanding and bad-tempered than ever, and though 'Mama and I are not great friends', still Fanny paid her the respect and attention that was a mother's due, and was 'anxious to defend her from a charge so foreign to her character'[12] as that she had pursued Shelley and Mary like a hound after a fox, or Falkland after Williams. How nothing had been heard from Charles in months. How even Marshall, Godwin's unfailing assistant these thirty years and more, was now so deep in debts of his own that they seldom saw him.

Poor Fanny was torn between them, between her respect for her parents and her love for her sister, and torn apart by the hopelessness of their situation, the impossibility of the business's ever paying its way, the impossibility of reconciling Godwin and Mary. Her one comfort lay in the dreams and the memories that their visitors brought with them. The Wollstonecraft sisters had been to see her, and raised again the question of her joining them in Dublin. George Blood, to whose sister Fanny owed her name, and who had himself once been her mother's special favourite, had also been in town, and inspired and comforted her with praise of that altogether superior being. Even Robert Owen 'told me the other day that he wished our mother were living, as he had never before met with a person who thought so exactly as he did, or would so warmly and zealously have entered into his plans.'[13] Another regular caller, David Booth, might warn of the dreadful poverty and unemployment that followed the ending of the war with France, but Owen was as optimistic as ever, his recent *Address to the People of New Lanark* sounding in Fanny's summary more like *Political Justice* than *Political Justice* itself. He 'tells us to cheer up for that in two years we shall feel the good effect of his plans – he is quite certain that they will succeed'. But Fanny had heard it all before: 'I have no doubt that he will do a great deal of good, but how he can expect to make the rich give up their possessions and live in a state of equality is too romantic to be believed.'[14]

The discovery that Claire was pregnant brought Shelley and Mary back to England after all, to Bath, so that Claire might have her baby in secret. But Shelley had to go up to London to visit the money-lenders and there, in that familiar haunt of them both, he met Fanny more than once. He knew that she felt her father's difficulties as keenly as did Godwin himself; he knew that she blamed him for Godwin's inability to get on with the novel he had promised Constable; he knew that she was as distraught as Godwin when Shelley had been unable to raise the £300 he had promised. But he did not know just how deep her despair went:

> Friend had I known thy secret grief
>
> Her voice did quiver as we parted,
> Yet knew I not that heart was broken
> From whence it came, and I departed
> Heeding not the words then spoken
>   Misery – O misery
> This world is all too wide for thee
>
> Some secret woes had been mine own
> And they had taught me that the good –
> The pain –
> And that for whom the lone and weary
> The load of life is long and dreary;
> Some hopes were buried in my heart
> Whose spectres haunted me with sadness.

On Monday 7 October Fanny Godwin left London for Ireland, or so she told her fellow-travellers. Perhaps she met Shelley as she passed through Bath and Bristol, perhaps she did not, but she did write letters, letters so alarming that both Godwin and Shelley went separately in search of her. Godwin could find nothing and returned home, writing to Mary and to Claire as he did so, but without calling on either. But Shelley followed the trail to Swansea, and came back to Mary on the Saturday morning 'with the worst account'. That day the Swansea *Cambrian* carried a report of 'a melancholy discovery'. A most respectable looking young female had arrived on Wednesday and been found next morning dead from an overdose of laudanum, the drug that Shelley had used in his own dramatic gesture at suicide. By the body there was a note,

> I have long determined that the best thing I could do was to put an end to the existence of a being whose birth was unfortunate, and whose life has only been a series of pain to those persons who have hurt their health in endeavouring to promote her welfare. Perhaps to hear of my death will give you pain, but you will soon have the blessing of forgetting that such a creature ever existed as . . .[15]

But the signature was torn away. All that remained to identify the body were her clothes, the letters 'M.W.' on her stays, and a 'G' marked on her stockings.

'I did indeed expect it', Godwin wrote wretchedly to Mary.

> I cannot but thank you for your strong expressions of sympathy. I do not see however that sympathy can be of any service to me: but it is best.
>
> My advice, and earnest prayer is, that you avoid doing any thing that leads to publicity. Go not to Swansea. Disturb not the silent dead. Do nothing to destroy the secrecy she so much desired, that now rests upon the event. It was, as I said, her last wish. It was the motive that led her from London to Bristol, and from Bristol to Swansea.
>
> I said your sympathy could be of no use to me. But I retract the assertion. By observing what I have just recommended to you, it may be of infinite service. Think what is the situation of my wife and myself, now deprived of all our children but the youngest; and do not expose us to those questions, which to a mind in anguish is one of the severest of all trials.
>
> We are at this moment in doubt whether during the first shock we shall not say that she is gone to Ireland to her aunts, a thing that had been in contemplation. Do not take from us the power to exercise our own discretion. You shall hear again tomorrow.
>
> What I have most of all in horror is the public papers; and I thank you for your caution as it might act on this.
>
> We have so conducted ourselves, that not one person in our house has the smallest apprehension of the truth. Our feelings are less tumultuous than deep: God knows what they may become.
>
> The following is one expression in her letter to us, written from Bristol on Tuesday. 'I depart immediately to the spot from which I hope never to be removed.'[16]

The secret was well kept: friends were told that Fanny had died in Ireland from a disease of the lungs, and it took three years for Crabb Robinson to hear that Fanny had died in Wales, by hanging it was said. But while Godwin was understandably anxious not to fuel the malicious rumours that still circulated round him, there was more to his deception than that. For most of his life he had contrived to control his emotions by repressing them, by reporting their outbreak in careful French or Latin, by stressing the role of reason in all things, and cultivating a calm detachment. Now, overwhelmed by calamities private and public, and with not the remotest idea how to deal with them, he simply closed up and tried to ignore what was happening, his feelings less tumultuous than deep. Shelley, too, had preferred not to disturb the silent dead: he actually saw the body but turned away, saying nothing. And Fanny Imlay, dutiful, sensitive Fanny, was buried nameless in a pauper's grave.

Why had she done it? Surely not from shame at her illegitimacy, for she must always have known that familiar fact. Scarcely because she was unable to return with her aunts to Ireland, for there is no sign that she either wanted to or was prevented from it. Perhaps because, 'a very plain girl and odd in her manners and opinions',[17] she feared growing into another Aunt Everina or Eliza, a nervous, awkward, eccentric old maid barely tolerated by those around her, and living only through the joys of others – she had already written to Mary that she thought of her nephew as a son of her own, and looked 'forward to the time of my old age and his manhood'.[18] Possibly because she too had been in love with Shelley, the explanation favoured by Mrs Godwin and one that Godwin later endorsed. But most probably because she could absorb no more of the miseries of Skinner Street, her father's inability to pay his debts or write his books, her mother's unending irritability and spitefulness. For Fanny blamed everything, the scandal of Mary and Shelley too, on herself, on the personal inadequacies that had brought only pain and suffering to those who had tried to help her. Once a letter from Aunt Everina had gone astray, and Fanny wrote nervously of the guilt she had felt:

> I have been made very unhappy by your long silence; which I feared would never be broken. I . . . assure you how much affected I am by the return of your confidence and affection, which I trust my conduct and character will secure to me through life, even under the greatest misfortunes.[19]

When George Blood had hoped that the daughter of Mary Wollstonecraft would prove worthy of her, it 'in some degree roused me from my torpor. I have determined never to live to be a disgrace to such a mother. I have always found that if I endeavour to overcome my faults, I shall find beings to love and esteem me.'[20] Or again, when Mary Jane told her she was the laughing stock of Shelley and Mary, the 'constant beacon of your satire',[21] she wrote sadly to assure them that whatever they might think of her, her love for them would always be sincere. Fanny's report of Godwin standing for hours in morbid depression beside Sheridan's grave, tells us as much about her own state of mind.

But whatever the reason, Shelley clearly felt some special guilt of his own. His health, Claire said, was completely broken by the event, and he told Byron that he felt 'a far severer anguish' at this than at the second suicide that followed two months upon the first, though it was more clearly his responsibility. On 10 December the body of Harriet Shelley, the golden girl-child who had always shared his fascination with self-destruction, was taken from the Serpentine. But in her case the reason was all too evident: she was far advanced in pregnancy, and it could not be by Shelley.

Godwin learnt the news six days later, and grasped at this means of bridging the abyss of dependence and recrimination that had separated him from his daughter, his disciple, and the grandson that bore his name. Shelley and Mary must marry at once, that was the gist of his letters to them both, and of Shelley's two-hour conversation with Mrs Godwin, who is supposed to have told him that if they did not he would have a third suicide – Godwin's – on his conscience. But Shelley had powerful reasons of his own for marrying quickly after Harriet's death, a point of etiquette on which Godwin took expert advice, for he wanted to claim Harriet's children, who by rights were his. That had been in his mind, and in Mary's too, even before they broke the news to Godwin.

So it was that Shelley and Godwin faced each other again on 27 December 1816, after an interval of some two-and-a-half years. The next day they went together to obtain a marriage licence, as they had once gone to get one for Harriet, and the day after that Mary came home to Skinner Street, for a formal dinner of reconciliation. On the 30th they were married, at St Mildred's in Broad Street, with Godwin and his wife for witnesses. Shelley tried hard to be nonchalant about this 'ceremony so magical in its effects', and wrote to Claire that 'nothing could be more provoking than to find all this unnecessary. However they will now be satisfied and quiet.' But Godwin's kindness and concern, his evident wish to forgive and forget all that had passed between them, genuinely moved him, even if Mrs Godwin appeared to him still 'in her real attributes of affectation, prejudice and heartless pride'.[22] Claire's baby was due next month, but the Godwins did not even know that she was pregnant.

Godwin's account of the day is even more demeaning. It is always possible to find some excuse for his shameless borrowings, his petty weaknesses and conceits, his vacillation and chicaneries, his arrogance towards Shelley, his hardness towards Mary, his deception over Fanny. It is easy to understand his relief and delight that Mary was at last married to her young gentleman of talent and fortune. But there is little to say in defence of the letter he sent his brother, Hull Godwin, on the occasion of his daughter's wedding:

The piece of news I have to tell, however, is that I went to

church with this tall girl some little time ago to be married.
Her husband is the eldest son of Sir Timothy Shelley, of Field
Place, in the county of Sussex, Baronet. So that, according to
the vulgar ideas of the world, she is well married, and I have
great hopes this young man will make her a good husband.
You will wonder, I dare say, how a girl without a penny of
fortune should meet with so good a match. But such are the
ups and downs of this world. For my part I care but little,
comparatively, about wealth, so that it should be her destiny in
life to be respectable, virtuous and contented.[23]

It was a fittingly dishonest epitaph to Godwin's most dishonourable
years.

Yet even as he wrote that coyly deceitful note Godwin was giving
more honest and more adequate expression to the canker that had
eaten at his soul these past few years. On the surface he was still the
same mild, quiet, dreary old gentleman, his manners 'polite, almost
cringing', but within him seethed emotions that he concealed even
from himself. Three days after the ceremony he awoke with an
imprecation from a 'vehemently impassioned dream', and the novel
he was writing for Constable would be equally revealing of his true
state of mind. It would be a story of malignity and hatred, and a
malevolence that tips into insanity, a story of black bile and bitter
gall, the story of *Mandeville*.

Set in Godwin's favourite period, the time of the Civil War, it tells
of a man whose childhood and schooldays combine to turn him into
a morose and forbidding misanthrope who makes the whole world
his enemy. But as Godwin always reminds us, all men need some
object of love and affection, and in Mandeville's case these feelings
focus with peculiar intensity on a single individual, his sister
Henrietta. His hatred, equally, fastens on one man, the talented and
honourable Clifford, and the more open, the more amiable, the more
admirable Clifford is, the greater is Mandeville's malevolence
towards him, and the more anxious he is to see him disgraced and
reviled. So when Mandeville discovers that Clifford and Henrietta
have fallen in love, his loathing slides into madness, he is determined
to keep them apart by any means in his power, and the stage seems
set for an obsessive pursuit like that in *Caleb Williams*. But it is already
the close of Volume III. There is a thwarted attempt to abduct
Henrietta, a fight between her brother and the man who has now
become her husband, and Mandeville's face is slashed open by a
blow from Clifford's sword. The novel closes with him staring at his
disfigured features in a mirror, fit symbol of his ravaged soul, his
whole being churning with re-intensified hatred.

It is clear enough that the adventures of Mandeville do not end here, that Godwin's story has scarcely yet begun, and in an Advertisement for a projected second edition he explained that he had found it impossible to complete the novel in the three volumes originally planned though 'whether I shall ever be enabled to complete my original purpose, depends on a variety of circumstances, many of which are placed beyond my control.' One, of course, was whether he would live to write the further three volumes he thought the story needed; but another was whether he could find a publisher to finance them. Constable, no doubt, thought himself lucky to have anything to publish at all, though this time the problem had been not whether Godwin would write him a novel, but whether he would ever stop writing it. The old long-windedness, the obsession with detail and reluctance to pass over anything that might usefully be explained or elaborated, the store of miscellaneous learning, all had contributed to drag the story out beyond endurance.

So the task of completing *Mandeville* fell to another writer called Arnold, and another publisher. At first Volume IV, *Mandeville: The Last Words of a Maniac!*, By Himself, continues the story in the frenetic style of the original. But Arnold cannot keep the hysteria up, and soon relapses into straightforward narrative: Mandeville is consigned to an asylum, falls among mildly dotty Quakers, and celebrates his 21st birthday – which happens to fall on Guy Fawkes Day – by hanging and burning an effigy of the hated Clifford, finally shooting it through the heart and falling on the remains in a state of delirious ecstasy! After that there is some respite. Mandeville and his sister are reconciled, and he falls in love himself, only to discover on the eve of his wedding that the lady is Clifford's cousin. This sends him back to his ravings, his betrothed dies of a broken heart, and when Henrietta dies too, of the plague that is sweeping the country, everything is laid at Clifford's door. They meet by Henrietta's graveside, they draw their swords, they pierce one another through the heart: 'We fell together across the grave of Henrietta – we never rose again', except, it seems, to tell the tale. Godwin's novel could certainly have done with more of a story line. But it could have done without this.

In all probability, however, Godwin was not greatly disappointed to leave it where he did. The setting fascinated him, but the sluggish melodrama held no more interest for him than it does for us. It was the depiction of character that mattered, and there was little he could add to that. For here, even more than in *Caleb Williams*, Godwin wields his metaphysical dissecting knife to lay bare the deepest involutions of motive and personality, taking us within his character to feel what he feels, and hate what he hates. For all its faults, its verbosity and tedium, it is the relentless expression of this one dominating state of mind, an unrelieved hatred of everything that men might find good and pure and honourable, that makes *Mandeville* one of Godwin's most extraordinary works. His narrators do not always speak for their author – the Godwinian here is rather Clifford, the advocate of human brotherhood and the virtues of simplicity – but nowhere in his writing is there a figure whose actions, beliefs and innermost thoughts are so at variance with everything Godwin himself valued and admired. Somewhere within himself he found that store of spleen to draw upon; in *Mandeville* he gave vent to feelings he could articulate in no other way, not to his friends, not to his family, not to himself.

The effect was cathartic, and 1817 proved a much better year than most. Mrs Godwin, too, was in better health now, and instead of her usual rest cure at the seaside she spent the summer in France, visiting friends and relations and, mixing business with pleasure as always, arranging for a French edition of the forthcoming novel. Even young William seemed much improved in character and conduct, now he was at school in Greenwich with Godwin's customer Charles Burney. There still were money worries, of course, but they were less than they had been, less than Shelley's, less even than Marshall's, whom Godwin had now to rescue as Marshall had often helped to rescue him. In fact it was Place, highly mistrustful of Godwin's role in it all, who helped raise the few score pounds that Marshall needed.

Shelley, meanwhile, had failed to gain possession of Harriet's children, but by September there were three infants after all: William, Claire's daughter Allegra, and a daughter for Mary, too, named Clara after the unshakable sister. The William Godwins, father and son, were regular visitors, and though, despite the husband's protests, they preferred to keep the wife at arm's length, the Shelleys stayed from time to time at Skinner Street. Shelley introduced Godwin to the leading members of the Hampstead literary set, most notably Leigh Hunt and John Keats, but Godwin was unable to repay the compliment by introducing Shelley to his idol Coleridge. Once, back in August 1813, they had both called on Godwin on the self-same day, but Coleridge, too, 'often bitterly regretted in my heart that I never did meet Shelley.'[24]

Mandeville was published at the end of that year, on 1 December, with a dedication to 'the sincerest friend I ever had', John Philpott Curran, who had died that October. Shelley read the book with a sense of mounting relief. Perhaps it·was just hope that Godwin's talents might return to benefit the world once more, that Godwin might at last become his own man again, but it seemed to him to rival Godwin's very best work. He wrote to Godwin to tell him so, and was astonished to find the relevant 'Excerpt from a Letter from Oxfordshire' printed in the *Morning Chronicle* for 9 December. 'If I had believed it possible you should send any part of my letter to the Chronicle', Shelley wrote again, more amazed than annoyed, 'I should have expressed more fully my sentiments of Mandeville and of the Author.'[25] A more detailed appreciation in Leigh Hunt's *Examiner* soon gave him that opportunity. But it takes more than one enthusiast to make a popular success, and *Mandeville* proved too obsessive, too monotonous, for the majority of its readers. 'A morbid anatomy of black bile', declares a character in Peacock's gently mocking *Nightmare Abbey*, picking up a new novel called *Devilman* and hastily putting it down again. The reviewers agreed in finding it morbid and tedious, 'a very dull novel and a very clever book', and the proposed second edition was never realized.

No doubt Shelley's concern for *Mandeville* was fuelled in part by his anxiety for his own narrative poem *The Revolt of Islam*, published a month later, and when that proved no more successful than the rest he made up his mind once more to quit England for good, to travel to Italy for the sake of his health and Mary's, and to hand Claire and her child over to Byron, whose responsibility they were. All that kept them back was money, and the publication of Mary's first novel, a work whose reputation – if not, perhaps, its reading – would exceed that of all the books of Godwin and Wollstonecraft put together, and continue to do so even when the writings of her more famous husband are added to the balance. Mary had already published a diary of her elopement journey, her *History of a Six Weeks Tour*, inspired by her mother's *Letters from Scandinavia* that Shelley had read aloud as they floated down the Rhine. But *Frankenstein* would be her homage to her father. In Geneva with Byron that summer they had amused themselves with a book of ghost stories, and had agreed that they would write one each. Only Mary had been unable to think of anything until one evening, after listening to Shelley and Byron talk wonderingly of the experiments of a Dr Darwin who, they believed, had produced voluntary motion in – of all unlikely monsters – a piece of vermicelli, she had lain sleeplessly in bed, seeing as vividly as if he were in the room beside her

> the pale student of unhallowed arts kneeling beside the thing he had put together. I saw the hideous phantasm of a man stretched out, and then, on the working of some powerful engine, show signs of life, and stir with an uneasy, half vital motion . . . . Oh! if I could only contrive one which would frighten my reader as I myself had been frightened that night![26]

280 · A PAUPER'S GRAVE

It is a scene that Hollywood has since made its own, but for all the mounting horror with which she created it in her imagination, Mary took little interest in sheer mechanics. Just as her father had passed in silence over the manufacture of precious metals, the mixing of mysterious potions that bring eternal youth to St Leon, so she deals with the artificial creation of life in the space of a single sentence. Perhaps the idea alone was horrible enough to her readers; certainly those reared on the cinema will not find *Frankenstein* the terrifying book its contemporaries declared it to be. But Mary's real interests, like Godwin's, lay elsewhere: indeed they were Godwin's own. It has been suggested that, lacking a genuine father of her own, Mary created a substitute in her monster, but Godwin's influence on the novel he helped to revise is more basic, and more straightforward, than that. The idea of an obsessive pursuit, with Frankenstein staking his own survival against that of the monster, derives from *Caleb Williams*; the Swiss setting is reminiscent of *Fleetwood*, though based also on Mary's personal experience of that country; the Gothic horror, the themes of secrecy and the occult – and especially of *the* occult secret, the secret of life itself – come from *St Leon*. But more striking still, this is the story of a being cut off from mankind, anxious to put himself at the service of others but misunderstood, feared, hated, not for what he is but for what he seems to be; a story of the necessity of friendship if man, or monster, is to become all that he is capable of being; a story of a natural goodness corrupted and destroyed by prejudice and injustice, its moral, as Shelley said, 'Treat a person ill and he will become wicked.' It is the archetypal Godwinian novel, more Godwinian than many of Godwin's own.

In fact, had the anonymous publication not been dedicated to him, there is little doubt that Godwin – already one of several candidates for the Great Unknown, the mysterious writer of the hugely successful Waverley Novels – would have been cast as its author. Even when the name of Shelley began to be linked with the book, it never occurred to anyone that it might be *Mrs* Shelley. 'For a man it was excellent', marvelled *Blackwood's Magazine* five years later, when at length it discovered the truth, 'but for a woman it was wonderful.'[27] And not just a woman but a girl, not yet twenty! Many more books would be published by 'the Author of *Frankenstein*', but none would remotely approach that astonishing début. Her later novels are all thinly veiled autobiography, with Shelley, Byron, Claire, Godwin and the other characters of her life translated from one period setting to another, and written with an effusive grandiloquence that stands at the opposite extreme from the measured, almost deadpan prose that *Frankenstein* inherited from her father. It stands apart, in style, in theme, in originality. 'Most people felt of Mr Godwin', de Quincy would say, 'with the same alienation and horror as . . . of the monster created by Frankenstein.' Yet in a real sense, it was Godwin who created *Frankenstein*.

They left for Italy on the day that *Frankenstein* appeared, 11 March 1818. In January Shelley had sold another post-obit at a mere two for one, some £2,000 for a bond worth £4,500. Godwin's share was around £750, less than he had been promised, but enough. 'I acknowledge the receipt of the sum mentioned in your last letter,' he wrote. 'I acknowledge with equal explicitness my complete disappointment.' But for once he could allow himself the luxury of a little dignity:

> I am ashamed of the tone I have taken with you in all our late conversations. I have played the part of a supplicant, and deserted that of a philosopher. It was not thus I talked to you when I first knew you. I will talk so no more. I will talk principles; I will talk Political Justice. I would enlighten your understanding if I could, but I would not, if I could, carry things by importunity . . . . If you have the courage to hear me, come; if you have not, be it so. What I have to say I *must* say, if I ever stand in your presence again; but I had rather it were without a witness.[28]

Shelley, it seemed, did lack the courage, or the patience, and for a time preferred to ignore his father-in-law. But Godwin was with them continually the week before they departed, and attended the mass christening of all three grandchildren, and Shelley's last act in England was, appropriately enough, to send a final £150 from aboard ship at Dover. Then they were gone. Of those three adults and three children, only the two step-sisters would ever return.

23 ♣ The principle of populations

What matters what becomes of this miserable carcass, if I can
live for ever in true usefulness? And this must be the case in the
present instance: for whatever becomes of my individual book
if I am right the system of Malthus can never rise again, and
the world is delivered for ever from this accursed apology in
favour of vice and misery, of hard-heartedness and oppression.[1]

To Mary Jane Godwin, 1819

♣ The close of the war with France brought with it a curious echo of
twenty years before. Although the parliamentary Whigs had
remained in total disarray throughout, their only taste of power the
short-lived Ministry of All the Talents that followed Pitt's death in
1806, a tradition of more radical protest had survived, waxing and
waning with the state of the war-torn economy until more troops
had to be garrisoned in the industrial centres of England than were
serving under Wellington in Spain. Indeed it was to many a
disappointment that the assassination of the prime minister proved to
be the work of a mere maniac, and when demobilization brought
mass unemployment and even worse poverty, the followers of
Thomas Spence, advocate of 'agrarian equality' and an end to the
aristocracy, organized a series of huge public meetings on Spa
Fields, directly inspired by the gatherings of the Corresponding
Society in 1795 and with Henry 'Orator' Hunt stirring the crowds in
place of John Thelwall. But this time the mood was more bitter – on
one occasion the toast was drunk, 'May the last of Kings be
strangled with the guts of the last priest' – and at a meeting on 2
December 1816, a second of the crowd split away and marched to
the Tower to urge the troops to join them, breaking into gunshops
on the way. It was the nearest such rallies ever came to armed
insurrection, and the government responded quickly with another
pair of Gagging Acts. And although several leading Spenceans were
acquitted of treason the following June, the authorities had already
found their scapegoat. 'Governments, like poet-laureates, certainly
"*grow milder*" as they grow older,' sneered Hazlitt. 'Our government,
the other day, instead of six hundred citizens, taken at a venture
from the wards of Cripplegate or Farringdon-without, only sus-

pended Cashman and the Habeas Corpus.'[2] Godwin, however, said nothing, and it all happened outside his window.

John Cashman was a drunken, penniless Irish sailor – penniless because he had not received the £200 he claimed in prize monies and back wages for services rendered against the French, drunken because he had been drinking a mixture of beer, gin and rum on an empty stomach – and one of five accused of raiding Beckwith's, the gunsmiths that stood directly across Snow Hill from M. J. Godwin and Co. Others had played a more prominent part in the riot, but Cashman was the only one who could be found guilty, a verdict widely regarded as unfair even among those who deplored the rioting and the attempted treason. But to make his example even more of a warning, it was decided to have Cashman hung at the scene of his crime, the last time that this was done in England. Beckwith tried to get them to shift the gallows, a form of publicity he would prefer to do without, but on 12 March 1817 the execution took place at the junction of Skinner Street and Snow Hill. An angry, seething crowd filled both streets, held back by barricades and an 'immense force' of constables, while Cashman, evidently more concerned at being taken through the streets in a cart like a common criminal than at being hung by the neck until dead, urged the throng on from his vantage point. Two clergymen tried to prepare him for death, but he would have none of it. 'Don't bother me,' he told them, 'it's no use – I want no mercy but from God.' Then he turned to the crowd, 'Now you buggers, give me three cheers when I trip.' And finally to the hangman, 'Come Jack, you bastard, let go the jib-boom.' Cashman himself was cheering when he fell. The crowd, crying murder and shame, could not be dispersed for hours.

But this was not politics as Godwin knew it. His diary does record the riot at Beckwiths, and later an 'outrage at Manchester', the Battle of Peterloo in August 1819, when armed yeomanry charged a defenceless crowd, killing eleven and injuring maybe 600. But he had his eyes set on larger, nobler game, the sort that he could handle and defeat in the quiet of his study. What was needed was the rehabilitation of *Political Justice*, no less, or if not *Political Justice* itself then of what it stood for. The little skirmishing pamphlets, the novels of buffoonery and scandal, were forgotten now, as forgotten as his own *Reply to Parr*. But one of the manifold replies to Godwin had survived, and even taken his place in the firmament of reputation. 'While every body was abusing and despising Mr Godwin', wrote Sydney Smith, 'and while Mr Godwin was, among a certain description of understandings, increasing every day in popularity, Mr Malthus took the trouble of refuting him: and we hear no more of Mr Godwin.'[3] But now Godwin felt it was time to refute Malthus.

He seems to have forgotten that he had done so already. Perhaps that was because no one seemed to have noticed.

It was towards the close of *Political Justice* that Godwin had first confronted an 'Objection to This System from the Principle of Populations'. Thirty years previously Robert Wallace's *Various Prospects of Mankind, Nature and Providence* had outlined a system of equality that differed from Godwin's only in the central role it ascribed to the vigilance of the state. But 'having exhibited this picture, not less true than delightful', Wallace had gone on to uncover 'an argument that demolishes the whole'[4]:

> Under a perfect government the inconveniences of having a family would be so intirely removed, children would be so well taken care of, and everything become so favourable to populousness, that though some sickly seasons, or dreadful plagues in particular climates might cut off multitudes, yet in general mankind would increase so prodigiously, that the earth would at last be overstocked, and become unable to support its numerous inhabitants.

It was not, however, a difficulty that Godwin took very seriously, passing immediately to the suggestion that men, once born, might refuse to die.

> Three fourths of the habitable globe is now uncultivated. The parts already cultivated are capable of immeasurable improvement. Myriads of centuries of still increasing population may probably pass away, and the earth still be found sufficient for the subsistence of its inhabitants . . . . It would be truly absurd for us to shrink from a scheme of essential benefit to mankind, lest they should be too happy, and by necessary consequence at some distant period too populous.[5]

One among the many to be enchanted by Godwin's vision of pure justice was Daniel Malthus, a man who once had the distinction – and also the anxiety – of having Hume and Rousseau together as guests in his house. He passed on his copy of the *Enquirer* to his son Thomas, drawing his attention especially to the essay 'Of Avarice and Profusion', where Godwin again outlined the advantages to flow from a state of economic equality. But Malthus junior, a mathematician by training, thought he could detect an inescapable difficulty, and what began as a series of notes for his father, ended up a book, his 1798 *Essay on the Principle of Population*, 'as it affects the future improvement of society, with remarks upon the speculations of Mr Godwin, M. Condorcet, and other writers'. It was, like Godwin's, a work for its time, appearing at just the moment when a hopeless pesssimism began to replace the original optimism. But more crucially still, it too was equipped with arguments, proofs positive, providing a logical – even better, a mathematical – demonstration that Godwin must be wrong, that the nature of things, the nature of man himself, were such that poverty and hardship, misery and vice, are inescapable, and that visions of human perfection are misconceived, when they are not positively counter-productive.

The basis of Malthus's argument was that population and the means of its subsistence tend to grow at different rates. Experience in the newly settled countries of North America suggested that, with adequate resources, population tends to double every twenty or twenty-five years, while food and the other necessities of life can be expected to increase at a constant rate. Thus while resources increase in so-called arithmetical ratio (1, 2, 3, 4, 5 . . .) population will increase in geometric ratio (1, 2, 4, 8, 16 . . .). Left to itself population will soon outstrip the means of its support, and outstrip it at an ever-faster rate: after five steps in the series population has already grown three times more than subsistence; after another five it will be some 61 to 1. But of course this can never happen. Something must check the natural growth of population, keeping it down to the limits of subsistence. If all else fails, there is always the ultimate check of sheer starvation.

But Malthus did not, as is often thought, predict an ultimate fate of universal starvation. Rather, on his principles over-population will generate poverty before it generates famine, and it is poverty and hardship, what Malthus calls vice and misery, that keeps the population down. For Godwin it had been one of the major objections to private wealth that 'the established administration of property may be considered as strangling a considerable portion of our children in their cradle,'[6] but to Malthus that would be a positive, a necessary, advantage. This, then, is what has since been dubbed the Dismal Theorum, that in every country and in every age population will grow inexorably to the point which generates sufficient misery and vice to prevent it growing any further. And from this there follows in turn the Utterly Dismal Theorum, that attempts to improve social conditions must always be futile and probably self-defeating. 'Systems of equality' cannot make things better, they may even make things worse, by spreading the suffering among all members of the society, instead of restricting it to a single class. And chief among these, of course, is the system of Godwin. The moment that vice and misery were eliminated in a state of political justice, population would begin to grow to the point where the earth could support no more, and vice and misery would return as before:

Even if we allow it to be possible we may venture to pronounce with certainty that if Mr Godwin's system of society was established in its utmost perfection, instead of myriads of centuries, not thirty years could elapse before its utter destruction from the simple principle of population.

This is, moreover, not simply an unfortunate consequence of Godwin's theories; it is an objection that cuts at the very heart of his ideas. For we can see that it is a mistake to attribute 'all the vices and misery that are seen in civil society to human institutions'. Instead they are rooted in the human condition itself, in that very nature of things to which Godwin had looked for the perfectibility of man. The moral must be that perfection is to be found not in this world, 'a state of moral discipline and probation', but in another. The sins and sorrows that beset us are not social evils to be removed by truth and reason, but suffering which is necessary for the awakening of our souls and the softening of our hearts. They are, in short, the challenge that God has sent us. Malthus, we must indeed remember, was also an ordained minister in the Church of England.

Godwin knew from the first that he had in Malthus an opponent worthy of his respect, and in 1798, the year of Malthus's anonymous *Essay*, and again in 1801, the year of the *Reply to Parr*, the two met more than once to discuss their differences of opinion. Yet to Godwin the answer was so obvious as hardly to need making; indeed *Political Justice* had made it already:

> The gratifications of sense please at present by their imposture. We soon learn to despise the mere animal function, which apart from the delusions of intellect, would be nearly the same in all cases. The men therefore who exist, when the earth shall refuse itself to a more extended population, will cease to propagate, for they will no longer have any motive, either of error or duty, to induce them.[7]

As Hazlitt, himself the author of an answer to Malthus, pointed out, the case against Godwin rests on supposing that man is perfectible in every respect save one. But if men are rational enough to reach a state of justice they will surely be rational enough to keep their population within due bounds. Malthus is always more concerned to prove that population, left to itself, must outstrip productivity than to examine the factors that might restrain it. It is never clear, for example, whether he means to include the threat of starvation under the head of misery, or whether it is a separate factor; and the vice in question remains tantalizingly unanalysed. But more crucially, he offers no proof that the checks on population must always reduce to vice and misery, and if that assumption can be avoided then the Dismal and Utterly Dismal Theorums no longer follow. They follow only if the checks on population must without exception be dismal checks; so long as there are other, less distressing ways of holding population down, misery and vice will not be the inescapable lot of mankind, social reform need no longer be doomed to failure, and human perfectibility remains a genuine possibility.

This, then, was the point that Godwin had to make when he decided that Malthus needed an answer after all, and devoted a substantial portion of the *Reply to Parr* to that task. Even as things are 'virtue, prudence or pride' lead many people not to marry, because they feel unable to support a family, and in a state of justice and equality the same motives will influence the whole community. All that is needed is a change in public attitudes,

> such as, that it is the first duty of princes to watch for the
> multiplication of their subjects, and that a man or woman, who
> passes the term of life in a condition of celibacy, is to be con-
> sidered as having failed to discharge on the principal obligations
> they owe to the community. On the contrary it now appears to
> be rather the man who rears a numerous family, that has in
> some degree transgressed the consideration he owes to the
> public welfare.[8]

Nor need the restrictions be as great as Malthus might think. Each marriage could be allowed two children; or perhaps three, since one child in three may be expected not to survive into maturity; or even four, to compensate for those who do not marry; certainly no more, but there is no great hardship here!

It was a fair reply, which the history of the developed nations has more than borne out, much as the history of the underdeveloped countries might seem to support Malthus. But it was marred by a single tactical error that gave the massed ranks of Godwin's enemies all that they needed, and more. 'There is at the end one loathsome cursed passage for which I could in right vexation root up his nose', snarled Southey. 'His folly in thus eternally making himself a mark for abuse is inconceivable. Come kick me – is his eternal language.'[9] For Godwin happened to remark that some societies had avoided the problems of over-population by exposing their unwanted children and leaving them to die; and horrible though that might be, it may still be preferable to the checks that Malthus had in mind:

> Neither do I regard a new-born child with any superstitious
> reverence. If the alternatives were complete, I had rather such

a child should perish in the first hour of its existence, than that a man should spend seventy years of life in a state of misery and vice.[10]

Not, of course, that Godwin believes that the alternative is complete – 'I hope and trust, that no such expedient will be necessary to be resorted to, in any state of society which shall ever be introduced in this or the surrounding countries' – but his less sympathetic readers leapt gladly to the conclusion that he was advocating infanticide as a way of keeping families down to the permitted maximum of four.

'When all the gods and goddesses gave you each a good gift,' lamented Coleridge, 'Nemesis counterbalanced them all with the destiny that, in whatever you published, there should be some one outrageously, *imprudent* suicidal passage.'[11] Godwin was no less horrified at the misunderstanding – had not Malthus also listed infant mortality as one of the positive checks on population growth? – and he arranged for the *Monthly Magazine* to be sent an outraged letter in his defence. But it was too late to undo the harm, and the exposing of babies took its place alongside the free intercourse of the sexes, a world without death or disease, and the mechanical plough.

Nevertheless, on the main point at issue, Godwin had the better of the argument, and Malthus's second edition, so thoroughly revised as to constitute a whole new *Essay* almost four times the length of the first, duly allows a place for what Godwin had termed 'virtue, prudence or pride', what Malthus calls 'moral restraint', an 'abstinence from marriage, either for a time or permanently, from prudential considerations, with a strictly moral conduct towards the sex in the interval'. This, he reluctantly concedes, is an acceptable and 'virtuous means of avoiding the vice and misery which result so often from the principle of population':

> However powerful may be the impulses of passion, they are generally in some degree modified by reason. And it does not seem entirely visionary to suppose that, if the true and permanent causes of poverty were clearly explained and forcibly brought home to each man's bosom, it would have some and perhaps not an inconsiderable influence on his conduct.

And that concession is all that Godwin needs, for if moral restraint is a means of avoiding vice and misery, then a nation that practises moral restraint – or perhaps other forms of restraint that neither Malthus nor Godwin can bring themselves to contemplate – will be a nation that has no need of misery or vice to keep its population down.

Yet Malthus was not a man to abandon some hard-won conclusion merely because he had been dissuaded of the premises that led to it. His tactic, instead, was to minimize the controversy with Godwin, and insist as firmly as ever on an inevitable prospect of vice and misery. Indeed the second *Essay* went further than the first, passing from the Dismal Theorum to the more devastating Utterly Dismal Theorum, and replacing the attack on the outmoded doctrine of perfectibility with an attack on the system of Poor Laws. The health and happiness of society at large, Malthus argues, depends on the suffering of some: 'Private charity almost invariably leads to pernicious consequences'; 'We are bound in justice and honour to disclaim the right of the poor to support', for fear that their poverty will infect the rest of society; and if a man is unwise enough to marry when he cannot afford a family

> he shall be taught to know, that the laws of Nature, which are the laws of God, have doomed him and his family to suffer for disobeying their repeated admonitions; that he has no claim of right on society for the smallest portion of food, beyond that which his labour will fairly purchase . . .

It was, as Hazlitt said, the old conservative remedy, to take nothing from the rich and give it to the poor, made even less palatable by Malthus's distinctive brand of sanctimonious moralizing. 'I have, during my life, detested many men,' seethed Cobbett; 'but never anyone so much as you . . . . No assemblage of words can give an appropriate designation of you; and, therefore, as being the single word which best suits the character of such a man, I call you *Parson* . . . .'[12] But though writers as different as Hazlitt, Cobbett and Southey had raged against him across two decades, Malthus remained unruffled, thanks largely, as Godwin said, to 'the degree in which . . . the theory of this writer flattered the vices and corruption of the rich and great, and the eager patronage it might very naturally be expected to obtain from them.'[13] He could concede moral restraint, he could even concede that the evidence was that the Poor Laws did not in fact encourage marriage and procreation among the poor, and 'should this be true, many of the objections which have been urged in the Essay against the poor-laws will be removed'. But nothing would persuade him to moderate his conclusions. To Godwin, in particular, it was galling. Once he had refuted Malthus, and Malthus had accepted the refutation, yet to the world and to Malthus himself it was as if he had never written. The fame and influence of the *Essay* spread more widely with every successive edition, each one longer and less compromising than the last, while *Political Justice* had been consigned to the scrapheap of forgotten theories. Worse still, Malthus's most recent edition, in 1817, had replaced a chapter on the *Reply to Parr* with one on Robert Owen, and explained that although he had been urged to dispense altogether with any discussion of Godwin and his ilk 'as having in a considerable degree lost its interest', he thought there might still be some small value in the one chapter that remained, 'independently of its being natural to me to have some little partiality for that part of the work which led to the inquiries on which the main subject rests'.

Perhaps it was that patronizing paragraph that goaded Godwin into action, and for twelve months after *Mandeville* he was constantly dipping into Malthus and beginning to write, then going back to Malthus and starting to write again, at least six times in all. By December of 1818 he was ready to advertise a book, though it would be the best part of two years before *Of Population* actually appeared. His spirits were high. His tone was that of the man who had written *Political Justice*, who had no doubt that this new masterwork would again make the age, and all ages to come, his own. But his hopes were those of the man who wrote *Antonio*: for once he would make no contracts and accept no advances; this time nothing would be allowed to dilute either the prestige or the profits.

It was the irresistible force of pure mathematics, the unmistakable difference between the arithmetic and geometric ratios, that made Malthus's argument seem so compelling. Yet through all the statistics and the case studies the suspicion lingers that it is, in the words of John Stuart Mill, an 'unlucky attempt to give numerical precision to things which do not admit of it.' For who is to say what the rate of population growth might be, if all checks were removed? Who can decide what is the 'natural' rate of increase in the means of subsistence? These are questions that have no answer, much less a mathematical one. But as Mill also says. 'Every person capable of reasoning must see that it is wholly superfluous to his argument.' All that Malthus needs is the assumption, reasonable enough, that unless something holds it back, population will tend to grow faster than the resources which support it. The greater the difference the sooner we will reach the limit set for us by poverty and famine; but whatever the difference that limit will be reached sooner or later, just so long as population tends to outstrip subsistence. The actual arithmetic, Malthus's beloved ratios, is entirely irrelevant. What is not irrelevant is the nature of the checks that hold population down. Godwin's initial response, therefore, was the right one: 'I admit the ratios of the author in their full extent, and . . . I do not attempt in the slightest degree to vitiate the great foundations of his theory. My undertaking confines itself to the task of repelling his conclusions.'[14]

But this time he will take nothing for granted. He turns his back on moral restraint; he forgets entirely the *Reply to Parr*; he plunges into the jungle of statistical calculation, and disappears from view.

Godwin's guide through this unfamiliar territory was David Booth, a Scotsman and also, by coincidence, a member of the Glassite Church, which is to say a Sandemanian. He had corresponded with Godwin since the turn of the century, and had introduced to him his wife's family, the Baxters, with whom Mary Godwin had lived in Dundee. In fact when Booth's first wife, the eldest Baxter daughter, had died in 1814 Booth immediately replaced her with her youngest sister, Mary's special friend Isabella, in defiance of both his church and the law – though that had not prevented him refusing Isabella any contact with Mary and Shelley, even after they had married. Seven years older than her father and almost thirty years older than Isabella herself, less than five foot tall and with red, watery eyes staring out of a dark, impish face, Booth was by all accounts a husband bad-tempered to the point of cruelty. But he was a statistician as well as a brewer, and the 'Mathematical Dissertation' which he included in Godwin's book was an important technical contribution, introducing such factors as age distribution into population studies.

However, Godwin's main target was the famous geometric ratio, the claim that left to itself population will double every generation. Malthus had gone to ever greater lengths to demonstrate that this is the natural tendency, but Godwin answers that since approximately half of the children that are born die before maturity, the geometric ratio would require an average of eight births per family, and of this there is no evidence, neither in Europe nor in North America. Instead families seem to average only four births, of whom two survive to bear children of their own, so the natural tendency is actually for population to remain constant. As for the means of subsistence, its current limits 'arise out of civil institutions, the inequality of mankind, and the accumulation of property, landed property especially, in few hands.'[15] If all land were cultivated as intensely as it is in China, for example, the earth could support fifteen times its present population, and the best current methods of husbandry, applied generally, could double that number again, to 18,000 million. England and Wales alone could support as many as 20 million. (A census in 1800 put the population of England and Wales at less than 9 million, but it had reached 22 million by 1871, due more to a falling death rate than a rising birth rate. By March 1976 the estimated population of the earth had reached only 4,000 million.)

But all this, Godwin thinks, is sheer fantasy. 'His numbers will go on smoothly enough . . .' he wrote, returning to the topic eleven years later,

> but restiff and uncomplying nature refuses to conform to his dicta . . . . Morse, in his American Gazateer, proceeding on the principles of Malthus, tells us that, if the city of New York goes on increasing for a century in a certain ratio, it will by that time contain 5,237,493 inhabitants. But does anyone, for himself or for his posterity, expect to see this realised?[16]

Unhappily Greater New York did reach that figure almost exactly a century later, but that proves nothing, except that the figures prove nothing, for the question is how and why New York grew as it did. Malthus believed that the American figures settled the matter, coming as they did from a country where there were as yet no constraints on food or living space. But as Godwin points out, Malthus took no account of immigration. In the event the population of the United States did more or less double every twenty-five years for the rest of the century, but the cause was immigration, not procreation. The truth lay more with Godwin.

Nevertheless, all this grubbing about among the population studies was quite beside the point, and Godwin's own argument is a revealing indication of the dangers that lay hidden there. The crucial question is not the average size of families, but what it would naturally tend to, were you to remove the checks of misery and vice. No reference to the new-found land America could settle that issue, for however congenial its settlers might find it, it was certainly not a Godwinian utopia. The most that might be ascertained with any degree of certainty is the total number of children that a normally healthy couple might produce in a marriage of average length. But whether that number – many more than four! – would be in any sense natural, is quite another matter. It is, moreover, no answer to Malthus to say as Godwin does, that 'till human affairs shall be better or more auspiciously conducted than they have hitherto been under the best of governments, there will be no absolute increase in the numbers of mankind.'[17] For it is precisely Malthus's point that if human affairs were better conducted, population would grow until vice and misery returned again. Indeed when Godwin argues that families naturally tend to four births, not eight, that actually favours Malthus. Only remove the vice and misery of infant mortality, and the geometric ratio is immediately reinstated!

Of Population has its strengths, in particular its probing beneath the vague verbiage of 'vice and misery' to get at the factors – war, famine, disease – that actually check population growth. But it has its weaknesses too, its long-windedness, its bickering tone, its reluctance to leave any point unmade, and whatever its successes of detail, on the main issue between them it can no more disprove Malthus's geometric ratio than Malthus can verify it. The best answer to Malthus, the true Godwinian answer, lay elsewhere, in the *Reply to Parr* which *Of Population* fails even to mention. Godwin may have been better advised to have left well alone; the effect of his second reply is to diminish the force of the first.

The effect was diminished in another way also. There was a time when Godwin had admired Malthus's work, and had declared himself flattered by the attentions of so acute a critic: 'For myself I cannot refuse to take some pride, in so far as by my writings I gave the occasion, and furnished an incentive, to the producing so valuable a treatise.'[18] But now the bitterness of *Mandeville* welled within him again, and this new book is one long-drawn-out sneer at a man who approves of vice and misery as a means of keeping poor families in their place, who credits no one with wisdom or benevolence, who has no sense of consistency and no understanding of statistics. Lamb once joked that in his writings Godwin never expressed himself disrespectfully of anyone, except his Maker. But that was before the Answer to Malthus:

> I own I am pleased with the condition in which the author of the Essay on Population has dismissed his subject. He who has written three volumes expressly to point out to us the advantage we obtain from the presence of vice and misery, would naturally leave the question in all the confusion in which Mr Malthus has left it. This is as it should be. It is scarcely conceivable that the man who recommends to us such bosom-friends and companions, should have much discrimination and choice as to the different species and degrees of each.[19]

In thus descending to the level of personal abuse Godwin was simply asking for the same sort of vituperation he had had to endure in the past. To someone like James Mill *Of Population* might appear beneath contempt, but the *Edinburgh Review* delivered itself more forcibly:

> It appears to us, we confess, the poorest and most old-womanish performance that has fallen from the pen of any writer of name, since we have first commenced our critical career. So long as Mr Godwin's judgement remained in sufficient vigour to repress useless ebullitions of anger against Mr Malthus, he seems to have bit his lips in silence; and this laudable restraint lasted twenty years. But the sight of a fifth edition of the Essay on Population, operating, as we must

suppose, upon an enfeebled judgement, was at length too much for him.[20]

Given the solar system itself to review, said one contributor, Sydney Smith, the *Review* would surely damn it: 'bad light – planets too distant – pestered with comets – feeble contrivance; – could make a better with great ease'.[21] But when Godwin discovered that this was actually the work of Malthus himself – though both he and the *Review* had taken care to conceal the fact – he was understandably infuriated. Still, it was hardly for the man who had once said that of Malthus's 'book and the spirit in which it is written I can never speak but with an unfeigned respect'[22] to complain now that

> Mr Malthus's unmanly article . . . shows how easily the mask of good manners may be put on, and how easily it may be put off. The wretched trick of dispensing twelve thousand copies of his animadversions under the solemn hypocrisy of an impartial examination of the book, can only be equalled by the glaring desertion of all character on the part of the Review that gave it insertion. The article is unworthy of any further notice from me.[23]

Officially that was Malthus's reaction too. Secure in his reputation and his ratios he could simply dismiss *Of Population* in a single paragraph added at the end of his next edition. The character of this book, he writes,

> both as to matter and manner, is such, that I am quite sure that every candid and competent enquirer after truth will agree with me in thinking that it does not require a reply. To return abusive declamation in kind would be as unedifying to the reader as it would be disagreeable to me; and to argue seriously with one who denies the most glaring and best attested facts . . . would evidently be quite vain with regard to the writer himself, and must be totally uncalled for by any of his readers whose authority could avail in the establishment of truth.

Godwin met Malthus on two further occasions, the first with such emotion that the diary records it in Latin: '*adv.* Malthus, *dextrae conjunctio*'. On the second he was silent.

Godwin himself described his book as 'rough, smooth, and impenetrable, like a globe of hardest steel',[24] but to the bulk of his readers it was dense, heavy, and mammothly boring, 'the longest answer to the shortest argument', albeit less than half the length of the massive three-volume treatise into which Malthus's original slim essay had by then grown. But as Godwin wrote on his own final page, 'I am sensible that what I have written may be regarded in some respects as a book about nothing.'[25] No amount of nit-picking, however careful, however valid, could counteract the persuasive simplicity of those famous ratios. Godwin sent copies to those he thought might benefit from it – Bentham, Coleridge, Mrs Inchbald – but the world yawned, when it did not sneer, and passed him by, and *Of Population* sank under the weight of its acrimony and verbiage, leaving barely a ripple to show where it had been.

Godwin himself tried to keep the debate simmering with letters in the *Morning Chronicle*, and Booth published his own reply to the more technical criticisms of the *Edinburgh Review*. But only one writer would pay Godwin's arguments any further attention, and that was the man who now seemed almost obsessed by his inconsistencies: Francis Place, whose *Illustrations and Proofs of The Principle of Population* was published in 1822. Exaggerating out of all proportion an occasional favourable reference in the House of Commons, Place seemed to think that Godwin had succeeded in damaging Malthus where all else had failed. So he adopted the simple, if not entirely fair, expedient of quoting Godwin against himself, the *Reply to Parr* against *Of Population*: in the one, for example, 'Everyone, whose attention is for a moment called to the subject, will immediately perceive that the principle of multiplication in the human species is without limits';[26] but in the other it is 'a multiplication, which it is difficult for human imagination; or (as I should have thought) for human credulity to follow'.[27]

But although Place accepts Malthus's ratios, he does not accept his conclusions; his position, rather, is that of the *Reply to Parr*, rescuing mankind from a fate of misery and vice by an appeal to moral restraint: it is, in effect, the earlier Godwin replying to the later. And he interprets that restraint in a way that neither Godwin nor Malthus nor anyone else had yet dared, to include 'such precautionary means as would, without being injurious to health, or destructive of female delicacy, prevent contraception'. To Place at least the honour of introducing birth control into the debate.

24 ♣ A notice to quit

Nothing can be more worthy of regret, than the manner in which property is at present administered, so far as relates to courts of justice. The doubtfulness of titles, the different measures of legislation as they relate to different classes of property, the tediousness of suits, and the removal of causes by appeal from court to court, are a perpetual round of artifice and chicane to one part of the community, and of anguish and misery to another. Who can describe the baffled hopes, the fruitless years of expectation, which thus consume away the strength and lives of numerous individuals? . . . The imbecility of law is strikingly illustrated, by the vulgar maxim of the importance of possession. Possession could not be thus advantageous, were it not for the opportunity that law affords for procrastination and evasion.[1]

Political Justice, 1798

♣ 1817 had been a good year, as years had recently been, but 1818 had promised even better. Money seemed no longer a problem. The shop might take only a pound or two a day, but for once they were living on the Juvenile Library instead of its living on them, leaving Godwin free to pursue Malthus through his forest of figures. But he knew it could not be for long. 'You will, I dare say, be glad to hear I am now head and ears in my answer to Malthus,' Godwin wrote to Mary that summer,

That painful complication of circumstance which for four or five months suspended my labours, seems at present to have dispersed itself like a summer's cloud. But I know that all these appearances are fallacious. I know that the tempest is brewing in the distance, and that at no very remote period it will pour all its fury upon my devoted head. But this very consciousness gives new energy to my exertions.[2]

And the tempest lay nearer than he was saying: a fortnight earlier, on 23 June, there had come a clerk from Tilson, the solicitor, with notice to quit.

When Shelley's friend Hogg visited Skinner Street he had felt 'the crazy floor of the ill-built, unowned dwelling house . . . shake and tremble'[3] under Shelley's impatient tread, and several of those ramshackle buildings had never been occupied, even then. But No. 41 had proved a better bargain than Godwin had ever dared hope: those first two quarters' rent in 1807 had been the only rent he had ever paid. The property had gone up for lottery as planned, but the lucky ticket-holders, a pair of stockbrokers called Walsh and Nesbitt, had gone bankrupt before the formalities could be completed, and thereafter it had been entirely unclear to whom, if anyone, the house belonged. From time to time the question of rent would come up, but it was a question that Godwin could well afford to ignore, partly because he could not possibly pay it, but also because where two parties were claiming it would be foolish to give anything to either. It was not until August 1817 that a man named Read established a clear claim to the title, but for five years more, through threats and lawsuits, Godwin clung grimly on, unable to pay and unwilling to vacate. It would take the most desperate means to shift him.

They first came before the courts in February 1819, with Read suing for as much as £2,000 in damages for unpaid rent, followed by a second suit for possession of his property. But the verdicts, whatever they were, left Godwin sitting comfortably where he was, still working at Malthus, his enthusiasm rising and falling with the strength of his arguments and the state of his health. The fainting fits that had dogged him for years had gone for the moment, to be replaced by something still more sinister, an occasional paralysis, a dead little right finger on one day, torpor of the left hand on another. But while health and happiness allowed he wrote on. The further he could get before Read struck again, the nearer he would be to that great moment when fame and fortune would again be his. And in a crisis he could always turn to Shelley.

Shelley, meanwhile, had crises of his own. Mary had never really shaken off her illness at Clara's birth, and with a young family to protect she found it less and less easy to tolerate the restless, shiftless existence that Shelley forced upon them, much less the ambiguous presence of Claire. Allegra had been sent on directly to her father's palazzo in Venice, but the stories they heard of life in that warren of sensuality convinced Claire and Shelley that they must get her back. They went to Venice together to see what could be done, and Byron, in conciliatory mood so long as he did not have to face Claire, offered them all the use of his summer villa. Shelley sent for Mary and the children to join them, but no sooner had they arrived than Clara, barely a year old, contracted dysentery. Ignoring the local doctors Shelley rushed her on to Venice, but before they could get help the child had died.

Consciously or not Mary thereafter blamed Shelley, his recklessness and his pursuit of Claire, as it seemed to her, for their daughter's death. She idealized her husband, the more so when he was dead, just as she had idealized her father, but the hopes and passion that had carried her away from Skinner Street and through their first turbulent years together had faded, and Mary never again felt for Shelley what she had felt for him once. Then nine months later, in June 1819, William Shelley, their precious Willmouse, the most lively and the most loved of all Shelley's children, died in Rome of a sudden fever. Mary had been pregnant three times, and seen three children die; the fact that she was pregnant again was calculated more to increase her depression than diminish it.

In the circumstances Godwin's response seems almost brutal. 'You should, however, recollect that it is only persons of a very ordinary sort, and of a pusillanimous disposition, that sink long under a calamity of this nature', he wrote at Clara's death. 'I assure you such a recollection will be of great use to you. We seldom indulge long in depression and mourning except when we think secretly that there is something very refined in it, and that it does us honour.'[4] It was advice he had himself followed at the death of her mother and the suicide of her sister, to bury himself in his work and forget, to conquer his feelings by ignoring them. But it is hard to think of anything more likely to increase Mary's dejection, her sense of isolation and rejection, than Godwin's severe incomprehension. And it was hardly to be endured that he should choose the death of William to reproach Mary with falling from the class of those qualified to support their family and friends into the class of those who need the support of others, and yet at the same time revive his demands on Shelley. 'I have no consolation in any quarter,' Mary wrote wretchedly to Amelia Curran, daughter of Godwin's sincerest friend, 'for my misfortune has not altered the tone of my father's letters.'[5]

Her only relief lay in writing, in the novella *Mathilda* which she wrote between William's death and the birth of another son, Percy Florence, in November 1819. It was the story of a girl whose mother dies at her birth, and who does not meet her father until she is sixteen. They live together for a time blissfully content, but when a handsome youth is attracted to Mathilda her father turns mysteriously sour and miserable, and finally spurns her entirely. At length all is explained. The father confesses his passion for his daughter, and kills himself, but before her own death from sorrow and remorse Mathilda manages to find some comfort in a platonic friendship with a beautiful, gifted and equally unhappy young poet called Woodville. Mathilda, of course, is Mary herself, and Woodville her romanticized portrait of her husband, loved and admired, but no longer loved physically. But the nameless father is an amalgam of the distant Godwin and the passionate Shelley that Mary, too, met when she was sixteen. Nowhere does she make it more obvious how she sought her father in her lover, and lost them both.

. Mary eventually sent the story to Godwin, to sell for whatever it might bring, but the idea of incest, common enough in Shelley's poetry, was less familiar to him than it was to her. He pronounced the subject 'shocking and detestable', and urged the addition of a preface so that the reader could know from the start that the heroine does not suffer a fate worse even than the fate worse than death. But realizing that a book so obviously autobiographical would be readily misunderstood, and fearing fresh scandals, he did nothing about its publication. Three years later Mary was still trying, unsuccessfully, to get her manuscript back.

Shelley had begun to think he would have to go back to England to sort out his own and his father-in-law's affairs, and Mary felt that her father should sell up while he still could and come to join them in Italy. But Godwin would have none of it, suddenly bubbling over with cheerfulness and good humour. 'I consider the day on which I entered on this business as one of the most fortunate days of my life,' he wrote, his unusual optimism quite defeating his memory. After *Political Justice, Caleb Williams*, and the rest he had been in need of some respite. Not that he had remained idle in the meantime, but

> Blessed . . . and thrice blessed was the interval which enabled me to renew my strength! I did not begin Mandeville till 1816, and I have ever since felt that I have gained a new tenancy of my intellectual life. I write and I plan works, and I feel all the vigour of youth, that I shall never leave off writing again, till the infirmities of nature, or some terrible convulsion in my circumstances, shall perhaps put an end to my literary career for ever.[6]

It could not last, of course, and soon the monster with the maw was at him again. 'Better than a sop to Cerberus or the music of Orpheus to the furies is £100 to a philosopher!!' mused Claire. 'An english philosopher it would seem to mean . . . .'[7] But the amount Godwin needed was £500, and Shelley could promise no more than £50 each quarter from his own allowance. Mary wrote anxiously to their friends the Gisbornes, who were currently in London, to see if they could help, but Shelley attached a letter of his own: they must beware 'Godwin's implacable exactions . . . his boundless and plausible sophistry';[8] they must be sure to get a properly signed receipt; and unless they can be sure that the money is going where it is meant to, they must let him have nothing at all. It was the very next day, 1 July 1820, that Shelley copied out another *Letter to Maria Gisborne*, in verse this time, with its reference to

> That which was Godwin,* – greater none than he
> Though fallen – and fallen on evil times – to stand
> Among the spirits of our age and land,
> Before the dread tribunal of *to come*
> The foremost, – while Rebuke cowers pale and dumb.

The past tense, the sense of an obituary almost, was not accidental, and when later that year Shelley supplied his cousin Tom Medwin with a list of the titles that were all a good library needed, no contemporary work was among them, not even *Political Justice*. The intellectual father of his youth was his father no longer.

Maria Gisborne, of course, was the former Maria Reveley who, as Godwin put it in the letter of introduction Mary took with her to Italy, 'may perhaps recollect an unfortunate female infant, of which I was the father, that you took into your house, and were kind enough to protect for a week, a very few days after its birth.'[9] 'I have not seen her I believe these twenty years,' he had written again, delighted to have news of the woman who had once been more than a favourite; 'I think not since she was Mrs Gisborne.'[10] Now Maria was in London again, finding Godwin older and plumper than she remembered him, but only mildly embittered towards his untrustworthy son-in-law:

> Mr Godwin has never yet spoken with any violent degree of
> bitterness respecting S. but he accuses him of immorality, and
> says that he has deceived him, and failed in a solemn promise
> on the performance of which Mr G. had depended. He asserts
> also that S. has a particular enmity against truth, so that he
> utters falsehoods and makes exaggerations even when no end is
> to be answered by them; he represents him as a lover of
> falsehood.[11]

On one occasion Godwin ponderously cross-examined her about Claire, but remained 'still incredulous as to the real author of her misfortune'.[12] He could not credit it was Byron; he felt sure it must be Shelley; at any rate he told Maria that all 'three girls were in love with ———— and that the eldest put an end to her existence owing to the preference given her younger sister.'[13] But if Godwin blamed Shelley, his wife still blamed Mary, and when she learnt that the Gisbornes not only knew her step-daughter but admired her im-

---

*When Mary published Shelley's *Posthumous Poems* in 1824 she altered this phrase to 'Your old friend Godwin'.

mensely, she became almost hysterical, so agitated that she could not speak. Thereafter she avoided them, assuring Maria through intermediaries 'of her extreme good will toward me, but at the same time the impossibility of seeing or conversing with any person who should be attached to Mrs S. the author of all her misery.'[14] It was a topic on which she was clearly unbalanced.

The conduct of the other member of the household, William junior, seemed no less odd:

> It seems that William is the happiest mortal alive; his limbs are in perpetual motion, the house (Mr G. says) cannot contain him; he knows not how to give vent to his playful feelings; all this I believe, produced by his present state of complete idleness; his father appears to have no objections.[15]

From school William had gone to commercial college, and then to a private tutor to study mathematics. He had been examined for entrance to the School of Naval Architecture, and then apprenticed as an engineer with Maudsley of Lambeth, but had had to give that up after losing a finger in an accident. Now he sat – or more accurately, tumbled – about Skinner Street, trying to think of some other career. Eventually he chose architecture, and when Godwin sought the advice of the royal architect, John Nash, then 'finishing a street that winds its way from Carlton House to Portland Place, about three quarters of a mile, and . . . the only truly magnificent thing by the name of a street I ever saw', London's Regent Street, Nash suggested that William might like to work for him. Even better, 'in consideration of my literary reputation and character he was willing to waive' his usual fee of 500 guineas. William began there on 28 December, 'in transports with his situation'.[16] But that would not last either.

William was indeed, as Godwin lamented to Mary, of 'unsteady and roving disposition', unable to control the temper he had inherited from his mother, spoilt, selfish, and unstable to the point that his father habitually describes in almost contradictory terms: hyperactive yet 'inexpressibly idle', fiery yet affectionate, stubborn yet impetuous, self-contained yet talkative. Even into his twenties William's 'ill-bred' behaviour and 'rough and noisy ways' would spoil the games of whist with Lamb or Crabb Robinson, and once when Robinson called on the Lambs they did not let him in, for fear it was young Godwin. 'And at any rate', Godwin concludes, 'he is no smiler, no consoler.'[17] But this moody, feckless, exhausting seventeen-year-old was the only child who remained to see his aged parents through the final crises of the Juvenile Library.

It took Godwin almost a month to lose his reticence before the

Gisbornes 'I observed many times that Mr. G. was on the point of saying something that seemed to require a great effort,' Maria noted; 'but at length he overcame his reluctance and began . . . .' He had been quite ill with worry, Godwin said, not just by the affair of the house but by

> S's cruel and unjust treatment of him. He said that, to use a vulgar phrase, S. would certainly be the death of him; that he acted in the most equivocal unmanly unintelligible manner, that he was perpetually leading him into expectation, and never coming to any conclusion.[18]

Shelley was a lover of novelty, with as much mysticism in his conduct as Coleridge had in his poetry, with 'high mental endowments, and a heart well-disposed to do good, but neither constancy nor perseverance. This was the utmost he could say in his favour.' Two weeks later, with the Gisbornes about to return to Italy, Godwin called again. There was some further talk of Shelley, his restlessness, his ceaseless travels, his unreadable poetry, but Godwin seemed uneasy, as if he wanted to say more than he had so far, and when the time came to say goodbye, he left more agitated than ever. So the Gisbornes got ready to depart, not much wiser about the true state of Godwin's affairs than when they arrived. There had evidently been no suggestion, on either side, that they might lend him something.

In the meantime Godwin was still angrily pursuing Shelley and Mary. 'Do not let me be led into a fool's paradise', he complained.

> It is better to look my ruin full in the face than to be amused for ever with promises, at the same time that nothing is done. If Shelley will not immediately send me such bills as I propose and you offer, my next request is, that he will let me alone, or not disturb the sadness of my shipwreck by holding out false lights, and deluding me with appearances of relief when no relief is at hand.[19]

(I have been unable to trace the original of this letter. Dowden's *Life of Shelley* locates it at the end of 1819, but Ford K. Brown's biography of Godwin dates it, more plausibly, as 13 June 1820, in which case it will be the letter which provoked Claire's remark about the sop to Cerberus. Yet its tone suggests the letter of 21 July, to which Shelley now replied.)

So it was on 7 August, the same day that Godwin had first unburdened himself to the Gisbornes, that Shelley's patience and respect, worn to a thread by demands and accusations which would long since have destroyed a friendship between mere equals, snapped finally and irrevocably. It was the last letter he would ever address to the man of whose existence and dwelling he had heard with such inconceivable emotion only seven-and-a-half years before:

> I have given you within a few years the amount of a considerable fortune, and have destituted myself, for the purpose of realising it, of nearly four times the amount. Except for the *good will* which this transaction seems to have produced between you and me, this money, for any *advantage* that it ever conferred on you, might as well have been thrown in the sea. Had I kept in my own hands this £4 or £5000 and administered it in trust for your permanent advantage I should have indeed been your benefactor. The error however was greater in the man of mature age, extensive experience and penetrating intellect than in the crude and impetuous boy. Such an error is seldom committed twice.[20]

He had never promised Godwin more than the £50 each quarter; he had said only that he would raise £500 if he could, and only if it were guaranteed to settle all Godwin's debts. So far as he could tell Read was actually owed some £2,000, and £500 now would simply be more good money flung after bad. In any case this futile, unending importuning must stop, for Mary's sake as well as his own. At her request he was keeping her father's letters from her; on no account must he write to her about money again, for 'on one occasion, united to other circumstances agitation of mind produced through her a disorder in the child similar to that which destroyed our little girl two years ago.' But on second thoughts Shelley deleted the reference to 'other circumstances'. He knew well enough that Mary's illness had been as much his doing as Godwin's, but the implacable father-in-law made a handy scapegoat.

This letter reached London on 25 August. Aggrieved to the point of illness, desperate for someone to justify himself to, Godwin went at once to the Gisbornes, but they were not in. He left a note saying he must see them at once and, because their sailing had been delayed, they invited him to tea three days later. This time Godwin said all that he had wanted to say before, but had been prevented from revealing by the presence of Shelley's friend Henry Reveley. He told them about the house, the lawsuit, the understanding with Shelley. He gave them a paper with the whole dismal story set out in writing. Then he apologized for imposing on their time and patience, and left. Exactly what he said, exactly what grounds he had for accusing Shelley, we do not know. But for whatever reason, the Gisbornes' attitude to Shelley was never the same again.

Yet there was still something to be salvaged from the wreck, for on

1 September Horace Smith came to call, the same Horace Smith whose gently mocking *Horace in London* had once reported 'My Godwin' slumbering peacefully in St Paul's Churchyard, the Horace Smith who was now, in effect, Shelley's financial agent. With Smith to assist him, with no new threat from Read, with *Of Population* almost ready at the printers, the world seemed suddenly a calmer place. And so the great Answer to Malthus, the hope of mankind's future and of Godwin's own, made its appearance on 1 November 1820. It cost him, Godwin had told Shelley, as much effort as anything he ever wrote; and so it had, except for the unhappy precedent of *Antonio*. But now it seemed that 'I shall be a loser, not a gainer, by my labours.'[21] There was a French edition in 1821, but when Godwin wrote to Henry Grattan for news of its reception in Ireland, Grattan could find nothing to tell him, and by the end of that year he could find a profit of only £40 7s. 8d. It had been no answer to Malthus, and it would be no answer to Read.

In fact Read's suit for ejectment did not come up until July of 1821, but this time the unanimous decision was that Godwin must lose:

> The whole bar were loud in their declarations, that it was a
> most dishonest proceeding to live 14 or 15 years in a house
> without paying rent (they entirely overlooked that there was no
> person who had the shadow of a claim to receive it) . . . . My
> own counsel perpetually exclaimed, that I had not 'a leg to
> stand on, that they had not an argument to offer in my
> behalf'.[22]

The upshot was that it was left to the judges of the King's Bench to decide 'whether I had a right to the established courtesy of a note to quit', though from the attitude of the trial judge that seemed a mere formality. All that stood between him and the sale of his stock and consequent beggary was the £400 that Horace Smith had left at his disposal, when to Godwin's 'astonishment and utter confusion' three junior judges, meeting without the trial judge on 24 October, 'unanimously pronounced in my favour. I have not yet recovered from my surprise, and can hardly yet say that I believe what has passed.'[23] What would happen next he did not know; everyone seemed to have forgotten that he had already received the established courtesy of a note to quit, more than three years before!

There had been a time when these pressures would have made it impossible for Godwin to write, but despite Read, despite the virtual failure of both *Mandeville* and *Of Population*, something of his regained enthusiasm remained. He had even found time to complete that child's *History of Greece*, abandoned in 1809 and now the last of the books of Baldwin. Ideally he would then have prepared an 'improved and finished edition of Political Justice', but if no one would read Godwin on Malthus, who would read Godwin on Godwin, so he decided instead on a history of his favourite period, a *History of the Commonwealth*. In December he agreed £250 for each of two volumes with the publisher Henry Colburn, and on 4 January he began to write. Through law-suit and trial, through eviction and bankruptcy, he worked stolidly away at it, through four volumes and seven years, as long as *Antonio* and *Of Population* put together, though it cost him far less effort than either. It was not just a source of income; it was also a means of escape.

So Godwin went into 1822 still clinging on to Skinner Street. But Read's suit was heard again on 16 April, and this time there could be no avoiding the verdict. Two weeks later the judgment was signed, and leave to appeal rejected. At once Read took out two writs, one for eviction, the other for possession of goods to cover his legal costs of £135 – and so impaled the Godwins on a dilemma such as only the law could devise. On the one hand they were given two days to move, on pain of being thrown into the street, and as William later explained to his sister, this had to be understood quite literally: 'At a pianoforte makers in Tottenham Court Road, where an ejectment was served, which he refused to obey, they actually tossed his pianofortes, finished and unfinished, from the second floor into the street.'[24] But on the other hand there were two men guarding the house, to ensure that nothing was moved until the £135 was paid!

Godwin's response was to rush frantically to and fro between his solicitor and Read, and even Mrs Read, to throw himself on their mercy. But the others were more practical. William sat up all night preparing a list of their best stock until the auctioneer was satisfied that the £135 would be forthcoming, and Mrs Godwin supervised their move, the remaining stock into a warehouse in nearby Gunpowder Alley, themselves into lodgings in Pemberton Row, by Gough Square. There they stayed for six weeks until Godwin's printer Macmillan and his stationer Curtis could get him back into business, postponing their own bills, discounting others, and finding fresh funds so that he could lease new premises. Perhaps they feared that, in the current recession, Godwin's collapse would carry them down too. But they surely would not have done it had not the Juvenile Library been paying its way at last, just as Godwin claimed it was. Without Read and the Skinner Street rent, they might have been safe after all.

So M. J. Godwin and Co., the French and English Juvenile and School Library, survived precariously to publish new editions from 195 (St Clement's) the Strand, and on 26 June they moved into their new shop, one storey smaller but far nicer and much better situated than the old. The only disadvantage was the rent, payable this time, and payable at the awful rate of £210 per annum. 'How we shall get on God only knows', wrote William, managing to sound unconscionably like his father: 'I have some fear it is true, but like Pandora's box, I still find hope at the bottom.'[25] But No. 41 Skinner Street was closed for good. The children who loved to peer into the wonderland of its long curving windows could hardly believe what had happened. What could it mean? Why was it closed? They expected it to reopen any day, but it never did. 'Gradually the glass of all the windows got broken in, a heavy cloud of black dust, solidifying into inches thick, gathered on the sills and doors and brickwork, till the whole frontage grew as gloomy as Giant Despair's Castle.'[26] The decline of Skinner Street, which had begun before it was yet new, gathered pace until, almost wholly derelict, it was torn down in the 1860s to make room for Holborn Viaduct and the Metropolitan Railway. The property Read had won so arduously was never used again; only the carving of Aesop, over the door, remained to puzzle the passer-by.

Read might have his property but he wanted his pound as well, not flesh but rent, £200 of it per annum, and with the full force of the law behind him now the only question was whether Godwin could keep his income ahead of Read's demands. Charles Lamb sent £50 the moment he learnt of the eviction, saying 'pay me when you can', and Crabb Robinson sent a more reluctant £30 a month or so later, convinced both that he would never see it again, and that it would do Godwin no good either. The sharp practice in the matter of rent was for him the final straw in a friendship that had always been marred by Godwin's irritating demands, and no less irritating because they were always too petty to justify an outright confrontation. But with Read claiming rent at least back to 1820, and possibly back to 1817, these were but trifles. Inevitably, Godwin turned again to thoughts of Shelley. He did not know it yet, but Shelley could not help him now.

When the verdict had finally gone against him Godwin had sent to Italy one last despairing note, part reproachful, part regretful:

The die, so far as I am concerned, seems now to be cast; and all that remains is that I should intreat you to forget that you have a father in existence. Why should your prime of youthful vigour be tarnished and made wretched by what relates to me? I have lived to the full age of man in as much comfort as can reasonably be expected to fall to the lot of a human being.

What signifies what becomes of the few wretched years that remain? For the same reason I think I ought in future to drop writing to you. It is impossible that my letters can give you any thing, but unmingled pain. A few weeks more, and the formalities which still restrain the successful claimant will be over, and my prospects of tranquillity must, as I believe, be eternally closed. Farewel.[27]

But a fortnight later he was back again, only slightly shamefaced at rising so rapidly from the grave: Skinner Street was lost but the business might be saved, if he can find the £400 that Read is demanding; and only a few hours before Read had obtained his writs for eviction and costs, the man who had bought Shelley's 1818 post-obit had come to ask whether Shelley might be interested in more on the same terms as before. 'What does this mean?', despairs Godwin. 'In the contemplation of such a coincidence, I could almost grow superstitious. But alas, I fear, I fear, I am a drowning man clutching at straws.'[28]

Used though he was to Godwin's cries of desperation, Shelley hardly knew what to make of these cryptic laments. In any case he had troubles enough of his own. The day of Godwin's first farewell, 19 April, had been the day that Allegra had died in the convent near Ravenna where Byron had sent her, for her protection and his convenience. Mary's insistence that the child be taken to Italy to her father could not have turned out more disastrously. Increasingly wretched, suffering from her fifth pregnancy in eight years, she sat brooding over all their dead children, and watching with as much detachment as she could muster Shelley's pursuit of Jane Williams, the latest in that succession of planets, comets and shining stars that adorned the universe of which Shelley himself was always the centre. To those who met her at this time she seemed a prim, sour, carping presence in that devastatingly bohemian circle, her dejection a continual brake on her husband's exuberant genius. But Mary's depression had reached the dimensions of a major illness that Shelley could neither understand nor cope with. The tensions between them were evident to all.

Nothing would persuade Shelley to write to Godwin, but he did write to Mary Jane, to say that Mary's health was such that he could tell her nothing yet, but that he had asked Horace Smith whether he could find the £400. But Smith proved bluntly unforthcoming: what could be the point of giving Godwin money now, when it would only end up in the hands of 'strangers, commissioners, assignees, who care not two pence about it, who have no individual interest in the matter'; 'the interest of former loans is . . . enough to run away with all the profits of the business, besides keeping them in hot water all their lives'; he had told Godwin himself that the only honourable course was to take refuge in the Insolvency Act and declare himself bankrupt. 'It is unworthy to exclaim about being ruined – he *is* ruined, and it is only by acknowledging the fact to all the world that he can get relief.'[29] Indeed for all that Shelley knew, Godwin was bankrupt already.

Mary knew nothing of all this when she lost her baby, and would certainly have died herself had not Shelley stopped the bleeding by siting her in a tub filled with ice, while everyone else looked on in helpless horror. She was still convalescing when Shelley and Edward Williams went off in their new boat to Livorno, to welcome Leigh Hunt. She was waiting nervously for news with Jane Williams when, twelve days later, a letter arrived from Hunt and addressed, ominously, to Shelley. 'Pray write to tell us how you got home', it said, 'for they say that you had bad weather after you sailed on Monday, and we are anxious.' 'Then it is all over,' said Jane. Shelley had left Livorno on 8 July, with Williams and a boat boy; it was another week before a body was found cast up on the sand, the flesh eaten entirely from hands and face but the clothes, and the volumes of poetry in the pockets, marking it as his. Shelley had been twenty-nine; Mary was twenty-five; their one surviving child, Percy Florence, was not yet three.

Strangely, significantly, this ultimate tragedy seemed to shock Mary out of her depression of the past five years, suggesting that her husband was more its cause than either would ever have admitted. Her father, too, found a vein of sympathy and understanding that had been so wretchedly absent at the deaths of Clara and William. At first he seemed hurt that he had had to hear the news from a third party, and then began to wallow in self-pity, almost glad to have someone else share in his misery. But gradually he became more supportive, less obsessed with his own troubles, and even sent Mary money, though he had need enough of it himself. Shelley's father, on the other hand, remained as unconcerned in his son's death as he had been in his life, unwilling to provide the slightest assistance. He would maintain Percy, who stood next in line after Harriet's son Charles, only on condition that he be placed 'with a person I shall approve', a condition that Mary naturally rejected. And when at length he was persuaded to send an occasional one or two hundred pounds, it was explicitly marked as an advance against her inheritance under Shelley's will. The biographers have no qualms in ridiculing the penurious publisher whose demands drove Shelley and Mary literally to destruction; the wealthy baronet, concerned only to keep the family fortune entire, is of course free from any such complaint.

Exhausted though he was himself, Godwin had not yet exhausted old friendships, and now it was the oldest ally of all, James Marshall, who came to his rescue. Somehow Marshall persuaded John Murray, son of the man for whom Godwin had written in the 1780s, to organize a subscription that might meet Read's demands, and so protect Godwin's property and papers while he got on with the *History of the Commonwealth* which would surely see him through the few years that remained to him. 'If the subscription fills', Godwin wrote to Mary, 'I shall perhaps be safe; if not, I shall be driven to sea on a plank.'[30] Perhaps Murray remembered how his intransigence had cost Godwin the £600 that Byron had intended for him; at any rate that was the sum he now set himself to raise among those who remembered William Godwin. And many and various they proved. Lamb's £50 and Robinson's £30 were converted from loans into gifts, Murray contributed 10 guineas of his own, Byron added another 25, and though Wordsworth declined to contribute, Sir Walter Scott sent £10 on condition that it be anonymous, 'because I dissent from Mr Godwin's theory of politics and morality as sincerely as I admire his genius'[31] – a remark that the man in question found so insulting that he was tempted to return the money. There were some illustrious names from Godwin's past: Basil Montagu, Sir James Mackintosh, Sir Anthony Carlisle, Sir Thomas Lawrence, who had sketched Godwin sitting side by side with Holcroft at the 1794 treason trials, and painted a formal portrait in the following year. And there were names from his future: Lamb's friend John Rickman, and the Honourable William Lamb, husband of the notorious Lady Caroline.

In fact it was Lady Caroline herself, her bizarre affair with Byron dead but not forgotten, least of all by her, who persuaded her husband to contribute his £10. She had made herself known to Godwin back at the beginning of 1819 when she was throwing her restless energies behind the parliamentary candidature of her brother-in-law George. Godwin, in principles a Republican but in practice a Whig, had declined to help. He was always willing to discuss political theory, he told her, but he would take no part in active politics: 'I do not mix in the business of the world, and I am now too old to alter my course, even at the flattering invitation of Lady Caroline Lamb.'[32] Intrigued, she sought him out and they struck up a close, unlikely friendship, the venerable thinker and the flighty lady, that lasted until her death in 1828. Godwin became something of a confidant and adviser, and flattered as ever by the attentions of aristocracy, he had spent several relaxing days at her

L

country house, Brocket Hall, only a fortnight before the trial that finally turned him out of Skinner Street.

But unhappily the contributors proved more distinguished than the contributions, and by July of 1823 they had raised only £220, of which Godwin had already had £100. Personally he blamed this lack of success on Murray's indifference and inefficiency, and doubtless he could have made a better job of it himself – certainly he had had the practice – but although the subscription now went public under Mackintosh's supervision, it was still stuck at only half way, around £300, when the final reckoning came.

In December 1822 Read had been awarded £373 6s. 8d. in arrears of rent between 1820 and Godwin's eviction. Perhaps it was a 'writ of error' in January that enabled Godwin to hold him off that little bit longer, or perhaps he settled the bill with the £400 he received from Mary's novel 'Castruccio' which he published as *Valperga* that February. Mary had sent it to him a year before, but he had hung on to it because, he said, he feared that publishers would take advantage of his difficulties, but also, as always, because he thought he could see some small improvements here and there. 'I have taken great liberties with it', he had to admit,

> and I am afraid your *amour propre* will be proportionally shocked. I need not tell you that all the merit of the book is exclusively your own. The *whole* of what I have done is merely confined to taking away things which must have prevented its success.[33]

The romantic plot comes from Mary Shelley sure enough, but the literary style, the self-conscious erudition, even the spelling, mark it as equally a work by Godwin.

Later in 1823 there was also a request from an Edinburgh publisher for a second edition of the *Enquirer*, twenty-five years late but flattering none the less. And fortunately, in view of his recent long-windedness, Godwin could find neither time nor spirits to carry out his usual meticulous alterations. 'Alas! to what does it all amount?' he asked, looking back over a lifetime of theories meant to shape the world, and novels meant to shake it:

> The toys of childhood, the toys of manhood, and the toys of old age are still toys; and if it were hereafter possible for me to look upon them from a future state, I should find them all alike to be laborious trifles. As it is, and seeing with my present imperfect organs, I am more than half inclined to despise them. But I know not that I could have done any better.[34]

Even so there was one essay which, 'not willing to contribute, however slightly, to give permanence to notions which now appeared to me erroneous', Godwin felt he did have to rewrite completely, the essay 'Of English Style'. Gone are the pernickity criticisms of the great writers of the last two centuries, gone are the asterisks which disfigured the original text, but gone too is the cool definition of an elegant prose style, no longer so true of his own.

It was in November 1823 that Read and Godwin came to a final agreement, to set the rent owing from 1817 to 1820 at £430. With £250 available immediately from the subscription, the remainder covered by four notes of £45 each to fall due at six-monthly intervals, and Murray still holding a balance of £41 5s. od., Godwin seemed safe for a year at least. Suddenly he was all good humour again, bubbling over with relief and gratitude to those who had dragged him from the quicksand at the last. Characteristically he felt no need to worry until the second bill fell due. Equally characteristically, by then it was too late. In February 1825 there was yet another trial for use and occupation, and within the month Godwin had himself declared bankrupt. It was a bad time for businesses generally – at the end of that year more than seventy banks would have to suspend their payments – and the book trade was no exception. Soon even Constable would collapse, destroyed by the very forces that had beggared Godwin, lack of capital and the need to borrow at rates that ran away with all the profits and more beside. If a giant like Constable's could fall, dragging down with it James Ballantyne and Sir Walter Scott, then a mere Juvenile Library could hardly survive, and after several months haggling with the accountants, Godwin's bankruptcy was certified. It would take another six years to sort the mess out, to realize such assets as there were.

So it had come at last, the fate that Place had thought him absurdly terrified of, the fate that Horace Smith had urged as the only honourable solution to his problems, the fate against which he had struggled so doggedly and so disreputably for nigh on twenty years. Was it an end to his precarious happiness, his security, his life? Not a bit of it. Godwin simply shrugged the catastrophe off, and went back to writing his *History of the Commonwealth*. Mary Jane, it was said, had kept him at the business because she knew she would survive him, and she wanted some means of support in her old age. Yet it was only when the firm miscarried that they were free at last from the monster with the maw.

Was it then all a mistake, all unnecessary, the borrowing and the discounting, the whining and the wheedling, the manoeuvring and the misrepresentation, the disgrace and the downright dishonesty? What might have happened had Place, for example, persuaded him those many years before to the step that was now forced upon him? What might his reputation have been, to his contemporaries and to us, if he had not had to estimate every acquaintance, old and new, for his capacity to lend, postpone repayment, then lend again? What might Shelley have done for him – or he for Shelley – if they had not had to struggle with the burden of a decade's accumulated debt? Perhaps, as Godwin told Place, he could not see any alternative to the Library, now that the public no longer looked with favour on works that bore his own name. Yet its death was his regeneration. It left him to his own work as he had not been since the death of Mary Wollstonecraft. At last he was his own man again.

25 ♣ A virtue of necessity

I regard you as vicious, but I do not consider the vicious as
proper objects of indignation. I consider you as a machine; you
are not constituted, I am afraid, to be greatly useful to your
fellow men; but you did not make yourself; you are just what
circumstances irresistibly impelled you to be. I am sorry for
your ill propensities; but I entertain no enmity against you,
nothing but benevolence.

Caleb Williams, 1794

♣ The immediate result of the bankruptcy was that the Godwins
had to abandon their three-storeyed shop in the Strand for a smaller,
cheaper home – a mere £50 per annum, instead of 200 guineas – at
44 Gower Place, on what is now the edge of London's University
College. They shifted in, just the two of them now, at the end of May
1825, though it was the best part of a fortnight before a carpenter
had erected shelves and Godwin could order his books and return to
the writing which the bankruptcy itself had scarcely interrupted. His
health was worse than ever, with spells of nervousness and vomiting,
day after day of fainting fits, and even, in 1827, a period of twelve
days when he was by his own account 'unhinged'. When Sir Walter
Scott caught sight of him in the street a year later he noted that
Godwin had grown old and thin, though by that time he was
actually on the mend, despite a house so cold and damp that the
frost sometimes formed right in their bedroom. His diary determinedly lists every deliquium and deorsum, giddiness and numb-
ness, indisposition and vomitio, constipation and diarrhoea, and
once even 'void a large worm', but by 1828 Godwin had to admit
himself sometimes 'bien' or, with slight surprise, in 'perfect health 8
days', and from then on he was as in good health as a man in his 70s
could reasonably hope to be.

Meanwhile, that labour of love, his *History of the Commonwealth*,
was still growing inexorably beneath his pen. A first volume had
appeared in February 1824, bearing an epigraph from Burke which
was intended to be doubly appropriate: 'To attend to the neglected,
and to remember the forgotten.' His publisher Colburn, worried at
what he had let himself in for, had tried to demur at a second
volume, but Godwin persuaded him to another advance, and what
had been planned as two, at most three, ended up as four, and did

313

not get beyond the death of Cromwell even then. It was, none the less, a thoroughly respectable piece of work, with Godwin again plotting a course that others would follow. His novels had always been concerned to lay bare the innermost thoughts, feelings and motives of his characters, and here he extends the technique into history, trying to set each agent in the context that shows how his actions seemed to him, at the time, the reasonable and rational thing to do. It is an early example of empathy or *verstehen*, of historical understanding arrived at by thinking yourself into the position of another, backed up by a comprehensive grasp of the historical sources, many of which – as with the *Chaucer* – Godwin was the first to utilize. He had, after all, his acquaintances in high places who could open doors closed to the general public – George Canning, for example, once an acquaintance through Sheridan, then an editor of the *Anti-Jacobin*, but now the nation's Foreign Secretary and soon to be its Prime Minister.

The villain of the story, of course, is Charles I.

> Crime . . . is that act of a human being, in possession of his understanding and personal freedom, which diminishes the quantity of happiness and good that would otherwise exist among human beings; and the greatness of a crime consists in the extent to which it produces this effect. Liberty is one of the great negative advantages that can fall to the lot of man; without it we cannot possess any high degree of happiness, or exercise any considerable virtue. Now Charles, to a degree which can scarcely be exceeded, conspired against the liberty of his country.

But although 'it is not easy to imagine a greater criminal than the individual against whom the sentence was awarded', Godwin was in some difficulty over Charles's execution. *Political Justice*, of course, had argued that since, strictly speaking, we are none of us responsible for our actions – 'The assassin cannot help the murder he commits, any more than the dagger'[1] – punishment can never be deserved, can only be justified, if at all, in terms of its good effects:

> The only measure of equity is utility, and whatever is not attended with any beneficial purpose, is not just . . . . Why do I inflict suffering on another? If neither for his own benefit nor the benefit of others, can that be right? Will resentment, the mere indignation and horror I have conceived against vice, justify me in putting a being to useless torture?[2]

So, forgetting that he had also argued that men cannot be deterred by punishment, only by persuasion, the 'proper lesson' taught by

Charles's fate would have to be 'that no person, however high in station, however protected by the prejudices of his contemporaries, must expect to be a criminal against the welfare of the state and community, without retribution and punishment'. Yet if we take the long-term Utilitarian view, as Godwin in theory must, we must still conclude that the execution was not justified, for the shock and the stain of the regicide were such, 'I am afraid, that the day that saw Charles perish on the scaffold, rendered the restoration of his family certain.'

For a hero, more surprisingly, Godwin chose Cromwell, or 'Cromwel' as he calls him, with his habitual aversion to the final double 'l'. His own sympathies lay most with Vane, the republican parliamentarian who 'designed that every Englishman should be a King; or, in other words, that none of his countrymen should have a master'; and the *coup d'état* by which Cromwell overthrew Vane and his supporters would be for Godwin the great lost opportunity in English history. But Vane is too shadowy a figure in the narrative to hold our attention, and Winstanley and the Diggers, who might be thought to anticipate Godwin's own anarchism, are dismissed in a single page as 'scarcely indeed worth to be recorded, except so far as their proceedings may tend to illustrate the character and temper of the age.' Instead it is Cromwell who appears from the start as 'one of the greatest geniuses of the times in which he lived.' Volume II, dealing with the establishment of the Protectorate, might charge Cromwell with deceit and intrigue, 'obliquity and ambition', and 'deserting the principles on which he began his career'. But by the close of Volume IV he emerges again as a glowingly heroic figure, warts and all, his death a fitting climax to the drama that has gone before.

The *History of the Commonwealth* came to its uncertain end in October 1828, with Godwin still hoping for another volume, or perhaps a *History of the Restoration*, and that same month there was something of a family reunion in the little house in Gower Place. Mary Shelley had come home five years before, to find that she could endure only a couple of weeks in the shop on the Strand, not – as she had feared – because of her step-mother's animosity, which seems to have vanished in her presence, but because 'my father's situation, his cares and his debts, prevent me from enjoying his society'.[3] She had wanted to go back to Italy, but Godwin had persuaded her to stay, and now she eked out a living from novels and journalism, her prospects much improved when the death of Charles Shelley left her own son next in line to the family fortune. Young William was making his own way in the world too, at last. 'In our family', Claire said, sympathizing with the pressures on W. Godwin's only *son*, 'if you cannot write an epic poem or a novel that by its originality knocks all other novels on the head, you are a despicable creature, not worth acknowledging,'[4] but towards the end of 1823 William had astonished his father by having some small essays accepted by Hunt's *Literary Examiner*, and three years later he became a professional journalist and part-time art critic. 'It seems to me that it is at a later period than is usually imagined, that a youth for the most part manifests original powers of mind,'[5] was the thankful verdict of the father, who had once written whole essays to demonstrate the sure signs of genius that were manifest from earliest childhood.

Then, in July 1828, Charles Clairmont had come home too, with an Austrian wife and two small daughters, having survived the scrutiny of Metternich's secret police, on account of his sinister family connections, to become a successful teacher of English. And now Claire had joined them, all the way from Moscow where she worked as a governess. For the first time in fourteen years the Godwins and the Clairmonts were together again. Only Fanny was missing, somewhere in her nameless pauper's grave.

Claire stayed almost a year, before going to meet her charges in Dresden. Charles's plan to open a hostel for students at the new University College had come to nothing, nor could Godwin interest Colburn in a 'proposition . . . growing out of his intimate acquaintance with German Literature', so in November 1829 Charles returned to Vienna, borrowing the fare from Mary, who could ill afford it. But there he prospered again, becoming a professor at the university and tutor to the royal family, his pupils including Franz Joseph's two younger brothers, one to become the Emperor Maximilian of Mexico, the other the father of that Archduke Franz-Ferdinand who would figure in an incident at Sarajevo. And perhaps Godwin had had his hopes of University College also. His diary carefully records the laying of the foundation stone at the end of April 1827, and its formal opening on 1 October of the following year. In the interval he called on Birkbeck and on James Mill, both closely associated with Bentham in the project, and, with the *History of the Commonwealth* then drawing to its close, he may well have been hoping for an appointment that would suit his scholarly interests and talents. But Mill, for one, did not see him.

So Godwin was at something of a loose end as he sat listening to his family's talk of foreign lands. He took careful note, did his habitual careful research, and a mere fortnight after Claire's arrival began a novel that starts out, somewhat irrelevantly, in Russia, before moving to Italy for its main plot. The title changed too as he wrote, from 'Mowbray' to 'Delamere' to *Cloudesley*, and so does the narrator, until we end up with a tale told by two minor characters and named after a third! It seems clear enough that Godwin had little idea in advance where his story was taking him, but after the clumsy change of setting and narrator it settles down to be his most readable novel since *St Leon*: better written than the others, said Hazlitt, in a final appreciation before his death in 1830, but unimaginative and unnecessarily drawn out by the elaboration of minor and often entirely trivial points.

And so he had come back to the old trade, writing if not to order then at least on demand, living precariously from one contract to the next. 'If I can agree with these tyrants in Burlington Street for £300, £400 or £500 for a novel', he complained to Mary,

> and to be subsisted by them while I write it, I probably shall not starve for a fortnight to come. But they will take no step to bring the thing to a point, and I may go thither one, two or three times, and catch them if I can.[6]

But though *Cloudesley*, published in March 1830, managed one more edition than *Fleetwood* and *Mandeville*, the new partnership of Bentley and Colburn could not be tempted again. They were more interested in *Caleb Williams* and *St Leon* for their series of Standard Novels, a daring new venture inspired by the runaway success of the collected Waverley Novels. The plan was to cover the whole range of classic novels in English, in authoritative, well-printed one-volume editions, at a mere six shillings each, and *Caleb Williams* would be their second number, followed not only by *St Leon* but by *Fleetwood* and Mary's *Frankenstein*. Godwin gratefully accepted the offer, and the £100 that went with it, but he was anxious to go over the text himself because, as he said, 'I have sufficient experience in the matter of proofs to know, that if I do not, the edition will not fail to exhibit a certain number of disgraceful errors.' But to his intense irritation, they took no notice of his alterations.

But if the world had forgotten that little bald-headed old man buried amongst his books and his papers, he had not become entirely a recluse. He could still be seen in his regular place at the theatre,

> with his arms folded across his chest, his eyes fixed on the stage, his short, thick-set person immovable, save when some absurdity in the piece or some maladroitness of an actor caused it to jerk abruptly forward, shaken by his single-snapped laugh;[7]

and when the managements tried to remove his name from the Book of Life which entitled him to his free place, his angry response soon convinced them that he was not yet among the dead. Charles Lamb visited no more, perhaps finding it with Crabb Robinson 'a relief to be disburthened of his acquaintance', but Marshall and Hazlitt, Booth and Kenney, still came for a regular game of whist, joined by other friends from the distant past, John Thelwall, James Northcote, Richard Phillips.

And there were new friends too, like Frederick Reynolds, who dedicated his own Godwinian novel *Miserrimus* to his mentor; or David Uwins, a physician at the Peckham Lunatic Asylum who combined an interest in the neurological bases of insanity with a less reputable interest in homeopathy, the theory that a disease can be cured by artificially reproducing its symptoms; or Mary's friends and would-be suitors, Edward Trelawney, the Cornish companion of Byron and Shelley, and the American novelist Washington Irving; or the poet and editor Thomas Campbell; or Harriet Martineau, one of the most successful essayists and story-tellers of her day, whose admiration for Godwin more than compensated her misgivings about his first wife; or Claire's friend Mary Gaskell, an enthusiastic friend, of all things liberal, who kept a school and collected celebrities. But especially there was Edward Bulwer, later Lord Lytton. They had met originally in 1826 at the home of Caroline Lamb, who had adopted Bulwer, then aged twenty-one, as a latter-day Byron, a role he was only too happy to fill, but it was not until after Lady Caroline's death two years later that he and Godwin became close friends. What sealed their acquaintance, apparently, was Bulwer's praise of *Cloudesley* and Godwin's equal enthusiasm for Bulwer's first novel, *Paul Clifford*. (A biography by Bulwer's son suggests that Godwin was the 'gentleman of considerable distinction in literature' to whom his father said he owed the idea for *Paul Clifford*. But it is clear from Bulwer's other remarks that the anonymous gentleman was Scots, probably the Thomas Campbell who was also a friend of Godwin. It was *Eugene Aram* that Bulwer owed to Godwin.) For Bulwer was a novelist very much in the Godwin mould, perhaps his closest follower after the 'American Godwin', Brockden Brown. It was Godwin who gave Bulwer the idea of a novel based on the true story of Eugene Aram, the man cited in *Caleb Williams* as having been executed for a murder committed fourteen years before, despite having lived blamelessly in the meantime; it was Godwin who encouraged Bulwer in his attempts to enter parliament; and it was at Bulwer's, one day in 1832, that Godwin found himself in the distinguished company of Augusta Leigh, Byron's half-sister and the subject of a scandal that lingers still, the diarist Tom Moore, a young political hopeful called Benjamin Disraeli, whose father had once written satires of William

Godwin, and an Indian Prince, Ramahoun Roy, whom he would soon be consulting about Eastern Magic.

They all found Godwin easy now, as easy, Hazlitt said, as an old glove, dictatorial and quibbling no longer and, according to one, 'with a gracious suavity of manner which many a "fine old English gentleman" might envy'.[8] When James Fenimore Cooper had visited London in 1828 his very first caller had been an odd little chap who introduced himself as William Godwin and enquired whether Cooper might possibly be the son of his former pupil Thomas. Not the least put out by his error, he had then sat himself down to chat happily about American literature. 'I felt several times during his visit', Cooper recalled 'as if I wished to pat the old man's bald head and tell him "he was a good fellow".'[9] But to the one or two who still came to seek out the oracle, even now, this mild, grandfatherly figure was something of a disappointment. 'William Godwin was then 70 years old, but he seemed to me older then Bentham,' reports Robert Owen's son, who met them both in 1826.

> Feeble and bent, he had neither the bright eye nor the elastic step of the utilitarian philosopher . . . . His conversation gave me the impression of intellect without warmth of heart; it touched on great principles, but was measured and unimpulsive; as great a contrast to Bentham's as could well be imagined.[10]

Five years later the young Thomas Carlyle devoted the better part of an evening to working his way closer and closer until, just as he had cornered his prey and was about to open up on him, Godwin went merrily off to a game of whist which '*I* had already flatly declined'.[11]

Ten years before, and ten years before that, Godwin had seriously doubted whether he would live to write another book, but now that he survived and even prospered in his study in Gower Place he had no lack of ideas: the new novel he had already plotted; a *History of the Restoration* to complete that of the Commonwealth; a *Lives of the Necromancers*; a fourth edition of *Political Justice*; a book on Shakespeare; and 'when I have got to the end of writing on my own inventions, may I not find a resource in piece-work – Lardner's Pocket Encyclopedia . . . Murray's Family Library.'[12] The hope was that he might support himself as an essayist, like Hazlitt or Mackintosh, and 1830 was accordingly devoted to 'a collection of ten new and interesting truths, illustrated in no unpopular style . . . the fruits of thirty years meditation (it being so long since I wrote the "Enquirer") in the full maturity of my understanding.'[13] But

Lardner advised him they would be better published together as a book, and it was only at the eighth attempt that Godwin found himself a publisher, and an advance of £100, in one Effingham Wilson. By the time that these *Thoughts on Man*, 'His Nature, Productions and Discoveries, interspersed with particulars respecting the author', actually appeared, in February 1831, the ten new and interesting truths had grown to twenty-three.

Godwin thought it probably 'the most faultless book I ever printed . . . It contains some egotism, but kept perhaps within proper bounds.'[14] But to those who know the old Godwin it is curious indeed, as floridly ornate as a novel by Mary Shelley, as rhetorically pious as an atheist, or pantheist, could ever hope to be. 'The sweepings of his study', thought Crabb Robinson's brother Thomas, and certainly it is the work of an old man, garrulous, nostalgic, meandering, jejune, so that the occasional insight – a penetrating criticism of the 'chilling and wretched philosophy of the reign of Louis the Fourteenth', the doctrine of self-love, or praise for the obscure and unfashionable poetry of Donne, a taste that Godwin possibly acquired from Coleridge – comes as something of a shock. In desperation we turn to those 'particulars respecting the author': an essay 'Of Diffidence', for example, which traces Godwin's history of alternating awkwardness and arrogance in company, or some understandably bitter reflections on 'The Durability of Human Achievements and their Productions'.

Yet there is no biography in the essay 'Of Phrenology', the currently fashionable craze pursued in some thirty or more amateur societies up and down the country. Godwin had had Mary assessed at only nineteen days by his friend William Nicholson; in 1820 he had been assessed himself, with extraordinary accuracy, via his portrait by that other William Nicholson of Edinburgh (see plate XVI); indeed after his death it would be thought worthy of note that his bald head was 'singularly wanting in the organ of veneration (for the spot where the phrenologists state that "bump" to be was on Godwin's head an indentation instead of a protuberance.)'[15] But here he will have none of this nonsense, not just because it is pseudo-science, based on inadequate evidence and special pleading – 'The human head, that crowning capital of the column of man, is too interesting a subject to be made the proper theme of every dabbler'![16] – but more especially because 'it is all a system of fatalism':

> It assigns to us organs . . . which are entailed upon us from our birth, and which are altogether independent, or nearly so, of any discipline or volition that can be exercised by or upon the individual who drags their intolerable chain . . . . Independently

of ourselves, and far beyond our control, we are reserved for good or evil by the predestinating spirit that reigns over all things.[17]

Yet *Political Justice*, too, had been a system of fatalism, and these same *Thoughts on Man* insist that 'human creatures are born into the world with various dispositions',[18] that

> when a genuine philosopher holds a new-born child in his arms, and carefully examines it, he perceives in it various indications of temper and seeds of character. It was all there, though folded up and confused, and not obtruding itself upon the remark of every careless spectator. It continues with the child through life, grows with his growth, and never leaves him till he is at last consigned to the tomb.[19]

So why should the genuine philosopher succeed, when the phreno-logical dabbler must fail? The answer, it emerges, is that 'many of Gall's organs are a libel on our common nature.' Whereas the phrenologists 'remark the various habits and dispositions, the virtues and the vices, that display themselves in society as now constituted, and at once and without consideration trace them to the structure we bring into the world with us,' the 'scrupulous and exact' philosopher will be 'extremely reluctant to believe that some men are born with a decided propensity to rob, and others to murder'.[20] Men are not born evil; evil is the product of society. We are predisposed to virtue, not to vice: 'Every child that is born has within him a concealed magazine of excellence. His heart beats for everything that is lovely and good; and whatever is set before him of that sort in honest colours, rouses his emulation.'[21] It is a noble faith, wholly in keeping with the *Thoughts on Man*'s effusive humanism. But unhappily Godwin no longer has any reason to believe it true.

Once, of course, there had been arguments: that men are rational by nature; that reason will lead them to truth; that truth will lead them to justice. But those arguments had disappeared, and the *Thoughts on Man* seems to go out of its way to mock the premises on which its conclusions ought to depend, almost as if Godwin recognized that his own life was a refutation of his theories. Truth, for instance, is no longer the talisman it once was. 'Frankness has its limits', warns the old advocate of total sincerity, 'beyond which it would cease to be advantageous or virtuous. We are not to tell everything.'[22] Reason, too, has lost something of its power:

> It is however the rarest thing in the world, for anyone to found his opinion, simply upon the evidence that presents itself to him

of the truth of the proposition which comes before him to be examined. Where is the man who breaks loose from all the shackles that in his youth had been imposed upon him, and says to Truth, 'Go on; withersoever thou leadest, I am prepared to follow'?[23]

It is almost apologetically that Godwin admits that he had once tried to be just such a man. But the destruction of perfectibility goes further than this:

> Those persons who favour the opinion of the incessant improvableness of the human species, have felt strongly prompted to embrace the creed of Helvetius, who affirms that the minds of men, as they are born into the world, are in a state of equality, alike prepared for any kind of discipline and instruction that may be afforded them, and that it depends upon education only, in the largest sense of that word . . . whether we shall be poets or philosophers, dancers or singers, chemists or mathematicians, astronomers or dissectors of the faculties of our common nature. But this is not true; . . . the talent, or, more accurately speaking, the original suitableness of the individual for the cultivation, of music or painting, depends upon certain peculiarities which we bring into the world with us.[24]

True, Godwin had already modified the creed of Helvetius in *Political Justice*'s second edition, had doubted it in the memorandum on the *First Principles of Morals*, and refuted it through the key experiment of Milton and his nephews. But in its place he now has nothing to offer but the bland assertion that we have each of us our own special excellence, a distinctive area in which we will stand out as others stand out in theirs. We need, therefore, a more selective and differentiated approach to education, so that we can discover in each child the particular talent that nature had given him. We must not rely on some single, uniform method of instruction, but always be ready to try a new approach if the old one fails to reveal the particular genius of the particular child. As the *Account of A Seminary* had said those many years before, the pupil must go first and the master follow. But there is this crucial difference. Once Godwin had seen an equal education, providing the same opportunity for each to develop his essential human rationality, as the means to equality and justice. But now equality of a sort, of status but not of talents, is to be attained by differential education. While still emphasizing the role of the three Es – environment, experience, education – Godwin has come to stand at the opposite extreme from the Helvetianism with which he began. Where Helvetius had believed that an identical environment would make all men the same, Godwin is arguing that a different environment, different training, is necessary to make men different, if each is to be talented and deserving in his own distinctive way.

Now this is all very well, and no doubt productive of good educational practice. But Godwin offers no argument or evidence that we each of us do have our own special sphere of excellence; worse still, that unproven assumption quite destroys the argument for perfectibility. For if one man's excellence lies in the exercise of reason and the discovery of truth, another's, equally, may not, and truth will not after all be available to everyone. Indeed this is a difficulty strikingly illustrated elsewhere in the same *Thoughts on Man*. For Godwin follows up his attack on the foolishness and gullibility of the phrenologists with another, no less forthright, on the absurdity and pretension of the astronomers who, in a world where philosophers cannot even prove the existence of the bodies we seem to see before us, nevertheless claim to know that the sun is some 95 million miles from the earth, a million times larger and immensely hot; that there are thousands of such suns, each surrounded by planets of their own which might well support intelligent life very different from our own; that some are so enormously distant that a cannonball travelling at 480 miles an hour would still take more than 700,000 years to reach them; and other equally incredible things! How can men believe such nonsense? Only on authority: 'Is it not enough? Newton and his compeers have said it.'[25] If only we trusted in our own reason we would never fall into such errors.

To be fair, when we see some of the fanciful speculations which the astronomers of his day mingled with their more enduring discoveries, Godwin's scepticism may not seem quite so misplaced. But there is surely a lesson here, that there are some facts we have to accept on authority, some arguments too complex to be explicable to all, some truths not everyone can grasp. Godwin himself, all too evidently, is in just this position when it comes to the discoveries of Newton and his compeers. And if some are unable to comprehend the calculations of the astronomers, or the proofs of the philosophers, how can we rely on the omnipotence of truth?

Yes it is in an essay 'On the Liberty of Human Actions' that the *Thoughts on Man* most dramatically undermine the doctrines of *Political Justice*. It was 'Godwin on Necessity' that Wordsworth advised his Temple student to read, and for all that the relevant discussion is tucked away in *Political Justice*'s miscellaneous Book IV, with the advice that the reader 'who is indisposed to abstruse speculations' – supposing that such a one would have picked the book up in the first place – might prefer to skip those chapters,

Godwin was derided in his time as much as a 'necessarian' as a republican. Not that his opinions were particularly original, as he was himself careful to point out: the psychology comes from Hartley, and so from Locke; the account of necessity from Hume; the critique of free will from Johnathan Edwards. But here, it seems, Godwin was a popularizer as much as a prophet, and it was through his text that their ideas reached a wider public.

Godwin is clear that, like everything else in the natural world, the human mind must be 'a system of mechanism', where 'every incident requires a specific cause, and could be no otherwise in any respect than as the cause determined it to be',[26] so that any particular input, mental or physical, will lead by invariable physical or psychological laws to a particular output. It is only because we do not understand how thoughts affect actions, how mind can influence body, that we think that our behaviour is not causally determined like that of planets or rivers, and so believe that there is room for individual decision, for freedom of the will and a liberty to act at variance with the laws of nature. But in fact we no more understand the connection between one inanimate event and another. As Hume has shown, the necessity that governs physical phenomena consists in nothing more than regularity and predictability, in which like follows like: 'All that, strictly speaking, we know of the material universe, is this succession of events . . . . But the principle or virtue by which one event is conjoined to another we never see.'[27]

This means, then, that in so far as human behaviour (and the connection between thought and action) is regular and predictable, it will exhibit the same necessity that we find in inanimate matter. Moreover, the fact that we sometimes cannot predict someone's behaviour with certainty demonstrates not his liberty but our ignorance. A scientist cannot predict the outcome of his experiment until he has accurate and detailed knowledge of the conditions which might affect it, and typically we do not have this knowledge of the opinions and preferences of our fellow human beings. But if we did, we would be in a position to predict their behaviour as we can predict our own, and so demonstrate the necessity that governs it all. Indeed the liberty claimed by the advocates of free will is an impossibility, an absurdity 'To ascribe freedom to our voluntary actions, is an express contradiction in terms,'[28] for a voluntary action is precisely one that is determined by our intentions, by our foresight of the consequences to follow from it. Once allow that our actions are determined by our wills, as they surely must be, and we have admitted necessity into human conduct. For if our motives did not determine our conduct, as the advocates of liberty seem to imagine, they would not be motives at all, but idle fancies with no direct bearing on what we actually do. The inevitable result of a freedom which consisted in the possibility of acting independently of our desires and intentions, would be conduct so erratic and unmotivated as to be incapable of moral assessment!

> Freedom of the will is absurdly represented as necessary to render the mind susceptible of moral principles; but in reality, so far as we act with liberty, so far as we are independent of motives, our conduct is as independent of morality as it is of reason, nor is it possible that we should deserve either praise or blame for a proceeding thus capricious and indisciplinable.[29]

Godwin's necessity is, therefore, a 'moral necessity': without it there can be no voluntary action and no morality, and more to the point, no perfectibility. Without necessity we could no longer rely on the omnipotence of truth: it would be possible for men to recognize the facts of the matter, and yet act at variance with them. 'A mysterious philosophy taught men to suppose, that, when the understanding had perceived any object to be desirable, there was need of some distinct power to put the body in motion,' and so was introduced 'a distinction where there is no difference, to wit, a distinction between the intellectual and the active powers of the mind.'[30] But once we recognize that our opinions causally determine our behaviour, just as everything in the universe is causally determined, we can see that the perfectibility of man is as inevitable as the motion of the planets:

> Man being, as we have here found him to be, a simple substance, governed by the apprehensions of his understanding, nothing further is requisite but the improvement of his reasoning faculty, to make him virtuous and happy. But did he possess a faculty independently of the understanding, and capable of resisting from mere caprice the most powerful arguments, the best education and the most sedulous instruction might be of no use to him. This freedom we shall easily perceive to be his bane and his curse; and the only hope of lasting benefit to the species, would be, by drawing closer the connection between the external motions and the understanding, wholly to extirpate it.[31]

In the most literal possible sense, Godwin makes a virtue of necessity.

But here too Godwin had changed his mind. In February 1800 he had added a further note to the 1798 memorandum on future works:

> Too much stress is, I apprehend, laid in the Enquiry concerning Political Justice, on the inferences from the doctrines of

necessity. That doctrine may perhaps be beneficially applied towards extirpating the odious sentiment of revenge, and to moderating the fury of political and private animosities. But . . . we should lose the noblest emotions and sentiments of our nature by an indiscriminate application of the vulgar maxim, 'it will be the same thing an hundred years hence', and the moral feeling of approbation and disapprobation, in the finest tones, would be extinguished within us, if we constantly viewed our fellow men in the light of machines.[32]

Not that Godwin wants to deny that human conduct is subject to natural necessity. On the contrary, the *Thoughts on Man* continue to insist that this can be demonstrated, and demonstrated by the arguments of *Political Justice*. But we can never rid ourselves of the delusive sense of liberty, which is moreover of the utmost importance to human dignity and virtue. It encourages us to exert ourselves, to do what we can, instead of resigning ourselves to our fate, and leaving what will be to the ineluctable workings of cause and effect. Once he had argued that freedom of the will would undermine morality, by enabling individuals to act contrary to what they explicitly recognize to be in their best interests. But now he insists that there can be no morality without freedom, that without it duty becomes 'a term that can scarcely be said to have a meaning'.[33] So what are we to do, if reason establishes necessity, but morality and common sense require liberty? The answer lies in that old maxim of the philosophers: we must think with the learned, but talk with the vulgar!

It is hard to imagine a conclusion more subversive of the teachings of *Political Justice*. There will always be a tension between the doctrine of necessity and the demands of morality, a tension originally resolved by Godwin's identification of duty with doing what unbiased reason will inevitably lead us to do. But now he sees morality as requiring a choice between one course of action and another, irrespective of the workings of cause and effect. Once he had argued that, in terms of moral responsibility, a man is no different from a knife, both equally the pawn of necessity. Now he explicitly rejects the comparison: 'Duty is the performance of what is due, the discharge of a debt . . . But a knife owes nothing, and can in no sense be held to one sort of application rather than another.'[34] But it is not just that Godwin has altered his view of man and morality, leaving room for private whim to subvert the cause of reason and truth. It is not simply that he no longer recognizes the virtue of necessity as a guarantee of perfectibility and political justice. It is not even that he is here conceding that there is something which reason can demonstrate as true, but which cannot affect our conduct. He is actually recommending that we disregard what reason tells us, and base our words and deeds on what we know to be false! So much for the value of sincerity, the power of reason, the omnipotence of truth. The *Thoughts on Man* are distressing enough for the way in which rhetoric replaces argument, and optimism replaces proof. It is appropriate that of all Godwin's theoretical writings, it should be the most romantic in style. But without his apparently realizing the fact, this 'most faultless book I ever printed' is in fact the repudiation of the principles of a lifetime.

26 ♣ For services rendered

If it gives, as you say, universal suffrage, that is pain to my heart. Without the spirit of prophecy, I can anticipate the most disastrous effects from that. England is not yet ripe for universal suffrage, and, as I have often said, if it were established here, the monarchy probably would not stand a year.[1]

To H. B. Rosser, 1820

♣ After three decades of repression and prosecution, treason trials and Gagging Acts, parliamentary reform, the cause of Godwin's youth, was in the air again. In 1828 that litmus test of radical opinion, the repeal of the Test and Corporation Acts, had scraped through both Lords and Commons, followed a year later by Catholic emancipation. 'It is a bad business', admitted Lord Wellington, faced with the certain prospect of an Irish rebellion if he did nothing, 'but we are aground'. And it was worse than he thought. The Emancipation Bill had to be forced through against the wishes of the die-hard Tories who regarded him as their leader, and against the feelings of most Englishmen, as fervently anti-Papist as ever. Men of every political persuasion were thus presented with proof positive, both of the power of public pressure to upset the existing order, as had happened in Ireland, and the power of politicians to use a corrupt parliament to force their wishes on the nation, as had happened at Westminster. What, indeed, could be clearer, when Robert Peel was defeated at an Oxford by-election because of his involvement in the Emancipation Act –

> Oh! Member for Oxford! you shuffle and wheel!
> You have altered your name from R. Peel to Repeal

– but was found another seat and returned to the Commons, before a single week had passed? A system acceptable neither to radicals or reactionaries could endure no longer.

The Whigs, to be sure, had almost lost interest in the subject. Long years of absence from power had meant that the advocation of parliamentary reform had become with them more ritual than belief. But the pressure of public opinion carried them along, half afraid of losing their place in the balance of power, half afraid that the alternative to a Whig reform might be one even more radical, if not outright revolution. George IV was dying; his death would bring a general election, and a monarch who was not determined to prevent a government headed by Grey. But still Parliament refused to create new seats for the industrial cities of Manchester, Birmingham and Leeds, or even to transfer to them seats lost by electorates whose corruption so exceeded the norm that they had to be disqualified.

In the event the election of July 1830 brought little change in the overall position of the parties, and the most prominent reformer, Lord John Russell, actually lost his seat. But the tone of many an election battle demonstrated a growing feeling that the landed gentry could no longer look upon parliamentary seats as as much their personal property as their houses or their estates, to be disposed of as they felt inclined. When Wellington, old and deaf, sheltered in the Lords from the new ideas wafting through the Commons, and so far out of touch that he did not realize he was out of touch, delivered a fiercely uncompromising rejection of any suggestion of change, the fall of his government became only a matter of time. On 15 November he was defeated on a financial vote, and resigned. After almost half a century of Tory rule which stretched back virtually unbroken to the disastrous Fox–North coalition that Godwin had once defended against its critics, the Whigs were in again.

It was indeed Godwin's party. The new Prime Minister was the dandified George Grey he had met at Sheridan's in 1786; the Home Secretary, Lord Melbourne, had been William Lamb, Lady Caroline's husband, whom Godwin had met at Brocket Hall in 1822; the Chancellor of the Duchy of Lancaster was the Lord Holland who had contributed to the Juvenile Library subscription of 1808; and even James Mackintosh, a Privy Councillor thanks to his work on the legal reforms that had swept many an outdated capital offence from the statute book, held a minor place in the administration. The reform of Parliament stood at the top of their agenda, and the sense of an approaching triumph brought even John Thelwall from retirement, to join Place's National Political Union. But Godwin, carefully recording in his diary the result of each crucial division, still held himself aloof.

Outside Parliament the demand was the traditional demand: annual elections, manhood suffrage, a secret ballot. But the reform Grey had in mind was a more modest affair, which might save the situation by satisfying public opinion without damaging the structure of Parliament as he knew it. 'The principle of my Reform', he said, 'is to prevent the necessity for revolution'; and again, 'there is no one more decided against annual parliaments, universal suffrage and the ballot, than I am. My object is not to favour, but to put an end to

330 · FOR SERVICES RENDERED

such hopes and projects.' And that was Godwin's position too. It was somewhere around this time that he was approached by the artist Martin, anxious to enlist his support since he had once been 'all for knocking down the aristocracy and for throwing the whole power of the nation into the hands of the people'. 'If I said that', said Godwin, quietly getting on with his game of whist, 'then I was wrong', later adding 'I don't think a whole people can think.' 'Then you throw up the democratic principle?' urged the horrified Martin. 'Perhaps I do,' said Godwin, and calmly took his trick.

And of course he did. He distrusted Paine's common man as much as he distrusted Paine's rights and constitutions; he had explicitly rejected popular assemblies and the demagogy that went with them; he had put his faith in an educated elite, not the will of the masses. 'If you refer every public question to the people at large, and give everybody a vote,' he had warned the youthful readers of his *History of Rome*, 'the ignorant and brutish will always outnumber the well-informed and humane. The people see but a little way before them, they are governed by their passions more than by their reason.' In fact *Political Justice* had been opposed to voting of any sort, 'that intolerable insult upon all reason and justice, the deciding of truth by the casting up of numbers,'[2] but it was the secret ballot that he objected to most of all, no less than Grey, no less than the Lords, no less than the King himself:

> It is scarcely possible to conceive of a political institution that includes a more direct and explicit patronage of vice . . . . A feeble and irresolute character might before be accidental; ballot is a contrivance to render it permanent, and to scatter its seeds over a wider surface . . . . To tell men that it is necessary that they should form their decision by ballot, is to tell them that it is necessary they should be vicious.[3]

Accordingly the *Thoughts on Man*, appearing only a fortnight before Lord John Russell introduced the first Reform Bill to the Commons, contained a single essay devoted to practical politics, to this threat of a new Gagging Act, every bit as evil as the old:

> Little did I and my contemporaries of 1795 imagine, when we protested against these acts in the triumphant reign of William Pitt, that the *soi-disant* friends of liberty and radical reformers, when their turn of trumph came, would propose their Gagging Acts, recommending to the people to vote agreeably to their consciences, but forbidding them to give publicity to the honourable conduct they had been prevailed upon to adopt![4]

The argument was, of course, that unless men were free to vote in secret they were not genuinely free to vote as they pleased. But that for Godwin was the same old error, of thinking that deception and secrecy might be a means of political progress. And it is still an arguable question, albeit one that it is never argued, whether our political opinions might not be more sincere, and better grounded, if we had to declare them publicly, and if needs be, defend them.

In the event Russell's Reform Bill dropped the original proposal for a secret ballot – among other disadvantages it would make it possible for voters to take bribes from more than one candidate without fear of detection. But although the Bill stood very much for things as they were, altering the means by which Members entered Parliament but doing its best to ensure that the final composition would be much the same, it passed its second reading by a single vote, and when the inevitable defeat came, early in the morning of 20 April 1831, Grey went to the country, hoping to return with a majority of between 50 and 100, but in fact coming back with one of more than 130. The Commons was now no problem, but there were still the Lords, and when the Bill reached them on 22 September, it was rejected by 41 votes. The result, predictably, was rioting in Derby, Nottingham and Bristol, crystallizing public opinion and forcing a number of wavering Lords to make up their mind between reform and revolution. Grey's second and 'not less efficient' Bill included a number of technical alterations designed to reassure the doubtful, and with William IV evidently willing to create enough new peers to get the measure through, it passed its second reading in April 1832 by 9 votes. Yet when a procedural defeat presented a reluctant monarch with the prospect of having to create as many as fifty or sixty new Lords he refused, and Grey resigned. The Commons passed an immediate vote of confidence in the outgoing administration; Peel, recognizing that a Tory government would have to introduce a Reform Bill of its own, and remembering the débâcle of Catholic emancipation, refused to serve; and public feeling, running at fever pitch through those Days of May – splendidly master-minded by Francis Place – made it impossible for Wellington to form a government. Within the week Grey was back, the Tory peers stayed home, and the Reform Bill passed into law by 106 votes to 22.

It seemed to Godwin a propitious moment to prepare a Prospectus for a new edition of *Political Justice*:

> after many memorable vicissitudes, it became apparent that the cause of improvement and equality would finally triumph. Of late years in particular great strides have been taken in this respect; and it seems evident that, at least in these islands,

sentiments favourable to human liberty and happiness will go
forward with a tide no power can resist.[5]

But despite the overwhelming triumph of the Whigs at the election
that followed, the reform movement had reached its peak – Russell
himself was known as 'Finality Jack' because he was convinced that
his reform must be the last reform – and a year later an exhausted
Grey was only too glad of an excuse to resign, to be followed by the
cantankerous old Melbourne, his favourite complaint 'Why can't
they leave things alone?' The final triumph of reason, truth and
justice lay still in the future.

Godwin, even so, could not afford to abandon his pursuit of the
publishers, offering here a *History of the Protestant Reformation*, there a
Lives of the Necromancers, anything that he might write and they might
sell, and so see himself and his wife through to the next project and
the next advance. For the moment there was another novel, which
Bentley had rejected, twice, but still been prevailed upon to accept,
yet another tale of a human outcast, 'the most forlorn and odious of
men. All pleasures of life have at length deserted me; and every
calamity and misery is heaped on my head. I have no friends . . . .'
Early on in the book there is an account of a marriage like that in *St
Leon*, and a wife who dies in childbirth, that take Godwin back
across half a lifetime to the moments that had meant most, and cost
most, of all. (A passage is quoted at pp. 131–2 above.) From there we
turn to a story of relentless pursuit and constant escape which was
clearly intended to rival *Caleb Williams*, but succeeded only in being
boring and contrived. Godwin had anticipated no difficulty in
providing 'incidents of hair-breadth escapes and adventures' with
which to pad out the three volumes, but after he had been working
on it for a year he had to complain to Mary that he had been stuck
fast for weeks, and when *Deloraine* finally appeared, in February
1833, it bore all too obviously the marks of its laborious composition.
Both *Cloudesley* and the later *Necromancers* are written smoothly and
elegantly, but *Deloraine* is turgid and unbearably pompous, its plot
both tortuous and tedious, its characterization absurd. Worse still,
Godwin's handling of emotion, never very sure, goes lamentably,
even laughably, astray, until what is meant as tragedy approaches
farce, in a way that even *Antonio* cannot rival.

After that came the much-heralded *Lives of the Necromancers*,

the object of which was to trace the subject biographically, and
to endeavour to ascertain by what steps Roger Bacon, Cornelius
Agrippa, and a multitude of other eminent men came to be
seduced into the profession of magic, or to have magical power
imputed to them.[6]

Not that Godwin believes these tales of sorcery that he relates with such gusto, tales culled from the Bible, the Ancient World and the Far East as well as from medieval Europe. But it was a topic that had always fascinated him, as witness *St Leon* and footnotes to many another work, and the information is so intrinsically interesting, so thoroughly researched and clearly presented, that this proves to be one of Godwin's most readable books, favourably reviewed by that connoisseur of the occult, and admirer of Godwin's novels, Edgar Allen Poe. First published in June 1834, and running into several editions, especially in North America, it was the last of Godwin's works to appear in his lifetime.

It was a meagre existence, full of uncertainty and strain, yet Godwin always managed to get by, struggling uncertainly from one publisher to the next, and averaging almost a book a year through his seventies. Their wants were few, the monster with the maw had died with the Juvenile Library, and they, miraculously, were still alive. May 28 1831, had been a date to record with particular pride, for he then equalled the age of Dr Johnson, seventy-five years and eighty-six days. Mary Jane, too, 'an old vivacious lady', seemed to have thrown off the ailments and debilities of the past two decades. But death was to strike where they least expected it.

In 1832 the country had been gripped not just with the debate over the Reform Bill but with an epidemic of cholera so severe that Mary Shelley received a panic-stricken letter from Claire, now living in Pisa, urging her and Percy to flee the country while they could. 'I am nearly mad with fear about the cholera . . .,' she wrote. 'I have taken it into my head you will surely have it.' But though Mary and her son escaped the disease, to Claire's equal anguish their half-brother William did not. That idle, meddlesome, ill-mannered boy had grown into a relaxed, cheerful, good-humoured young man, married but without family, a parliamentary reporter for the *Morning Chronicle* – a position, once held by Hazlitt, in which he would be followed by his colleague, Charles Dickens – and founder and leading light of a Shakespearean club called 'The Mulberries' whose members would include Thackeray as well as Dickens. But on the night of 4 September, at the age of twenty-nine, William fell suddenly ill, and died four days later at 5.30 in the morning, leaving a play with the tempting title of *The Sleeping Philosopher*, which Godwin tried without success to get performed, and a Gothic novel, *Transfusion, or the Orphans of Unwalden*, published in 1835 accompanied by the father's memoir of his son. The younger William had finally begun to reveal what had always been expected of him, too impatiently perhaps. But Godwin took this fresh disappointment with his usual resignation, and returned to the drudgery of *Deloraine*.

Soon he would be free at last from the necessity of writing for a living.

Among those many institutions and conventions condemned by *Political Justice*, Godwin had found space for a passing attack on the habit of rewarding political services with an official salary or pension. The reward for public position should be the honour it carries with it; a salary would be either what the office deserves, in which case 'how are we to be sure he will not have more regard to the salary than the public', or a mere token by which we merely demean the post, 'a service, first degraded by being paid, and then paid with an ill-timed parsimony'.[7] Instead those who would serve the public must look for their support to private wealth and patronage. It might seem to conflict with that independence and self-sufficiency that Godwin elsewhere so approves; but this support of the great by the rich is no more than justice demands.

Yet circumstances alter cases, and experience modifies opinion, and Godwin was no longer so convinced of the immorality of public assistance, or so certain that a man of extraordinary talents, lacking riches of his own, will inevitably find someone to be his patron. With the encouragement of Mackintosh and Bulwer, who had finally entered Parliament in the General Election of 1831, he had written to Grey and to Melbourne to see if a man of his age and lifelong adherence to the party of Fox, a man known personally to half the members of the present administration, might be found a position suitable his remaining talents and meagre needs. In December of 1831 he had come up with a more specific proposal, for men were being appointed to go through the accumulated mounds of official records and decide which were worthy of publication, a task to which his experience and character made him well suited. But nothing had come of it. His diary does list a 'Hereditary Peerage rejected' on 27 December, but it is beyond belief that the natural interpretation can be the correct one, and with Parliament and country convulsed in the debate over the Reform Bill, the Whigs had other matters on their mind. But by 1833 things were different, and on 15 April Prime Minister Grey offered the pathetic little gentleman, for services rendered in an illustrious past, the post of Office Keeper and Yeoman Usher of the Receipt of the Exchequer, a title carrying with it a stipend of £200 a year and free accommodation in the Palace of Westminster.

History, yet again, seems to go out of its way to mock his principles, to prove that the last person capable of abiding by his extraordinary opinions, was William Godwin himself. It was Johnson's *Dictionary* that defined a pension as 'An allowance made to anyone without an equivalent. In England it is generally understood to mean pay given to a state hireling for treason to his country'; and when Godwin had attacked Thelwall in 1795 there had been those who wondered aloud whether he had been won over by the usual method of an official salary. More recently Cobbett, praising *Of Population*, had declared that 'Mr Godwin, who has lived to the age of pretty near four score I believe, and who has as much talent in his little finger as Malthus has in his whole body, has no pension from the government.'[8] But now, in defiance of all that *Political Justice* might say, Godwin had gratefully accepted, indeed had eagerly sought out, his position as a servant of the state.

Nevertheless *Political Justice* had explicitly, if rather reluctantly, exempted those minor officials among whom he now numbered, the 'clerks and tax-gatherers, whose employment is perpetual, and whose subsistence ought, for that reason, to be made the result of their employment',[9] though once there were no other state salaries to pay, no wars to finance, no expenditure to administer, no accounts to render and no taxes to collect, the need for these functionaries would disappear. At seventy-seven he could not be expected to keep going for ever through his single-handed exertions, and justice surely demanded that he receive an income from somewhere, even if it could come only through political favour. And though the chroniclers, both sneering and sympathetic, universally describe the position as a sinecure, it was far from being that:

To keep safe in his own custody the keys of the Outer doors of the Exchequer; to open them every morning, and to lock them again after the business of the day is over.

To attend to the duties of his situation as Yeoman Usher in the Tally Court, to keep the keys thereof, and to attend strictly to its Security.

To take care of the clocks in the Tally Court.

To keep the Fire Engine, and to take care that it be at all times fit for use.

To pay persons for sweeping and dusting the Offices, lighting the fires and sweeping Chimnies; and to provide Coals for sundry Offices if required.

To give notice, under the direction of the Heads of the Departments, to pay the Clerk of Works when repairs may be wanted.

To pay Money Porters for moving cash.

To provide the Official Gown for the Porter at the Exchequer.

To provide Necessaries in the Tally Court at Easter, and at Michaelmas for the Cursitor Baron.

To Provide an Account of his Expenditure Quarterly, or
Annually, together with the vouchers thereof.

To collect and produce Quarterly, or Annually, as may be
required, the Bills of Tradesmen employed in the service of the
Exchequer together with their vouchers for the Articles
furnished, and for the works performed by them.

To produce Quarterly to the Receiver of the Fees in the
Exchequer an account of any Fees or Emoluments which he
may have received; and to pay the same over to the Receiver of
the Fees.

Also generally to obey, according to the requisition contained
in his appointment all such orders as he may receive from the
Principal Acting Officers of the Exchequer, for the execution of
his duties.[10]

It was a post instituted in 1817 to replace one once held by Horace
Walpole, and Godwin was its third, and final, occupant. His one
regret was that James Mackintosh, who had tried so often to make
proper amends for his treachery of 1799, had died a year too soon
to celebrate this final success.

So on 4 May 1833 the Godwins moved again, from their little
house in Gower Place to 13 New Palace Yard, in the corner by the
Speaker's gateway and close to the entrance of Old Westminster
Hall, recently cleared of its clutter of coffee shops and ale-houses.
And there the ancient enemy of established institutions enjoyed
himself hugely, proudly showing his visitors the richly decorated
ceiling of the Star Chamber, and carrying about with him the
emblem of his office, an enormous key with which, perhaps, to open
the legendary Chests of the Exchequer, from which the monarch had
once made his official disbursements. He had rooms for himself and
his books, musty historic rooms that suited both of them equally; he
had a job to do, and an income to earn from it. One day a man called
Perry, 'the man who several years ago did no good to the portrait of
Bradshaw for the lives of the Phillipses', called 'in the last degree of
distress, without a shirt.'[11] In his mild prosperity Godwin was able
to give him three shillings to get his clothes out of pawn, then a coat
of his own and another five shillings, so that poor Perry could find
himself a job.

Yet this unaccustomed situation made little difference to his
familiar way of life. Godwin still found time to read and to write, and
to carry out his researches. He would call on friends, and they on
him, and a month or two after the move his new neighbour and
fellow employee, John Rickman, was able to end the misunderstanding that had separated Elia and the Professor. In July Godwin,

Lamb and Rickman dined happily together at the Bell, near Lamb's home at Edmonton. Mary Jane had had an attack of painful spasms in one arm, and after unsuccessful treatment with poisons, she was sent to recuperate with a sister at Herne Bay, but Godwin's own health was remarkably good. His spirits were high. He was happy now. But it could not last; he would soon discover that uninterrupted happiness was not for him.

On 16 October a roaring fire swept through the Palace of Westminster, almost completely devastating the site. Ironically, it was the most antiquated department of all, Godwin's own Exchequer, that was responsible. Only three months earlier he had been showing Harriet Martineau the old wooden tallies, piled high in cupboards and corners, that had once been used to keep the accounts. Now the spirit of reform had reached even there, and the tallies were being burnt, not outdoors as instructed, but in the fireplaces. Blocked flues began to smoulder, old timbers began to burn, and soon the flames were raging through the Houses of Parliament. Members rolled up their sleeves, manned the pumps, and managed to save Old Westminster Hall and Godwin's lodgings along with it. According to Miss Martineau he had come home from the theatre knowing nothing of what had happened, to discover that his wife had packed and removed all his books and manuscripts by herself – a colossal task, surely – rather than disturb him. But in fact he had left the theatre after only two acts of Richard III, and according to Mary the fire came nowhere near him, 'they were not even inconvenienced'.[12] Luckily, too, no one seems to have noticed that the lighting of fires, the sweeping of chimneys, and the care of the fire engine, were all under his supervision, so that the destruction of the Mother of Parliaments might perhaps have been blamed on the father of anarchists!

But though he had survived the fire, Godwin seemed unlikely to survive the Whigs. His letter of appointment had been careful to inform him

> that as the establishment of the Exchequer Office has been for some time under the consideration of the Government he must not expect compensation in the case of any arrangement being made which may affect his appointment,[13]

and in August 1833 the reformist MP Joseph Hume had proposed, and then withdrawn, a motion on sinecures, anxiously noted in Godwin's diary. But now, only four days before the fire an act had come into force regulating the scores of antiquated, superfluous, titular posts that governments had always had at their disposal. And Godwin's was among them.

It meant a return to those beseeching letters he had thought he would never have to write again, and Godwin prepared careful draft after careful draft. The understanding with Grey had been that the appointment was for life, what little remained of it; he could hardly be expected to find fresh employment and new accommodation in this his 79th year of age; in any case everyone agreed that whatever became of the title, someone would still have to carry out the duties. But though Melbourne, who had replaced Grey as Prime Minister, was prepared to be sympathetic, he would come to no decision, doubtless trusting that if he delayed long enough, the problem of Godwin would solve itself. And so 10 October came and went, with Godwin still not knowing how long his salary would continue, or whether he would have to vacate his rooms. There was no question that his post had been abolished, and some officers had been dismissed already. The uncertainty that suited Melbourne was the cruellest torment to him, and he wrote again to say so, to receive much the same reply.

A month later William IV seized eagerly at a pretext to be rid of the Whigs, and appointed Sir Robert Peel in their place. It was a difficult situation, for the men who had abolished Godwin's position might have wanted to keep him in his place, but the Tories who would have retained the post of Yeoman Usher would surely want to be rid of Godwin! Godwin cautiously introduced himself to Peel as the author of *Caleb Williams* and *St Leon*, and not *Political Justice*, but Sir Robert, it emerged, knew and admired them all:

> I will not defer the assurance, that whatever I can do consistently with my public duty, to prevent a measure of Official Retrenchment from bearing hardly upon one so far advanced in years, and so distinguished by his literary character, I will do as well from a sense of Justice, as from a grateful recollection of the pleasure I have derived from those Works to which, with a just Pride, you have referred.[14]

On 9 February 1835 Godwin received the letter for which he had been waiting, and was left savouring the irony of it all: the destroyer of pensions had survived the destruction of pensions; the Jacobin, threatened by the Whigs, was saved by the Tories!

27 ♣ A last judgment

Religion is among the most beautiful and most natural of all things; that religion which 'sees God in clouds and hears him in the winds', which endows every object of sense with a living soul, which finds in the system of nature, whatever is holy, mysterious and venerable, and inspires the bosom with sentiments of awe and veneration. But accursed and detestable is that religion by which the fancy is hag-rid, and conscience is excited to torment us with phantoms of guilt, which endows the priest with his pernicious empire over the mind, which undermines boldness of opinion and intrepidity of feeling, which aggravates a thousand-fold the inevitable calamity, death, and haunts us with the fiends and retributory punishments of a future world.[1]

Undated manuscript note

♣ Godwin no longer needed to pursue the reluctant publishers with new projects, but he could not easily abandon the habit of a lifetime, and there was one topic he had still to deal with, the topic that had dominated his youth and shaped his character, the topic of religion. It was a subject his published works had made surprisingly little reference to, but time and again, in his manuscript notes, he had carefully detailed the evolution of his religious beliefs – and once even drawn up a list of 'Reasons why I will not become a Papist' – from Calvinist to Sandemanian at the hands of Newton, from Sandemanian to Deist under the influence of D'Holbach's materialistic *Système de la Nature*, from Deist to Socinian after reading and corresponding with Joseph Priestley, from Socinian to Atheist under the guidance of Holcroft, and finally, in conversation with Coleridge, from Atheist to Pantheist, who found his divinity in Nature itself.

Most of these shifts of opinion, more interesting to Godwin than they are to us, took place in the ten years after leaving Hoxton, but ever since then he had hoped to explain and expound his convictions. Among the works projected in September 1798 had been *Two Dissertations on the Reasons and Tendency of Religious Opinion*, whose object would be

to sweep away the whole fiction of an intelligent former of the world, and a future state; to call men off from those incoherent and contradictory dreams that so often occupy their thoughts and vainly agitate their hopes and fears, and to lead them to apply their whole energy to practicable objects and genuine realities.[2]

In 1806 he had written for the Juvenile Library, and perhaps published, his *Rural Walks, or First Impressions of Religion*, as an introduction to his own faith in terms that a child might comprehend: 'I listen to the wind, and observe the motion of every leaf, and I say, This is God! I look up at the blue heavens, and the clouds, and these too (sic) I perceive the presence of God.'[3] In 1818 he had begun an autobiographical essay 'Of Religion', opening with the round declaration 'I am an unbeliever.' And at Coleridge's death in 1834 he had thought of writing a memoir, which could hardly fail to have discussed the faith that Coleridge had taught him. Now, after the publication of the *Necromancers* and contemplating in his bed a 'Life of Swift', he decided it was time to deal with the topic as it deserved, in detail and in public.

After the effusive piety of both *Deloraine* and the *Thoughts on Man* – one of whose complaints against the astronomers was precisely their lack of respect towards the work of God – and as the day grew irrevocably closer when Godwin himself might have to face his maker, we naturally expect some further change in his opinions, some movement back to the religion of his youth and the idea of an omniscient judge who might hopefully temper knowledge with mercy. But not a bit of it. Godwin borrows both title and treatment from a work by D'Holbach he may not actually have read, *The Genius of Christianity Unveiled*, and that genius is an evil genius. Godwin sets himself to show that 'Christianity, like all the sallies of mortal enthusiasm, is a mass of contradictions,' vicious in its doctrines and pernicious in its effects. There is no sign here of the positive beliefs acquired from Coleridge, only a bitterly outspoken attack on orthodox Christianity and all its works.

Yet for all its strength of conviction and spirited insolence, the posthumous *Essays*, as they came to be called, suffer from one single overwhelming defect, their repetitiveness, as Godwin uses a massive overdose of Biblical quotation to make every point, and often enough the same quotation to make the same point. What he has to say might well have been said more effectively at a fraction of the length, in two or three essays instead of the fifteen, plus fragments, that he actually wrote. It is charitable to think that had he lived to complete his manuscript he would have organized it more coherently, eliminating much of the wearing repetition. But it is unlikely. He is a terrier at the throat of Christianity and, shaking it this way and that, nothing will persuade him to let go.

Godwin was well aware that this new book must renew the odium and execration that he had finally managed to escape. Almost nothing that Shelley had done caused such outrage as when, irritated by the fervent pieties that clogged the visitors' books among the natural beauties of Switzerland, he had signed himself 'P. B. Shelley . . . atheist'. Byron, horrified at so direct an affront to God's majestic creation, had tried to erase one such entry. More recently Godwin himself had come in for criticism for treating Biblical miracles with the same scepticism as the other allegedly magical occurrences discussed in the *Lives of the Necromancers*. But once before he had been prepared to speak the truth without fear of the consequences, for the good it might do mankind, whatever it might cost him personally, and now he was willing to do so again. At one point he wrote a Preface, which both outlined his own positive faith and defended himself against the 'aversion and abhorrence' he knew his book would generate. But a week before he died, as his cold turned to fever, he wrote 'rejected' across it, almost as if he wanted no apologies in this final confrontation with truth. The *Thoughts on Man* make one dread the prospect of a fourth edition of *Political Justice*; the posthumous *Essays* encourage us to hope again.

The indictment that Godwin drew up against the religion of his fellows was a formidable one. There are first the manifest inconsistencies of Christian dogma: the uncertainty whether we are to act from benevolence and a love of our neighbours, or from self-love and a fear of the consequences of sin; the uncertainty whether we are to be saved by faith or by works, by a belief in God the father and Christ the son or by actually doing some good in the world; the uncertainty whether God is kind and loving as the Christians tell us, or stern and vindictive as the Bible actually portrays him; the absurdity of the doctrine of atonement, according to which a God who is justice itself saves the guilty by punishing with the greatest cruelty the only man who is wholly innocent. Then there are the manifold evils that Christianity has caused, warfare, persecution, repression and injustice:

> Religion is naturally the equaliser of mankind. The rich and the
> poor are together in that future state, the belief of which is
> taught in our churches. Whatever distinctions of rank are
> imposed in our political constitutions, they are all put to an end
> by death . . . . It is therefore too bad that this great equaliser
> should be used, as in modern policy it is, as the main instru-
> ment to keep down the illiterate in the state of subjection to
> which we doom them.[4]

M

Indeed religion, no less than the political institutions attacked in *Political Justice*, has been a major obstacle to the progress of truth:

> It has imposed a tissue of falsehood upon the human mind for eighteen hundred years; nor do we yet see when the imposture will be at an end . . . . Oh, when shall the mind of man again be free, shake off the chains that fasten it to its dungeon, and soar unrestricted in its native element?[5]

But worst of all is the Christian ethic, with its doctrine of original sin which contradict's man essential dignity and worth: 'The first lesson of a sound philosophy is self-reverence. The first lesson of the Scriptures is self-abasement';[6] its doctrine of predestination which makes men the mere playthings of their maker; and its doctrine of eternal punishment, at once central to the Christian faith and absolutely destructive of genuine morality.

It is this last, in particular, to which Godwin returns obsessively again and again. At first sight the idea of an after-life seems the obvious way of reconciling God's alleged benevolence and justice with the manifest sufferings and injustices of this present life: everything will be compensated in the world to come. But instead we are told to beware a fate alongside which our present misfortunes fade into nothing, and a fate most likely to be meted out to those who have suffered most already. It is evil circumstance that makes men evil; 'it ought, therefore, in a certain sense, to be the circumstances, and not the man, that should be called into judgment.'[7]

> Is it just, then, that men should be punished hereafter because their lot in life was unfavourable to their moral character, while others, purely inasmuch as their fortune was propitious here, shall be crowned with the favour of God and the joys of heaven to all eternity? The lot of a great proportion of human creatures is miserable here, and, purely because of the fierce pressure of their misery, they become vicious. What equity can we discern in their being made for ever miserable hereafter, because it was their fate to be miserable in this transitory state?[8]

And such punishment! The arguments of *Political Justice* had shown that punishment is both unjust and unjustifiable, treating men as responsible for their character and their conduct, and attempting to make them better through force and fear, instead of through reason and truth. But here we have a punishment which is unbelievably savage, everlasting, and almost universal, a punishment not only out of all proportion to any crime, but meted out with a crudity that divides the whole of mankind into the sheep and the goats, the blessed and the damned, in a way that cannot possibly do justice to the merits of the individual case:

> Cases have been recorded, where a great number of persons accused have been given in charge to one jury, to be disposed of by one sweeping verdict. But what is this compared with what is announced to us of the judgment of the last day![9]

Once Coleridge had got so carried away in a description of the Devil that a listener remarked that he made the Devil sound like God. 'Madam,' Coleridge replied, 'the Devil *is* God.' But if we believe what the Bible tells us, Godwin comments, the proper conclusion is that God is the Devil! The idea of a just being who punishes at all, let alone one who inflicts such appalling, indiscriminate, unmerited punishment as this, is the most manifest of Christianity's contradictions, corruptive of morality and of man himself.

For true morality must rest on a recognition of what is good, not a fear of future suffering, on benevolence and not self-interest. So when Harriet Lee had presented Godwin's lack of religion as the main obstacle to their marriage, his unromantic remonstrance sprang not from mere arrogance, a refusal to believe that she could reject such a one as he for such a reason as that. It sprang from his conviction that she was the victim of a simple error that made her exaggerate the difference between them, a mistake that he could easily and convincingly demonstrate. If she refused to accept the proof, then religious prejudice – 'bigotry', he called it – was the only possible explanation:

> You tell me that, if it were not for your religion, and your ideas of a future state, you believe you should adopt a system of conduct selfish and licentious. I do not credit you when you say this; if I did it would be impossible for me to have the smallest regard for you . . . . Every parent and preceptor perfectly knows that a conduct adopted from the hope of reward or the fear of punishment is not virtue.[10]

But now Godwin recognizes that her error lay at the very heart of her religion, that Christianity tells us we must be virtuous – if virtue it be – not for virtue's sake, nor even for the benefits it brings, but simply from fear of a cruel, powerful and vindictive deity, as weak and irrational as he is vicious:

> If He knew what was right, could He not communicate that knowledge to the delinquent? Could He not enlighten His understanding, and thus correct His errors? He has probably tried the experiment . . . and failed. And to supply His

deficiency in logic and demonstration, he has resorted to brute force. Brute force is in no way adapted to enlighten the under-standing; the best thing it can effect is to produce servility, a fawning and cowardly protestation of soul before Him that is mightier than we are.[11]

(These capital Hs are the work of Godwin's anonymous editor; they are not in the original manuscript.)

In a book of sermons notable for its evangelical praise of Christ and his lessons for the world, Godwin had nevertheless insisted that 'God himself has not the right to be a tyrant.'[12] But now he comes to the only possible conclusion, 'as calmly', marvelled the *Fortnightly Review*, 'as if he were speaking of George III':[13] 'to say all in a word, since it must finally be told, the God of the Christians is a tyrant!'[14] No fear of hell-fire there!

In the end the great fire that destroyed the old Palace of Westminster did force the Godwins out of New Palace Yard. The entire site was to be rebuilt, and those minor buildings that had escaped the blaze were to be pulled down to make room for the new Houses of Parliament. So in November of 1835 the Godwins were moved into rooms in the new Exchequer Office in Whitehall Yard, almost adjoining the Banqueting Hall, and so close to the spot where Charles I had been executed that friends wondered whether Godwin should not be afraid of the ghost. It was there that he celebrated his eightieth birthday, still holding a post that no longer existed, still writing his essays on religion. Soon after, on 26 March, he made a final entry in the thirty-second volume of his diary, brought up to date the four-page farewell he had drafted almost two years before, complete with its footnote reference to *Hamlet*, Act IV Scene V, and pasted it in the cover:

With what facility have I marked these pages with the stamp of rolling weeks and months and years – all uniform, all blank! What a strange power is this! It sees through a long vista of time, and it sees nothing. All this at present is mere abstraction, symbols, not realities. Nothing is actually seen: the whole is ciphers, conventional marks, imaginary boundaries of un-imagined things. Here is neither joy nor sorrow, pleasure nor pain . . . . Here are fevers, and excruciating pains 'in their sacred secundine asleep'. Here may be the saddest reverses, destitution and despair, detrusion and hunger and nakedness, without a place wherein to lay our head, wearisome days and endless nights in dark and unendurable monotony, variety of wretchedness; yet of all one gloomy hue; slumbers without sleep, waking without excitation, dreams all heterogeneous and perplexed, with nothing distinct and defined, distracted without the occasional burst of energy and distraction. And these pages look now all fair, innocent and uniform. I have put down eighty years and twenty-three days, and I might have put down one hundred and sixty years.[15]

Outside it was snowing. He had a cough, felt feverish, suffered no illusions. A week later he was put to bed, and a week after that, on Thursday 7 April 1836, he was dozing peacefully, a little after seven in the evening, with his wife and daughter sitting by the fire, when they heard a slight rattle. They went to his side. William Godwin, the worn-out philosopher who had survived his philosophy, was dead.

He was buried, as he had asked to be, as close as possible to the remains of Mary Wollstonecraft, and the funeral might have passed entirely without public notice were it not for the remarkable fact that her coffin, placed in the ground some forty years before, was found to be in a state of almost complete preservation, with remnants of the original shroud still visible. There was a mere handful of mourners, the minor friends of his final years, for the great names from his past had preceded him to the grave. There was young Shelley, now sixteen; James Kenney; David Uwins; Thomas Campbell; the Rev. J. H. Caunter, who had adapted *St Leon* for the stage the previous year; and Edward Trelawney.

Mary's first concern was for her step-mother, no longer the enemy of her youth. There was a mere £100 in the house, to which were added the proceeds from Sotheby's sale of Godwin's library, but it seemed unlikely that a salary artificially prolonged for the husband could be retained indefinitely by the wife. Godwin had left a note urging his daughter to publish the incomplete *Genius of Christianity Unveiled*, not only for its intrinsic importance but because its value might be all of £1,000, but Mary, already anxious to protect both her father and her husband from their follies while alive, preferred to ignore it, and instead an agreement was signed with Henry Colburn for the *Memoirs and Correspondence of William Godwin*, as edited by Mary Shelley for the sum of 350 guineas. But in death as in life the contract was unfulfilled: the book was advertised, and Mary worked on it for a year or more, but during some trouble over Percy's admission to university, on account of his – or her – irreligion, the project was abandoned and she never went back to it.

By then, however, Mary Jane was free from the need to live by her husband's writings. Her step-daughter had approached the Prime Minister, now Melbourne once more, through the medium of their mutual friend Caroline Norton, whose husband would shortly cite

Melbourne in a suit for divorce. And though Melbourne had replied that it was not in his power to continue the salary for a position that had been abolished, he was able to offer Mrs Godwin £300 a year from the Royal Bounty Fund, that existed for just such a purpose. Yet even that lapsed within the year, at the death of William IV, and Mary had to go back to Mrs Norton, to find that her access to the Prime Minister was now more restricted. Edward Bulwer, MP, had to be her intermediary instead.

So Mary Jane Godwin, 'crony – rheumy – rheumatic and phythisicky', lived on near Mary in Kentish Town until 1841, when she too was buried in Old St Pancras Churchyard. It was three years after that that the death of Shelley's father freed Mary, too, from the necessity of writing for a living. Percy inherited the baronetcy, and his father's legacies were paid at last, including, to Mary's disgust, a mistaken double payment of £6,000 to Claire Clairmont, who survived in a state of increasing piety until 1879 and the age of ninety-one, growing ever more ashamed of her disreputable past. The girl whose relentless pursuit had astonished even Byron now tried to erase all mention of him and their daughter from her journals, and even contemplated writing a book to 'illustrate, from the lives of Shelley and Byron, the dangers and evils resulting from erroneous opinions on the subject of relations between the sexes.'[16]

Mary, meanwhile, had died in 1851, but with Old St Pancras Churchyard about to be desecrated by a new railroad line, the remains of her father and mother were taken with hers to Bournemouth, where Percy Shelley had his home. Despite complaints at a gravestone that cited such infidel works as *Political Justice* and *A Vindication of the Rights of Women*, they were buried there together, all three, in St Peter's Churchyard, and there they lie still. Mary Jane, it seems, was left behind, to be ploughed up by the Midland Railway. Shelley had descendants enough, for his eldest child Ianthe produced seven children. But Godwin's line came to an end in 1889, with the death of the childless Sir Percy. 'A loutish youth', Crabb Robinson had lamented,

> quite unworthy of in his external appearance his distinguished literary ancestors. If talent descended, what ought he not to be, he who is of the blood of Godwin, Mrs Wollstonecraft, Shelley and Mrs Shelley! . . . . He is in Parliament. His moral character is highly spoken of. Of his abilities nothing is said.[17]

Godwin's inheritance would have to lie elsewhere.

It was on 21 October 1824, the day after he received the final injunction from Read that would end in his bankruptcy, that Godwin had opened Hazlitt's *Spirit of the Age* and found himself celebrated there among the first and foremost of his time, more gifted and less pedantic than Bentham, more rational and less capricious than Coleridge, more profound and more significant than either, massively famous once, almost forgotten now, but certain to live again and forever as the author of *Caleb Williams* and *Political Justice*. And no less than Hazlitt, Godwin would have liked to believe it was so. All his life, as far back as he could remember, he had been obsessed with fame, with reputation, and there was more to that obsession than mere pride or conceit, or the need of approval that had moulded him from childhood. 'How beautiful a passion is the love of fame,' he noted once; and again, anticipating a further revision of *Political Justice*, 'The love of fame is the love of the future; so is the love of individual and general advancement; the love of fame therefore is the ape of the best of passions.'[18] For the love of fame is the desire to stand out among our fellows, to be recognized by them for the good that we have done; like the best of passions, benevolence itself, it is a desire directed at the benefit of all. One day this love of fame will replace our present corrupt love of wealth and possessions, until it in its turn gives way to the love of all mankind, the love of justice itself. Others might ridicule Godwin's petty conceits, but to him it was almost a virtue. A posthumous fame would recognize not merely his talents but his contributions, the good he had done his fellows.

Some obituaries were obviously the work of friends, but there were those, like the *Gentleman's Magazine* who still linked the name of Godwin with Hardy, Tooke, Thelwall and the other plotters of Jacobin treason. Admittedly *Caleb Williams* is 'perhaps the most powerful novel in our language', and even *Political Justice* 'was a bold and outstanding piece of writing, a very master-stroke of levelis-ation, pardonable only as having been conceived in the madness of a distracting period in the history and affairs of Europe.' But the Wollstonecraft *Memoirs* were a warning, to over-ambitious women and their biographers alike, and the *Magazine* is forced to the 'painful tho' certain conclusion, that it might have been better for mankind had he never existed.'[19] Nevertheless, for a time it seemed that posterity might yet restore the prestige that had once been his. With something of the excitement of the 1790s the Chartists were eagerly reading the excerpts from *Political Justice* printed in their English and Scottish *Circulars*, and the long-delayed fourth edition appeared as a result in 1842. But there its direct influence ended, and *Political Justice* was not republished again, in full and in English, until the scholars' edition of 1946. Burke and Paine, rooted solidly in the issues of their day, remained at the centre of political debate, but Godwin, who sought to put the principles of politics on an immovable basis, had become only a subject for academic research.

Of all Godwin's doctrines it was his critique of private property that fared best, and for a considerable time *Political Justice* was available in English only in the form of a reprint of Book VIII, 'Of Property', in its most extreme, first edition, version. For that, no doubt, he had the impact of Marx to thank. 'Godwin may be regarded as the first scientific socialist of later times,' a weighty German treatise on man's right to the full produce of his labour declared at the end of the century: 'the germs of all the ideas of later socialism and anarchism are to be found in his work. He wielded the most powerful influence over Hall, Owen and Thompson, and through them upon the development of socialism.'[20] But though there are many respects in which Godwin anticipated Marx, their differences are no less than their similarities. The roots of Marx's theories lie in economic analysis; Godwin's lie in Christianity, if not in ancient Greece. Marx is the product of the industrial revolution; Godwin belonged to an earlier, more individualistic, more aristocratic age. Where Marx anticipates the creation of wealth for all, Godwin looks to its replacement in a world of austere simplicity. Where Marx puts his hopes on an oppressed proletariat, Godwin puts his in an educated elite. And where Marx trusted in social and economic control, Godwin trusted in the nature of man himself.[21]

For Godwin was utterly and explicitly opposed to any form of state interference or supervision, even to social security and state education:

> He that should command a conflagration to cease or a tempest to be still, would not display more ignorance of the system of the universe, than he, who, with a code of regulations, whether general or minute, that he has framed in his closet, expects to restore a corrupt and luxurious people to temperance and virtue.[22]

'It is not the office of the state to feed the souls it contains,' adds a magistrate in *St Leon*; 'it could not do that without making them slaves. Its proper concern is to maintain them in that security and freedom of action, which may best enable them to support themselves.' Clearly the author of *Political Justice* would be as critical of the state socialisms of our day as he was of the monarchies and aristocracies of his own, and for much the same reasons. It is even possible that he would have seen in them the refutation of his theories:

> It is nevertheless essential that we should at all times be free to cultivate the individuality, and follow the dictates, of our own

judgment. If there be anything in the scheme of equal property that infringes this principle, the objection is conclusive. If this scheme be, as it has often been represented, a scheme of government, constraint and regulation, it is, no doubt, in direct hostility with the principles of this work.[23]

What has survived, then, is not Godwin's philosophical anarchism but Owen's economic socialism, and for a Marxist estimation of Godwin we can turn to the index of Engels's *Condition of the Working Class in England*. Shelley, whose *Queen Mab* Engels once tried to translate, is hailed as 'Shelley the genius, the prophet, Shelley'. But Godwin is dismissed, all too accurately, as an 'English petty-bourgeois publicist, rationalist; exercised great influence on Robert Owen; one of the founders of anarchism'. And although both Marx and Engels had read *Political Justice*, that book was virtually lost to the main anarchist tradition. Proudhon and Bakunin seem not to have known it at all, and Kropotkin came to it only after he had developed his own theories. The only subsequent thinker to have and acknowledge a direct debt to Godwin is that curiously peripheral figure, whatever his other claims on our attention, Leo Tolstoy, whose theories of private reason and moral perfectibility, of political institutions and educational practice, all have an authentically Godwinian ring. But as a living political theorist, Godwin is unquestionably dead.

As a novelist, too, Godwin is read now more for historical than for literary reasons, for his impact and influence on Poe, Wilkie Collins, and even Charles Dickens, who extended the social concern he found in both Godwin and Holcroft, though without modelling himself on either. Godwin's own school came to an early end with Brockden Brown and Bulwer-Lytton, its only lasting memorial in his daughter's *Frankenstein*. His innovations were many, but they were of a sort quickly assimilated into the literary mainstream, there losing all trace of their origin, and his reputation has become that of a shadowy figure who wanders into the stories of Coleridge, Lamb and Hazlitt, the whining scoundrel who haunts the romance of Shelley and Mary, the shameless sponger, the butt of the literary anecdotalists.

This, then, is Godwin's posthumous reputation: remembered primarily by the literary historians for his contacts with, and perhaps his influence on, other more enduring writers; remembered by the political theorists as the original anarchist whose influence, such as it was, was via Robert Owen to a Marxist communism that stands at the opposite extreme from his own beliefs; remembered more obscurely by the political economists as the man who provoked

Malthus's celebrated *Essay on Population*; but among the philosophers, where he most deserves to be, remembered not at all. Most academic philosophers, never noted for their historic sense, barely know the name. It does not appear in the most authoritative contemporary *History of Philosophy*; it is not so much as mentioned in a current anthology of his period, *Between Hume and Mill*. Yet Godwin is a philosopher's philosopher, and the very faults that make his contributions to politics and economics now of only historical interest might be expected to ensure his philosophical reputation. His fault lay in being too much the philosopher, too logical in defiance of common sense, too viciously persuadable by an impressive argument. But philosophical theories do not date as do those of politics and economics, nor is their impracticality any obvious barrier to their interest or importance: the omnipotence of truth and the immorality of the private affections are not notably more outrageous claims than the non-existence of material bodies or the unprovability of other minds. Godwin's reply to Hume is worth considering in its own right, even if he did not recognize it as such himself; his argument for a rational benevolence is both more interesting and more plausible than Bentham's simplistic appeal to sensations of pleasure and pain. He is not, of course, a Hume or a Mill in the history of philosophy – in the somewhat disconcerting image of one editor, Godwin stands 'among the smaller giants'[24] – but he is a thinker of interest and originality, in his conclusions if not in his premises. And the question remains why he should have been so massively famous once, so totally ignored now.

The explanation of Godwin's success lay, as he knew it did, in the way he captured the unreasoning optimism of the early 1790s and provided it with a basis in argument. But the force that carried him up, carried him down again. Just as Bentham's *Introduction to the Principles of Morals and Legislation* got lost in the excitement that greeted the Revolution in France, so *Political Justice* was abandoned in the fury that accompanied its passing. Godwin was, he once said, the martyr of that book, though it was Sir James Mackintosh, ironically enough, who recognized the point most clearly, when the *Lives of the Phillipses* gave him the opportunity to do Godwin more justice than he had done in 1799:

> Had it appeared in a metaphysical age, and in a period of
> tranquility, it would have been discussed by philosophers, and
> might have excited acrimonious disputes; but they would have
> ended, after the correction of erroneous speculations, in assign-
> ing to the author of that status to which his eminent talents
> entitled him . . . . But the circumstances of the time, in spite of

the author's intention, transmuted a philosophical treatise into a political pamphlet. It seemed to be thrown up by the vortex of the French Revolution, and it sunk accordingly, as that whirlpool subsided; while by a perverse fortune, the honesty of the author's intentions contributed to the prejudice against his work . . . . Intending no mischief, he considered no consequences; and in the eye of the multitude was transformed into an incendiary, only because he was an undesigning speculator . . . . The moment for doing full and exact justice will come.[25]

Yet the French Revolution was not the only rock on which Godwin foundered. He had his failures, both political and philosophical, both aesthetic and financial, but he also had a positive gift for misjudgment and mistiming. 'If I had time, which I have not', Coleridge wrote to him once,

I would write two or three sheets for your sole Inspection, entitled History of the Errors and Blunders of the literary life of William Godwin. To the world it would appear a Paradox to say, that you are all too persuadible a man, but you know yourself that to be the truth.[26]

There was the *Defence of the Rockingham Party*, followed within months by the collapse of the Fox-North coalition and the exclusion of the Whigs from office for decades thereafter; the *Internal Affairs of the United Provinces* arguing against the foreign intervention that came only a week later; *Political Justice*'s first edition, supremely confident in the imminent arrival of a universal brotherhood of man, followed by repression in Britain and a reign of terror in France; *Political Justice*'s second edition, with its proof positive of the power of truth, appearing at just the moment when government and radicals alike refused to listen to Godwin's arguments; the *Considerations*, published two days before the passage of the Gagging Acts; the *Memoirs* of Mary Wollstonecraft, insisting that her tragedy would still the voices of gossip and scandal, but only adding fuel to their fires; the *Reply to Parr*, putting its trust in Napoleon to preserve democracy; the *Letters of Verax* defeated at Waterloo even before it was published . . . . The list stretches on, even into the grave. 'The human mind is now a considerable state of preparedness to receive the sentiments, and to consider the evidence, which I have endeavoured to prepare,' Godwin assured his daughter, urging her to publish the *Genius of Christianity Unveiled* as soon as she could:

The political world is rapidly on the advance to shake off its shackles. And a great portion of mankind is disposed soberly to examine the evidence of things, which for a vast length of time have been suffered to pass unquestioned.[27]

But the age that followed within the year, the age of Victoria, was hardly one for questioning established opinion, especially when the subject was religion. Godwin's last work did not appear until 1873, and then only under the cautious title *Esays: Never Before Published*. By then a book by Godwin would create little stir.

Godwin's massive misjudgments, in his private life as well as his writings, seem evidence enough of the total impracticality of which friend and foe alike accused him. Indeed, if *Political Justice* seeks to prove that political justice is not only possible but inevitable, what more decisive refutation could it possibly receive? Political justice, as Godwin conceived it, is as far away as ever; people might take him seriously in 1793, but who could take him seriously now? Yet the failure to achieve political justice, our failure even to pursue it, does not by itself prove that Godwin was mistaken. For men have never been trusted with their own judgment in the way Godwin believed necessary if justice is to prevail; men have never been educated in the way that, he believed, would lead them to trust in truth and reason; men have never been free from the impostures and coercions of political institutions. Who is to say what men might be capable of, should such things ever come to pass?

Nor does Godwin's own change of opinion, his rejection of his own premises, the undermining of his own argument, prove that *Political Justice* is founded in error. The ultimate difficulty for his theories, their ultimate impracticality, lies deeper than that, in the controversy with Thelwall and the dilemma of things as they are. Far from being hopelessly idealistic Godwin was, if anything, only too well aware that men are not yet wholly rational, not yet bound by truth, not yet ready for justice. Unlike some later anarchists, he did not think that the abolition of political institutions would be enough by itself to bring about the millennium. Instead he insisted on the necessity of government, perhaps even of coercion, until reason and truth can come into their own. But how, then, are we to bridge the gap between things as they are and things as they are capable of being, trapped forever in the circle that men cannot be wholly rational so long as governments exist, and that governments must exist until men have become rational? Without an answer to that problem, without some positive practical programme, political justice remains an impossible, unattainable ideal – not because men are as they are, but because society is as it is. Perhaps Godwin is right about the power of reason and truth; but that power can never be exercised. The real objection is not that his theories have been tested and refuted; the objection is that they cannot be refuted, because they cannot be tested. Only his arguments remain, his deductions of sound reasoning and truth; and they have never been properly assessed. The moment for doing full and exact justice has still not come.

The streets of London are dotted with circular blue plaques which commemorate the residences of the famous, from Dick Whittington to Harold Schlupp, fatrender and cyclist. But Godwin's name appears nowhere, vanished like the homes that he lived in. Some old buildings survive at the bottom of Chalton Street, but the area is now of more interest to the student of the evolving ugliness of British council housing, such as the complex that has replaced the Evesham Buildings, than to the student of William Godwin. The Polygon, one of the most distinctive residential buildings in all London, was demolished in the 1870s to provide housing for railway workers, four starkly rectangular blocks which bore the wholly inappropriate name of Polygon Buildings, until they in their turn gave way to yet more council housing, which may endure rather better than its neighbours. Skinner Street was demolished in 1867 to make room for the Holborn Viaduct, so that No. 41 now lies 15 feet below the forecourt of a modern office block. No. 195 the Strand, near St Clements, is a luxury hotel; 44 Gower Place was another victim to the railroad, in the form of the Amalgamated Society of Railway Workers, whose office is now that of the National Union of Railwaymen; 15 New Palace Yard was pulled down so that Big Ben might be built.

Even Old St Pancras Church, dating back to the eleventh century and possibly the oldest Christian church in London, is no longer as Godwin knew it, having been substantially altered and rebuilt in 1848, and virtually abandoned now. But when the Midland Railway built its St Pancras line through the graveyard in 1866, some tombs and graves were moved into the public gardens beside the church, and there you can see a square stone pedestal inscribed on three sides: to William Godwin, Author of Political Justice; to Mary Wollstonecraft Godwin, Author of a Vindication of the Rights of Women; and to Mary Jane, second wife of William Godwin. Even it may not be the original, for a newspaper report of 1851 describes the monument as lying in pieces, presumably destroyed when Godwin and Mary were moved to Bournemouth, where they had never been before. But apart from that Godwin's only London memorial is Godwin Court, an unpleasant brick pile near the top of Chalton Street, graffiti and broken windows where once there were market gardens.

There is, however, one way in which posterity, and the Greater

London Council in particular, might make amends for this neglect, gratifying both Godwin's love of distinction and his sense of irony: by fixing to the walls of the new Houses of Parliament one of its familiar blue plaques, with the inscription

William Godwin
Anarchist
Lived Here 1833–1835

Chronology

(Publications are by Godwin, unless otherwise stated.)

1756
3 March   Birth of William Godwin at Wisbech in
                   Cambridgeshire

1758
Autumn   Godwin's family moves to Debenham in Suffolk

1759
27 April   Birth of Mary Wollstonecraft in London

1760
October   Godwin's family moves to Guestwick in Norfolk
25 October   Accession of George III

1761   Godwin attends village school of Mrs Gedge

1764
31 March   Death of Mrs Gedge; Godwin attends Akers'
                   school in Hindolveston

1766
27 April   Birth of Mary Jane Clairmont (née Vials?)

1767
September   Godwin becomes pupil of Samuel Newton at
                   Norwich

1770
June   Godwin returns to Akers' school

1771
March   Godwin returns to Newton
December   Godwin leaves Newton, becomes usher in Akers'
                   school

1772
12 November   Death of Godwin's father, John Godwin

1773
April   Godwin rejected by Homerton Dissenting

	Academy; spends summer in London, Gravesend and Stockbury
September	Godwin enters Hoxton Dissenting Academy

1776
| 4 July | American Declaration of Independence |

1777
| June–July | Godwin preaches at Yarmouth and Lowestoft |

1778
| 25 May | Godwin graduates from Hoxton Academy |
| June | Godwin becomes minister at Ware in Hertfordshire; meets Joseph Fawcett |

1779
| August | Godwin leaves Ware, lives in London |
| December | Godwin becomes minister at Stowmarket in Suffolk |

1781
| | Godwin meets Frederick Norman, who introduces him to the writings of the French *philosophes* |

1782
April	Godwin expelled from his church in Stowmarket; lives in London
30 November	End of American War of Independence (Treaty of Versailles, 3 September 1783)
December	Godwin becomes minister at Beaconsfield in Buckinghamshire

1783
29 January	*Life of Chatham* published (written July–November 1782)
2 April	Fox–North coalition formed under Duke of Portland
5 May	*Defence of Rockingham Party* published
June	Godwin leaves Beaconsfield and abandons the ministry
2 July	*Account of the Seminary* published
4 August	Planned opening of Godwin's school at Epsom in Surrey
17 November	*Herald of Literature* published (written July–October 1783)
26 November	*Sketches of History* published
18 December	Fall of Fox–North coalition

1784

5 January	*Instructions to a Statesman* published (completed December 1783)
January–February	*Damon and Delia* published (written November 1783)
February	Godwin employed by *English Review*
29 June	Hannah Godwin writes about Miss Gay as a prospective wife
1 July	Godwin employed by *New Annual Register*
10 July	*Italian Letters* published (written December 1783)
11 July	*Imogen* published (written January–May 1784)

1785

March	Godwin takes Willis Webb as a private pupil for a year
1 July	Godwin employed by *Political Herald*

1786

?	Godwin meets Thomas Holcroft
Summer	Godwin becomes acting editor of *Political Herald*
December	Collapse of *Political Herald*

1787

24 January	Godwin applies for post at British Museum
9 May	Outbreak of civil war in Netherlands
6 September	*History of the Internal Affairs of the United Provinces* published
13 September	Prussians intervene in Netherlands

1788

April	Godwin begins his diary
13 July	Godwin meets George Dyson
25 July	Tom Cooper comes to live with Godwin
November	Andrew Kippis addresses centennial meeting of London Revolution Society

1789

4 May	Three Estates assemble at Versailles
14 July	Storming of the Bastille
4 August	St Bartholomew of the Privileges
6 October	March on Versailles; Royal Family escorted back to Paris
4 November	Richard Price addresses London Revolution Society, *On the Love of Our Country*
15 November	Suicide of William Holcroft

1790

1 November	Burke's *Reflections on the Revolution in France* published

29 November	Mary Wollstonecraft's *Vindication of the Rights of Man* published

1791

22 February	Paine's *Rights of Man*, Part I, published; withdrawn and republished 12 March
30 June	Godwin proposes 'Political Principles' to Robinson; contract signed 10 July
14 July	Anti-Dissenter riots in Birmingham; Joseph Priestley's home and laboratory destroyed
13 November	Godwin and Mary Wollstonecraft meet at Joseph Johnson's

1792

January	Mary Wollstonecraft's *Vindication of the Rights of Women* published
25 January	London Corresponding Society formed
16 February	Paine's *Rights of Man*, Part II, published
4 March	Godwin meets James Mackintosh
11 April	Society of the Friends of the People formed
20 April	France declares war on Austria
May	Holcroft's *Anna St Ives* published
21 May	*Rights of Man* banned, Paine charged with sedition
22 July	Tom Cooper joins Stephen Kemble's company in Edinburgh; returns to London 10 September
4 August	Birth of Percy Bysshe Shelley
10 August	Attack on Tuileries Palace; French Royal family placed under detention
2 September	Massacres in Paris prisons
13 September	Paine flees to France
21 September	French National Convention meets; Prussian army halted at Valmay
22 September	France declared a Republic
29 October	Godwin meets Elizabeth Inchbald
18 December	Paine sentenced to death by English court
26 December	Godwin moves into 25 Chalton Street

1793

8 January	Trial of Daniel Crichton
21 January	Execution of Louis XVI
1 February	France declares war on Britain
10 February	Godwin meets Tom Wedgwood
14 February	*Political Justice* published (written 15.9.91– 19.1.93)
24 March	Godwin meets John Thelwall

April	Mary Wollstonecraft meets Gilbert Imlay in Paris
6 May	Grey's motion for parliamentary reform defeated 282 votes to 41
25 May	Cabinet discusses prosecution of *Political Justice*
17 July	Execution of Charlotte Corday marks beginning of Reign of Terror
September	Scots radicals Muir and Palmer sentenced to transportation for sedition
21 September	Godwin meets Maria Reveley
19 November	British Convention assembles in Edinburgh

1794

2 February	Godwin meets Samuel Parr
10 March	Trial of Joseph Gerrald
12 May	Arrest of Hardy and Adams, followed by others including Thelwall and Horne Tooke
14 May	Birth of Fanny Imlay at le Havre
26 May	*Caleb Williams* published (written 24.2.93–8.5.94)
27 June	Godwin meets Amelia Alderson in Norfolk
25 July	Execution of Robespierre
17 September	Godwin meets William Hazlitt
2 October	Lord Chief Justice presents charge to Grand Jury
5 October	Godwin leaves for Warwickshire
6 October	Holcroft and other indicted
7 October	Holcroft presents himself in court
13 October	Godwin returns to London
21 October	*Cursory Strictures* published (written 16–19 October)
5 November	Hardy acquitted
22 November	Horne Tooke acquitted
1 December	Holcroft discharged without trial
5 December	Thelwall acquitted
21 December	Godwin meets Samuel Coleridge

1795

27 February	Godwin meets William Wordsworth
April	Mary Wollstonecraft returns to London
May	Mary Wollstonecraft's first suicide attempt
6 June	Birth of Charles Clairmont
26 June	Mass meeting of London Corresponding Society
October	Mary Wollstonecraft's second suicide attempt
19 October	Tom Cooper appears as Hamlet at Drury Lane
26 October	Second mass meeting of London Corresponding Society; Directorate established in France
6–9 November	Pitt and Grenville introduce Bills outlawing

	Treasonable Practices and Unlawful Assemblies
21 November	*Considerations* published (written 16–19 November)
25 November	Godwin meets Mary Hays
26 November	*Political Justice*, second edition, published (revised 24.12.94–10.10.95)

1796

8 January	Godwin meets Mary Wollstonecraft at Mary Hays's
February	Final break between Mary Wollstonecraft and Gilbert Imlay
12 March	First performance of George Colman's *Iron Chest*
14 April	Mary Wollstonecraft calls on Godwin
22 April	Godwin entertains '3 Parrs, 4 Mackintoshes, Inchbald, Imlay, Dealthy & Holcroft'
1–24 July	Godwin visits Norfolk
10 July	Godwin makes proposal to Dr Alderson
21 August	Godwin and Mary become lovers
12 September	Tom Cooper leaves for United States

1797

18 February	Godwin meets Robert Southey
27 February	*Enquirer* published (written 1.8.96–28.1.97)
29 March	Godwin and Mary marry at Old St Pancras Church
6 April	Godwins take apartment at 29 The Polygon; Godwin takes rooms at 17 Evesham Buildings, Chalton Street
April	Godwin's translation of *Memoirs of Simon, Lord Lovatt* published (written 1784)
April–June	Navy mutinies at Spithead and at Nore
26 May	Grey's motion for parliamentary reform defeated 258 votes to 63
4–20 June	Godwin visits Warwickshire and Staffordshire with Basil Montagu
7 July	Death of Edmund Burke
30 August	Birth of Mary Godwin
10 September	Death of Mary Wollstonecraft; funeral on 15 September
26 October	Napoleon appointed Commander-in-Chief of the Army of Britain
20 November	First issue of *Anti-Jacobin, or Weekly Examiner*; becomes monthly *Anti-Jacobin Review* in July 1798
December	*Political Justice*, third edition, published (revised 11.3.97–30.7.97)

1798

29 January	*Memoirs* of Mary Wollstonecraft published (written 24.9.97–3.12.97), plus *Posthumous Works*
February	Thomas Green's *Examination of the New System of Morals* published
?	W. C. Proby's *Modern Philosophy and Barbarism* published
6 March	Godwin meets Harriet Lee at Bath
27 April	Birth of Jane Clairmont
24 May	Rebellion of United Irishmen
9 June	Godwin's 'conference' with Harriet Lee
June	Malthus's first *Essay on Population* published
7–20 July	Lee sisters visit London
31 July	Harriet Lee sends Godwin a final rejection
August?	Wollstonecraft *Memoirs*, second edition, published (revised June 1798)
1 September	Memorandum on projected works, including *First Principles of Morals*

1799

February–June	Mackintosh gives lectures on the *Law of Nature and of Nations*, repeated following year
1 July	Holcroft leaves England for Hamburg
6 July	Death of Willey Reveley
25 July	Hazlitt calls on Godwin
10 October	Godwin meets John Philpott Curran
October/November	Robert Hall delivers sermon on *Modern Infidelity Considered*
9 November	*Coup d'état* makes Napoleon First Consul of France
30 November	Coleridge calls on Godwin
2 December	*St Leon* published (written 31.12.97–23.11.99)

1800

?	C. Findlater's sermon on *Liberty and Equality*
7 February	Godwin meets Charles Lamb
15 April	Parr's Spital Sermon
29 May–19 August	Godwin visits Curran in Dublin
3 June	Incident of Dyson and Louisa Jones
13 December	*Antonio* performed (written 3.7.97–22.11.00), published 22 December

1801

5 May	Godwin meets Mrs Clairmont
12 June	*Reply to Parr* published (written 18–25 May)
10 September	*Abbas, King of Persia* submitted to Drury Lane; rejected 23 September
1 October	Truce between Britain and France; Peace of Amiens 25.3.02

3 November	Godwin's application for passport rejected
21 December	Godwin marries Mrs Clairmont, twice

1802

4 April	Mrs Godwin has miscarriage, or still-born baby
2 August	Napoleon becomes Life Consul of France
September	Mrs Godwin's translation of Voltaire's *Pensées* published
September	Holcroft returns to England from Paris

1803

7 March	Tom Cooper appears as Hamlet at Drury Lane
28 March	Birth of William Godwin junior
12 May	Resumption of War with France
13 October	*Life of Chaucer* published (written 3.5.01–23.9.03)

1804

2 February	Row with Coleridge at Lamb's
18 May	Napoleon proclaimed Emperor; coronation on 2 December

1805

15 February	*Fleetwood* published (written 1.3.04–11.3.05)
24 June?	Godwins open shop in Hanway Street
10 July	Death of Tom Wedgwood
21 October	Battle of Trafalgar; Baldwin's *Fables* published (written 22.2.05–2.7.05)
October	Marcliffe's *Looking Glass* published (written 19.7.05–15.9.05)
2 December	Napoleon defeats Austrians and Russians at Austerlitz

1806

23 January	Death of William Pitt; Coalition Ministry of All the Talents until 26.3.07
?	Marcliffe's *Life of Lady Jane Grey* published (written 8.11.05–1.12.05)
2 June	Baldwin's *History of England* published (written 18.1.06–21.3.06)
13 September	Death of Fox
24 October	Sir Francis Burdett rejects Godwin's suggestion that he become his patron
15 December	Baldwin's *Pantheon* published (written 22.3.06–28.8.06)
?	*Rural Walks* published? (written 23.9.06–6.10.06)

1807

January	Lambs' *Tales from Shakespeare* published
25 March	Abolition of the slave trade

18 May	Godwins open shop at 41 Skinner Street
13 November	Godwins move to 41 Skinner Street
16–19 December	*Faulkener* performed (written 25.10.03–23.11.07)

1808

1 January	Mary Godwin's *Mounseer Nongtongpaw* published
7 April	Godwin and Marshall open subscription for Juvenile Library, eventually raise some £1,400–£1,500

1809

11 February	*Essay on Sepulchres* published (written 27.11.08–3.2.09)
23 March	Death of Thomas Holcroft
13 July	Baldwin's *History of Rome* published (written 30.3.09–1.6.09)
13 August	Death of Godwin's mother, Ann Godwin
?	Baldwin's *New Guide to the English Tongue* (written 29.7.09–19.9.09) included in Mylius's *School Dictionary* and in Hazlitt's *Grammar*
20 December	Death of Joseph Johnson

1810

5 February	Godwin meets Francis Place
19 June	Godwin meets Patrick Patrickson
June/July	Baldwin's *Outlines of English Grammar* published (written 6.4.10–25.6.10)
27 October	Bankruptcy of Sir Richard Phillips

1811

January–June	Godwin revises Mylius's *School Dictionary*
March	Place, Lambert and Hammond begin to raise £3,000 for Godwin
11 March	First Luddite riots in Nottingham
25 March	Shelley expelled from Oxford
25 August	Shelley elopes with Harriet Westbrook
3 November	Charles Clairmont leaves for Edinburgh to join Constable's

1812

3 January	Shelley writes to Godwin
May–October	Napoleon invades Russia
18 September	Godwin arrives at Lynmouth to find Shelleys gone
14 October	Godwin and Shelley meet in London
11 November	Shelley meets Mary Godwin

1813

24 January	Godwin meets Robert Owen
17 February	Spy's report on Skinner Street bookshop
May	Shelley's *Queen Mab* published privately
4 August	Godwin meets Lord Byron
2 October	Shelley sells post-obit for £500, probably for Godwin

1814

22 January	Charles Clairmont returns from Edinburgh
4 March	Auction of Shelley's second post-obit; raises £1,250 for Godwin; transaction completed on 6 July
24 March	Shelley and Harriet repeat their marriage
31 March	Russian and Prussian armies enter Paris
6 April	Napoleon abdicates
13 May	Shelley and Mary meet for second time
26 June	Shelley and Mary declare their love for one another
6 July	Shelley informs Godwin
28 July	Shelley and Mary elope, accompanied by Jane
10 August	Suicide of Patrickson
10–12 August	William Godwin junior runs away
August–September	Negotiations with brothers Stone, over purchase of half-share in Skinner Street business
September	Quarrel with Francis Place
14 September	Shelley, Mary and Jane return to England
2 December	Shelley provides post-obits for Place, Lambert and Taylor

1815

6 January	Death of Shelley's grandfather
22 February	Birth of Mary's baby; dies 6 March
1 March	Napoleon escapes from Elba
11 May	*Lives of Phillipses* published (written 16.2.13–6.5.15)
13 May	Provisional settlement with Shelley's father; Shelley arranges for Godwin to receive £1,200, but keeps £200 for himself
25 May	First 'Letter of Verax' published in *Morning Chronicle*
18 June	Battle of Waterloo
22 June	*Letters of Verax* published (written 2.5.15–9.6.15); Napoleon abdicates for second time

1816

21 January	Byron suggests that Murray give £600 of his royalties to Godwin; Murray declines
24 January	Birth of William Shelley

23–24 March	Shelley calls at Skinner Street, Godwin refuses to see him
April	Claire Clairmont begins affair with Byron
7 April–3 May	Godwin visits Edinburgh
April?	Charles Clairmont leaves England
2 May	Shelley, Mary and Claire leave London for Geneva
7 July	Death of Sheridan
8 September	Shelley, Mary and Claire return to England
9 October	Suicide of Fanny Godwin
2 December	Mass meeting at Spa Fields, followed by rioting and march on Tower of London; Beckwith's gunshop in Skinner Street broken into
7 December?	Suicide of Harriet Shelley
27 December	Godwin and Shelley meet; Mary joins them on 29th
30 December	Marriage of Shelley and Mary

1817

12 January	Birth of Claire's daughter Alba, later named Allegra
12 March	Execution of John Cashman at corner of Skinner Street and Snow Hill
8 May–10 July	Mrs Godwin holidays in France
13 August	Read establishes his title to 41 Skinner Street
22 September	Birth of Clara Shelley
14 October	Death of John Philpott Curran
18 November	Godwin meets John Keats
1 December	*Mandeville* published (written 31.5.16–18.10.17)
?	Two volume *Scripture Histories* published?

1818

31 January	Shelley post-obit raises around £750 for Godwin
March	*Letter of Advice to Young American* published in *Edinburgh Magazine* (written 4.2.18–9.2.18); reprinted for private distribution
11 March	Mary Shelley's *Frankenstein* published; Shelleys leave for Italy with Claire and Allegra
23 June	Clerk from Tilson with notice to quit Skinner Street
24 September	Death of Clara Shelley

1819

2 February	Trial for damages
2 March	Tilson elects to have suit for ejectment heard before special jury
13 May	Godwin meets Lady Caroline Lamb
7 June	Death of William Shelley
16 August	Peterloo Massacre

18 October	Trial in ejectment
12 November	Birth of Percy Florence Shelley
31 December	Suicide of Elton Hammond

1820

29 January	Accession of George IV, previously Prince Regent
10 June	Gisbornes call on Godwin
25 August	Godwin receives Shelley's last letter to him
1 November	*Of Population* published (written 14.12.17–20.10.20)

1821

24 July	Trial for ejectment, reserved verdict
1 August	Death of Elizabeth Inchbald
24 October	King's Bench decide Godwin cannot be evicted without 'established courtesy of note to quit'
?	Baldwin's *History of Greece* published (written 2.6.09–15.7.09 and 23.3.21–13.10.21)

1822

31 January	Godwin accepts Mary's offer of Castruccio
16 April	Trial in ejectment
19 April	Death of Allegra
30 April	Judgment signed
1 May	Leave to appeal refused; Read obtains writs for eviction and for costs
4 May	Godwins leave Skinner Street
16 June	Mary Shelley has miscarriage
26 June	Godwins move to 195 The Strand; shop opens 4 July
8 July	Shelley drowned
18 September	Murray agrees to organize subscription for Godwin
23 December	Trial for damages, Read obtains judgment for £373 6s. 8d. for rent between 1820 and 1822

1823

27 January	Writ of error
19 February	Mary Shelley's *Valperga* published (revised by Godwin 18.4.22–10.1.23)
9 July	Public committee for arrears headed by Mackintosh
July?	*Enquirer*, second edition, published (revised 12.6.23–12.7.23)
25 August	Mary Shelley returns to London
7 November	Read settles claim for rent from 1817 to 1820 at £430

CHRONOLOGY · 367

1824

26 February	*History of the Commonwealth*, Volume I, published (written 4.1.22–21.2.24)
20 October	Injunction served
21 October	Godwin reads Hazlitt's *Spirit of the Age*

1825

22 February	Trial for use and occupation
17 March	Godwin bankrupt; certified 5 July
31 May	Godwin leaves Strand for 44 Gower Place

1826

| 26 January | Godwin meets Edward Bulwer |
| 24 April | *History of the Commonwealth*, Volume II, published (written 13.3.24–11.3.26) |

1827

| 13 June | *History of the Commonwealth*, Volume III, published (written 13.3.26–1.6.27) |

1828

28 April	Repeal of Test and Corporation Acts
11 July	Charles Clairmont and family arrive in London
16 October	Claire Clairmont arrives in London
25 October	*History of the Commonwealth*, Volume IV, published (written 5.6.27–11.10.28)

1829

4 April	Catholic Emancipation Act
18 September	Claire Clairmont leaves for Dresden
14 September	Charles Clairmont leaves for Vienna

1830

4 March	*Cloudesley* published (written 29.10.28–16.1.30)
26 June	Accession of William IV
18 September	Death of William Hazlitt
16 November	Grey becomes Prime Minister

1831

22 February	*Thoughts on Man* published (written 3.2.30–14.2.31)
1 March	Lord John Russell introduces Reform Bill
20 April	Government defeated on Reform Bill; parliament dissolved
14 June	New parliament with large Whig majority
8 October	Reform Bill defeated in Lords

1832

7 May	Revised Reform Bill defeated in Lords; Grey resigns 9 May; recalled 15 May
30 May	Death of Sir James Mackintosh
7 June	Reform Bill receives Royal Assent
8 September	Death of William Godwin junior
22 October	Death of James Marshall

1833

12 February	*Deloraine* published (written 20.4.31–11.11.32)
15 April	Godwin offered post of Office Keeper and Yeoman Usher of the Receipt of the Exchequer
4 May	Godwins move to 15 New Palace Yard

1834

17 February	Death of John Thelwall
2 June	*Lives of Necromancers* published (written 18.10.32–26.5.34)
25 July	Death of Samuel Coleridge
10 October	Godwin's post abolished
16 October	Fire destroys old Houses of Parliament

1835

9 February	Godwin permitted to retain his position
1 May	William Godwin junior's *Transfusion* published, with memoir by Godwin
6 November	Godwins move to Exchequer Building in Whitehall Yard

1836

7 April	Death of William Godwin

1841

17 June	Death of Mary Jane Godwin

1842

Political Justice, fourth edition, published

1849

21 April	Death of Tom Cooper

1850

Death of Charles Clairmont

1851

1 February	Death of Mary Shelley; remains of Godwin, Mary Wollstonecraft and Mary Shelley moved to St Peter's, Bournemouth

1873

Posthumous *Essays* published (written 29.8.34–15.2.36)

1879
19 March   Death of Claire Clairmont

1889
6 December   Death of Percy Florence Shelley, last descendent
                            of William Godwin

References

Burton R. Pollin's monumental *Godwin Criticism: A Synoptic Bibliography* (1967) makes a detailed bibliography unnecessary, but a personal short-list of works about Godwin would include: for general background and context, H. N. Brailsford, *Shelley, Godwin and Their Circle* (1931), and R. G. Grylls, *William Godwin and his World* (1953); for Godwin's theories, C. H. Driver, 'William Godwin', in *Social and Political Ideas of the Revolutionary Era*, ed. F. J. C. Hearnshaw (1931), and David Fleischer, *William Godwin: A Study in Liberalism* (1951); for Godwin's writings, J. B. Boulton, *The Language of Politics* (1965), Ch. 11; for Godwin himself, Ford K. Brown, *William Godwin* (1926); and for Mary Wollstonecraft, E. Flexner, *Mary Wollstonecraft* (1972), and C. Tomalin, *The Life and Death of Mary Wollstonecraft* (1974). C. Kegan Paul, *William Godwin: His Friends and Contemporaries* (1876, repr. 1970), contains a wealth of source material from the Abinger Mss, but is often misleading and frequently inaccurate.

The bulk of Godwin's unpublished manuscripts, including the diaries, are in the collection of Lord Abinger, currently being transferred on loan to the Bodleian Library, Oxford. References are to the Abinger Mss. The Henry Crabb Robinson Mss are in the Dr Williams's Library, London; the Place and Peel Mss in the British Library; the Wedgwood Mss in the Library of Keele University; the James Losh Diaries at Tullie House, Carlisle. I am extremely grateful to all of these, and especially to Lord Abinger, for permission to use and quote from manuscript material.

In giving references I use the following abbreviations and short titles:

Coleridge, *Letters*: *Collected Letters of S. T. Coleridge*, ed. E. L. Griggs (1956–71).

Crabb Robinson: *Henry Crabb Robinson on Books and Their Writers*, ed. E. J. Morley (1938).

G&M: *Godwin and Mary: Letters of William Godwin and Mary Wollstonecraft*, ed. R. M. Wardle (1967).

Gisborne and Williams: *Maria Gisborne and Edward Williams: Their Journals and Letters*, ed. F. L. Jones (1951).

Hazlitt, *Works*: *Complete Works of William Hazlitt*, ed. P. P. Howe (1931).

KP: C. Kegan Paul, *William Godwin: His Friends and Contemporaries* (1876).

Lamb, *Letters*: *Letters of Charles and Mary Lamb*, ed. E. V. Lucas (1935).

Mary Shelley, *Letters*: *The Letters of Mary Wollstonecraft Shelley*, ed. F. L. Jones (1944).

Memoirs: W. Godwin, *Memoirs of the Author of the Vindication of the Rights of Women*, ed. W. Clark Durant (1927).

OP: W. Godwin, *Of Population* (1820).

PJ: W. Godwin, *Enquiry concerning Political Justice*, ed. F. E. L. Priestley (1946), see below.

RP: W. Godwin, *Thoughts Occasioned by a Perusal of Dr Parr's Spital Sermon*, also called the *Reply to Parr* (1801), reprinted in *UW* pp. 281–374, page references to former.

S&C: Shelley and his Circle, 1773–1822, ed. K. N. Cameron, subsequently Donald H. Reiman (1961–).

S&M: Shelley and Mary, ed. Lady Jane Shelley (1882).

Seminary: W. Godwin, *An Account of The Seminary* (1783), reprinted in *Four Early Pamphlets, 1783–84*, ed. B. R. Pollin (1966), page references to latter.

Shelley, *Journals: Mary Shelley Journals*, ed. F. L. Jones (1947).

Shelley, *Letters: The Letters of Percy Bysshe Shelley*, ed. F. L. Jones (1964).

Southey, *Correspondence: The Life and Correspondence of Robert Southey*, ed. C. C. Southey (1850).

Southey, *Letters: New Letters of Robert Southey*, ed. K. Curry (1966).

TM: W. Godwin, *Thoughts on Man* (1831).

UW: W. Godwin, *Uncollected Writings, 1785–1822*, ed. J. W. Marken and B. R. Pollin (1968).

The Priestley edition of *Political Justice* is in three volumes, the first two a facsimile of the third edition (1798), the third giving variant readings and chapters from the first (1793) and second (1796) editions. I refer to these three editions as (A), (B) and (C) respectively, so that *PJ*(A), II, p. 149 will refer to a passage from the first edition retained, very possibly with verbal alterations, until the third, while *PJ*(A), III, p. 149 will refer to a passage from the first edition deleted in the second, or possibly the third. Similarly *PJ*(B), II, p. 149 will refer to a passage added in the second edition and retained in the third; *PJ*(B), III, p. 149 will refer to a passage added in the second edition but deleted in the third; and *PJ*(C), II, p. 149 will refer to a passage added in the third edition. *PJ*(A&C), II, p. 149 refers to a passage from the first edition expanded in the third; *PJ*(A), II, p. 149 and III, p. 276 refers to a passage from the first edition partially retained in the third edition and partially deleted; *PJ*(A), III, p. 149 and II, p. 276 refers to a passage from the first edition relocated in the second or third. In every case I have used the earliest wording of the passage quoted, which may sometimes differ substantially from that of the third edition (these variants are given in Priestley's third volume). References to *PJ*, III, pp. 1–133 are to Priestley's own analytical essay.

Chapter 1 **Reason, truth and justice**

1 *PJ*(A), III, p. 282.
2 Hazlitt, *Works*, XI, p. 17.
3 KP, I, p. 67.
4 *PJ*(A), III, p. 247.
5 *PJ*(A), I, p. 119.
6 *PJ*(A), III, p. 282.
7 *PJ*(A), II, pp. 184–5.
8 *PJ*(A), III, p. 279.
9 *PJ*(A), II, p. 324.
10 *PJ*(A), II, p. 401.
11 *PJ*(A), II, p. 337.
12 *PJ*(A), I, p. 221.

13 *PJ*(B), II, p. 506.
14 *PJ*(A), II, pp. 501–2.
15 *PJ*(A), II, p. 504.
16 *PJ*(A), III, p. 146.
17 *PJ*(A), III, p. 252.
18 *PJ*(A), I, p. 134.
19 *PJ*(A), I, p. 217.
20 *PJ*(A), I, p. 129.
21 R. Bisset, *Life of Burke* (1800), II, p. 429.
22 *PJ*(B), I, p. 161.
23 *PJ*(A), I, p. 135.

24 *PJ*(A), II, p. 487.
25 *PJ*(A), II, p. 484.
26 *PJ*(A), II, p. 528.
27 *PJ*(A), II, p. 503.
28 *PJ*(A), III, p. 140.
29 *PJ*(A), II, pp. 364–5.
30 J. Churton Collins, *Posthumous Essays* (1912), p. 69.
31 Abinger Mss.
32 *Public Characters for 1799–1800* (1801), pp. 363–4.
33 Hazlitt, *Works*, XI, pp. 16–17.

Chapter 2 **The most powerful instrument**

1 *PJ*(B), I, p. 45.
2 Autobiographical quotations are from the Abinger Mss, some printed in KP, Ch. 1.
3 *TM*, p. 143.
4 *Enquirer* (1797), p. 154.
5 Abinger Mss.
6 *PJ*(A), III, p. 206.
7 J. W. Ashley-Smith, *The Birth of Modern Education* (1954), p. 186.
8 *Monthly Review*, January 1784.
9 *Life of Chaucer* (1803), II, p. 216.
10 KP, I, p. 29.

11 J. R. Green, *A Short History of The English People* (1895), p. 788.
12 *Gentleman's Magazine*, August 1783.
13 *Enquirer*, p. 79.
14 *Enquirer*, pp. 5–6.
15 *Enquirer*, p. 31.
16 *Enquirer*, p. 102.
17 *Enquirer*, p. 96.
18 *Enquirer*, p. 81.
19 *Enquirer*, p. 67.
20 *Seminary*, pp. 172–3.
21 *PJ*(B), I, p. 43.

Chapter 3 **Sincere friendships**

1 *PJ*(A), III, p. 292 and (B), I, p. 329.
2 Hazlitt, *Works*, XI, p. 27.
3 Abinger Mss.
4 KP, I, p. 47.
5 *Enquirer* (1797), p. 86.
6 *Enquirer*, pp. 91–2.
7 KP, I, p. 51.
8 Hazlitt, *Works*, III, pp. 132–3.
9 Quoted in E. Colby, *A Bibliography of Thomas Holcroft* (1932), p. 15.
10 KP, I, pp. 49–50.
11 KP, I, p. 360.
12 KP, I, p. 37.
13 KP, I, pp. 38–9.

14 KP, I, p. 39.
15 Coleridge, *Letters*, I, p. 214.
16 *PJ*(A), III, p. 293.
17 *PJ*(A), III, p. 296.
18 *PJ*(A), III, p. 294.
19 *PJ*(A), III, p. 296.
20 *PJ*(A), III, p. 306.
21 *PJ*(A), III, p. 307.
22 *PJ*(A), II, p. 405.
23 *PJ*(A), II, p. 63.
24 *PJ*(B), I, pp. 348–9.
25 KP, I, p. 45.
26 *Dictionary of American Biography*, II, pp. 416–17.

Chapter 4 **The great debate**

1 KP, I, p. 61.
2 J. Holland Rose, in *Social and Political Ideas of the Revolutionary Era*, ed. F. J. C. Hearnshaw (1931), p. 59.

3 Quoted in J. Boulton, *The Language of Politics* (1963), p. 147.
4 *PJ*(A), III, p. 273.

Chapter 5 **A true euthanasia of government**

1 *Enquirer* (1797), p. 27.
2 *The Correspondence of Robert Southey with Caroline Bowles*, ed. E. Dowden (1881), p. 52.
3 KP, I, p. 69.
4 KP, I, p. 67.
5 *Fleetwood* (1832), Preface.
6 KP, I, p. 65.
7 KP, I, pp. 64–5.
8 KP, I, p. 67.
9 Mary Shelley, KP, I, p. 79.
10 *PJ*(A), I, p. viii.
11 *PJ*(A), III, p. 249 and (B), I, p. 124.
12 Abinger Mss.
13 *PJ*(A), III, p. 140.
14 *PJ*(A), III, p. 237.
15 *PJ*(A), III, p. 147.
16 *PJ*(A), I, p. 186.
17 *PJ*(A), I, p. 189.
18 *PJ*(A), I, pp. 215–6.
19 *PJ*(A), III, p. 276 and (B), I, p. 246.
20 *PJ*(A), II, p. 122.
21 *PJ*(A), II, p. 205.
22 *PJ*(A), II, p. 2.
23 *PJ*(A), II, p. 205.
24 *PJ*(A), II, p. 197.
25 *PJ*(B), I, p. 238.
26 *PJ*(A), II, p. 119.
27 *PJ*(A), II, p. 212.
28 *PJ*(A), II, p. 409.
29 Hazlitt, *Works*, XI, p. 17.
30 KP, I, p. 80.
31 *Public Characters for 1799–1800* (1801), pp. 363–4.
32 KP, I, p. 71.
33 *Analytical Review*, August 1793.
34 *New Annual Register*, 1793.
35 *Monthly Review*, March–May 1793.
36 *Critical Review*, April–October 1793.
37 *British Critic*, July 1793.
38 R. Bisset, *Life of Burke* (1800), II, p. 429.
39 KP, I, p. 116.
40 KP, I, p. 116.
41 KP, I, p. 84.
42 KP, I, p. 85.
43 KP, I, p. 295.

Chapter 6 **Things as they are**

1 *Enquirer* (1797), p. 136.
2 *TM*, p. 141.
3 Unidentified quotations on the composition of *Caleb Williams* are from the Preface to the 1832 edition of *Fleetwood*.
4 Hazlitt, *Works*, XI, p. 24.
5 *Analytical Review*, January 1795.
6 KP, I, p. 89.
7 KP, I, p. 139.
8 *British Critic*, July 1794.
9 *Iron Chest* (1796), Preface.
10 *Fleetwood* (1832), Preface.
11 *British Critic*, July 1795.
12 'William Godwin', in *Notes on Gilfillan's Literary Portraits* (1859).
13 *PJ*(C), II, p. 546.

Chapter 7 **A case of constructive treason**

1 *UW*, pp. 195–6.
2 *UW*, p. 135.
3 *UW*, p. 141.
4 *UW*, p. 140.
5 *UW*, p. 157.
6 *Public Characters for 1799–1800* (1801), p. 364.
7 *PJ*(A), I, p. 297, III, p. 159, III, p. 161.
8 *UW*, p. 116.
9 *PJ*(A), I, pp. x–xi.
10 *UW*, p. 112.
11 Mrs Thelwall, *Life of Thelwall* (1837), I, p. 206.
12 W. Hazlitt, *Life of Thomas Holcroft*, ed. E. Colby (1925), II, p. 67.
13 *UW*, p. 146.
14 Abinger Mss.
15 Hazlitt, *Works*, III, p. 206.
16 Hazlitt, *Works*, XI, p. 52.
17 KP, I, p. 147.
18 Abinger Mss.

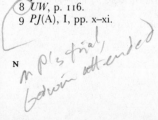

Chapter 8 **The firmament of reputation**

1 KP, I, p. 118.
2 TM, p. 349.
3 Southey. *Letters*, I, p. 86.
4 S. T. Coleridge, *Collected Works*, II, ed. L. Patton (1970), p. 196.
5 Coleridge, *Letters*, I, p. 141.
6 S. T. Coleridge, *Collected Works*, I, ed. L. Patton and P. Mann (1971), p. 164.
7 S. T. Coleridge, *Collected Works*, II, p. 196.
8 Coleridge, *Letters*, I, p. 293.
9 Hazlitt, *Works*, XI, p. 17.

10 *Letters of William and Dorothy Wordsworth, The Early Years*, ed. E. de Selincourt (1967), pp. 170–1.
11 *PJ*(A), III, p. 227.
12 *PJ*(A), III, p. 160.
13 *PJ*(B), I, p. xvi.
14 Thomas de Quincey, 'William Godwin', in *Notes on Gilfillan's*

Literary Portraits (1859).
15 *Seminary*, p. 200.
16 *TM*, p. 457.
17 *PJ*(A), III, pp. 203–4.
18 *PJ*(A), III, p. 141.
19 *PJ*(B), I, p. 86.
20 *PJ*(A), I, p. 174.
21 *PJ*(B), I, p. 91.
22 *PJ*(B), I, p. 88.
23 *PJ*(B), I, p. 93.
24 *PJ*(B), I, p. 56.
25 *PJ*(A), II, p. 121.
26 *PJ*(B), I, p. 73.
27 *PJ*(B), I, p. 80.
28 *PJ*(B), I, pp. 81–2.
29 *PJ*(B), I, p. 424.
30 *PJ*(A), III, p. 315.
31 *PJ*(B), I, p. 71.
32 *PJ*(B), I, pp. 79–80.
33 *PJ*(B), I, p. 79.
34 *PJ*(B), I, p. 92.

Chapter 9 **Genial and benignant power!**

1 KP, II, pp. 204–5.
2 *UW*, p. 202.
3 *UW*, p. 215.
4 *UW*, pp. 211–12.
5 *Tribune* (1796), Preface.
6 *PJ*(B), I, p. 244.
7 *PJ*(A), I, p. 99.
8 *PJ*(A), I, pp. 295–6.
9 *UW*, pp. 457, 462.
10 Crabb Robinson Mss.
11 Abinger Mss.
12 *Tribune* (1796), Preface.
13 *PJ*(A), II, p. 208.
14 *PJ*(A), II, pp. 366–7.
15 *PJ*(A), II, pp. 361–2.
16 *PJ*(B), I, pp. 238–9.
17 T. N. Talfourd, *Final Memorials of Charles Lamb* (1848), p. 140.
18 Southey, *Correspondence*, I, p. 306.
19 *PJ*(A), II, p. 511.
20 *PJ*(A), III, p. 86.

21 *PJ*(A), III, pp. 220–1.
22 KP, I, pp. 161–2.
23 *Dictionary of National Biography*, X, p. 425.
24 KP, I, p. 74.
25 KP, I, p. 74.
26 Abinger Mss.
27 Coleridge, *Letters*, I, p. 589.
28 KP, I, p. 162.
29 KP, I, p. 162.
30 Coleridge, *Letters*, I, p. 214.
31 KP, I, pp. 335–6.
32 Abinger Mss.
33 KP, I, p. 162.
34 C. L. Brightwell, *Memorials of A. Opie* (1854), p. 43.
35 C. L. Brightwell, *Memorials of A. Opie*, pp. 56–7.
36 Abinger Mss.
37 *The Love Letters of Mary Hays*, ed. A. F. Wedd (1925), p. 227.

Chapter 10 **A salutary and respectable institution**

1 *Memoirs*, p. 63.
2 *The Love Letters of Mary Hays*, ed. A. F. Wedd (1925), p. 232.

3 *Annual Necrology for 1797–98* (1800), p. 460.
4 *Memoirs*, p. 100.

5 *G&M*, p. 8.
6 *Memoirs*, pp. 99–100.
7 *G&M*, p. 15.
8 *Memoirs*, p. 101.
9 *PJ*(A), III, p. 219.
10 *PJ*(A), II, p. 507 and III, p. 219.
11 *PJ*(A), III, p. 220; *PJ*(B), II, p. 508.
12 *G&M*, p. 60.
13 *KP*, I, p. 235.
14 *KP*, I, p. 240.
15 *The Love Letters of Mary Hays*, ed. A. F. Wedd, p. 241.
16 *G&M*, p. 68.
17 *G&M*, pp. 29–30.
18 KP, I, p. 240.
19 KP, I, p. 237.
20 Quoted *Memoirs*, pp. 313–14.

21 *Memoirs*, p. 110.
22 *Enquirer* (1797), p. 370.
23 *PJ*(C), I, p. xviii.
24 *PJ*(A), III, p. 227.
25 *PJ*(B), III, p. 227.
26 *PJ*(B), III, p. 220.
27 *PJ*(C), II, pp. 509–10.
28 *G&M*, p. 46.
29 *G&M*, p. 57.
30 *G&M*, p. 64.
31 *G&M*, p. 62.
32 *G&M*, p. 107.
33 *G&M*, p. 118.
34 *G&M*, p. 76.
35 KP, I, p. 361.
36 *G&M*, pp. 92, 102.
37 *G&M*, p. 82.
38 *Deloraine* (1833).

Chapter 11 **The empire of feeling**

1 Abinger Mss.
2 KP, I, p. 276.
3 *Monthly Review*, May 1798.
4 'The Shade of Alexander Pope' (1799).
5 *G&M*, p. 30.
6 *G&M*, p. 111.
7 *European Magazine*, April 1798.
8 *Letters of Robert Southey*, ed. J. W. Warter (1856), p. 180.
9 *Fraser's Magazine*, October 1834.
10 KP, I, p. 325.
11 *Memoirs*, p. 101.
12 *Memoirs*, p. 101.
13 *Memoirs*, p. 130.
14 *Memoirs*, p. 56.

15 *TM*, p. 295, cf. *UW*, pp. 435–6, *Chaucer* (1803), II, p. 133.
16 KP, I, p. 294.
17 KP, I, p. 284.
18 KP, I, pp. 294–5.
19 *PJ*(B), I, p. 26.
20 *PJ*(B), I, p. 38.
21 *PJ*(B), I, p. 42.
22 *PJ*(C), II, p. 87.
23 *Enquirer* (1797), pp. 24–5.
24 KP, I, p. 294.
25 Abinger Mss.
26 *PJ*(B), I, p. 55.
27 *PJ*(B), I, p. 81.
28 *PJ*(B), I, pp. 79–80.
29 KP, I, pp. 294–5.

Chapter 12 **Domestic and private affections**

1 Abinger Mss.
2 Abinger Mss.
3 *Memoirs*, pp. 127–8; *St Leon* (1799), Preface; *RP*, pp. 25–6.
4 Abinger Mss.
5 Hazlitt, *Works*, XI, p. 24.
6 KP, I, p. 281.
7 KP, I, p. 276.
8 KP, I, pp. 276–7.
9 KP, I, p. 277.
10 KP, I, p. 279.
11 KP, I, p. 279.
12 James Losh Diaries, March 1798.

13 KP, I, p. 299.
14 KP, I, p. 301.
15 Abinger Mss.
16 KP, I, p. 303.
17 Abinger Mss.
18 Abinger Mss.
19 KP, I, p. 308.
20 KP, I, pp. 306–7.
21 KP, I, p. 333.
22 KP, I, p. 333.
23 KP, I, pp. 335–6.
24 KP, I, p. 338.
25 KP, I, p. 338.

Chapter 13 Apostasy and calumny

1 Abinger Mss.
2 'London Reminiscences,' *Tait's Edinburgh Magazine*, 1837.
3 T. Mathias, 'The Shade of Alexander Pope' (1799).
4 *Port Folio*, 17 July 1802.
5 *RP*, pp. 1, 9, 51.
6 *RP*, p. 9.
7 Hazlitt, *Works*, XI, p. 98.
8 *RP*, p. 16.

9 Charles Lamb, 'To James Mackintosh' (1800).
10 *RP*, p. 10.
11 W. Derry, *Dr. Parr* (1966), p. 161.
12 KP, I, pp. 375–6.
13 *Edinburgh Review*, October 1802.
14 *G&M*, p. 85.
15 KP, I, p. 383.
16 *Enquirer* (1797), p. 232.
17 *The Times*, 26 January, 1802.

Chapter 14 The famous fire cause

1 *Essays* (1873), p. 155.
2 *Anti-Jacobin Review*, December 1802.
3 R. Hall, *Modern Infidelity Considered* (1799).
4 *PJ*(B), I, p. 132.
5 Lamb, *Letters*, I, p. 237.
6 *PJ*(A), I, pp. 126–8.
7 *PJ*(A), I, p. 125.
8 *RP*, p. 34.
9 *PJ*(B), I, p. 126.
10 *PJ*(A), I, pp. 126–7.
11 *PJ*(A), I, p. 127.
12 *RP*, p. 42.
13 *PJ*(C), I, p. xxv.
14 G. Ticknor, *Life, Letters and Journal* (1877), I, p. 294.
15 *Crabb Robinson*, I, p. 3.
16 *PJ*(B), I, p. 121.
17 Abinger Mss.
18 *PJ*(B), I, p. 441.

19 *Enquirer* (1797), p. 104.
20 C. Lloyd, *Lines Suggested by the Fast* (1799).
21 J. Austen, *Letters* ed. R. W. Chapman (1952), I, p. 133.
22 *PJ*(A), III, p. 285.
23 *PJ*(B), I, p. 342.
24 *PJ*(B), I, p. 440.
25 *Essays* (1873), p. 226.
26 *Seminary*, p. 197.
27 *TM*, p. 209.
28 *PJ*(B), I, pp. 426, 425.
29 *PJ*(B), I, p. 427.
30 *TM* p. 212.
31 *PJ*(B), I, pp. 447–8.
32 Abinger Mss.
33 *PJ*(A), III, pp. 319–20 and (B), I, pp. 436–7.
34 KP, I, pp. 294–5.

Chapter 15 Antonio, a tragedy

1 KP, II, pp. 289–90.
2 KP, II, p. 5.
3 *Mandeville* (1817), Dedication.
4 Coleridge, *Letters*, I, p. 215.
5 Coleridge, *Letters*, I, p. 557.
6 Coleridge, *Letters*, I, p. 549.
7 Coleridge, *Letters*, I, p. 553.
8 Coleridge, *Letters*, III, p. 315.
9 S. T. Coleridge, *Notebooks*, ed. K. Coburn (1962), I, p. 910.
10 KP, I, pp. 357–8.
11 Coleridge, *Letters*, I, p. 549.
12 Coleridge, *Letters*, I, p. 621.

13 Lamb, *Letters*, I, p. 36.
14 Lamb, *Letters*, I, p. 174.
15 Lamb, *Letters*, II, p. 114.
16 Lamb, *Letters*, I, p. 250.
17 Hazlitt, *Works*, XI, p. 27.
18 Hazlitt, *Works*, XI, p. 235.
19 KP, I, p. 296.
20 *S&C*, I, p. 228.
21 KP, I, p. 48.
22 Abinger Mss.
23 *S&C*, I, p. 230.
24 *S&C*, I, p. 256.
25 KP, I, p. 365.

26 *S&C*, I, p. 237.
27 Abinger Mss.
28 *London Magazine*, April 1822.
29 Lamb, *Letters*, I, p. 237.
30 Coleridge, *Letters*, I, pp. 656–7.
31 KP, II, p. 26.
32 Lamb, *Letters*, I, pp. 230–1.

33 Lamb, *Letters*, I, p. 231.
34 *British Critic*, April 1801.
35 *Anti-Jacobin*, January 1801.
36 KP, II, p. 77.
37 KP, II, p. 65.
38 KP, II, p. 65.

Chapter 16 **The best qualities of a reply**

1 *RP*, pp. 11–12.
2 R. Hall, *Modern Infidelity Considered* (1799).
3 W. C. Proby, *Modern Philosophy and Barbarism* (1798).
4 S. Smith, *Works* (1848), I, p. 4.
5 S. T. Coleridge, *Collected Works*, I, ed. L. Patton and P. Mann (1971), p. 46.
6 S. T. Coleridge, *Collected Works*, I, p. 164.
7 T. Green, *An Examination of the Leading Principles of the New System of Morals* (1798).
8 T. Green, *Extracts from the Diary of a Lover of Literature* (1810), p. 209.
9 *RP*, p. 41.
10 *RP*, p. 60.
11 *RP*, p. 41.
12 KP, I, p. 294.
13 *RP*, p. 41.
14 *RP*, pp. 36–7.

15 *RP*, p. 29.
16 *RP*, pp. 26–7.
17 *RP*, p. 51.
18 *RP*, pp. 11, 19.
19 *RP*, p. 8.
20 *RP*, p. 22.
21 *UW*, pp. 296–7.
22 *Memoirs of James Mackintosh*, ed. R. J. Mackintosh (1835), I, p. 134.
23 Southey, *Letters*, I, p. 246.
24 Southey, *Letters*, I, p. 389.
25 *S&C*, I, p. 283.
26 Coleridge, *Letters*, I, p. 636.
27 *RP*, p. 6.
28 *Letters of Robert Southey*, ed. J. W. Water (1856), I, p. 184.
29 W. Austin, *Letters from London* (1804), p. 203.
30 J. C. Cabell, quoted in *Keats-Shelley Journal*, 1971.
31 Abinger Mss.

Chapter 17 **The immortal Godwin, I presume**

1 Lamb, *Letters*, I, pp. 273–4.
2 KP, II, pp. 76–7.
3 KP, II, pp. 98–9.
4 KP, II, pp. 187–8.
5 KP, II, p. 190.
6 KP, II, p. 180.
7 *Crabb Robinson*, I, p. 235.
8 C. L. Brightwell, *Memorials of A. Opie* (1854), p. 141.
9 Lamb, *Letters*, I, p. 304.
10 Lamb, *Letters*, I, p. 317.
11 Southey, *Correspondence*, II, p. 268.
12 Coleridge, *Letters*, II, pp. 1072–3.
13 *Edinburgh Review*, January 1804.

14 *Letters of Sir Walter Scott*, ed. H. J. Grierson (1932), I, p. 216.
15 *Annual Review for 1803* (1804).
16 Southey, *Letters*, I, p. 354.
17 *Anti-Jacobin Review*, July 1804.
18 Abinger Mss.
19 *S&C*, II, p. 545.
20 *Eclectic Review*, October 1807.
21 *S&C*, II, p. 599.
22 T. W. Thornbury and E. Welfourd, *Old and New London* (1889–90), II, p. 489.
23 A. F. Wedd, *The Fate of the Fenwicks* (1927), p. 215.

Chapter 18 **M. J. Godwin and Co.**

1 Abinger Mss.
2 *Monthly Visitor*, October 1797.
3 R. G. Grylls, *Claire Clairmont* (1939), p. 169.
4 KP, I, p. 290.
5 KP, II, p. 214.
6 KP, II, p. 98.
7 S&C, III, p. 76.
8 T. J. Hogg, *Life of Shelley* (1906), p. 567.
9 KP, II, p. 271.
10 W. Thornbury and E. Welfourd, *Old and New London* (1889–90), II, pp. 489–90.
11 S. C. Hall, *Book of Memories* (1871), p. 63.

12 *PJ*(A), II, pp. 379–80.
13 Abinger Mss.
14 Coleridge *Letters*, III, p. 43
15 Abinger Mss.
16 *Satirist or Monthly Meteor*, January 1808.
17 *European Magazine*, December 1807.
18 Lamb, *Letters*, II, pp. 59–60.
19 KP, II, p. 174.
20 Abinger Mss.
21 *London Magazine*, October 1823.
22 KP, II, p. 128.
23 KP, II, p. 164.
24 Lamb, *Letters*, II, pp. 53–4.
25 Abinger Mss.
26 Abinger Mss.

Chapter 19 **The monster with the maw**

1 *Enquirer* (1797), pp. 268–9.
2 *Crabb Robinson*, I, p. 118.
3 Abinger Mss.
4 KP, II, p. 183.
5 *Crabb Robinson*, I, p. 14.
6 *Crabb Robinson*, I, pp. 138, 135.
7 *Crabb Robinson*, I, p. 175.
8 T. N. Talfourd, *Final Memorials of Charles Lamb* (1848), pp. 145–6.
9 *PJ*(A), II, pp. 418–19.
10 *PJ*(A), I, p. 135.
11 KP, II, p. 186.
12 W. Peck, *Shelley* (1927), II, p. 414.

13 W. Peck, *Shelley*, II, pp. 415–16.
14 'A Greybeard's Gossip about a Literary Acquaintance', *New Monthly Magazine*, 1848.
15 Abinger Mss.
16 Place Mss.
17 Place Mss.
18 Place Mss.
19 *PJ*(B), I, p. 167.
20 *PJ*(B), I, p. 205.
21 *PJ*(B), I, pp. 207–8.
22 *PJ*(B), I, p. 197.

Chapter 20 **A young gentleman of fortune**

1 Public Record office: Domestic, Geo. III, 1813, January to March, No. 217.
2 *UW*, p. 445.
3 Place Mss.
4 Crabb Robinson Mss.
5 Shelley, *Letters*, I, p. 220.
6 Shelley, *Letters*, I, p. 80.
7 Shelley, *Letters*, I, p. 233.
8 KP, II, p. 207.
9 Abinger Mss.
10 Shelley, *Letters*, I, p. 327.

11 Shelley, *Letters*, I, p. 337.
12 Shelley, *Letters*, I, p. 311.
13 Shelley, *Letters*, I, p. 372.
14 Shelley, *Letters*, I, p. 341.
15 *Gisborne and Williams*, p. 45.
16 T. J. Hogg, *Life of Shelley* (1906), p. 567.
17 *Revolt of Islam* (1818), Dedication.
18 H. Buxton-Forman, *The Elopement of Shelley and Mary* (1911), p. 10.
19 E. Dowden, *Life of Shelley* (1886), II, p. 545.

Chapter 21 The venerable horseleech

1 H. Buxton-Forman, *The Elopement of Shelley and Mary* (1911), p. 10.
2 W. Peck, *Shelley* (1927), II, p. 416.
3 Shelley, *Journals*, p. 21; Shelley, *Letters*, I, p. 408.
4 Shelley, *Journals*, p. 43.
5 Shelley, *Journals*, p. 25.
6 *Keats-Shelley Memorial Bulletin*, 1970.
7 *The Journals of Claire Clairmont*, ed. M. K. Stocking (1968), p. 59.
8 Crabb Robinson, I, pp. 162, 196.
9 Lamb, *Letters*, II, p. 196.
10 E. Dowden, *Life of Shelley* (1866), I, p. 521.
11 Shelley, *Letters*, I, p. 442.
12 Lord Byron, *Works*, ed. R. Prothero (1889), III, p. 255.
13 Lord Byron, *Works*, III, p. 257.
14 E. Dowden, *Life of Shelley*, II, p. 332.
15 Shelley, *Letters*, I, p. 447.
16 Shelley, *Letters*, I, p. 450.
17 Shelley, *Letters*, I, p. 459.
18 Shelley, *Letters*, I, p. 460.
19 Shelley, *Letters*, II, pp. 202–3.

Chapter 22 A pauper's grave

1 *PJ*(C), I, pp. 138–9.
2 KP, II, pp. 235–6.
3 Shelley, *Letters*, I, pp. 472–3.
4 Lord Byron, *Works*, ed. R. Prothero (1899), III, p. 348.
5 *S&C*, I, p. 253.
6 J. Boaden, *Memoirs of Mrs Inchbald* (1883), II, pp. 222–3.
7 *S&M*, III, p. 580B.
8 Crabb Robinson Mss.
9 *S&M*, I, p. 186.
10 Abinger Mss.
11 *S&M*, I, p. 95.
12 *S&M*, I, p. 143.
13 *S&M*, I, p. 107.
14 *S&M*, I, p. 106.
15 KP, II, p. 242.
16 *S&M*, I, p. 148.
17 *Crabb Robinson*, I, p. 203.
18 *S&M*, I, p. 113.
19 Abinger Mss.
20 *S&M*, I, p. 94.
21 *S&M*, I, p. 94.
22 Shelley, *Letters*, I, pp. 524–5.
23 KP, II, p. 246.
24 R. Holmes, *Shelley: The Pursuit* (1974), p. 94.
25 Shelley, *Letters*, I, pp. 576–7.
26 *Frankenstein* (1831), Introduction.
27 *Blackwood's Magazine*, March 1823.
28 Shelley, *Letters*, I, pp. 597–8.

Chapter 23 The principle of populations

1 KP, II, p. 260.
2 Hazlitt, *Works*, XIX, p. 186.
3 S. Smith, *Works* (1848), I, p. 16.
4 *PJ*(A), II, p. 515.
5 *PJ*(A), III, p. 223, cf. (C) II, p. 518.
6 *PJ*(A), II, p. 467.
7 *PJ*(A), II, p. 528 and III, p. 227.
8 RP, p. 62.
9 Southey, *Letters*, I, p. 246.
10 RP, p. 65.
11 Coleridge, *Letters*, II, p. 761.
12 *Weekly Register*, 8 May 1819.
13 OP, p.v.
14 *RP*, p. 61.
15 *OP*, p. 485.
16 *TM*, p. 395.
17 *OP*, p. 625.
18 *RP*, p. 56.
19 *OP*, pp. 523–4.
20 *Edinburgh Review*, July 1821.
21 S. Smith, *Letters* (1953), I, p. 121.
22 *RP*, p. 10.
23 Abinger Mss.
24 Abinger Mss.
25 *OP*, p. 626.
26 *RP*, p. 56.
27 *OP*, p. 4.

Chapter 24 A notice to quit

1 *PJ*(C), II, pp. 412–13.
2 *S&M*, II, p. 296.
3 T. J. Hogg, *Life of Shelley* (1906), p. 567.
4 *S&M*, II, p. 338A.
5 Mary Shelley's *Letters*, I, p. 79.
6 KP, II, p. 271.
7 *The Journals of Claire Clairmont*, ed. M. K. Stocking (1968), p. 153.
8 Shelley, *Letters*, II, p. 208.
9 *S&C*, V, p. 512.
10 *S&M*, II, p. 279.
11 *Gisborne and Williams*, p. 38.
12 *Gisborne and Williams*, p. 48.
13 *Gisborne and Williams*, p. 39.
14 *Gisborne and Williams*, p. 42.
15 *Gisborne and Williams*, p. 45.
16 *S&M*, III, pp. 580A–B.
17 Abinger Mss.
18 *Gisborne and Williams*, p. 43.
19 E. Dowden, *Life of Shelley* (1886), II, p. 322.
20 Shelley, *Letters*, II, p. 225.
21 Abinger Mss.
22 *S&M*, III, p. 704A.
23 *S&M*, III, p. 704B.
24 KP, II, p. 276.
25 KP, II, p. 277.
26 W. Thornbury and E. Welfourd, *Old and New London* (1889–90), II, p. 490.
27 Shelley, *Letters*, II, p. 423.
28 KP, II, p. 278.
29 Shelley, *Letters*, II, p. 426.
30 *S&M*, III, p. 904B.
31 W. Scott, *Letters*, ed. H. C. C. Grierson (1932–37), VII, p. 252.
32 KP, II, p. 266.
33 KP, II, p. 277.
34 *Enquirer* (1823), Preface.

Chapter 25 A virtue of necessity

1 *PJ*(A), II, p. 324.
2 *PJ*(A), II, pp. 324–5.
3 Shelley, *Journal*, p. 192.
4 R. G. Grylls, *Claire Clairmont* (1939), p. 193.
5 'Memoir of William Godwin Junior', in W. Godwin jnr, *Transfusion* (1835).
6 KP, II, pp. 309–10.
7 C. and M. Cowden Clarke, *Recollections of Writers* (1878), p. 58.
8 T. N. Talfourd, *Final Memorials of Charles Lamb* (1948), p. 140.
9 H. W. Boynton, *James Fenimore Cooper* (1931), p. 176.
10 R. D. Owen, *Threading My Way* (1874), pp. 207–8.
11 J. A. Froude, *Thomas Carlyle* (1882), p. 172.
12 Abinger Mss.
13 Abinger Mss.
14 Abinger Mss.
15 C. and M. Cowden Clarke, *Recollections of Writers*, p. 36.
16 *TM*, p. 358.
17 *TM*, pp. 372–3.
18 *TM*, p. 29.
19 *TM*, p. 270.
20 *TM*, p. 370.
21 *TM*, p. 457.
22 *TM*, p. 302.
23 *TM*, pp. 245–6.
24 *TM*, p. 41.
25 *TM*, p. 398.
26 *PJ*(A), I, p. 399.
27 *PJ*(A), I, pp. 364–5.
28 *PJ*(A), I, p. 376.
29 *PJ*(A), I, p. 383.
30 *PJ*(A), I, p. 381.
31 *PJ*(A), I, pp. 382–3.
32 Abinger Mss.
33 *TM*, p. 236.
34 *TM*, p. 237.

Chapter 26 For services rendered

1 KP, II, p. 265.
2 *PJ*(A), II, p. 205.
3 *PJ*(A), II, p. 319.
4 *TM*, p. 327.
5 Abinger Mss.
6 KP, II, pp. 311–12.

REFERENCES · 381

7 *PJ*(A), II, p. 308.
8 *Weekly Register*, 18 June 1831.
9 *PJ*(A), II, p. 314.
10 Public Record Office, E403/2499.

11 Abinger Mss.
12 Mary Shelley, *Letters*, II, p. 440.
13 Public Record Office, E403/2499.
14 Peel Mss.

Chapter 27 **A last judgment**

1 KP, I, p. 28.
2 KP, I, p. 296.
3 Abinger Mss.
4 *Essays* (1873), pp. 7–8.
5 *Essays*, pp. 207–8.
6 *Essays*, p. 86.
7 *Essays*, p. 62.
8 *Essays*. pp. 66–7.
9 *Essays*, pp. 169–70.
10 KP, I, p. 305.
11 *Essays*, pp. 253–4.
12 *Sketches of History* (1783).
13 *Fortnightly Review*, April 1873.
14 *Essays*, p. 72.
15 KP, II, p. 331.
16 R. G. Grylls, *Claire Clairmont* (1939), p. 213.

17 *Crabb Robinson*, II, p. 569.
18 Abinger Mss.
19 *Gentleman's Magazine*, June 1836.
20 A. Menger, *The Right to the Whole Produce of Labour*, trans. M. E. Tanner (1899), p. 40.
21 *Enquirer* (1797), p. 177.
22 *PJ*(B), III, p. 190.
23 *PJ*(A), II, p. 497.
24 A. E. Rodway, *Godwin and the Age of Transition* (1952), p. 7.
25 *Edinburgh Review*, October 1815.
26 Coleridge, *Letters*, II, p. 736.
27 Abinger Mss.

Index

Publications listed by title, not by author; philosophical and theoretical discussions listed by topic, not by work.